NATIONAL GEOGRAPHIC

ATLAS *of* NATURAL AMERICA

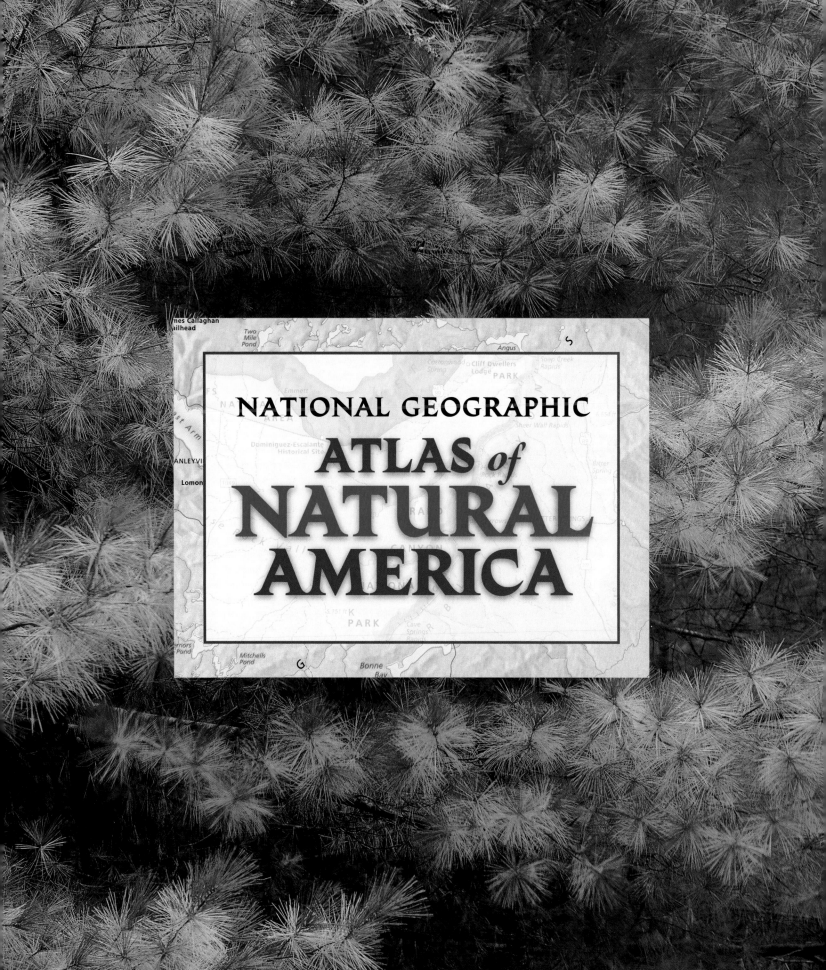

NATIONAL GEOGRAPHIC
ATLAS *of* NATURAL AMERICA

TABLE of CONTENTS

*Trunk of aged giant swallows visitors to
Sequoia National Park, California.*

Introduction

BY KENNETH R. YOUNG

Department of Geography, University of Texas, Austin

Geographers and other scientists subdivide North America into units that share common characteristics such as physical features, predominant vegetation types, and climate. Additionally, geologists demarcate these regions according to their stratigraphic and structural history, factors that are, for example, the basis of physiographic provinces such as the Colorado Plateau and the Basin and Range in the West.

In this volume, location in the continental United States and in Canada was a principal means to create a regional classification for the chapters. In addition, a combination of geologic features, such as mountain ranges, and climate characteristics help to separate one region from another. Although necessarily artificial, this jigsaw arrangement tends to put similar sites together, thus allowing the armchair traveler to plan (or at least dream of) forays into areas preserved to some degree in their natural state. The regions are illustrated and discussed from east to west, and then north to the higher latitudes.

Within each of the six regions, as shown in maps on the following pages, natural parklands, forests, and other preserves serve as icons of the wonders nature can create. In many cases, these are locations where humans and their activities are at a minimum. Often the land is cloaked in the vegetation expected given the particular climate of that place: cactuses in deserts, massive temperate rain forests on the windward side of the coastal ranges of the Pacific Northwest. Of course, "wilderness" is in the eye of the beholder, as is the degree to which any spot on the Earth can be said to be "natural" in these times of near ubiquitous human influence. For that matter, there have always been natural processes that modified these landscapes, proving the adage that nothing is so constant as change. In fact, it is through the changes wrought by volcanoes, earthquakes, fires, and floods that the Earth renews itself as a dynamic, living planet.

Although surrounded by the built and grown environments created by human artifice in cities and farmland, the natural landscapes featured in this book still contain native plants and animals that interact according to the rules of ecology—competition, predation, mutualism, and more. Their distributions and abundances are affected by the maxims of biogeography. Typically, these natural areas are protected, established by legislative intent and administered by national, regional, or local governance. They provide a hint, and frequently more than a hint, of nature's wildness. Look and reflect, drive the roadways, walk the trails, paddle the rivers, and scale the mountains.

The book begins with "The East," a chapter that encompasses eastern portions of Canada and the U.S. Here, the Appalachian highlands, the Coastal Plain, and the Piedmont, although dissimilar, are related. The second chapter, "The Midlands," includes the boreal forests found on the ancient rocks of the Canadian Shield, the northern forests of the upper Midwest, the southern forests of the Ozarks and the Big Thicket, south to the Gulf of Mexico and then back north through

Sharp spines cushion crimson blossoms of a claret cup cactus in Big Bend National Park, Texas. Established in 1944 to preserve a Chihuahuan Desert ecosystem, Big Bend contains more than 45 species of cactuses.

northern plains grasslands and up to the lower reaches of tundra. After intense exploitation by human settlers, the natural landscapes that remain are often in scenic areas that were too marginal to farm or that have recovered after past logging.

"The Great Divide," Chapter 3, features the Rocky Mountains, which rise from the Great Plains—at one time creating a barrier to colonists from the East but also offering opportunities because of the abundant forest, hydrologic, and scenic resources. This is a region that continues to change in the present day as new settlers arrive each year, reshaping rangelands into approximations of suburbia. The natural landscapes include wilderness areas where fires govern forest dynamics and the grizzly bear imposes its own tenets. The highest peaks include glaciers and glacial cirques. Some of their vistas require weeks of walking to appreciate, while others beckon from the roadside or trailhead.

To the south lies the fourth region, "The Southwest." The Grand Canyon reveals deep time by exposing rocks a thousand million years old. In the deserts and in the highlands, large areas of accessible shrublands and forests reveal nature's solutions for adapting to lowland heat, drought, and flash floods—or to mountain chill and steepness.

The part of North America this book terms "The Far West" nestles next to the cool waters of the Pacific Ocean, with towering mountain ranges to the east. Natural landscapes are on the islands, on the flanks of the mountains, and on the volcanoes of the Cascade Range. Here, too, the climate becomes humid, and the vegetation changes to massive forests that clothe slopes. Some of the continent's most dramatic scenery and grandest forests occur here in the West and continue northward through Canada's far west and into Alaska, where the influence of humans diminishes and wilderness increases.

"The Arctic North" attracts few visitors and contains mostly natural landscapes. The glacial legacy can be seen everywhere, and permanently frozen subsoils are underfoot. Indigenous peoples use traditional methods to harvest food, while simultaneously debating which of modern life's conveniences should be incorporated into their evolving life-styles. Yet even here, in the far north, it is possible to feel the living tensions that connect these natural landscapes to those found at other latitudes. For example, the arctic terns that nest here in the summer fly to the southern tip of South America in the winter. There are also profound environmental concerns that link the Arctic North to the industrialized landscapes of the Midlands and the East: Global warming is driven by emissions of carbon dioxide from the south, although the most dramatic consequences will be felt on the Arctic ecosystems, and thinning ozone layers in the high Arctic are caused by chemicals produced in the middle latitudes.

The natural areas of the United States and Canada contain secrets to be explored of how plants and animals are adapted to their respective environments. And they provide guidelines for the ecological restoration of degraded landscapes. These areas also represent our future—certainly the future of our needs for recreation, for learning, for reflection. Each of the authors of this book speaks to these concerns with his or her own distinct voice, style, and emphasis. By each of them, in turn, we are led deep into the heart of natural America.

Ever alert, a coyote in Colorado eyes possible prey in a mountain aspen grove. Clever and adaptable animals that once inhabited prairies and deserts, coyotes now roam throughout much of North America.

YUKON DELTA
NAT. WILDLIFE REFUGE, Alas.

ARCTIC
NAT. WILDLIFE REFUGE, Alas.
IVVAVIK N.P., Yukon Terr.
VUNTUT N.P., Yukon Terr.

DENALI NAT. PARK
AND PRESERVE, Alas.

U.S.
CANADA

ARCTIC CIRCLE

WRANGELL-ST. ELIAS
NAT. PARK AND PRESERVE, Alas.

KLUANE NAT. PARK RESERVE,
Yukon Terr.

NAHANNI
NAT. PARK
RESERVE,
N.W.T.

GLACIER BAY NAT. PARK
AND PRESERVE, Alas.

THELON WILDLIFE
SANCTUARY,
N.W.T., Nunavut

TONGASS
NAT. FOREST, Alas.

WOOD BUFFALO
NAT. PARK, Alta., N.W.T.

*Sites, here, are plotted
in the geographic center
of all respective features.*

JASPER
NAT. PARK, Alta.

YOHO N.P., B.C.
BANFF NAT. PARK, Alta.

NORTH
CASCADES
NAT. PARK, Wash.
KOOTENAY NAT. PARK, B.C.

PACIFIC RIM NAT. PARK
RESERVE, B.C.

OLYMPIC NAT. PARK and
OLYMPIC NAT. FOREST, Wash.

WATERTON-GLACIER
INTERNATIONAL
PEACE PARK, Mont., Alta.

MT. BAKER-
SNOQUALMIE
NAT. FOREST,
Wash.

QUETI
PRO
PAR
O

GRASSLANDS N.P., Sask.

CANADA
U.S.

VOYAGEURS
N.P., Minn.

MT. RAINIER NAT. PARK, Wash.

MT. HOOD NAT. FOREST, Oreg.

THE WILDERNESS
CORE, Idaho, Mont.

CHARLES M. RUSSELL
N.W.R., Mont.

SUPERIOR NAT.
FOREST, Minn.

HELLS CANYON
N.R.A., Idaho, Oreg.

LITTLE MISSOURI
NAT. GRASSLAND,
N.Dak.

APOSTLE ISLA
NAT. LAKESHORE,

CRATER LAKE NAT. PARK, Oreg.

REDWOOD NAT. PARK, Calif.

KLAMATH BASIN N.W.R.
Calif., Oreg.

SAWTOOTH N.R.A.
AND SAWTOOTH
WILDERNESS, Idaho

YELLOWSTONE N.P.,
Wyo., Idaho, Mont.

HART MT.
NATIONAL
ANTELOPE
REFUGE, Oreg.

GRAND TETON
NAT. PARK, Wyo.

BLACK HILLS NAT. FOREST,
S.Dak., Wyo.

ST. CRO
NAT. SCE
RIVERWA
Minn., W

BADLANDS
NAT. PARK, S.Dak.

GREAT BASIN
NAT. PARK,
Nev.

ROCKY MOUNTAIN
NAT. PARK, Colo.

YOSEMITE NAT. PARK, Calif.

INYO NAT.
FOREST,
Calif.,
Nev.

ARCHES
NAT. PARK,
Utah

WHITE RIVER NAT. FOREST, Colo.

BRYCE CANYON
N.P., Utah

BLACK CANYON OF
THE GUNNISON N.P., Colo.

SEQUOIA-KINGS CANYON NAT. PARKS, Calif.

DEATH VALLEY
NAT. PARK, Calif., Nev.

ZION N.P.,
Utah

CANYONLANDS N.P., Utah

FLINT HILLS
N.W.R., Kans.

CHANNEL ISLANDS
NAT. PARK, Calif.

PARIA CANYON-
VERMILION CLIFFS
WILDERNESS, Ariz., Utah

GRAND CANYON
NAT. PARK, Ariz.

OZARK NAT. FOREST and
BUFFALO NAT. RIVER,
Ark.

JOSHUA TREE
NAT. PARK, Calif.

COCONINO
NAT. FOREST,
Ariz.

PETRIFIED FOREST
NAT. PARK, Ariz.

WICHITA MOUNTAINS
WILDLIFE REFUGE, Okl

CABEZA PRIETA
N.W.R., Ariz.

SAGUARO
NAT. PARK, Ariz.

CARLSBAD
CAVERNS
NAT. PARK, N. Mex.

U.S.
MEXICO

GUADALUPE MTS.
NAT. PARK, Tex.

BIG THICKET
NATIONAL
PRESERVE, Tex.

BIG BEND
NAT. PARK, Tex.

SABI
N.W.
La.

ARANSAS
N.W.R., Tex.

PADRE ISLAND
NAT. SEASHORE, Te

ARCTIC NORTH

FAR
WEST

GREAT
DIVIDE

MIDLANDS

EAST

SOUTHWEST

MAP KEY

For Large-Scale Maps on Following Pages

National Lakeshore
National Monument
National Park
National Park Reserve
National Recreational Area
National Preserve
National Seashore
National Scenic Riverway

National Wildlife Refuge
National Wildlife Reserve
Wildlife Sanctuary

National Forest
State Forest

Provincial Park
State Park

Bureau of Land Management

Indian Reservation

Urban Area

Resthaven Icefield   Glacier

Salt Flat
Dry Lake

Intermittent Lake

Swamp
Marsh
Wetland

Land Exposed at Low Tide

Drainage

Intermittent Drainage

National Wild & Scenic River

Canal

Intracoastal Waterway

Ferry

Continental Divide

National Boundary
State Boundary

—90—   Interstate Highway (U.S.)

—1—   Trans-Canada Highway

20–47–14   Federal Highway
State Highway
Provincial Highway

261   Secondary Highway
Backroad

5   Unpaved Road

Bike Trail

Hiking Trail

National Marine Sanctuary Boundary

Wilderness Boundary

Buckskin □ Trailhead   Point-of-Interest

Mummy Pass 11,440 ft   Pass

Longs Peak + 14,255 ft   Mountain Peak Elevation Marker

○ Hot Spring   Natural Spring

Angel Falls   Waterfalls or Rapids

Town Bluff Dam   Dam

○ BELFAST   Town

∴ Rhyolite   Ruins

Grace Island △   Campground

Snake River   Overlook or Turnabout

Abbreviations

CAN.	Canada
Cr.	Creek
Fk.	Fork
Hdqrs.	Headquarters
Hwy.	Highway
I.R.	Indian Reservation
I., -s.	Island, Islands
Mon.	Monument
Mt., Mts.	Mount, Mountain(s)
Nat. Mon.	National Monument
Nat. For., N.F.	National Forest
N.H.P.	National Historic Park
N.H.S.	National Historic Site
N.P.	National Park
N.R.A.	National Recreation Area
N.S.	National Seashore
N.S.T.	National Scenic Trail
N.W.R.	National Wildlife Refuge
N.W.& S.R.	National Wild and Scenic River
Prov.	Province, Provincial
P.P.	Provincial Park
S.P.	State Park
U.S.	United States

UTTINIRPAAQ
(ELLESMERE ISLAND)
NAT. PARK, Nunavut

GREENLAND
(Denmark)

ARCTIC CIRCLE

BYLOT BIRD SANCTUARY,
Nunavut

AUYUITTUQ
NAT. PARK, Nunavut

GROS MORNE
NAT. PARK, Nfld.

CAPE BRETON
HIGHLANDS
NAT. PARK, N.S.

PUKASKWA
NAT. PARK, Ont.

LA MAURICIE
NAT. PARK, Que.

ISLE ROYALE
NAT. PARK, Mich.

MOOSEHORN N.W.R., Me.

ACADIA NAT. PARK, Me.

PICTURED ROCKS
NAT. LAKESHORE,
Mich.

WHITE MOUNTAIN
NAT. FOREST, N.H.

ADIRONDACK
PARK, N.Y.

SLEEPING BEAR
DUNES NAT.
LAKESHORE,
Mich.

GREEN MOUNTAIN
NAT. FOREST, Vt.

DELAWARE
WATER GAP
N.R.A., N.J., Penn.

CAPE COD
NAT. SEASHORE, Mass.

BOMBAY HOOK N.W.R., Del.

MONONGAHELA
NAT. FOREST, W. Va.

ASSATEAGUE ISLAND N.S., Md.
CHINCOTEAGUE N.W.R., Va.

SHENANDOAH
NAT. PARK, Va.

GREAT DISMAL SWAMP
N.W.R., N.C., Va.

MAMMOTH CAVE
NAT. PARK, Ky.

GREAT SMOKY
MOUNTAINS
NAT. PARK, N.C., Tenn.

CAPE HATTERAS
NAT. SEASHORE., N.C.

REELFOOT N.W.R.,
Tenn.

CAROLINA SANDHILLS
N.W.R., S.C.

CHATTAHOOCHEE
NAT. FOREST, Ga.

FRANCIS MARION
NAT. FOREST, S.C.

CAPE ROMAIN
NAT. WILDLIFE
REFUGE, S.C.

OKEFENOKEE
NAT. WILDLIFE
REFUGE, Ga.

CUMBERLAND ISLAND
NAT. SEASHORE, Ga.

LOWER SUWANNEE
NAT. WILDLIFE
REFUGE, Fla.

BIG CYPRESS
NAT. PRESERVE, Fla.

EVERGLADES
NAT. PARK, Fla.

BISCAYNE
NAT. PARK, Fla.

Cluster Area

Mapped site in cluster

Other site in cluster

| 0 | miles | 600 |
| 0 | kilometers | 900 |

NATURAL NORTH AMERICA

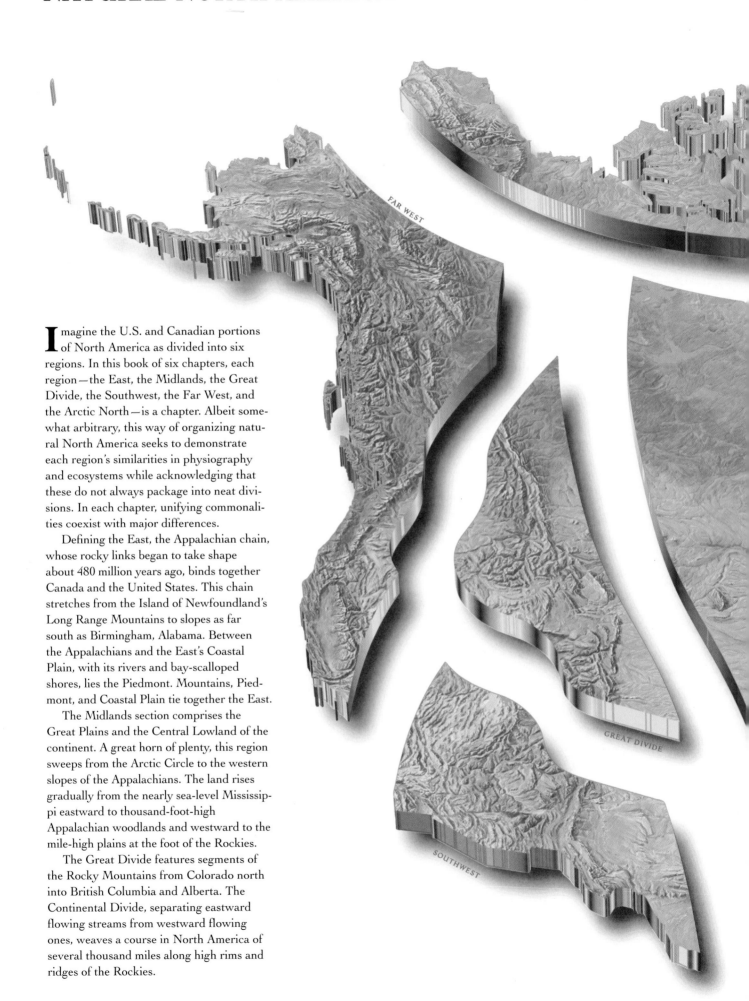

Imagine the U.S. and Canadian portions of North America as divided into six regions. In this book of six chapters, each region—the East, the Midlands, the Great Divide, the Southwest, the Far West, and the Arctic North—is a chapter. Albeit somewhat arbitrary, this way of organizing natural North America seeks to demonstrate each region's similarities in physiography and ecosystems while acknowledging that these do not always package into neat divisions. In each chapter, unifying commonalities coexist with major differences.

Defining the East, the Appalachian chain, whose rocky links began to take shape about 480 million years ago, binds together Canada and the United States. This chain stretches from the Island of Newfoundland's Long Range Mountains to slopes as far south as Birmingham, Alabama. Between the Appalachians and the East's Coastal Plain, with its rivers and bay-scalloped shores, lies the Piedmont. Mountains, Piedmont, and Coastal Plain tie together the East.

The Midlands section comprises the Great Plains and the Central Lowland of the continent. A great horn of plenty, this region sweeps from the Arctic Circle to the western slopes of the Appalachians. The land rises gradually from the nearly sea-level Mississippi eastward to thousand-foot-high Appalachian woodlands and westward to the mile-high plains at the foot of the Rockies.

The Great Divide features segments of the Rocky Mountains from Colorado north into British Columbia and Alberta. The Continental Divide, separating eastward flowing streams from westward flowing ones, weaves a course in North America of several thousand miles along high rims and ridges of the Rockies.

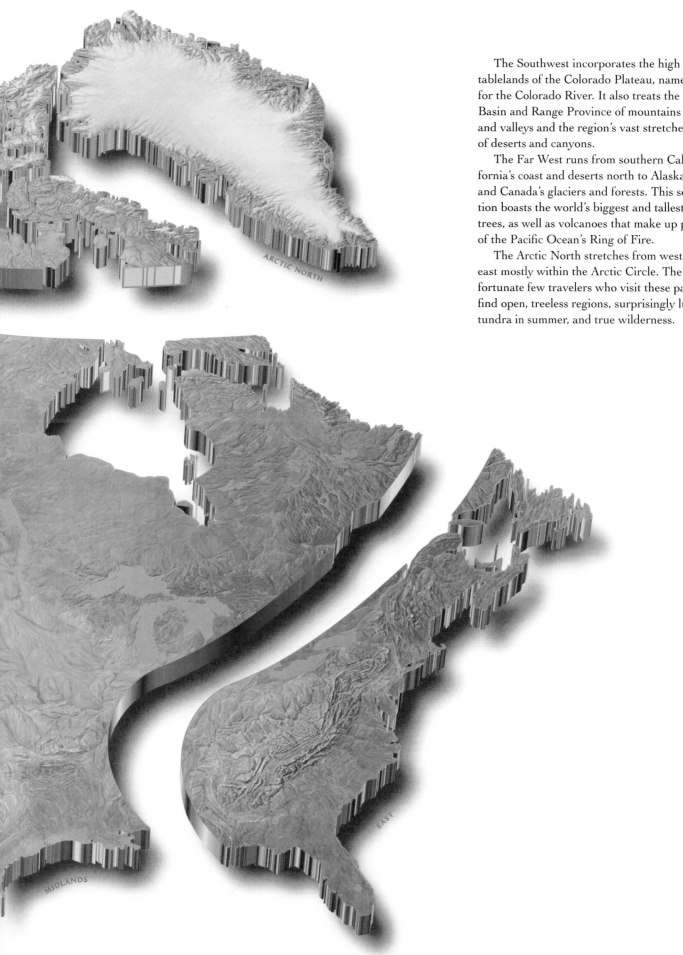

The Southwest incorporates the high tablelands of the Colorado Plateau, named for the Colorado River. It also treats the Basin and Range Province of mountains and valleys and the region's vast stretches of deserts and canyons.

The Far West runs from southern California's coast and deserts north to Alaska's and Canada's glaciers and forests. This section boasts the world's biggest and tallest trees, as well as volcanoes that make up part of the Pacific Ocean's Ring of Fire.

The Arctic North stretches from west to east mostly within the Arctic Circle. The fortunate few travelers who visit these parts find open, treeless regions, surprisingly lush tundra in summer, and true wilderness.

ARCTIC NORTH

MIDLANDS

EAST

Glaciers shaped the coast of Cape Cod, Massachusetts, and
winds and waves continue to change the peninsula.

BY MEL WHITE

You might be hard pressed at first to think of any unifying bond between Georgia and Newfoundland—between the warm South of alligators and bald cypresses and the chilly North of caribou and black spruce. But there it is on a relief map, curving up eastern North America like a crooked spine: the 1,800-mile line of the Appalachian Mountains, linking—geologically speaking—two otherwise disparate places.

The Appalachians dominate the natural character of much of eastern North America. Their peaks stand as several states' highest points, and a number of their most significant features are protected within some of the East's most popular parks. Rivers that run from Appalachian slopes provide recreation and wildlife habitat as well as superb scenery. Their lofty elevations offer an environment for "northern" species to extend their ranges far southward, which gives nature-watchers the chance to see common ravens in North Carolina, snowshoe hares in West Virginia, and alpine plants in Vermont.

Geologists say the Appalachians were pushed up by collisions of tectonic plates somewhere around 600 to 300 million years ago, a movement that enclosed the ancestral pre-Atlantic Ocean, known as Iapetus, and formed the continent of Pangea. As the slow-motion impacts ended and Europe, Africa, and North America began separating, forming the present Atlantic,

A laughing gull fishes in Florida's Everglades National Park.

the Appalachians rose to heights rivaling today's Rockies. Eons of erosion have worn them down to the more modest elevations and rounded outlines we see now.

The Appalachians encompass many of the natural areas covered in this chapter, from Great Smoky Mountains National Park on the Tennessee-North Carolina line, one of the world's great temperate forests, to Gros Morne National Park on the Island of Newfoundland, listed as a World Heritage site for its superb geologic features. In between, locations such as West Virginia's Monongahela National Forest and Vermont's Green Mountains rank with the East's finest examples of lands managed for the public good.

Other areas apart from the Appalachians reveal the great variety of this eastern region. Everglades National Park lies atop some of the youngest land in North America, and no part of this subtropical "river of grass" rises more than ten feet above sea level. In contrast to the ancient Appalachians, Cape Cod National Seashore occupies a fragile and eroding barrier peninsula, formed by glacial deposition only about 18,000 years ago. Reelfoot Lake, an important wetland in western Tennessee, was created by an earthquake as recently as 1812; its bottomland forest exemplifies the popular image of a southern swamp.

From the tundra atop Mount Washington, in New Hampshire, to the depths of Kentucky's Mammoth Cave, this chapter's sites make up an intriguing and rewarding selection of eastern North America's parks, national forests, and wildlife refuges. As you travel from Canada's maritime provinces to the tip of Florida, you will encounter whales in Nova Scotia, loons in the Adirondacks, huge flocks of shorebirds in Delaware Bay, bald eagles in Tennessee, wolves in South Carolina, and endangered crocodiles in the Everglades. You will bundle up against the Canadian wind and splash on repellent to fight off Okefenokee Swamp mosquitoes. But above all, you will encounter the marvelous diversity nature presents in eastern North America and learn of the varied and delightful opportunities that exist to enjoy it.

Spanish moss drapes from trees in Okefenokee Swamp, Georgia.

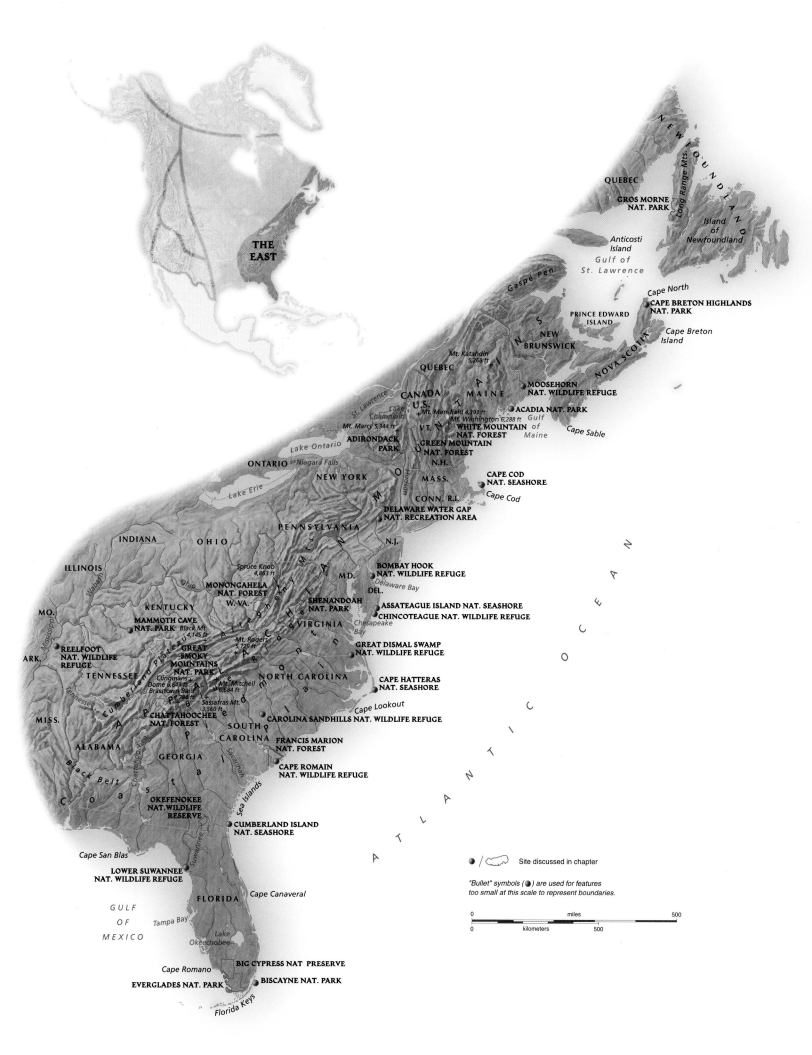

THE EAST

QUEBEC

GROS MORNE NAT. PARK

Long Range Mts.

NEWFOUNDLAND

Island of Newfoundland

Anticosti Island

Gulf of St. Lawrence

Gaspé Pen.

Cape North

CAPE BRETON HIGHLANDS NAT. PARK

PRINCE EDWARD ISLAND

NEW BRUNSWICK

NOVA SCOTIA

Cape Breton Island

Mt. Katahdin 5,268 ft

MAINE

MOOSEHORN NAT. WILDLIFE REFUGE

QUEBEC

CANADA U.S.

St. Lawrence

Lake Champlain

Mt. Mansfield 4,393 ft

Mt. Washington 6,288 ft

ACADIA NAT. PARK

Gulf of Maine

Cape Sable

Mt. Marcy 5,344 ft

WHITE MOUNTAIN NAT. FOREST

VT.

ADIRONDACK PARK

GREEN MOUNTAIN NAT. FOREST

N.H.

Lake Ontario

ONTARIO

Niagara Falls

NEW YORK

MASS.

CAPE COD NAT. SEASHORE

CONN. R.I.

Cape Cod

Lake Erie

Hudson

DELAWARE WATER GAP NAT. RECREATION AREA

PENNSYLVANIA

INDIANA

OHIO

N.J.

Spruce Knob 4,863 ft

MD.

BOMBAY HOOK NAT. WILDLIFE REFUGE

ILLINOIS

Ohio

MONONGAHELA NAT. FOREST

W. VA.

DEL.

Delaware Bay

Wabash

SHENANDOAH NAT. PARK

ASSATEAGUE ISLAND NAT. SEASHORE

MO.

KENTUCKY

Black Mt. 4,145 ft

CHINCOTEAGUE NAT. WILDLIFE REFUGE

MAMMOTH CAVE NAT. PARK

VIRGINIA

Chesapeake Bay

Mississippi

REELFOOT NAT. WILDLIFE REFUGE

Mt. Rogers 5,729 ft

GREAT DISMAL SWAMP NAT. WILDLIFE REFUGE

ARK.

TENNESSEE

GREAT SMOKY MOUNTAINS NAT. PARK

Clingmans Dome 6,643 ft

Mt. Mitchell 6,684 ft

NORTH CAROLINA

CAPE HATTERAS NAT. SEASHORE

Tennessee

Cumberland Plateau

Brasstown Bald 4,784 ft

Sassafras Mt. 3,560 ft

Cape Lookout

MISS.

CHATTAHOOCHEE NAT. FOREST

SOUTH CAROLINA

CAROLINA SANDHILLS NAT. WILDLIFE REFUGE

ALABAMA

GEORGIA

FRANCIS MARION NAT. FOREST

Black Belt

Chattahoochee

CAPE ROMAIN NAT. WILDLIFE REFUGE

Savannah

Sea Islands

OKEFENOKEE NAT. WILDLIFE RESERVE

Coastal Plain

CUMBERLAND ISLAND NAT. SEASHORE

Suwannee

Cape San Blas

LOWER SUWANNEE NAT. WILDLIFE REFUGE

FLORIDA

Cape Canaveral

GULF OF MEXICO

Tampa Bay

Lake Okeechobee

Cape Romano

BIG CYPRESS NAT PRESERVE

EVERGLADES NAT. PARK

BISCAYNE NAT. PARK

Florida Keys

ATLANTIC OCEAN

Site discussed in chapter

"Bullet" symbols (●) are used for features too small at this scale to represent boundaries.

0 — miles — 500

0 — kilometers — 500

15

ANCIENT BEDROCK, HIGH PLATEAUS

GROS MORNE
NAT. PARK,
Newfoundland

CAPE BRETON
HIGHLANDS
NAT. PARK,
Nova Scotia

GROS MORNE NATIONAL PARK

The landscape of Gros Morne National Park on the Island of New-foundland reveals its beauty at first sight: tall cliffs rising from the Gulf of St. Lawrence, uplands covered in balsam fir, black spruce, and white birch; lakes ringed by lofty rock walls, mountaintops, waterfalls, and cobble beaches.

But underlying all this splendor is something not so obvious. To a trained eye, the park's 697 square miles encompass clear evidence of Earth's tur-bulent past, of a continental collision, and a vanished ancient ocean. In fact, Gros Morne's geologic significance was the primary reason UNESCO designated the park a World Heritage site in 1987. Scientists come from around the world to study our planet's history here, where they can walk on rocks that take them millions of years back in time.

Set on Newfoundland's rugged west coast, Gros Morne offers rewards to all sorts of visitors. Those who simply drive through the park on High-way 430 (the Viking Trail, so called because it leads north to a thousand-year-old Norse settlement at L'Anse aux Meadows) will find plenty of postcard views of seacoast and mountains. Wildlife lovers can search for notable species, including arctic hare, woodland caribou, lynx, rock ptarmigan, and harlequin duck, or watch for whales from shoreline look-outs. Hikers can explore more than 50 miles of trails ranging from easy strolls to challenging high-country wilderness backpacking trips.

The park takes its name from the peak at its heart. Gros Morne (French for "big dreary")—at 2,644 feet, Newfoundland's second highest point—is part of the Long Range Mountains, which stretch the length of the island's northwestern peninsula. An outlying range of the Appalachians, these highlands were pushed up in a collision of tectonic plates from 600 to 300 million years ago. As a result of this slow-motion impact, a section of ocean floor now lies exposed at the Tablelands, in the southwestern part of the park. Here, on the surface, can be seen the boundary between the ancient Earth's crust and mantle: The meeting point is a version of today's Mohorovičić discontinuity, which lies from 6 to 20 miles beneath the Earth. Igneous rocks, with high mineral content, support only sparse vegetation, giving a suitably otherworldly aspect to the terrain.

Farther north, at Green Point, geologists study one of the continent's most complete sequences of rocks showing the end of the Cambrian and the beginning of the Ordovician periods, about 490 million years ago. Even older is the rock of the Long Range highlands in the eastern part of the park, where gneiss and granite date back a billion years or more.

The events that gave the park its present shape, though, occurred only yesterday, in geologic terms. In the most recent of several ice ages, gla-ciers blanketed the land from 25,000 to about 10,000 years ago, cutting deep, steep-sided valleys running down to the Gulf of St. Lawrence.

Barren sedimentary rocks jut into the Gulf of St. Lawrence at Green Point, in Canada's Gros Morne National Park. The landforms of the park on the rugged northwestern coast of Newfoundland record Earth's turbulent geologic history and earned it designation as a World Heritage site in 1987. Visitors hike more than 50 miles of trails over terrain up to a billion years old.

You will see one such glacier-carved feature at Bonne Bay—a true fjord that cuts into the southern section of the park. So great was the weight of the glacial ice that when it finally melted the land slowly rebounded upward. This rising action cut off some of the valleys from the sea, resulting in land-locked fjords such as majestic Western Brook Pond, one of Gros Morne's most popular destinations.

A 1.9-mile trail leads from Highway 430 to Western Brook Pond, passing over black spruce bogs and climbing small ridges before arriving at the departure point for boat tours of the park's largest lake. ("Pond," the term used in Newfoundland for most bodies of fresh water regardless of size, seems a misnomer for this nine-mile-long body of water.) The two-hour cruise passes along high cliffs adorned with waterfalls dropping into the deep, cold lake. Landlocked Atlantic salmon live here, though their numbers have declined seriously in recent decades.

Those who would rather explore Gros Morne by their own foot power will find excellent opportunities for hiking. The trail to Green Gardens, south of Bonne Bay, wanders along cliff tops, through coastal meadows, and passes sea stacks rising from the ocean, a coastal waterfall, and a sea cave accessible at low tide. The Lookout Trail, near Woody Point, leads to one of the park's best views of coast and mountains.

The summit of Gros Morne itself is reached by a strenuous nine-mile hike. On the way up you will pass through forests of black spruce stunted and twisted by strong, frigid winds and extreme weather conditions; called krummholz (crooked wood), this tree line forest is locally known as tuckamore. Above it lies ground-hugging alpine vegetation, including mosses, lichens, plants in the heath family such as blueberry and laurel, and a variety of wildflowers. Here a lucky hiker might find a rock ptarmigan, a grouselike bird, at the southern edge of its range in the park. The look-alike willow ptarmigan is found at lower elevations; male willows are redder than rocks, but the females are very hard to distinguish. Watch also for arctic hare—almost three times larger than the more common snowshoe hare. The arctic hare, though uncommon on the Island of Newfoundland, is seen often on Gros Morne.

Experienced backpackers can obtain a permit to trek through the Long Range Mountains, on routes that can range up to 21 miles through remote and rugged backcountry. Severe weather in the highlands makes this a journey for summer only—and only for accomplished hikers able to plot their own route with map and compass.

From leisurely boat rides to expeditions, a visit to Gros Morne National Park can include activities as multifaceted as its landscape. And while beauty is ever present and exhilarating, taking the time to learn the history beneath the scenery will make a visit here an even richer experience.

CAPE BRETON HIGHLANDS NATIONAL PARK

The most imposingly rugged terrain in Nova Scotia can be found within Cape Breton Highlands National Park, which spans the province's northernmost peninsula—on Cape Breton Island—from the Gulf of St. Lawrence to the Atlantic Ocean. This 366-square-mile park is easily accessible along the Cabot Trail, a scenic highway named for John Cabot (Giovanni Caboto), the Italian navigator who explored the northeast coast of North America for England and who may have landed on the island in 1497.

The greater part of the park is a high plateau averaging more than 1,100 feet above sea level, rising to a crest at 1,745-foot White Hill. Boreal forests of balsam fir and black spruce dominate much of this upland, though the highest areas comprise barrens of stunted trees and low shrubs.

Rich woodlands flourish in steep, protected valleys, made up of hardwoods including sugar maple, red maple, beech, and yellow birch, often with conifers such as balsam fir, hemlock, white pine, and white spruce intermixed. Adding to the park's diverse landforms are bogs on the highland plateau, deep faulted valleys, small ponds, lakes, brackish estuaries, and beaches both cobble and sand.

More than two dozen trails allow travelers to experience Cape Breton Highlands' varied habitats. The Lone Shieling Trail, in the Grand Anse Valley, explores an impressive forest of centuries-old sugar maples, while the Bog Trail follows a boardwalk through a wetland where orchids and carnivorous pitcher plants grow. To learn about Cape Breton geology, stop at the west side's Cap Rouge exhibit, or walk the Green Cove Trail along a rocky headland on the east coast.

You may see black bear, white-tailed deer, moose, red fox, and snowshoe hare—or, with luck, a lynx or pine marten. Bald eagles and common loons breed here, as do several species much sought after by birders, including spruce grouse, Bicknell's thrush, and the black-backed woodpecker. Find a comfortable seat overlooking the sea, and a pilot, finback, or minke whale might appear in the waters below. Any of these creatures could be the highlight of your visit to Cape Breton Highlands.

Fall ignites forested uplands of the Cape Breton Highlands National Park in Nova Scotia. Annually the park attracts some 300,000 visitors.

WOODLANDS, FJORDS, PEAKS

WHITE MOUNTAIN
NAT. FOREST, N.H.

GREEN MOUNTAIN
NAT. FOREST, VT.

MOOSEHORN
N.W.R., Maine

ACADIA NAT. PARK,
Maine

ACADIA NATIONAL PARK

Places, like people, often take on their own personalities, made up of sights and sounds, of pleasures and disappointments, of the cumulative experiences of repeated visits. For many travelers, Maine's Acadia National Park shines in the memory with its own very distinctive character. If places had faces, Acadia's would be open, cheerful, appealing—not to mention exceptionally attractive. Its mountains and lakes are accessible, its trails mostly gentle and inviting, its coastline as scenic as any in America. Indeed, it seems a singularly friendly spot on the map of our natural areas.

Anthropomorphic fancies aside, Acadia offers very real pleasures for lovers of the outdoors, as well as a history that truly can be called unique. While many national parks were created from near-pristine wilderness areas, what is now Acadia—the first national park east of the Mississippi—was designated in a region already thoroughly civilized, thanks to the help of some very influential friends.

Mount Desert Island, off the central Maine coast, became a popular resort in the 19th century, attracting wealthy families looking for escape from eastern cities. Quaintly called "rusticators," the back-to-nature set included names such as Astor, Carnegie, Ford, Vanderbilt, and Rockefeller. These socialites built mansions they called "cottages" along the island's eastern shore; by 1880, 30 hotels accommodated vacationers of lesser means. Over time, concern grew about development on Mount Desert: One affluent island-lover in particular, George B. Dorr, was to devote more than four decades and much of his family fortune to conservation efforts that eventually led to the creation of a national park. Parcels of land were added piecemeal until today Acadia protects more than 46,000 acres. It comprises about half of Mount Desert Island, plus outlying sections on Schoodic Peninsula, to the east, and Isle au Haut, about 15 miles to the southwest.

There is a grand view of Mount Desert and its surroundings from atop Cadillac Mountain, reached by road from the town of Bar Harbor, or on foot by means of segments of the park's 120-mile trail system. At 1,530 feet, Cadillac is the highest point along the Atlantic Coast—and, in a bit of geographic trivia, from October to March its summit is the first place in the United States to be touched by the rays of the rising sun each morning. The nearly barren granite tops of Cadillac and adjacent mountains inspired explorer Samuel de Champlain in 1604 to call this spot *l'isle des monts-déserts* (the island of bare mountains).

You can learn a lot about Acadia from Cadillac's summit: You will see how highways and villages intermingle with parkland on the island and how smaller islands (some of them part of the national park) dot the sea around Mount Desert. If you've studied a bit of local geology, you will note how glaciers carved north-south valleys across the island, gouging

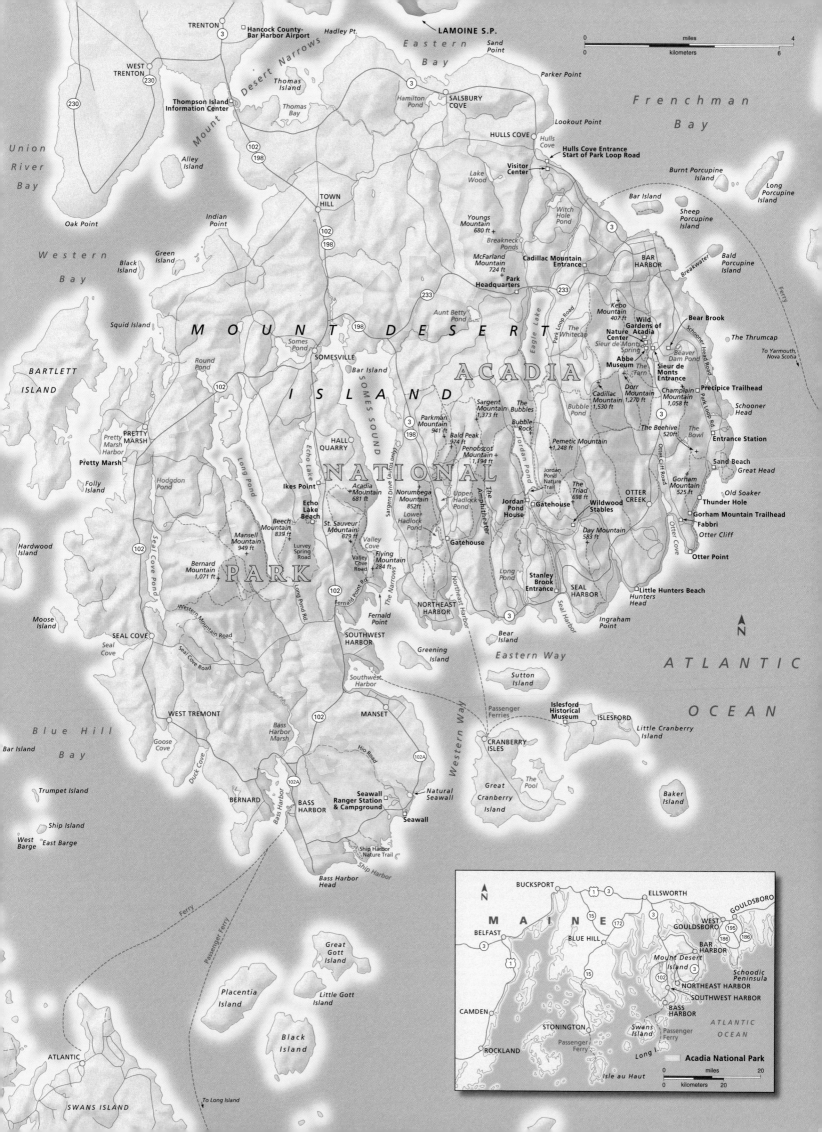

depressions that later became lakes. One glacial feature, Somes Sound, is considered the only true fjord on the Atlantic shore of the U.S.; this long bay nearly splits the island in two from the south.

Maine's famously rugged coast is the main attraction on Acadia's loop road, which hugs a shoreline lined with rock ledges and sea cliffs. Stop to scan the Atlantic and you may spot a common eider or black guillemot bobbing in the waves, an osprey flying overhead, a harbor seal lounging on a ledge, or a porpoise swimming offshore. When the surf is high, great

spouts of water can erupt at the eroded recess of Thunder Hole; Little Hunters Beach is a must stop, to admire its shoreline of colorful rounded stones called cobbles and to hear the clatter they make when waves roll in.

You will find a fascinating mini-universe in the intertidal zone at Acadia, where, between the extremes of high and low tide, life has adapted to a partly dry, partly submerged existence. Seaweed, barnacles, sea anemones, sea stars, periwinkles, limpets, and sea urchins are among the specialized dwellers in this narrow coastal belt. Make their acquaintance on a ranger-led nature walk to a tide pool, where you will learn about the complex interrelationships in this ever changing environment.

When you are ready to explore Acadia's inland habitats, your first stop might be the Acadia Wild Gardens, a botanical garden that introduces many of the island's trees, shrubs, and wildflowers. Then you will be ready to take advantage of what may be the park's most unusual feature: a system of roadways known as carriage roads.

The name of industrialist-philanthropist John D. Rockefeller, Jr., deservedly stands out among Acadia's greatest benefactors. Not only did he donate nearly 11,000 acres to the park, he also built a network of broken-stone roads that meander throughout the eastern part of Mount Desert Island. Automobiles have always been banned from these roads, which today are perfect for quiet strolls through woodland and alongside streams and ponds. Forty-five miles of carriage roads are found within the national park, crossing 16 picturesque stone bridges (also financed by Rockefeller), each custom designed for its particular location.

From several park lookouts, there is graphic evidence of a great conflagration that burned 17,000 acres of Mount Desert Island in 1947. A woodland of red and white spruce, hemlock, white pine, and balsam fir covers terrain spared by the fire, while fast-growing deciduous species such as yellow and paper birch, aspen, and red maple dominate burned areas. Even a half-century later, the boundary between the two zones remains in some places as clear as a line on a map.

The diverse habitats created by Acadia's coast, lakes, marshes, bogs, and woodland host an intriguing array of birds, from tiny boreal chickadees to elusive spruce grouse to bald eagles, which breed along the coast.

Sunrise silhouettes wind-blown spruce trees in Maine's Acadia National Park on Mount Desert Island. Six thousand acres of Mount Desert, once the playground of turn-of-the-century socialites, in 1919 became the first national park east of the Mississippi. The original name—Lafayette—was redesignated as Acadia in 1929, and more than 40,000 acres of land have been added to the park.

Swamp irises wave like
pennants in the marshes
and bogs of Moosehorn
National Wildlife Refuge
in eastern Maine. Two
divisions of the refuge
foster wildlife habitat
that also includes lakes,
hills, and hardwood and
conifer forests.

Peregrine falcons, threatened in recent decades by pesticides and persecution, have returned to nest on Mount Desert cliffs, and certain trails
may occasionally be closed to protect their breeding sites. For many naturalists, the most appealing avian group is the wood warblers; more than
20 species of these colorful birds nest on the island, including such beauties
as magnolia, Blackburnian, Nashville, chestnut-sided, and black-throated
blue warblers.

Acadia's great popularity and its compact size often lead to crowded
conditions in summer, when park roads can be distressingly congested.
To escape Mount Desert's multitudes, visit Isle au Haut, a disjunct district
of the park accessible by boat from the town of Stonington. Visitation is
limited on this small island, which offers many of the attractions of its
larger neighbor with the pleasures of greater solitude.

Though it may not match some national parks in size or wilderness
character, Acadia is unexcelled in beauty, charm, and ease of access. Plan
a trip at the right time of year—October is a favorite time for many—and
be sure to leave the highways to explore trails and carriage roads. Odds
are you will join those who have fallen under the spell of this lovely park's
forests, lakes, and rocky coast.

MOOSEHORN NATIONAL WILDLIFE REFUGE

Situated within the bulge of land where the St. Croix River winds into
Passamaquoddy Bay, separating Maine from New Brunswick, Canada,
Moosehorn National Wildlife Refuge is the easternmost major natural
area in the continental United States. Apart from that geographic distinction, Moosehorn's diversity of habitat earns it a prominent place
among Maine's finest wildlife-watching sites.

The refuge's two divisions—one just southeast of the St. Croix River and
Meddybemps Lake and the other a few miles south on Cobscook Bay—total
more than 25,000 acres of rolling hills, marshes, lakes, bogs, and woodland.
Moosehorn's forests vary from northern hardwoods such as birch, maple,
and aspen, with spruce and balsam fir intermixed, to stands of white pine.
Much of the refuge is carefully managed to improve wildlife habitat, but both
divisions also include wilderness where nature takes its own course.

Moosehorn is known for its population of American woodcock, a
rotund shorebird that breeds in scrubby woodland with scattered clear-
ings. In spring, the male woodcock performs a spectacular courtship
flight in which he ascends as much as 275 feet into the air before dropping back to the ground to mate with an appropriately impressed female.
The refuge's Woodcock Trail offers good viewing of this amazing display
at dawn and dusk in April and early May.

Black bear, found fairly commonly on the refuge, feed on ripe fruit in
summer and fall. Moose are sometimes seen browsing in open areas, or
belly deep in water. Bald eagles and ospreys, majestic raptors making a
comeback after population declines, nest here, searching refuge waters
for fish. Common loons give their weird laughing cry in summer, when
the odd "pumping" call of American bitterns can be heard from marshes. Canada geese and nine species of ducks nest on the refuge, and many
more types of waterfowl stop in migration.

More than 50 miles of dirt roads, closed to vehicles, make it easy to
explore Moosehorn—on foot, by bike, or in winter on snowshoes or

cross-country skis. Any time of year, you will find plenty to see in a refuge that is truly a wildlife wonderland.

WHITE MOUNTAIN NATIONAL FOREST

Opportunities for adventure abound in the White Mountain National Forest, which covers nearly 800,000 acres in north-central New Hampshire and southwestern Maine. And while backpackers will find challenges in five wilderness areas and on more than 1,200 miles of hiking trails, the national forest is not just for people experienced in the outdoors. Scenic drives and short interpretive trails make the beauty and wildlife of the region accessible to just about everyone.

White Mountain National Forest encompasses some of the wildest and most rugged topography in the eastern United States, with dozens of peaks over 4,000 feet. Foothills and slopes are covered in forests of beech, paper and yellow birch, red maple, hemlock, red spruce, and balsam fir, among many other species.

Topping them all, Mount Washington rises to 6,288 feet—the highest point in the Northeast. Notorious for its extreme winter weather (winds of 231 miles per hour have been recorded here), Washington can be ascended on foot, by car, or by a cog railway.

For naturalists, the greatest fascination of the White Mountains may

In Tuckerman's Ravine, climbers traverse wind-scoured snow blanketing 6,288-foot Mount Washington, the highest mountain in the Northeast. Washington anchors White Mountain National Forest, which encompasses nearly 800,000 acres in north-central New Hampshire and southwestern Maine. 1,200 miles of hiking trails crisscross an area larger than Rhode Island. One of more than 150 national forests that stretch from Alaska to Puerto Rico, White Mountain attracts about six million visitors each year.

be the vegetation found atop Mount Washington and other lofty summits: alpine tundra, above the wind-stunted trees at the highest elevations, where the harsh environment supports only the hardiest vegetation, including lichens, mosses, and a few dwarf shrubs and herbs.

The national forest is home to around eight square miles of alpine vegetation, the largest such life zone east of the Rocky Mountains. If you choose to explore the tundra on Mount Washington or elsewhere, stick strictly to established trails. Severe conditions mean the fragile vegetation grows extremely slowly here. A bit of moss displaced by a boot might take decades to regrow. In July, watch for the Melissa Arctic, a small, very dark mottled butterfly that often rests on lichen-covered rocks; this species is found in the United States only on a few of the White Mountains' highest peaks.

The Kancamagus Scenic Byway (New Hampshire Route 112), which

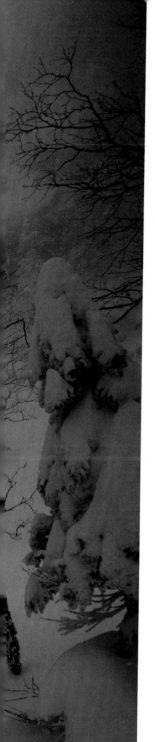

runs 34 miles from Conway west to Lincoln, offers terrific views and easy access to wild areas. The Boulder Loop Trail, about six miles west of Conway, interprets forest ecology with 18 numbered stops on its three-mile route; at the Ledges, you will have a fabulous view of the Passaconaway Valley, a thousand feet below. The popular Lincoln Woods Trail, about five miles east of Lincoln, leads three miles north to scenic Franconia Falls, continuing to the 45,000-acre Pemigewasset Wilderness, one of the largest wilderness areas in the eastern United States.

For advice on hiking in New Hampshire, visit the Appalachian Mountain Club's Pinkham Notch Visitor Center, on New Hampshire Route 16 south of Gorham. Books, maps, and experienced staff members will help you decide which of countless destinations you are most likely to enjoy.

GREEN MOUNTAIN NATIONAL FOREST

Vermont was named for the Green Mountains—*monts verts*, in French—and today these highlands symbolize the state's wild nature. The 375,000 acres of Green Mountain National Forest encompass a substantial part of the range in southern and central Vermont, attracting nature enthusiasts with 600 miles of trails, six wilderness areas totaling nearly 60,000 acres, and the White Rocks National Recreation Area.

The national forest is crossed by the Long Trail, a 265-mile path that runs the length of the state and coincides in part with the famed Appalachian Trail. The Long Trail was begun in 1910 by the Green Mountain Club, an influential group still active in Vermont's outdoor scene, and an excellent source for natural history information. While hiking the entire route would be, of course, a major undertaking, it is easy to select short sections for backpacking or day hikes. The Long Trail and national forest paths provide access to Green Mountain ecosystems ranging from lakes and bog to northern hardwood forests to spruce-fir woodland to alpine tundra.

Green Mountain summits make popular destinations for hikers, offering great views and a sense of accomplishment in return for sometimes strenuous ascents. From 3,835-foot Bread Loaf Mountain, in the 21,480-acre Breadloaf Wilderness, you can see Lake Champlain to the west and beyond it the Adirondacks in New York.

About ten miles north, 4,006-foot Mount Abraham is topped by a small tract of alpine tundra, one of only three such areas in Vermont. The cliffs of Mount Horrid, near Goshen, provide a home for peregrine falcons, a magnificent raptor whose numbers are only now recovering from decimation by pesticides in the mid-20th century. A steep trail to the cliffs offers a great view but is closed during peregrine nesting season.

Green Mountain National Forest's attractions could hardly be exhausted after years of exploration, but even a sampling will show why the Vermont peaks in this forest rank among the East's most scenic and rewarding wild places.

Shattered sunlight strikes a ring of ferns in the Lye Brook Wilderness Area of Vermont's Green Mountain National Forest. Few trails exist in the heavily wooded 15,680-acre wilderness. It ranks as the second largest of six in Green Mountain National Forest.

Winter snow weights evergreens on 4,393-foot Mount Mansfield, highest peak in the Green Mountains (left). A range of the Appalachians, the mountains march from Canada through Vermont into western Massachusetts.

SHAPED BY ICE, WAVES, WIND

CAPE COD
NAT. SEASHORE,
Massachusetts

CAPE COD NATIONAL SEASHORE

Cape Cod has long held a special mystique for travelers, a beguiling aura conferred upon it by both geography and history. Only a short distance from the great metropolis of Boston, it feels far more remote than it is. Connected to the mainland and home to a fascinating range of plants and animals, it nonetheless seems to belong in large part to the sea. Although the Cape still holds wild landscapes, it has also seen sweeping human-induced changes to its natural environment.

Quaint towns and superb beaches attract millions of visitors each year to this renowned vacationland, yet lovers of nature and solitude can still find ways to escape the crowds and enjoy the sights, sounds, and smells of duneland, marsh, and woods. Some of the best getaways lie within Cape Cod National Seashore, which protects nearly 44,000 acres of the narrow, curving peninsula that Henry David Thoreau famously described as "the bared and bended arm of Massachusetts."

Crowds were most assuredly not a problem when Thoreau walked the 30 or so miles along the shore from Eastham to Race Point in 1849. The writer-naturalist met oystermen, lighthouse keepers, and wreckers (men who searched beaches for driftwood and other debris) as he and a friend made their way northward, but for the most part they journeyed through a lonely landscape where "the solitude was that of the ocean and the desert combined."

Even then, though, Cape Cod was much changed from the place seen by settlers in the mid-17th century. Once thickly forested, the Cape had by the 1820s been so denuded that erosion and drifting sand were serious problems around towns and farms. Residents (sometimes under legal orders) planted pitch pines, black locust, and beach grass to try to restore stability to the dunes and keep the roads clear of drifts.

Change is a constant on Cape Cod, despite laws and control measures. The terrain here is young, in geologic terms: It was covered by glaciers toward the end of the last ice age, about 18,000 years ago, and it displays the capricious disposition of youth. Waves, winds, and storms continually reshape the peninsula, gnawing away at a beach in one spot, creating new land elsewhere, cutting off a spit to make an island here, joining one to the mainland there. Thoreau estimated that beaches on the eastern shore were disappearing at the rate of a few feet a year, and that observation remains true today. In 1996, two historic lighthouses, Highland Light and Nauset Light, were moved inland from eroding cliffs; without that human intervention, they would have collapsed before long as their foundations were eaten away.

You will find evidence of the glaciers that formed Cape Cod at Fort Hill, a popular hiking area in the middle of the national seashore near Eastham. The boulders scattered along the trails here are glacial erratics—large stones that were picked up by a glacier and carried along as it

moved slowly southward, then left far from their original locations when the ice melted. Nearby Red Maple Swamp, crossed by a boardwalk trail, is one of around 365 kettle ponds on Cape Cod. Each represents a spot where a huge chunk of ice melted, leaving a depression that later filled with fresh water. The red maples that give the swamp its name thrive in moist conditions, as do the black gums (or black tupelos) growing with them in this wetland.

Just north, the Salt Pond Visitor Center can provide maps, trail guides, and an array of other information on the national seashore. The Nauset Marsh Trail here loops down to a salt marsh where waterfowl, wading birds, gulls, and terns can be abundant. In winter, look for northern harriers flying slowly over the cordgrass and adjacent fields for prey; these medium-sized, long-winged hawks are easily identified by their white rump. From spring through fall, watch for ospreys, often known by the folk name "fish hawk." Once threatened by pesticides and persecution, these raptors have made a comeback in the years since DDT was banned.

History and nature meet at the national seashore's Marconi Station Site, a few miles farther north. Here, inventor Guglielmo Marconi demonstrated two-way transatlantic radio communication in 1903, transmitting messages between President Theodore Roosevelt and King Edward VII of England. (Although this event was trumpeted as the first such transmission, Marconi had actually sent test wireless messages across the ocean from Nova Scotia the previous year and had received a test in Newfoundland in 1901.)

Beginning at the Marconi site, the Atlantic White Cedar Swamp Trail offers a look back to Cape Cod's past. Extensive woodlands of Atlantic white cedar once grew throughout the Cape, but the tree's excellent wood made it a favorite of early shipbuilders; within a few generations, the old-growth white cedar stands were gone. Here, a boardwalk passes through a picturesque peat swamp where a new stand of the wetland-loving species has flourished.

Exploring more of the national seashore's 11 self-guiding nature trails will reveal additional aspects of Cape Cod's extraordinary history and ecology. The Beech Forest Trail, near Provincetown, passes through one of the few woodlands of its type remaining on the Cape. The Cranberry Bog Trail, as its name implies, skirts bogs that once were part of an active cranberry farm. The Great Island Trail, on the peninsula's west side, meanders along a spit separating Cape Cod Bay from Wellfleet Harbor. The "island" here—now connected to the mainland—was once a center of the local whaling industry. (Today, these magnificent sea mammals are sought not by harpoon boats but by whale-watching cruise ships, which depart from Provincetown harbor from April through October.)

Many people don't know that the Pilgrims landed first on Cape Cod in November 1620, before continuing to Plymouth Bay a month later. The national seashore's Pilgrim Spring Trail commemorates that historic landfall, leading to a spring representative of the one where the weary travelers "sat us downe and drunke our first New England water."

Dawn breaks over the Atlantic Ocean as waves lap a sandy beach on the Cape Cod peninsula of Massachusetts. Beyond the horizon, the next landfall is Europe.

While many visitors are content simply to lie in the summer sun on one of Cape Cod's splendid beaches, others find the greatest pleasure in more subtle matters: a glimpse of a red fox, looking back curiously as it crosses a field; harbor seals sunning themselves on shore; a least tern diving for fish in a marsh; the stunning pink flower of a lady's-slipper orchid; the cheery spring song of a yellow warbler; the smell of bayberry leaves.

October was Thoreau's favorite time on Cape Cod. Then, he wrote, "I never saw an autumnal landscape so beautifully painted as this was. It was like the richest rug imaginable...." Many experienced travelers—and locals, too—agree. Fall offers great rewards, from colorful foliage to an abundance of migrant waterbirds to strolls along uncrowded beaches, seeing what the sea has brought ashore. Every season, though, brings its own delights on Cape Cod, which is why so many people return year after year without feeling that they have exhausted its variegated charms.

While you are on Cape Cod, take time to visit two other excellent natural areas. The Massachusetts Audubon Society's Wellfleet Bay Wildlife Sanctuary encompasses 1,000 acres on Cape Cod Bay, with hiking trails through salt marsh, woodland, tidal flats, grassland, and other habitats. Monomoy National Wildlife Refuge, near Chatham at the Cape's "elbow," is home to nesting birds from the endangered piping plover to the elegant black skimmer. Tours to refuge islands are offered by Wellfleet Sanctuary and the Cape Cod Museum of Natural History in Brewster.

Gulls ride the skies above Cape Cod National Seashore, a 43,569-acre preserve of salt marshes, sand dunes, woods, and beaches that covers most of the upper arm of the narrow Massachusetts peninsula. Established in 1961 and administered by the National Park Service, the seashore logs nearly five million tourist visits each year.

HIGH PEAKS, STILL LAKES

ADIRONDACK PARK,
New York

ADIRONDACK PARK

There is an agreeable symmetry in the fact that the Adirondack Park is located in the same state as New York City. Just as the Big Apple holds a unique place among American cities—in its size, its colorful history, its diversity, and so variously on—this vast, and vastly renowned, park in upstate New York stands apart in many ways from other natural and recreation areas across the country. Even after the headlong growth of the 20th century, anyone so inclined can leave the intensely urbanized grid of Manhattan and, within a few hours, strike out on a trail leading into wild and remote terrain.

The Adirondack Mountains were at the center of much of our country's earliest debate on issues of preservation and exploitation, of natural beauty and economic development, of public lands and private-property rights. As timber companies, miners, and tourists moved deeper into the rugged backcountry west of Lake Champlain in the mid-19th century, New Yorkers who were concerned about the degradation of forests, wildlife, and water quality convinced the state to act to protect them.

As a result, the New York legislature in 1885 created a forest preserve of public lands in the Adirondacks, an area that the 1895 state constitution declared "shall be forever kept as wild forest lands." The Adirondack Park itself, which includes both the public preserve and intermingled private lands where development is controlled, has expanded over time to encompass nearly six million acres—an area more than twice as large as Yellowstone National Park. Of this, 43 percent is public; the remaining private land includes more than 130 towns and villages.

Apart from its sheer size, it is this patchwork of land use that helps give the Adirondack Park a distinctive place among other natural areas: Resort towns (including Lake Placid, which hosted the 1932 and 1980 Winter Olympics) are interspersed among 17 wilderness areas totaling more than a million acres and well over a million acres of other public forest. The park is crisscrossed by highways, as well as backcountry hiking trails and some of America's finest canoeing routes. Visitors can spend one night in a luxurious hotel and the next at a lakeside campsite where the alarm is the dawn yodeling of a loon.

Though located not far from the Appalachian chain, the Adirondacks are geologically distinct, associated with the great Canadian Shield stretching north across Canada. Peaks here once rose far higher than their present crest of just over a mile, but erosion has worn away overlying material to expose billion-year-old igneous and metamorphic base rock. In the most recent ice ages, immense glaciers scraped the entire landscape clean of vegetation and soil; evidence of their passing includes U-shaped valleys, glacial erratics, cirques (semicircular basins carved into mountainsides), and kettle ponds in depressions left by the melting of huge blocks of ice.

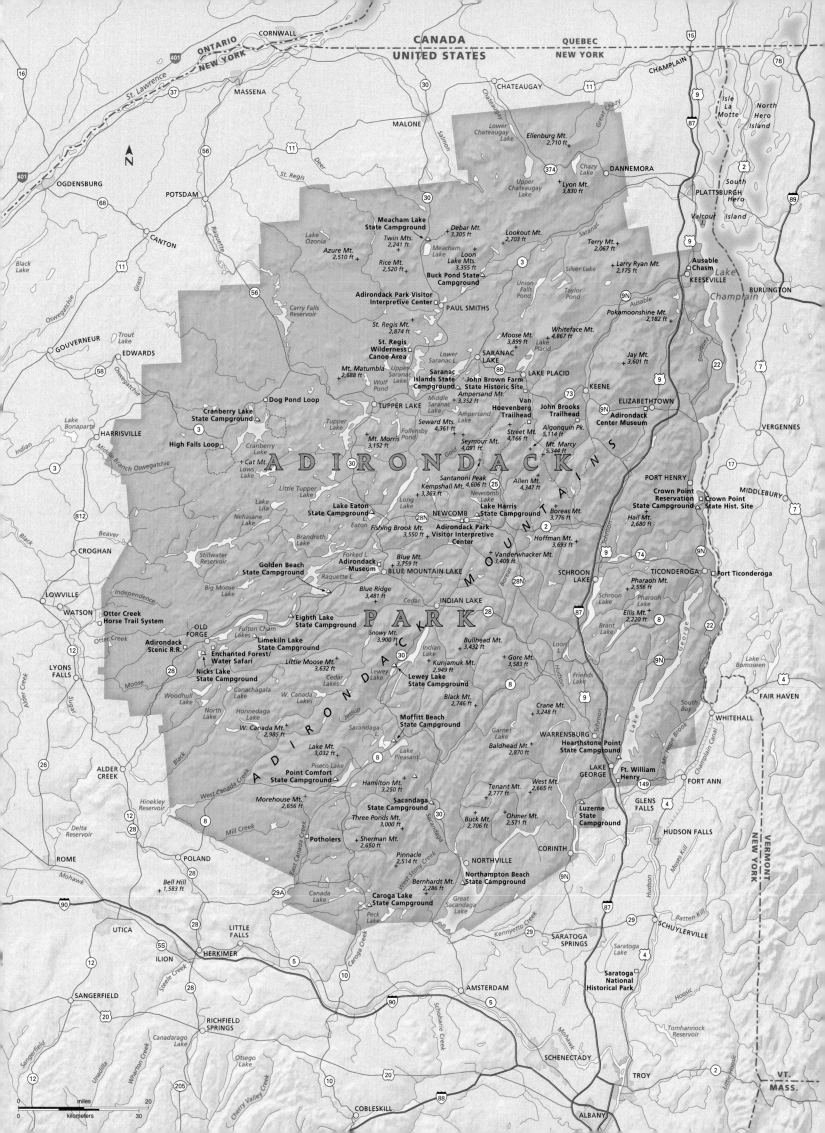

Because all this glacial activity ended only about 14,000 years ago, Adirondack soil is generally thin and infertile, as early settlers discovered when they tried to farm the land.

Countless Adirondack devotees revere the High Peaks region south of Lake Placid as the heart of the park. Here rise Mount Marcy, the highest point in New York at 5,344 feet, and many of the more than 40 other Adirondack mountains over 4,000 feet. The climb to Marcy's summit is, understandably, a popular trip—too popular, perhaps, on summer weekends. For many experienced hikers, the park's (and the state's) second-highest mountain ranks above Marcy as a destination. Algonquin Peak, at 5,114 feet, is famed for its views of the other High Peaks—a spectacular panorama that repays the fairly strenuous four-mile ascent.

As you hike up to a mountain summit, you will note changes in the surrounding vegetation. In the richer soil of lower elevations, northern hardwood forest is dominated by sugar maple, beech, and yellow birch. Higher, red spruce and balsam fir form the boreal forest, with burned or cleared areas covered in paper birch, a fast-growing pioneer species that is eventually shaded out by maturing conifers. And on nine Adirondack

peaks whose tops reach above tree line, you will find a true alpine environment, where plants struggle to survive a harsh climate of short summers, frigid winters, and constant moisture-stealing wind.

Just as much a part of the Adirondacks as its highlands are its lakes, ponds, and rivers, dotted throughout the park and sparkling in the vistas from its mountain crests. The Adirondack Park encompasses at least 2,800 lakes and ponds and around 1,200 miles of rivers designated by the state as wild, scenic, and recreational, plus many hundreds of miles more of smaller brooks.

The mighty Hudson River is born here, near Mount Marcy, while other park streams flow into Lake Champlain and the St. Lawrence, Black, and Mohawk Rivers.

These waterways and lakes offer an endless variety of canoeing opportunities, from a quick paddle around the perimeter of a placid pond to a multiday expedition along lakes and rivers that involves numerous carries — toting your boat and gear overland from a take-out point to the next put-in. The St. Regis Canoe Area, southwest of the settlement of Paul Smiths, is famed for its Route of the Seven Carries, a nine-mile itinerary that has been popular with Adirondack visitors for well over a century. Other favorite canoe trips include the Fulton Chain of Lakes, a 16-mile paddle in the southwestern part of the park, and the Raquette River route, which can stretch to 40 miles.

Though the beauty of these rivers and lakes is undeniable, scientists know that all is not well with Adirondack wetlands. The region's underlying rock and poor soil make it highly susceptible to the effects of acid rain, and in fact many lakes and ponds — especially smaller ones at high elevations — have become too acidic to support fish populations. The problem of acid deposition here has its origin in power plants and industrial areas west of the Adirondacks, and most ecologists believe the only long-term solution is a general heightening of air-quality standards throughout the country.

There is good news, though, elsewhere in the Adirondacks. Bald eagles, peregrine falcons, and ospreys are making a comeback here as they are all around America. Two shy and beautiful members of the weasel family, the fisher and the pine marten, have increased their numbers throughout recent decades. Lynx, killed off in the Adirondacks in the 19th century, may return to the boreal forests here if restocking efforts are successful.

The best places to learn about Adirondack ecology and history, and about the array of opportunities here, are the park's two visitor centers, at Newcomb and Paul Smiths, as well as the Adirondack Museum at Blue Mountain Lake. Exhibits and nature trails will introduce you to mountains and lakes, wildlife and vegetation, popular recreation spots and lonely wilderness areas. So huge is the Adirondack Park that one visit can reveal only a part of its diversity. But even that single visit will show that this great preserve remains, in the words of a 19th-century surveyor, "the wonder and glory of New York."

Still waters of Heart Lake reflect cottony clouds in northeastern New York's Adirondack Park. Created in 1885 as a forest preserve, the park is a quilt that pieces together public and private lands watered by at least 2,800 lakes, ponds, and streams.

BARRIER ISLANDS, DUNES, WETLANDS

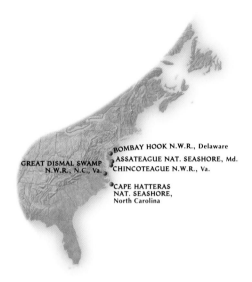

BOMBAY HOOK N.W.R., Delaware
ASSATEAGUE NAT. SEASHORE, Md.
CHINCOTEAGUE N.W.R., Va.
GREAT DISMAL SWAMP
N.W.R., N.C., Va.
CAPE HATTERAS
NAT. SEASHORE,
North Carolina

CAPE HATTERAS NATIONAL SEASHORE

As you walk the beach at Cape Hatteras National Seashore, the landscape around you seems a place of simple elements: sea, sand, sky, and the ever present wind. Add waterbirds and a bit of scrubby vegetation, and the picture appears complete. But as is so often the case in nature, more is going on here in North Carolina's Outer Banks than is apparent at first. The shore that looks so timeless and uncomplicated is in fact a dynamic and inconstant place, beset by powerful forces—terrain as precarious, in its own way, as exists anywhere on earth.

Hatteras and Ocracoke, along with other islands forming the 70-mile-long national seashore, are part of a chain of barrier islands that fringe the United States coastline from New York to Mexico. These long, narrow strips of land were built of sand carried seaward by rivers, then shaped by waves, wind, and currents. Here in the mid-Atlantic region, strong northeasters and regular hurricanes combine to push the islands to the south and west, in a slow but steady migration that's been continuing for thousands of years.

At Cape Hatteras's southeastern point, which forms the "elbow" of the Outer Banks, a lighthouse built in 1870 provides graphic proof of the islands' changeable character. The beach that once stretched more than 5,000 feet east of the first light built in 1803 gradually eroded until, by the 1990s, only about 120 feet remained; without intervention, this historic structure inevitably would have toppled into the ocean. In 1999, the lighthouse was placed on rollers and moved 2,900 feet inland—protecting it for the next century at the current coastal erosion rate. The black-and-white striped spire (at 208 feet, the tallest brick lighthouse in the country) still stands as the focal point for visitors to the national seashore.

In summer, Cape Hatteras is crowded with vacationers enjoying typical beach pastimes: swimming, sunbathing, sightseeing, surfing, and sampling seafood at local resorts. For those interested in nature, other times of year provide more opportunity for solitude and tranquil observation.

Many travelers find fall the best time on the Outer Banks. The great southbound migration of birds gets under way in September, bringing an array of species to beaches, thickets, and the marshes fronting Pamlico Sound, the shallow body of water between the islands and the mainland. Peregrine falcons are a common sight in fall, patrolling beaches with powerful wingbeats in search of shorebirds or waterfowl. Merlins (falcons smaller than peregrines) and Cooper's and sharp-shinned hawks also seek birds as prey, hoping to catch a warbler, thrush, or sparrow in scrub and scattered woodlands of live oak, red cedar, yaupon holly, and wax myrtle. Flocks of sandpipers, plovers, gulls, and terns feed along the shore, while out to sea pass ducks, loons, grebes, and gannets.

Contained within the national seashore, Pea Island National Wildlife

Refuge has long been a favorite destination for East Coast birders. Thousands of waterfowl congregate in shallow wetlands here from fall through spring, including tundra swans, Canada and snow geese, and two dozen or more species of ducks. Much of this variety is easily seen from trails and observation points a few miles south of Oregon Inlet, near the refuge visitor center. In spring, the great gatherings of waterfowl disperse northward, but the refuge remains a superb birding spot. Nesting birds in and near the refuge include great and snowy egrets, little blue and tricolored herons, white and glossy ibises, American oystercatcher, black-necked stilt, common moorhen, gull-billed and sandwich terns, and such

secretive species as clapper and king rails and marsh wrens. Piping plovers, endangered by beachfront development and off-road vehicles, breed in small numbers in protected areas in the Outer Banks and can sometimes be found in flocks of more common shorebirds.

The Cape Hatteras area marks the northernmost Atlantic nesting ground for the threatened loggerhead sea turtle, females of which come ashore in late spring and summer to lay their eggs on beaches. These huge reptiles, weighing as much as 350 pounds as mature adults, begin their lives as tiny hatchlings that scramble to sea as soon as they emerge from their buried nests. The sex of loggerheads is determined by the

Sea oats top dunes
that wind has sculpted
into sinuous curves on
Portsmouth Island,
one of three undeveloped
islands south of Cape
Hatteras that make
up Cape Lookout
National Seashore.

temperature at which the eggs are incubated; although relatively few nests are found in this northerly location, scientists believe they may provide a high percentage of the males in the entire Atlantic population.

One of the great pleasures of Cape Hatteras National Seashore comes from simply strolling the beaches, watching the small shorebirds called sanderlings chase the waves back and forth, feeling the salty breeze, and seeing what the ocean has brought to land. The ubiquitous sand dollars are the flat, bony tests, or skeletons, of a sea urchin that in life is covered with small brownish spines. You may come across hundreds of tiny, beautifully colored coquina clams, which range from pure white to red, orange, or purple, or may be striped in endless variations. With a field guide to sea creatures you can spend a day identifying all sorts of beach life, from barnacles and sea stars to occasional jellyfish washed ashore.

Just about anyplace you walk Cape Hatteras beaches, you will see anglers trying their luck in the surf. Red drum, bluefish, striped bass, flounder, speckled trout, croaker, and many other species make the Outer Banks one of America's most famous and productive fishing spots.

Just to the south, across Ocracoke Inlet, Cape Lookout National Seashore offers many of the same delights as Cape Hatteras, with the enhancement of far greater solitude. Reached only by boat, the 56-mile section of the Outer Banks comprises three main islands: Portsmouth Island, Core Banks, and Shackleford Banks. These undeveloped islands can be toured only on foot, by four-wheel-drive vehicle, or by private shuttle services. Rental cabins are available.

Visitors to Cape Lookout must be self-sufficient in their wanderings over the isolated islands; carrying adequate fresh water, sun protection, and insect repellent is especially important. But for those who arrive prepared, the chance to enjoy this world of marsh, beach, and surf in relative seclusion makes the effort of preparation more than worthwhile. Camped amid sand dunes topped with wind-blown sea oats, with only shorebirds for company, you will imagine the real world lies much farther away than the few miles across Core Sound.

ASSATEAGUE ISLAND NATIONAL SEASHORE AND CHINCOTEAGUE NATIONAL WILDLIFE REFUGE

About 135 miles north of Cape Hatteras, Assateague Island National Seashore beckons lovers of seascapes and wildlife. The seashore shares Assateague, a 37-mile-long barrier island at the Maryland-Virginia state line, with a state park and part of the Chincoteague National Wildlife Refuge. The seashore is a popular camping and recreational destination in the warmer months; crowds decrease from fall through spring, even though that is when the biting insects are least bothersome.

Short nature trails near the Maryland entrance station interpret the plant and animal life of the dunes, the marsh, and the forest, providing an excellent introduction to the barrier island environment. Whenever possible, take advantage of ranger-led tours to learn more about this deceptively vulnerable world, threatened in so many place by resorts, vacation homes, and other development.

Most travelers interested in natural history—and especially birders—spend most of their time at Assateague Island in Chincoteague National Wildlife Refuge, which is at the Virginia end of the island.

Renowned as one of the finest bird-watching sites on the Atlantic coast, the more than 14,000-acre refuge comprises beach, bay, mudflats, marsh, freshwater ponds, and pine forest, creating a mix of habitats that attract a wide range of species, from flocks of wintering waterfowl to terns, shorebirds, and wading birds such as herons and egrets.

The most popular animals on Assateague, however, are the island's famed "ponies"—small horses, actually. Inhabiting both the national seashore and Chincoteague, they delight visitors with their shaggy charm. The horses are descended from stock brought to the island in the 1600s by local planters; over the years, they have adapted well to the often harsh seaside environment. Their size is thought to be a result of a rather poor diet (mostly cordgrass and beach grass), and their chubby look comes from the amount of fresh water they must drink to offset the salt crystals consumed while grazing. While the ponies are appealing, they are wild. Enjoy them from a distance to avoid bites and kicks.

BOMBAY HOOK NATIONAL WILDLIFE REFUGE

The vast salt marshes that line the shores of Delaware Bay between Delaware and New Jersey, at the mouth of the Delaware River, embody

Cattle egrets keep watch as wild horses graze in Chincoteague National Wildlife Refuge. Chincoteague, more than 14,000 acres of beach, dune, marsh, and maritime forest, ranks as one of the most visited refuges in the United States. It is contained in Assateague Island National Seashore, part of the national park system since 1965.

a hybrid environment, neither solid ground nor open water. Sometimes dry, sometimes flooded, sometimes muddy, and laced with meandering tidal rivers, these wetlands seem inhospitable to humans but constitute invaluable wildlife habitat. Waterfowl congregate here in huge flocks from fall through spring, and many species of fish and invertebrates depend on the brackish shallows for all or parts of their life cycles.

The nearly 16,000 acres of Bombay Hook National Wildlife Refuge, northeast of Dover, are mostly salt marsh, which, along with woodland, old fields, and freshwater impoundments, make it a wonderfully productive place for wildlife observation. The 12-mile auto-tour route provides access to all the refuge habitat types, and hiking trails allow closer, more leisurely looks at flora and fauna.

Some refuge wildlife announces itself boldly: Bald eagles nest here, and it is impossible to miss summer multitudes of wading birds or cold-weather flocks of snow and Canada geese and ducks. You must look a little more closely for other varieties, though. In spring and fall, shrubs and trees can be alive with migrant songbirds, from diminutive kinglets and warblers to thrushes and orioles. Red foxes, river otters, muskrats, beaver, and white-tailed deer are among the refuge mammals, though you will need patience and good fortune to see many of them. Sitting quietly beside a swampy pond might reveal a turtle (several species are common, including snapping, red-bellied, and eastern painted), a bullfrog, or a northern water snake.

In late spring, horseshoe crabs—fearsome-looking but harmless creatures more closely related to spiders than to crabs—come to Delaware Bay's fringing shallows to lay billions of their tiny greenish eggs. Well over a million shorebirds stop here in their northbound migration to feast on this bounty, making the region a vital "refueling" station, essential to these birds' survival. More than 20 species can be found at times in spring, the most common of which are sanderling, red knot, semipalmated sandpiper, and ruddy turnstone.

In recent years, the increased harvest of horseshoe crabs (mostly for crab and conch bait) has caused concern for both horseshoe crab and shorebird populations. Conservationists are working with state and federal wildlife officials to protect this resource and assure the continuing health of one of the Atlantic coast's most prolific, if often little appreciated, ecosystems.

GREAT DISMAL SWAMP NATIONAL WILDLIFE REFUGE

The Great Dismal Swamp may have been "dismal" to early travelers who had to slog through its bogs, marshes, and flooded woods, but the naturalist who visits this wetland on the Virginia-North Carolina border today will discover a place of delight. Despite 300 years of drainage and logging, the more than 109,000-acre tract protected since 1974 within Great Dismal Swamp National Wildlife Refuge endures as home to varied flora and fauna.

History buffs who know the background of our first President may suspect a connection when they see the name "Washington Ditch" on the refuge map. Indeed, George Washington was involved in a company that partially drained and logged the swamp in the 1760s—one of the first of many operations that substantially altered the area's natural vegetation

Snow geese crowd a golden sky over salt marshes of Bombay Hook National Wildlife Refuge in eastern Delaware. The wetlands of the Delaware Bay afford prime habitat to migrating birds.

and water flow. Where wetland-loving species such as bald cypress, tupelo, and Atlantic white cedar once were dominant, trees more tolerant of drier conditions, especially red maple, have taken over large areas. Refuge management techniques, including controlling water movement, prescribed burning, and selective tree cutting and planting, are aimed at restoring as much of the swamp's original diversity as possible.

Hiking trails running alongside old drainage ditches provide plenty of opportunity for exploring the swamp, as does the mile-long Dismal Town boardwalk trail, at the Washington Ditch entrance. The careful, observant (and lucky) visitor may spot a black bear, river otter, bobcat, or canebrake rattlesnake, among sightings of more common species such as white-tailed deer, gray squirrel, and yellow-bellied turtle. Botanists note the presence of three special plants: log fern, a generally rare species that is more common here than anywhere else; dwarf trillium, which blooms in mid-March; and silky camellia, a tall shrub that opens its showy white blossoms in late May.

Birders, though, are the ones who may appreciate the Great Dismal Swamp most. Such wetland species as wood duck, American woodcock, barred owl, belted kingfisher, Louisiana waterthrush, and prothonotary warbler are common, as are typical forest birds such as the pileated wood-pecker, wood thrush, yellow-throated vireo, American redstart, ovenbird, and summer tanager. Birders also search here for Swainson's warbler, an uncommon bird of southern swamps and canebrakes, and the Wayne's subspecies of the black-throated green warbler, found only from south-ern Virginia to South Carolina.

In spring, when the songs of these and dozens of other species ring out throughout this great swamp, it seems anything but a dismal place.

Still waters in the Great Dismal Swamp, a more than 109,000-acre wildlife refuge on the Virginia-North Carolina border, mirror curving trunks and thick foliage of bald cypresses and other wetland-loving tree species.

APPALACHIAN HIGHLANDS

MONONGAHELA
NAT. FOREST,
W. Va.

• DELAWARE WATER GAP N.R.A.,
N.J., Penn.

• SHENANDOAH NAT. PARK,
Virginia

MONONGAHELA NATIONAL FOREST

No one who loves the outdoors—whether hiker, camper, photographer, bird-watcher, or one of any other inclination—could fail to be impressed with the range of opportunities available in the Monongahela National Forest. Sprawling over 909,000 acres of West Virginia's Allegheny Mountains, this rugged expanse can serve as an adventure arena, wilderness retreat, botanical garden, playground, scenic area, or outdoor classroom, depending on a visitor's interests.

From the observation tower on Spruce Knob, the state's highest point at 4,861 feet, the view takes in thickly forested mountains deeply cut by stream-carved valleys. Stands of red spruce at the higher elevations are reminiscent of Canadian forests. Dominating the lower slopes are the typical Appalachian hardwoods: oaks, hickories, beeches, magnolias, and maples, which in the fall create a colorful spectacle. Monongahela's wildlife checklist also includes species associated with more northern regions; birders especially enjoy the chance to see breeders such as northern saw-whet owl, olive-sided flycatcher, Swainson's thrush, and Blackburnian warbler.

Like most eastern forests, these Allegheny woods were thoroughly cut over beginning in the late 19th century, when ancient spruce, hemlock, and other timber trees fell to loggers' saws and axes. Fires swept across harvested areas, feeding on accumulated debris. Within a few decades, what had been magnificent mountain woodland became abused, nearly denuded barrens. Since the establishment of the national forest in 1920, timber harvest has been managed in a more careful, sustainable manner; today, maturing mixed woods reflect the goal of multiple use, providing for the needs of hikers, wildlife-watchers, hunters, anglers, and campers, among others.

In the southern part of the Monongahela, the Highland Scenic Byway makes a great introduction to the region. Winding for 43 miles eastward from Richwood to U.S. 219 north of Marlinton, the drive varies in elevation from 2,325 feet to over 4,500 feet; four overlooks offer superb panoramas of the mountains. Midway along the byway, stop at the Cranberry Mountain Visitor Center, where exhibits and programs interpret the environment you have been traversing.

Not to be missed: a visit to the nearby Cranberry Glades Botanical Area, a National Natural Landmark that preserves one of West Virginia's most fascinating and unusual environments. A half-mile boardwalk crosses peat bogs so acidic that only a limited array of plants can grow, including cranberry, mosses, lichens, and bog rosemary (found here at the southern limit of its range). Wildflowers flourish in delightful variety, from the early spring skunk cabbage (named for its fetid odor) to orchids to the brilliant golden-yellow swamp candle. Scrubby

Sandstone face of Seneca Rocks showcases a rising moon in Spruce Knob-Seneca Rocks National Recreation Area in the Monongahela National Forest, West Virginia. Established in 1965, it was the first national recreation area designated in a national forest. Seneca Rocks offers some of the best rock climbing on the East Coast.

woods of alder, hemlock, yellow birch, and black ash surround the open expanse of bog.

To the north of the glades extends the 35,864-acre Cranberry Wilderness, where rugged mountains are drained by a seemingly endless number of beautiful streams, and 60 miles of trails invite backpackers to find all the solitude they desire.

Solitude is not so easy to come by in the Dolly Sods Wilderness, a popular destination in the northern part of the Monongahela National Forest. On fair-weather weekends, hikers abound on trails in this 10,215-acre tract — but that is no reason to avoid it. Try to visit on a weekday or early in the morning to appreciate its distinctive environment. (By the way, this area's odd name has an explanation: It was once owned by a settler with the German name Dahle, and "sods" is a local name for a grassy area.)

In places, this high, wind-buffeted plateau takes on a stark, moorlike aspect, with rock fields, stunted trees, bogs, and extensive stands of azalea, rhododendron, blueberry, and mountain laurel. (The early-summer floral display here is one of the glories of the national forest.) As you hike, it requires little imagination to picture yourself somewhere in Canada, rather than on the same latitude as Washington, D.C. Just to the north of the wilderness, in the Dolly Sods Scenic Area, the short Northland Loop Trail features signs interpreting this boggy, high-elevation habitat.

A bit farther north, near the Red Creek Campground, volunteers have been trapping and banding southbound migrant birds every fall since 1961. From mid-August to October, visitors are welcome to watch the process, which provides an excellent chance to study warblers, vireos, flycatchers, sparrows, and other species that normally are only glimpsed in treetops and thickets.

In the central part of the national forest, the 4,460-foot peak called Gaudineer Knob offers a special treat. While most of the terrain here was cut and burned, a surveyor's error (and some good luck) left a small tract of old-growth red spruce standing untouched. In the 140-acre Gaudineer Scenic Area you will find trees rising more than 100 feet, with a diameter of three feet or more; these specimens are thought to be around 300 years old. And not only the trees are worth seeing here: The special environment is home to northern animal species including

snowshoe hare, rock vole (a mouselike rodent), and birds such as golden-crowned kinglet, veery, Swainson's thrush, blue-headed vireo, and magnolia warbler.

Mountain bikers, canoeists, and rock climbers will also find abundant opportunities in the national forest, with trails, streams, and cliffs offering all levels of challenge. So large and varied is the Monongahela that recreationists of all types can satisfy their desires here—there is plenty of room for everyone in these wild West Virginia mountains.

Arching antlers mark
a male white-tailed
deer in Virginia's
Shenandoah National
Park. The animals, once
scarce in an area settled
and logged in the 1800s,
have rebounded in the
protected ribbon of wild
country that stretches
along the Blue Ridge
Mountains of the
central Appalachians.

SHENANDOAH NATIONAL PARK

In their 1,800-mile course from Alabama to Canada, the Appalachian Mountains trend from southwest to northeast in parallel lines of wooded highlands, which from lookouts often resemble nothing so much as green waves stretching to the horizon. The Blue Ridge Mountains of the central Appalachians make up one of these waves; sitting atop their crest in northwestern Virginia stretches the slender strand of Shenandoah National Park.

Around 70 miles long and at times only a mile wide, Shenandoah each year attracts nearly two million visitors, who enjoy abundant wildflowers, picturesque waterfalls, brilliant fall foliage, and vast vistas from roadside overlooks. Skyline Drive, which meanders 105 miles through the park, provides easy access to attractions, but also gets crowded, especially during fall weekends. In Shenandoah, it is important to park the car, walk the trails, and enjoy the wilder territory away from the road.

The park's more than 500 miles of trails include easy interpretive walks, steep climbs, and 101 miles of the Appalachian National Scenic Trail (AT), which runs along the length of the park. Forty-one percent of Shenandoah has been designated official wilderness, and it is in this backcountry where you are most likely to find solitude.

Deciduous trees make up the predominant woodland in the park, among them oaks, hickories, maples, tulip poplars, beeches, ashes, and basswoods. Hemlocks are also common in the park, but they have suffered greatly in recent years from infestation by a tiny insect called the hemlock woolly adelgid, which has attacked stands of these conifers throughout the eastern United States.

Wildflowers and blooming shrubs brighten Shenandoah's woods and meadows in exciting diversity—from bloodroot, peeking out through dead leaves in early spring, on to the lady's-slipper orchids of late spring, mountain laurel of summer, and the goldenrods and asters of fall, to list only a few of the dozens of park species. Birders find Shenandoah a rewarding destination, especially in spring, when waves of migrants follow the Blue Ridge crest on their way north.

Stop at one of the park's three visitor centers. Ranger programs, covering subjects from history to birds of prey, will help you appreciate Shenandoah in ways you might not discover on your own.

DELAWARE WATER GAP
NATIONAL RECREATION AREA

Beginning in the early 1960s, a dam and reservoir were proposed that would have flooded a scenic stretch of the Delaware River along the Pennsylvania-New Jersey border. Citizens concerned about the environment responded quickly and forcefully. The Delaware Water Gap National Recreation Area was established in 1965, in anticipation of the reservoir being built. Protests led to years of controversy. Congress designated 40 miles of the Delaware River as a recreational and scenic river in 1978, resulting in the cancellation of the dam project in 1992. Today, boaters, anglers, and hikers give thanks for the turn of events every time they visit the park to enjoy its varied resources.

Located an easy drive from the metropolitan areas of New York, New Jersey, and Pennsylvania, Delaware Water Gap is named for the spot where the Delaware River bends though a gap in the Kittatinny Ridge of the Appalachian Mountains. In the 19th century many resort hotels in the area catered to guests escaping crowded eastern cities.

One of the best ways to see the park, quite naturally, is from the water. Local outfitters rent canoes and rafts that can be launched at landings spaced every eight to ten miles along the river. Shoreline campsites make overnight trips an appealing option. Hiking and nature trails (including 25 miles of the Appalachian Trail) wind through the park, offering a chance to enjoy the deciduous woodland covering the riverside hills. Popular routes climb Mount Tammany on the New Jersey side of the gap and Mount Minsi on the Pennsylvania side.

Excellent trails can be found at the Pocono Environmental Education Center, in the central part of the park on the Pennsylvania side. Here, a former honeymoon resort has been converted into a nature-study center presenting a variety of programs throughout the year. Twelve miles of trails at the center traverse forest, fields, and streamside hemlock ravines.

From the grace of a trillium flower to the spring song of a thrush to the sight of a bald eagle soaring over the river, Delaware Water Gap still brings the marvels of nature within reach of some of America's greatest urban centers, just as it did a century ago.

Below forested slopes of Mount Tammany, in New Jersey, the Delaware River winds into Pennsylvania. The Delaware Water Gap National Recreation Area preserves 40 miles of the river and adjoining acres of land where it cuts through a deep V-shaped gap in the Appalachians.

GREAT SMOKY MOUNTAINS, WILD RIVERS

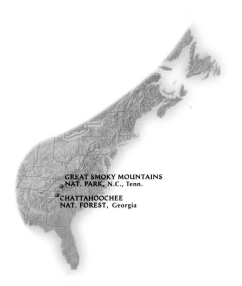

GREAT SMOKY MOUNTAINS
NAT. PARK, N.C., Tenn.

CHATTAHOOCHEE
NAT. FOREST, Georgia

GREAT SMOKY MOUNTAINS NATIONAL PARK

Tulip poplars soaring more than a hundred feet into the air, their trunks as straight as columns of a Greek temple. A stream shaded by the dense, green foliage of hemlocks. An open woodland dotted with an array of wild-flowers. The glistening spray of a waterfall. The startling drumroll sound of a male ruffed grouse in spring. The fragrance of spruce. The soul-inspir-ing view from atop one of the highest peaks in the Appalachians.

Sights, sounds, and smells like these only begin to tell the story of Great Smoky Mountains National Park, a place whose scenery is more than matched by its biological richness. Encompassing 800 square miles of some of the most rugged highlands in the East, the park remains a magnificent place for wilderness lovers, despite its popularity. More than nine million people visit this park on the Tennessee-North Carolina bor-der each year; far too few of them, though, leave paved roads and look-out points to experience the wonders of the landscape around them.

Facts and figures cannot portray Great Smoky's beauty, but they can help illustrate its uniqueness. Most important is the park's elevation, which ranges from 800 feet on its western boundary to 6,643 feet atop Clingmans Dome, the second highest mountain in the eastern U.S. Each thousand-foot gain in elevation is the equivalent of traveling north more than 250 miles—which means that ascending to the park's highest point is, environmentally speaking, like taking a trip to Canada.

This elevation span, combined with the park's high precipitation (more than 85 inches annually), creates a diversity matched in few temperate-zone locations around the globe. More than 4,000 species of plants grow in the park, in addition to more than 130 species of trees. The Smoky Mountains host one of the world's most varied populations of salaman-ders, with 27 species of these inconspicuous, moisture-loving amphibians present. Breeding birds range from such typical southeastern species as indigo bunting, white-eyed vireo, and yellow-breasted chat to others such as red-breasted nuthatch, Blackburnian warbler, and brown creeper that are usually associated with New England or Canada.

Within park valleys, the forest type called cove hardwood predomi-nates, with primary species including tulip poplar (despite its name, a member of the magnolia family), sweet gum, basswood, red maple, and black birch. Pines and oaks grow on dry ridges, while higher slopes are home to a hardwood forest of American beech, sugar maple, and yellow birch. Above 5,000 feet, spruce-fir woodland takes over. Open areas, called balds, top some peaks; the origin of these treeless expanses is debat-ed, but their splendor is unquestionable in spring and summer when mountain laurels, rhododendrons, and flame azaleas burst into bloom.

The park's most popular area is Cades Cove, a broad, low-lying val-ley in the west. Here, historic structures such as log cabins, country

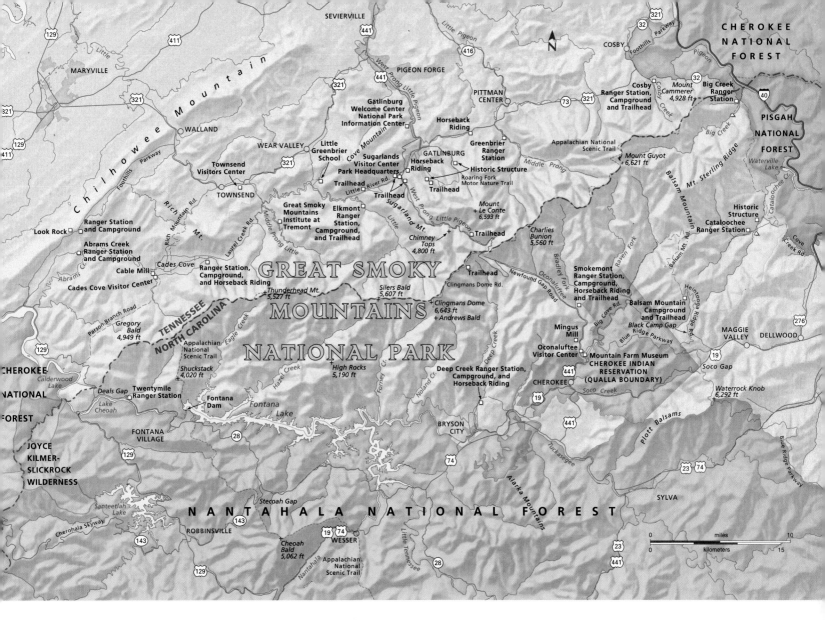

churches, and a working gristmill combine with splendid scenery to create a multifaceted destination. White-tailed deer, birds, and other wildlife are common in the open, parklike meadows around the 11-mile loop road. Unpaved Rich Mountain Road winds up oak-covered slopes northward to fabulous viewpoints back across the valley. While Cades Cove's popularity is justified by its many attractions, park rangers encourage visitors to consider a trip to Cataloochee Valley, in the eastern part of the park, which also boasts abundant wildlife and great scenery.

U.S. 441 bisects Great Smoky Mountains National Park, topping out at 5,088-foot Newfound Gap. From here, a side road leads to Clingmans Dome. This peak, straddling the Tennessee-North Carolina line, is reached by a half-mile trail from the road's end. Views from the summit in North Carolina are spectacular: On clear days seven states are visible.

On Clingmans, it is impossible to miss dramatic evidence of one of the great American ecological tragedies of recent decades. What was once a thriving forest of Fraser fir and red spruce is now a place of dead, bare trunks and dying trees. A tiny insect called the balsam woolly adelgid, accidentally introduced from Europe, has killed 95 percent of the region's firs. Control measures are laborious, costly, and only partly effective, and the resulting devastation has caused a major transformation of the southern Appalachians' environment.

With more than 850 miles of hiking trails, Great Smoky offers plenty

of ways to escape traffic, crowds, and noise. Even in often congested Cades Cove, trails off the scenic loop provide solitude. One of the park's most appealing trails, Gregory Ridge, begins on Forge Creek Road south of the cove. This strenuous hike climbs 3,000 feet in 5.5 miles, but the reward is a journey through old-growth forest with huge tulip poplars, topping out at Gregory Bald, where flame azaleas blossom in June.

The famed Appalachian Trail runs for 71.2 miles along park mountain crests. Most easily accessible at Newfound Gap, the AT offers excellent hiking possibilities. The four-mile (one way) walk eastward to Charlies Bunion provides great views in return for moderate effort. With a good trail map and advice from park rangers, you can find countless other routes to match your ability and interests. Some of the park's finest trails lead to its many waterfalls, appealing destinations for day hikes.

CHATTAHOOCHEE NATIONAL FOREST

Stretching across three-quarters of a million acres of northern Georgia, the Chattahoochee National Forest abounds with natural attractions, from the state's tallest peak to the southern terminus of the Appalachian Trail to one of the most famous rivers in the entire United States.

On clear days, four states can be seen from the summit of 4,784-foot Brasstown Bald, located in the northeastern part of the state less than ten miles south of the North Carolina line. This Georgia high point makes a good beginning for exploring the Chattahoochee, since the visitor center here offers interpretive exhibits and sells forest maps. Naturalists know Brasstown as a place to see nesting birds not found in the state outside the upland region, including ruffed grouse, common raven, veery, black-throated blue warbler, and dark-eyed junco.

Not far to the southeast, the twin cascades of Anna Ruby Falls make up one of the most dramatic of the national forest's many waterfalls. Southwest of Blairsville, the Sosobee Cove and Cooper Creek Scenic Areas make wonderful destinations to enjoy trails through hardwood forest; the former site includes a magnificent stand of old-growth tulip poplars.

Beginning at Springer Mountain, the Appalachian Trail passes through Georgia for 75.4 miles on its way north to Maine. Short sections of the trail are easily accessible and allow fine day hikes. One excellent example is the short, easy trail to Long Creek Falls, south of the town of Blue Ridge, which follows a section of the Appalachian Trail for most of its length. Also intersecting here, appropriately enough, is the Benton McKaye Trail, named for one of the most important of the Appalachian Trail's early supporters.

Bordering the Chattahoochee National Forest on the east and in part forming the Georgia-South Carolina line, the Chattooga River ranks near the top of America's wildest, most thrilling—and potentially most dangerous—whitewater streams. James Dickey's book *Deliverance* and the movie based on it made the Chattooga famous, attracting river-runners eager to challenge its ferocious rapids. But while the upper river is suitable for moderately skilled canoeists, the lower Chattooga challenges even the most accomplished. Joining a raft trip organized by an outfitter allows nonexperts to experience this spectacular river without risking life and limb. For a dry-land view, hike the Chattooga River Trail, which parallels the river upstream from the U.S. 76 bridge.

Dawn kindles gentle crests of the Great Smoky Mountains National Park, 800 square miles of rugged highlands that border Tennessee and North Carolina.

OLD-GROWTH PINES, SALT MARSH, SANDHILLS

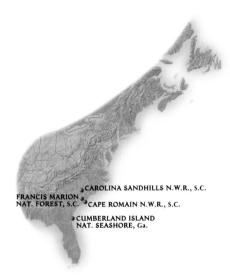

CAROLINA SANDHILLS N.W.R., S.C.

FRANCIS MARION
NAT. FOREST, S.C.   CAPE ROMAIN N.W.R., S.C.

CUMBERLAND ISLAND
NAT. SEASHORE, Ga.

CAPE ROMAIN NATIONAL WILDLIFE REFUGE AND FRANCIS MARION NATIONAL FOREST

Driving north up the Atlantic coast from the historic old city of Charleston, South Carolina, a nature enthusiast encounters a dilemma, although a pleasant one: Would it be more fun to visit a beach or a pine forest? A swamp or a salt marsh? Is it a day to stroll barefoot through the surf, looking for seashells? To scan a wetland for alligators? To hike a woodland trail in search of rare birds? Newcomers trying to decide among these choices should stop at the Sewee Visitor and Environmental Education Center, on U.S. 17 near the town of Awendaw. In an unusual cooperative effort, this site serves as the visitor center for both Cape Romain National Wildlife Refuge and the adjacent Francis Marion National Forest. Together, these areas offer a multitude of avenues for exploring the region's natural history. The exhibits, maps, and information available at the center will help travelers get started on their discoveries.

Cape Romain stretches for 22 miles along the South Carolina coast, its 64,000 acres taking in beach, salt marsh, ponds, woodland, scrub, and a maze of waterways winding among low barrier islands. Most of the refuge is difficult to reach except by boat, and it has no roads, trails, or facilities. One notable exception is Bull Island, a 6-by-2-mile tract with 16 miles of roads used only for hiking and a 2-mile national recreation trail. Commercial ferries run regular trips to the island, which is nearly 3 miles off the coast; the visitor center can provide a schedule.

Wildlife is ever present on Bull Island, from ubiquitous gulls and terns to fox squirrels (of the southeastern black form, with a characteristic pied face) scampering through the trees. Threatened loggerhead sea turtles nest on island beaches, females coming ashore in late spring and summer to excavate holes for their eggs—most of which are soon moved by refuge staff to predator-proof enclosures. Inland ponds are year-round home to alligators, otters, and wood ducks and from fall until spring to an array of other waterfowl. Sandpipers and plovers feed along the beach, and herons and egrets wade shallow marshes in search of fish and frogs.

In 1987, Cape Romain was chosen as a wild propagation site for red wolves, in one of the first steps in a program aimed at saving this critically endangered mammal. Since then, breeding wolves on the island have provided young for release at selected wild lands in the Southeast. Your chances of spotting this shy animal are low, but most visitors find it thrilling simply to know that the red wolf roams free here. (A special interpretive display at the Sewee Visitor Center includes captive wolves.)

Inland from the refuge, Francis Marion National Forest's 250,000 acres present a different set of habitats. Extensive sandy ridges (relict beaches from a time when the Atlantic extended farther west) encourage

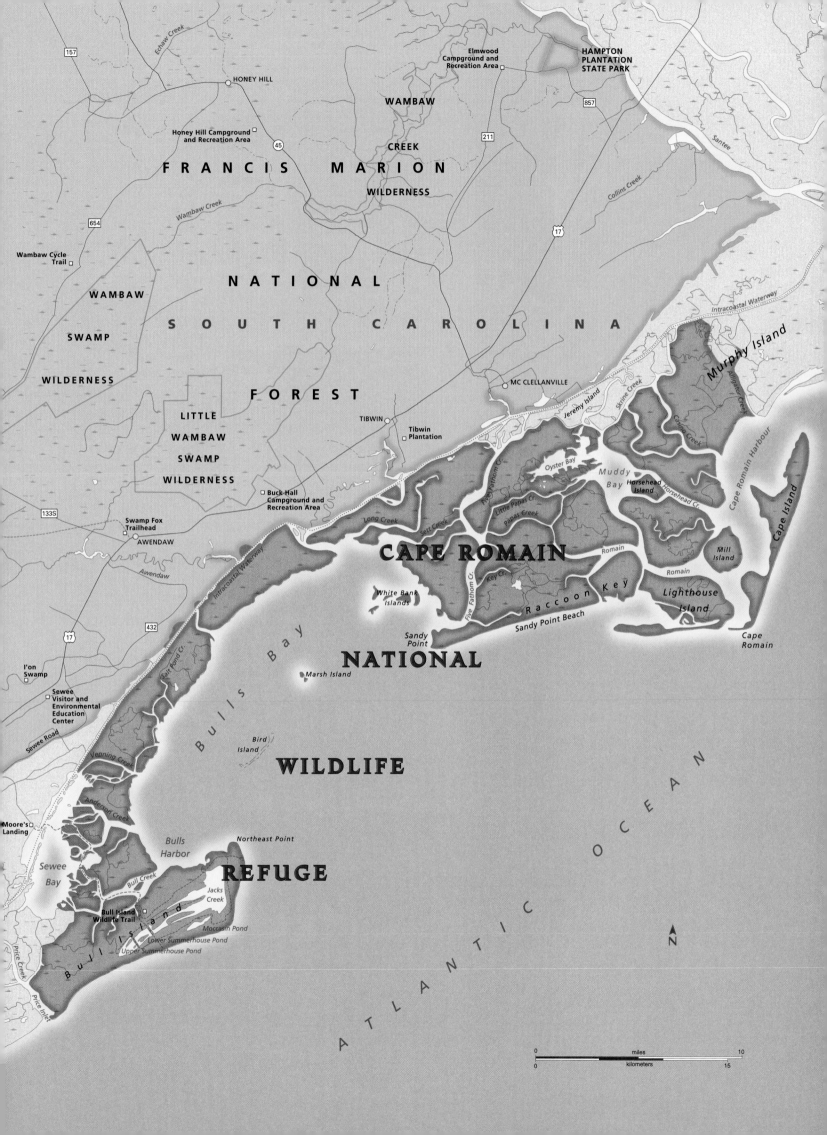

the growth of longleaf and loblolly pines, while bald cypress and water tupelo thrive in swampy lowlands. In certain places, the regionally distinctive oval depressions called Carolina bays—of unknown origin—support plant species that include pond pine, sweetleaf, and red bay and also carnivorous, species such as sundew and pitcher plants.

Swallow-tailed kites nest in the forest. In bottomland areas such as I'on Swamp, birds include barred owl, red-shouldered hawk, wood thrush, and prothono-

Like bleached bones, wave-worn tree trunks litter a beach on Bull Island, part of Cape Romain National Wildlife Refuge in South Carolina. Hurricane Hugo devastated the island in 1989, but it continues to recover and remains a vital part of the 64,000-acre tapestry of beach, salt marsh, scrub, woodland, and waterways that make up the reserve.

tary warbler. The I'on is famed among birders as the last place where Bachman's warbler is known to have been found. Last seen in the 1960s, the black-and-yellow bird is presumed extinct; a southern swamp specialist, it declined in the 20th century for reasons that remain unclear.

National forest personnel manage large areas to restore the longleaf pine ecosystem, once widespread in the South, which in its original state featured pines with an open, grassy understory. Regular burning was an essential part of the ecosystem, and today managed fires promote its recovery. Brown-headed nuthatches and Bachman's sparrows nest in such areas, but the most famous inhabitant is the red-cockaded woodpecker. The destruction of mature pinewoods, essential for the species' nesting success, brought this small woodpecker to endangered status. The Francis Marion is one of many southern forests striving to increase the red-cockaded woodpecker's numbers.

Both Cape Romain and Francis Marion were hit hard by Hurricane Hugo in 1989. But such devastating events have always been a part of the coastal environment; afterwards, the natural succession of plant species assures varied habitats to support diverse flora and fauna.

CAROLINA SANDHILLS NATIONAL WILDLIFE REFUGE

Millions of years ago, when sea levels were higher, ancient rivers formed a huge, sandy delta along the East Coast of North America. Later, when the ocean retreated, erosion created the rolling topography of the region now called the Carolina Sandhills, which spans 15 counties in North and South Carolina. Exceptional in both plant and animal species, this terrain of dry uplands and scattered swampy bottoms can be explored at Carolina Sandhills National Wildlife Refuge, northeast of Columbia.

Longleaf pine woodland dominated in the Sandhills, just as it once did throughout the Southeast from Virginia to eastern Texas. On the refuge, land managers use regular burning to reestablish the open, parklike pine landscape that existed before logging, agriculture, and fire suppression in large part obliterated it. As a result, Carolina Sandhills boasts the largest population of the endangered red-cockaded woodpecker of any national wildlife refuge.

This highly specialized species nests and roosts in small cooperative groups, excavating cavities only in mature pines. Once abundant in southern pinewoods, the red-cockaded woodpecker declined quickly as old-growth timber fell to the saw. Cavity trees on the refuge are marked with white bands of paint, and active cavity holes show fresh flows of shiny whitish sap. (Cavity pines are sometimes called candle trees for their distinctive appearance.) Refuge staff can direct you to sites to observe the birds, which are best seen at dawn as they leave to forage or at dusk when they return to roost.

Carolina Sandhills refuge is home to several of the dense, shrubby wetlands called pocosins, as well as streams, ponds, and bottomland-hardwood tracts. In spring, the rare pine barrens tree frog sounds its honking notes. Other habitats on the refuge's 45,348 acres include fields, cropland, and scrub oak areas, which together host an inviting range of species, from wild turkey to eastern fox squirrel and pygmy rattlesnake. Waterfowl are common on refuge lakes in winter, and raptors cruise open areas for prey. Roads, trails, and observation towers offer convenient ways to enjoy the wealth of wildlife of this extraordinary Sandhills environment.

CUMBERLAND ISLAND NATIONAL SEASHORE

The journey to Cumberland Island National Seashore requires a little more planning and effort than do trips to most national park areas. This barrier island off the south Georgia coast can be reached only by boat, and visitors must take care to provide all their own food and other essentials, whether they are camping or just spending a day enjoying the beach. But the reward for a bit of extra preparation is a seacoast world where nature and history blend to create a serene and fascinating environment.

Seventeen miles long and at most three miles wide, Cumberland Island has a long history of human occupation—from Indians, who left middens of discarded seashells, to Spanish explorers, British soldiers, and plantation owners with African-American slaves. At one point descendants of Thomas Carnegie, brother of wealthy industrialist Andrew Carnegie, owned most of the island and called it home. As a result, development was limited; when the national seashore was established in 1972, Cumberland's natural qualities remained mostly unspoiled.

A maritime forest with live oak as the dominant tree covers around 40 percent of the island, where white-tailed deer, raccoons, and pileated woodpeckers dwell. The many-fingered leaves of saw palmetto lend the woodland a tropical feel, enhanced by Spanish moss hanging from oak limbs. On the Cumberland Sound side of the island, extensive salt marsh provides a home for egrets, rails, marsh wrens, seaside sparrows, and crabs. The above-water uniformity of the marsh is deceiving: Countless varieties of sea life find a home in this productive environment, which serves as a "nursery" for shrimp, oysters, clams, and many species of fish.

Sunlight filigrees the needles of a longleaf pine in Carolina Sandhills National Wildlife Refuge. The sanctuary, which lies where the Piedmont Plateau meets the Coastal Plain in South Carolina, contains extensive longleaf forests. They are carefully managed to reestablish the open pine woodland that blanketed the Sandhills centuries ago.

Lightning sizzles above saw palmetto sentinels on Cumberland Island National Seashore. Unlike many other Atlantic barrier islands, Cumberland escaped development. It will remain unspoiled, thanks to residents who supported the establishment of the national seashore and national park regulations that limit visitors to 300 people a day.

On Cumberland's Atlantic coast, two lines of dunes topped with sea oats border the sandy beach. Between the primary dunes and the back dunes lies the interdune meadow, where wildflowers, grasses, and shrubs thrive, protected from salt spray.

Down on the beach, loggerhead sea turtles nest from May through August, females laying dozens or even hundreds of Ping-Pong-ball size eggs in cavities that they immediately cover with sand. If the nest is not

dug up by a hungry raccoon, young turtles eventually will emerge and scramble to the ocean.

Some of Cumberland's trails wind through its 20,000 acres of wilderness, whereas others lead to historic structures and ruins. The number of visitors is limited, so time spent almost anywhere on the island is likely to bring the solitude one needs to most appreciate the unique qualities of this barrier island sanctuary.

TREMBLING EARTH, COASTAL WETLANDS

OKEFENOKEE N.W.R.,
Georgia

LOWER SUWANNEE
RIVER N.W.R.,
Florida

OKEFENOKEE NATIONAL WILDLIFE REFUGE

The surprise experienced by many first-time visitors to the Okefenokee Swamp is, no doubt, a direct result of its name. "Swamp," people read, and arrive expecting a vast, shadowy jungle, where towering trees blot out the sky above tangles of vines and stagnant, fetid water.

It can be downright shocking, then, to discover that the Okefenokee encompasses expansive, grassy marshes spangled with wildflowers; that rivers are born here, flowing briskly along broad channels through the woods; that countless lakes, large and small, dot the landscape. Tall bald cypresses, oaks, tupelos, and other trees grow in abundance, to be sure, but only in parts of the Okefenokee do they create the kind of dense, dark forest often associated with southern swamps.

In short, the Okefenokee is a place of striking diversity, where in a matter of minutes a canoeist can pass from a narrow deep-woods channel into shrubby marsh and on into open water. The ranges of habitats here, and the variety of wildlife present, mean the Okefenokee truly deserves its reputation as one of the continent's great natural areas.

Covering about 438,000 acres in southern Georgia and northern Florida (of which 396,000 are protected within Okefenokee National Wildlife Refuge), the swamp sits in a basin that was once covered by sea. Trail Ridge, the slightly higher strip of terrain along the swamp's eastern edge, is a coastal terrace marking a high water level during an interglacial period. Underlying the wetland is river-borne sand, and atop that is a layer of peat, created by millennia of decaying organic material.

Though the hydrology of the swamp is not fully understood, even a quick look at a map will show that two major rivers arise from the Okefenokee: the Suwannee, which flows southward to the Gulf of Mexico, and the St. Marys, which heads eastward to the Atlantic, in part forming the boundary between Georgia and Florida.

As with so many wetlands, the Okefenokee has suffered greatly from human exploitation. In the late 19th century, speculators dug a canal to try to drain it. They failed; three years of effort led to the company's bankruptcy in 1897. Then began an era of intensive logging, during which staggering numbers of ancient bald cypresses and pines were cut. By 1927, virtually all the old-growth timber was gone. Ten years later, the national wildlife refuge was established, and the ecosystem began to recover.

Alligators, which were killed during the logging era and poached during the 1950s and 1960s, today are again abundant in the Okefenokee; the bellowing of males claiming their territories can be heard carrying across the still water in April. Black bears roam the woods, otters play on riverbanks, and pairs of wood ducks zoom overhead, the female giving her characteristic squealing call. In spring, prothonotary warblers—

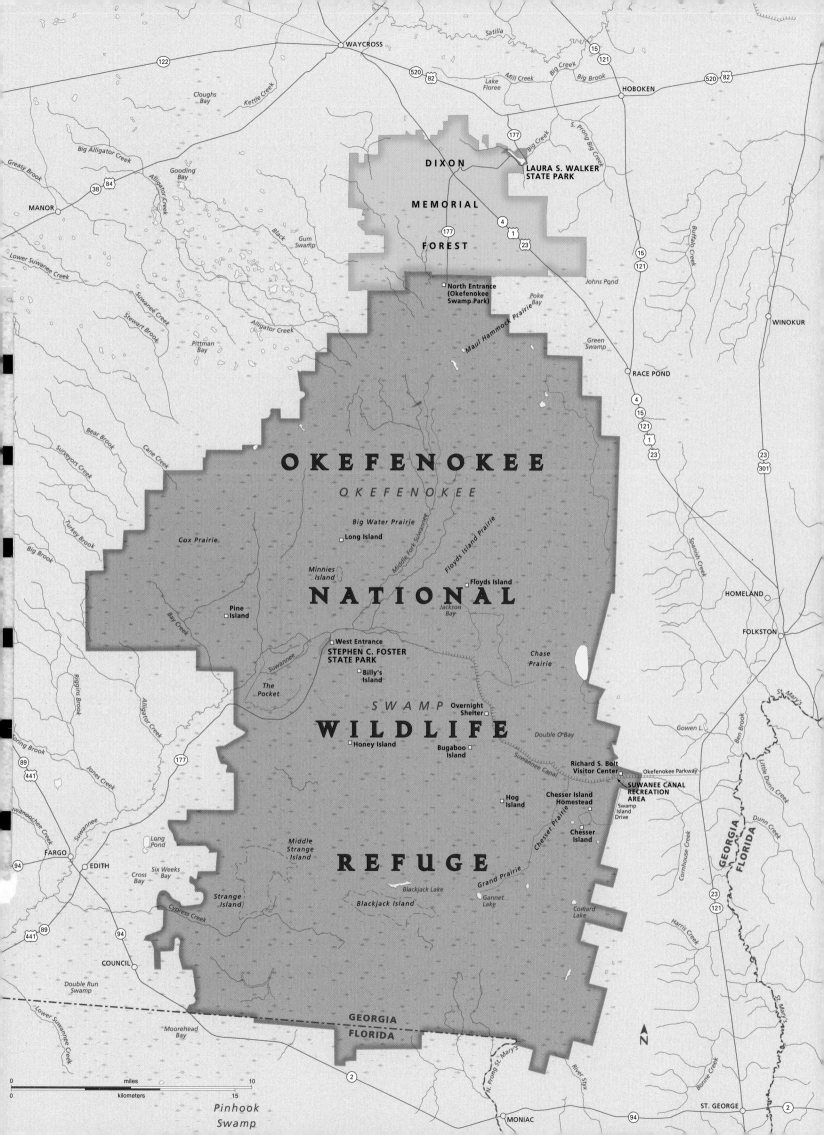

WAYCROSS

HOBOKEN

DIXON

MEMORIAL

FOREST

LAURA S. WALKER
STATE PARK

North Entrance
(Okefenokee
Swamp Park)

WINOKUR

RACE POND

OKEFENOKEE

OKEFENOKEE

Big Water Prairie
Long Island

Floyds Island

NATIONAL

HOMELAND

FOLKSTON

West Entrance
STEPHEN C. FOSTER
STATE PARK

Billy's
Island

Chase
Prairie

SWAMP

WILDLIFE

Overnight
Shelter

Honey Island

Bugaboo
Island

Richard S. Bolt
Visitor Center

Okefenokee Parkway

SUWANEE CANAL
RECREATION
AREA

Hog
Island

Chesser Island
Homestead

REFUGE

Middle
Strange
Island

Chesser
Island

Blackjack Lake

Blackjack Island

Gannet
Lake

Coward
Lake

FARGO

EDITH

GEORGIA
FLORIDA

Long Pond

Cross
Bay

Six Weeks
Bay

Strange
Island)

COUNCIL

Double Run
Swamp

GEORGIA

FLORIDA

0   miles   10

kilometers   15

Pinhook
Swamp

MONIAC

ST. GEORGE

MANOR

Big Alligator Creek

Greasy Brook

Cloughs
Bay

Gooding Bay

Kettle Creek

Black

Gum
Swamp

Alligator Creek

Lower Suwanee Creek

Suwanee Creek

Stewart Brook

Pittman
Bay

Bear Brook

Surveyors Creek

Cane Creek

Turkey Brook

Big Brook

Minnies
Island

Pine
Island

Bay Creek

Suwannee

The
Pocket

Riggins Brook

Alligator Creek

Goring Brook

Jones Creek

Suwannee

Suwanoochee Creek

Cypress Creek

Moorehead
Bay

Lower Suwannee Creek

Cox Prairie

Middle Fork Suwannee

Floyds Island Prairie

Jackson
Bay

Double O Bay

Suwannee Canal

Chesser Prairie

Grand Prairie

Satilla

Lake
Floree

Mill Creek

Big Creek

Big Brook

S. Prong Big Creek

Big Creek

Poke
Bay

Johns Pond

Maul Hammock Prairie

Green
Swamp

Buffalo Creek

Spanish Creek

Gowen L.

Cornhouse Creek

St. Mary's

Ben Brook

Little Dunn Creek

Dunn Creek

Harris Creek

St. Mary's

Bonne Creek

N. Prong St. Mary's

River Styx

brilliant golden birds often called swamp canaries—whistle in woodlands, while northern parula warblers buzz from the tops of tall trees.

Some of the Okefenokee's wild diversity can be seen at the Suwannee Canal Recreation Area, on the refuge's eastern side. Along the Swamp Island Drive, stop at the Upland Discovery Trail for a chance to see a red-cockaded woodpecker, an endangered species found only in open southern pine forests. At the end of the drive, a 4,000-foot boardwalk leads into the swamp itself, passing through shrubby woodland and the grassy marshes known in the Okefenokee as "prairies." Here you will see herons, egrets, ibises, and, occasionally, sandhill cranes. Greater sand-hills from the northern states and Canada winter in the Okefenokee, and smaller numbers of the Florida subspecies are permanent residents in the swamp's open areas.

Alligators and turtles sun themselves beside the trail, and if you look up you might spot a red-shouldered hawk or pileated woodpecker flying overhead. Green anoles are common along the boardwalk; these lizards are often called chameleons for their ability to change color from green to brown, though they're not related to the true chameleons of the Old World.

For the best Okefenokee experience, you will need to hop into a canoe for a day trip or an overnight journey into the heart of the swamp. Marked trails penetrate the interior, and campsites scattered along the routes let boaters enjoy the sights and sounds of dusk, night, and dawn in the Okefenokee. The refuge limits the number of campers (apply two months to the day before your planned trip), so you are likely to enjoy near-total solitude as you paddle the lakes and canal. If you lack boating or

Sandhill cranes stalk sedge marshes known as "prairies" in Okefenokee National Wildlife Refuge, which extends from southern Georgia into Florida. A red head patch and drooping feathers over its rump that resemble a bustle distinguish this tall bird from the great blue heron, another refuge inhabitant.

Pond cypresses arch above their reflection in the Suwannee River as it winds through Okefenokee Swamp (opposite). Nearly 400,000 acres of the swamp—90 percent of it— lie within the refuge, a wetland realm of grassy marshes, dark forests, and numerous lakes.

Curling past cabbage palms, the Suwannee threads delta flatlands near the Gulf of Mexico. The Lower Suwannee National Wildlife Refuge, which includes 20 miles of the river to its mouth, provides habitat for wading and shorebirds, migratory songbirds, and endangered wood storks, manatees, and Gulf sturgeons.

navigational skills, the refuge can provide names of local guides.

The beautiful water plant called golden club grows in abundance along Okefenokee waterways, and climbing heath winds up streamside trees (one look at the flowers and you will see why a local common name is "false-teeth bush"). The swamp is home to several species of insectivorous plants, including tall, trumpet-shaped pitcher plants, the attractive but inconspicuous sundew, and floating bladderworts. Some of the tree-covered higher spots, called islands, may be the origin of the swamp's mellifluous name: "Okefenokee" comes from Indian words meaning "trembling earth," and these places of seemingly solid ground are actually layers of peat that quake under heavy footsteps.

Spring and fall are the best times to see the Okefenokee; wildlife and flowers are less common in winter, and summers are usually too buggy. But whenever you arrive, you will find one of America's most extensive wetland wildernesses, containing within its borders a profusion of life.

LOWER SUWANNEE RIVER NATIONAL WILDLIFE REFUGE

The Suwannee River, which begins in the Okefenokee Swamp, reaches the Gulf of Mexico at Lower Suwannee River National Wildlife Refuge in Florida—about 115 miles south as the crow flies, or around 250 winding river miles.

Along the way, its tannin-stained dark water is transformed by the discharge of more than 50 springs and by the silty influx of muddy tributaries. By the time it reaches the refuge, the Suwannee flows as a typical meandering southern bottomland river, lined with bald cypress, tupelo, overcup and laurel oaks, sweet gum, and other wetland hardwoods.

Here ethereally beautiful swallow-tailed kites soar over the forest, and dozens of ospreys nest in riverside trees, along with small numbers of bald eagles. White ibises, black-crowned and yellow-crowned night-herons, and snowy egrets breed in the vicinity, alongside anhingas, the "snakebirds" that often swim with only their long, thin necks showing above water. Otters and alligators frequent the backwaters—the former always looking out for the latter, lest they end up as lunch. In the river's mouth, endangered manatees laze in the warm water from spring through fall.

A network of roads (some open only to bicycles and hikers) provides

access to woodland, the Suwannee banks, and the refuge's 20 miles of Gulf coastline. Visitors can walk several trails, including one that includes a midden, where enormous numbers of discarded oyster and clam shells and pottery form a large mound at an ancient campsite used from about 2500 B.C. to A.D. 1000.

The refuge has designated a canoe-kayak trail that follows the lower Suwannee and adjoining saltwater and brackish creeks, in optional loops that require from about an hour to more than three hours to complete. A quiet paddle through the coastal wetlands just might be the best way to enjoy this wildlife-rich refuge set at the intersection of river and Gulf.

RIVER OF GRASS, ESTUARIES, REEFS

BIG CYPRESS
NAT. PRESERVE, Fla.
EVERGLADES
NAT. PARK, Fla.
BISCAYNE
NAT. PARK, Fla.

EVERGLADES NATIONAL PARK

As befitting its location at the southeasternmost tip of the contiguous United States, Everglades National Park is a place of extremes. At more than 1.5 million acres, it makes up the largest subtropical wild landscape in the country. It is the only U.S. national park to be designated a World Heritage site, an international biosphere reserve, and a wetland of international importance; and it ranks among the most famous natural areas of not only the U.S. but the world.

Unfortunately, the Everglades also holds a place among the most endangered ecosystems. The flow of water that gives life to countless species, from microscopic aquatic organisms to tall royal palms to alligators and manatees, has suffered a century of disruption as southern Florida's human population has boomed. As a result, wading birds nesting in colonies, such as herons, egrets, ibises, and wood storks, numbering in the hundreds of thousands in the 1800s, have declined more than 90 percent since the 1930s. The waters of Florida Bay, once clear and healthy, have become murky and unproductive because of the reduced flow of fresh water. The bay's now too-salty water, which stresses plant and animal life, has resulted in persistent algae blooms, fewer seagrass beds, and declining populations of pink shrimp, lobsters, and game fish.

A ray of hope lights the Everglades' future, though. In what may be the world's largest ecosystem-restoration effort, governmental and private forces are attempting to reestablish much of the area's natural water flow and reduce pollution, in a project that will cost billions of dollars and continue for years to come. While it is too early to know how successful this monumental task will be, it is an auspicious sign that so many people have come to realize the irreplaceable value of the Everglades.

And, despite past abuse and future threats, Everglades National Park still rewards visitors with a unique and diverse environment, from marshes to pinelands to mangrove estuaries. Alligators still hunt the lakes, wood storks still stalk the swamps, and sea turtles still nest on the beaches. The Everglades endures as one of America's most wondrous wild places: the "river of grass" celebrated by the late Marjory Stoneman Douglas, whose book warning of threats to the region became a classic of the environmental movement. Douglas's *The Everglades: River of Grass* appeared in 1947, the same year the area was designated a national park, culminating decades of effort by activists.

The process that makes the Everglades work begins with summer thunderstorms that drench central and southern Florida, filling the Kissimmee River and Lake Okeechobee, northwest of Miami. From here, water drains across the flat, grassy landscape in a vast sheet, from six inches to three feet deep, southward into Florida Bay. In winter the

sloughs dry up, and what had been marshlands become broad prairies. The plants and animals of the Everglades have adapted to this cycle of wet and dry, which has too often been interrupted by human activities; one of the major goals of restoration efforts will be to renew its regular cycle of wet and dry.

While most visitors head straight to park headquarters near Homestead, a trip to the Everglades might better begin with a stop at the Shark Valley Visitor Center, on the Tamiami Trail (U.S. 41) west of Miami. Here, a ranger-guided tram tour leads into the heart of Shark Valley Slough, the main drainage from Lake Okeechobee—the true "river of grass." Even better, rent a bike and pedal around the 15-mile tram route; as you might expect in an area where the maximum elevation is eight feet above sea level, the route is perfectly flat and easy to ride. You will see alligators (no threat as long as you keep your distance), wading birds, and perhaps the endangered snail kite, a hawk that feeds only on the large apple snails that it plucks from sawgrass and cattails.

Having experienced the engine that drives the Everglades' watery ecosystem, take the 38-mile road from the park entrance west of Homestead to the Flamingo Visitor Center, on Florida Bay. Along the way, nature trails let you explore additional environments: open forests of slash pine with an understory of picturesque saw palmetto; hardwood hammocks (dense, shady stands of mahogany, gumbo-limbo, and live oak);

Like green sequins on blue velvet, mangrove isles dot Ten Thousand Islands in the northwestern section of Florida's Everglades National Park.

and "domes" of tall bald cypresses in wet depressions, with striking dwarf bald cypresses in dry prairie. Near the coast, mangrove forests crowd the edges of brackish estuaries where American crocodiles, endangered and numbering only a few hundred, laze on mudflats.

Consider taking a canoe along one of the well-marked trails through park wetlands. Short trails like the Nine Mile Pond Canoe Trail and the Noble Hammock Canoe Trail provide a true Everglades wildlife experience for a relatively small effort. On the more strenuous West Lake Canoe Trail, there is a chance of spotting a crocodile on Florida Bay. Longer trails lead far into the backcountry, where primitive campsites (some on elevated platforms called chickees) allow overnight wilderness trips.

While many Everglades visitors worry about alligators, snakes, or poisonous plants such as manchineel, with its blistering milky juice, the biggest threat to human well-being is far less dramatic. Be warned that, especially in summer, mosquitoes can make a trip to the 'Glades a real ordeal. Long sleeves and pants and plenty of repellent provide some protection; even so, you will spend a lot of energy shooing and swatting.

But when you spot a graceful swallow-tailed kite soaring above or hear

Roseate spoonbills vie for territory during mating season. Some 200 breeding pairs of the birds, once killed for their bright plumage, now nest in Everglades National Park.

Hiding in place, a trumpetfish mimics a stalk of flexible coral called gorgonian in Florida's Biscayne National Park. Biscayne protects the northernmost living reefs in the United States—and the most accessible in the world. They shelter more than 300 species of fish.

the hoot of a barred owl at dusk, or stop to watch a stunning roseate spoonbill fishing in the shallows, you will understand why the Everglades, despite its troubled past, remains such a precious place—and why so many people are fighting so hard to save it.

BIG CYPRESS NATIONAL PRESERVE

To the north of the national park, Big Cypress National Preserve protects another 729,000 acres of the Everglades ecosystem and provides additional opportunities for exploration and wildlife viewing. Drive the 26-mile loop road scenic drive, or make the loop north of the Tamiami Trail on Turner River and Birdon Roads, and you will see abundant birdlife and alligators. Egrets, wood storks, and white ibises wade in roadside wetlands, and long-necked anhingas perch on branches, drying their wings after diving for fish. For a closer look at a beautiful old-growth cypress swamp, walk the 2,000-foot boardwalk nature trail at Fakahatchee Strand State Preserve, just to the west.

In Big Cypress, a few critically endangered Florida panthers still roam the forests, hunting deer and wild boar. This eastern race of the mountain lion has suffered greatly from persecution, pollution, and loss of habitat; many panthers have been killed in the past by speeding vehicles, as well. While the chances of seeing a panther are slim indeed, the knowledge that the big cat survives here makes a visit to Big Cypress a singularly inspiring experience for any lover of America's wild places.

BISCAYNE NATIONAL PARK

Parts of Biscayne National Park, just south of Miami, match the environment of the nearby Everglades, including estuarine mangroves and lush hammocks of gumbo-limbo, mahogany, and strangler fig. But here the focus is on Biscayne Bay and what lies below it.

Water covers 95 percent of this 180,000-acre park, which encompasses the northernmost of the Florida Keys, the 150-mile-long chain of islands formed by ancient coral reefs. Here, too, are living reefs—the northernmost in the United States—swarming with marine life in a dizzying variety of forms. Hiking on eight-mile-long Elliott Key will bring sightings of birds, tropical plants, and butterflies; the real glory of Biscayne, though, lies beneath the waves. From park headquarters at Convoy Point, glass-bottom boats tour bay and reef. Boats also take scuba divers and snorklers out to explore the reef. Scuba diving and snorkling are by far the most satisfying ways to experience this diverse undersea world.

Floating silently over a reef, you will gaze down at fantastically shaped coral, brilliant Christmas tree worms, crabs, sponges, sea cucumbers, spiny lobsters, and a kaleidoscope of multicolored fish. Butterflyfish, parrotfish, damselfish, wrasses, angelfish, sergeant majors, and gobies are just a few of more than 300 species present, in hues that span the spectrum.

Lucky snorklers might spot a moray eel, a loggerhead sea turtle, a barracuda, or a shark. In winter, the bay is home to more manatees than in summer, those endearingly homely sea mammals that long-ago sailors mistook for mermaids.

Even a short visit will reveal why coral reefs are often compared to rain forests in the array of life they harbor—a diversity preserved here in one of America's least known, but most rewarding, national parks.

CAVE, SINKHOLE PLAIN, LAKE, WETLAND

MAMMOTH CAVE
NAT. PARK, Kentucky

REELFOOT N.W.R.,
Tennessee

MAMMOTH CAVE NATIONAL PARK

When it comes to truth in advertising, Mammoth Cave has absolutely no worries about the claim in its name. These interconnected caverns in southwest central Kentucky make up the longest known cave system in the world, with more than 350 miles of passages mapped by intrepid explorers. Scientists believe there may be literally hundreds more miles waiting to be found, as well. Mammoth, indeed.

Visitors to the cave see only a fraction of its total expanse, of course, but the range of tours offered—from easy strolls through spacious chambers to belly-crawls through constricted passages—makes a trip to Mammoth one of the most complete cave experiences available anywhere.

And it isn't just the subsurface scenery that places Mammoth among our most appealing national parks. History, both natural and human, adds complex layers of discovery to a journey through this granddaddy of America's underground wonders.

The Mammoth Cave story begins more than 350 million years ago, when what is now Kentucky lay near the Equator, and a warm, shallow sea spread across the entire Southeast. Over time, the shells of countless billions of marine creatures (composed of calcium carbonate) compacted on the ocean floor to form layers of limestone as much as 600 feet thick. Later, river-deposited sand added a mantle of sandstone above the limestone in some areas.

Much later, this region rose above the sea. Rainwater, made slightly acidic by naturally occurring carbon dioxide, seeped into cracks in the sandstone and limestone over millions of years, dissolving ever widening passages. As the nearby Green River cut into the land, the water table sank, allowing the process of cave formation to proceed deeper underground. Meanwhile, the harder sandstone cap protected higher caverns from collapsing as lower passages were hollowed out by underground rivers, forming karst topography, the term for limestone terrain riddled with caves, sinking creeks, and sinkholes.

To the east, where the sandstone caprock protects the Mammoth Cave limestone, lies a sinkhole plain. Here no rivers flow at the surface; rainwater quickly sinks into the porous rock. Though separated from the main cave by many miles, this region is intimately connected with Mammoth, since the water that flows through the cave and sustains its underground life filters down through the sinkholes—bringing with it pollutants from towns, roads, businesses, and farms. The Mammoth area is an important center for the study of karst ecology and hydrology, as scientists investigate ways to protect the cave from above-ground threats.

As long as 4,000 years ago, Native Americans entered Mammoth Cave, penetrating miles along its passages in search of gypsum and other minerals. Archaeologists do not know why these materials were so

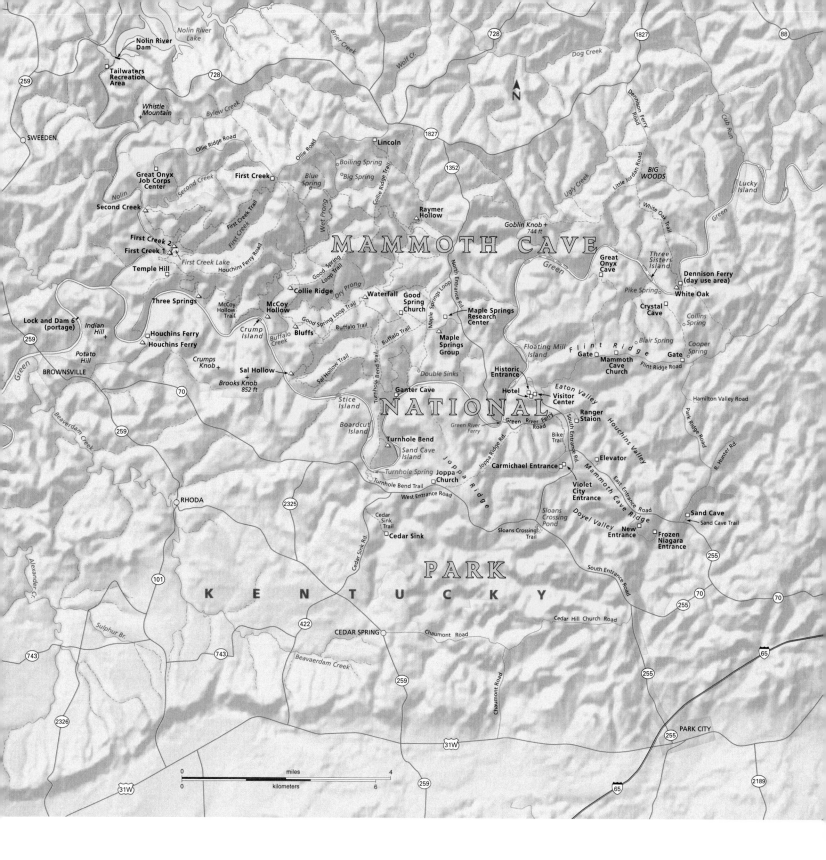

prized—decorative and medicinal uses are possibilities—but vast areas of the cave were mined by Indians using only hand tools and cane torches. Then, about 2,000 years ago, Indians stopped using the cave, and no humans entered until the natural passage was rediscovered in 1798. A new era of mining began in 1810, lasting five years, as saltpeter was removed for gunpowder. Soon enough, though, word of the cave's marvels spread, and Mammoth Cave became one of America's first real tourist attractions—a prominence it has held ever since, with two million visitors each year.

You can see evidence of prehistoric gypsum-diggers and 19th-century

Artificial light reveals the contours of Mammoth Cave, in southwest central Kentucky. This area, called New Discovery Borehole, contains fragile gypsum formations and is closed to the public, but rangers offer numerous tours of other sections of Mammoth. Although its caverns remain the centerpiece of Mammoth Cave National Park, visitors also enjoy 52,800 acres of woodlands.

miners as you tour the caverns, along with other signs of human activity. On the Violet City Tour you will pass huts once occupied by tuberculosis patients, dating from an era when doctors believed the cave air might effect a cure.

Not so apparent are signs of true cave dwellers: the animals that live here full- or part-time. Some, called troglobionts, have completely adapted to cave life, among them eyeless fish, eyeless crayfish, and a diminutive creature with the quite appropriate name Mammoth Cave shrimp. Other animals visit the cave for varying amounts of time but can also live on the surface: cave crickets (the animal you are most likely to spot underground), salamanders (look for the cave salamander, reddish with black spots), and bats (including the endangered Indiana and gray bats).

The same sandstone cap that has largely prevented roof collapses also keeps out the seepage that forms speleothems (cave formations), which means that the majority of Mammoth lacks the ornate natural sculptures common in many caverns. These formations aren't entirely absent, though; the Frozen Niagara Tour, for example, reveals stalactites, stalagmites, dripstones, and other beautiful configurations, as does the seasonally offered Great Onyx Cave Tour.

Other tour options include lantern tours, which re-create the lighting used by early explorers; the Making of Mammoth Tour, which focuses on geology from the cave's origins to its present-day evolution; and the Wild Cave Tour, which requires participants to wear helmets and crawl through tight spaces well off the regular tourist routes. (Only thin folks can take this tour: There's a maximum chest size of 42 inches.)

Back aboveground, the national park's 52,800 acres offer plenty of opportunity to explore a splendidly diverse hardwood forest. More than 70 miles of trails wind through the park—and, since most visitors concentrate on the cave, hiking here is often a blessedly solitary experience. In spring the woods are full of trillium, bloodroot, hepatica, dwarf crested iris, and dozens of other wildflowers; in fall the foliage of oaks, hickories, maples, and dogwoods creates a magnificent collage of reds and yellows. In the northeastern part of the park, the Big Woods area makes up one of the

few stands of old-growth forest still existing in this mostly cutover part of the country. Whether aboveground or underground, Mammoth Cave's attractions deserve far more time than most travelers allot for their visits. From vast passageways to a tiny cave cricket, the park tells a story as intriguing as it is ancient.

REELFOOT NATIONAL WILDLIFE REFUGE

Only a few natural areas have an origin as violent as that of Reelfoot Lake, a shallow, 15,000-acre body of water and wetlands in extreme northwestern Tennessee. In late 1811 and early 1812, a series of earthquakes that centered on the New Madrid Fault shook the central part of the United States, tremors as powerful as any that have occurred in North America in historic times. When the shocks were over, the Mississippi River had radically changed its course, and the few settlers in the region were surprised to find a sprawling new lake where dry land had been.

Today Reelfoot is known as one of the best wildlife-watching areas in the central Mississippi Valley, with huge flocks of waterfowl and 200 bald eagles wintering around its shoreline. In recent years nine pairs of bald eagles have returned to nest at Reelfoot, after decades of absence caused by pesticide pollution and persecution. In summer, this complex of wetlands — bald cypress swamp, hardwood forest, marsh, and mudflats — hosts breeding birds from great egrets and Mississippi kites to purple gallinules and prothonotary warblers.

Part national wildlife refuge, state park, and state game-management area, Reelfoot's bays and water-lily-covered backwaters can be explored by boat, or you can hike the trails in the state park and game management areas. In winter, eagle-watching tours depart daily from the state park. On the national wildlife refuge, the Grassy Island auto-tour route ends at an observation tower.

Still life with lilies, a fragrant flower and a tightly furled bud float amid lily pads in Reelfoot Lake, in the northwest corner of Tennessee. A mosaic of national wildlife refuge, state park, and state game-management area, 15,000-acre Reelfoot supports the largest population of wintering bald eagles in the contiguous 48 states.

Etched against a vermilion dawn (opposite), bald cypresses jut from glassy waters in Reelfoot Lake State Park.

The MIDLANDS

CHAPTER II

PUKASKWA   LA MAURICIE   ISLE ROYALE   SLEEPING BEAR DUNES

PICTURED ROCKS   APOSTLE ISLANDS   SUPERIOR   BOUNDARY WATERS   QUETICO

VOYAGEURS   ST. CROIX   OZARKS   BUFFALO NATIONAL RIVER   WICHITA MOUNTAINS   FLINT HILLS

BIG THICKET   PADRE ISLAND   ARANSAS   SABINE   BLACK HILLS   BADLANDS

WOOD BUFFALO   LITTLE MISSOURI   GRASSLANDS   CHARLES M. RUSSELL   THELON

Lake Superior has carved spectacular caves in sandstone off Squaw Bay

BY RON FISHER

Extremes of climate and landscape characterize the broad Midlands of North America—buggy tundra in the north, steamy bayous in the south. The oldest known rocks on earth—the Canadian Shield, dating back perhaps 3.96 billion years—sprawl across much of the Canadian north, and in the south saltwater marshes are home to pelicans and egrets.

The heavy hand of the glaciers sculpted much of the Midlands. Creeping down from Canada like spilled molasses, gargantuan sheets of ice as much as two miles thick reached as far south as Iowa. Beginning about three million years ago, they advanced and retreated in cycles, leveling topography, scouring out the Great Lakes, scraping the Canadian Shield clean, and pulverizing the land's surface. In spring and summer, their edges melted, sending torrents of water pouring off to form the Missouri, the Mississippi, and the Ohio River systems. Like veins of a leaf, these rivers pattern the heartland today.

When the ice finally retreated, its meltwater was trapped—on the south by the glacier's moraine, on the north by the glacier itself. It formed an enormous inland sea that stretched far north into Manitoba and lasted 3,000 years. It left behind a pancake-flat bed of layered sediment—the huge Canadian prairies.

Farther south, North America's plains and prairies rolled west to the Rocky Mountains in waves of grasses until settlers plowed them. Now only patches of the original grasslands survive. Several preserves and parks protect them.

Earlier, forests blanketed the heartland. It was said a squirrel could travel from the East Coast to the Mississippi River without ever touching the ground. Settlement ended those days, but still, from the Ozarks north to tree line far away in Canada, national forests enclose hundreds of thousands of acres. Wildlife refuges serve diverse North American animals and ecosystems. And those crown jewels of the preservationists—national parks in the heart of both the U.S. and Canada—keep immense tracts of land safe from encroachment.

The Midlands offers a subtler beauty than more spectacular parts of North America. The whisper of the wind in the tall prairie grass, the silent, chilling sweep of the aurora borealis in the far north, the liquid song of the meadowlark, the steady hiss and murmur of surf washing a white-sand beach. The farther north you go, the bigger the mosquitoes, the fiercer the wind, the greater the loneliness, the edgier the danger that remoteness can bring. There are loons on the lakes and beavers in the rivers. On Isle Royale, wolves and moose coexist in uneasy partnership. Ecosystems bump against one another in the Midlands: Southeastern swamps, eastern forests, central plains, and southwestern desert overlap, creating a wonderland of disparate plants and animals. Otters and alligators share the streams. Bluebirds nest near roadrunners. Overhead in the Midlands, the skies fill with birds as two of the four great North American migratory flyways funnel birds north in the spring and south in the fall. Among them are the endangered whooping cranes, resolutely coming back from near extinction, dodging power lines and goose hunters to make the trip.

The Lewis and Clark Expedition crossed much of the Midlands in 1804, charting a route to the Pacific Ocean. To Lewis the countryside seemed "one emence garden."

Bearberry brightens Canada's Thelon River Valley.

Bighorns traverse a cliff in Badlands National Park, South Dakota.

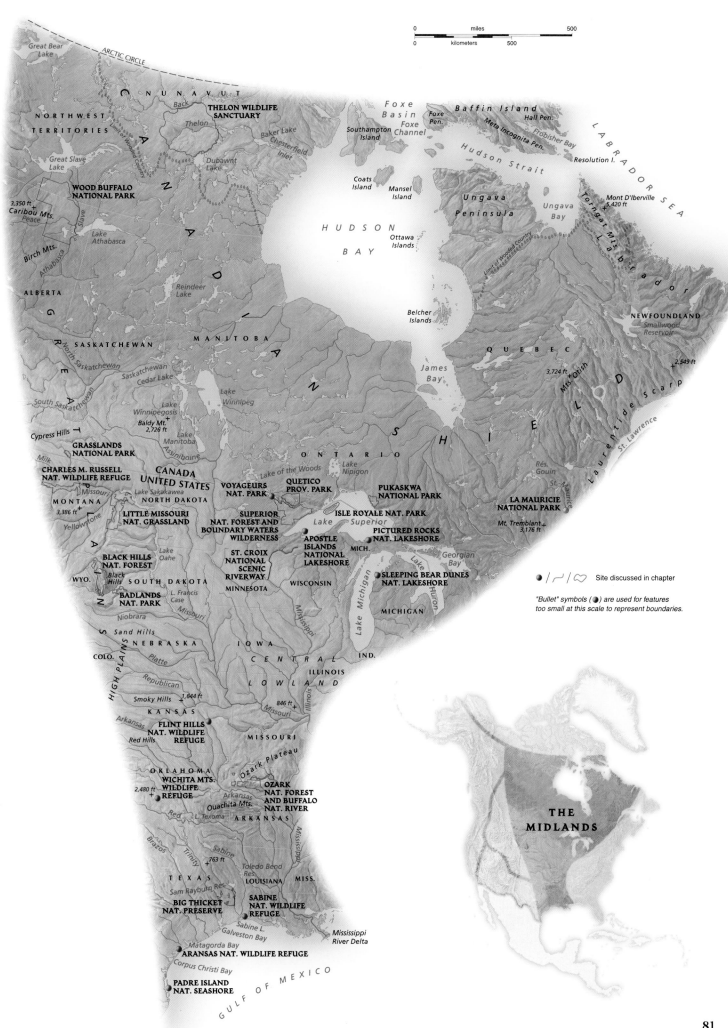

Great Bear
Lake

ARCTIC CIRCLE

N U N A V U T

Back
Thelon

THELON WILDLIFE
SANCTUARY

Foxe
Basin

Baffin Island

NORTHWEST

TERRITORIES

Baker Lake
Chesterfield
Inlet

Foxe
Channel

Foxe
Pen.

Hall Pen.

Meta Incognita Pen.

Frobisher Bay

L A B R A D O R   S E A

Limit of Wooded Country

Dubawnt
Lake

Southampton
Island

Hudson Strait

Resolution I.

Great Slave
Lake

WOOD BUFFALO
NATIONAL PARK

Coats
Island

Mansel
Island

Ungava
Peninsula

Ungava
Bay

Torngat Mts.

Mont D'Iberville
5,420 ft

3,350 ft
Caribou Mts.
Peace

H U D S O N

B A Y

Ottawa
Islands

Labrador

Birch Mts.
Athabasca

Reindeer
Lake

Belcher
Islands

NEWFOUNDLAND

Smallwood
Reservoir

ALBERTA

Lake
Athabasca

MANITOBA

James
Bay

Q U E B E C

Slave

C A N A D I A N

SASKATCHEWAN

North Saskatchewan

Saskatchewan

Cedar Lake

Lake
Winnipeg

3,724 ft Mts. Otish

2,549 ft

Laurentide Scarp

St. Lawrence

South Saskatchewan

Milk

Lake
Winnipegosis

Baldy Mt.
2,726 ft

Lake
Manitoba

Assiniboine

O N T A R I O

S H I E L D

Rés.
Gouin

St-Maurice

Cypress Hills

GRASSLANDS
NATIONAL PARK

Lake of the Woods

Lake
Nipigon

Laurentide Scarp

CHARLES M. RUSSELL
NAT. WILDLIFE REFUGE

CANADA
UNITED STATES

VOYAGEURS
NAT. PARK

QUETICO
PROV. PARK

PUKASKWA
NATIONAL PARK

LA MAURICIE
NATIONAL PARK

MONTANA
3,386 ft
Yellowstone

Missouri
Lake Sakakawea

NORTH DAKOTA

SUPERIOR
NAT. FOREST AND
BOUNDARY WATERS
WILDERNESS

ISLE ROYALE NAT. PARK

Lake   Superior

PICTURED ROCKS
NAT. LAKESHORE

Mt. Tremblant
3,176 ft

LITTLE MISSOURI
NAT. GRASSLAND

APOSTLE
ISLANDS
NATIONAL
LAKESHORE

MICH.

BLACK HILLS
NAT. FOREST

Lake
Oahe

ST. CROIX
NATIONAL
SCENIC
RIVERWAY

Georgian
Bay

Black
Hills

SOUTH DAKOTA

WISCONSIN

SLEEPING BEAR DUNES
NAT. LAKESHORE

WYO.

BADLANDS
NAT. PARK

L. Francis
Case

MINNESOTA

Lake Huron

Missouri

MICHIGAN

Niobrara

Sand Hills

NEBRASKA

I O W A

Lake Michigan

IND.

COLO.

Platte

C E N T R A L

Republican

ILLINOIS

L O W L A N D

Smoky Hills
1,644 ft

846 ft
Missouri

Illinois

K A N S A S

Arkansas

FLINT HILLS
NAT. WILDLIFE
REFUGE

M I S S O U R I

Red Hills

O K L A H O M A

Ozark Plateau

WICHITA MTS.
WILDLIFE
REFUGE
2,480 ft

Arkansas

OZARK
NAT. FOREST
AND BUFFALO
NAT. RIVER

Ouachita Mts.

Red

L. Texoma

A R K A N S A S

Mississippi

Brazos

Sabine

763 ft

Trinity

Toledo Bend
Res.

T E X A S

LOUISIANA

MISS.

Sam Rayburn Res.

Sabine

BIG THICKET
NAT. PRESERVE

SABINE
NAT. WILDLIFE
REFUGE

Sabine L.

Mississippi
River Delta

Galveston Bay

Matagorda Bay

ARANSAS NAT. WILDLIFE REFUGE

Corpus Christi Bay

PADRE ISLAND
NAT. SEASHORE

G U L F   O F   M E X I C O

0   miles   500
0   kilometers   500

● / ⌒ / ◡   Site discussed in chapter

*"Bullet" symbols (●) are used for features
too small at this scale to represent boundaries.*

THE
MIDLANDS

CANADIAN SHIELD, BOREAL FORESTS

PUKASKWA NAT. PARK,
Ontario

LA MAURICIE
NAT. PARK,
Quebec

PUKASKWA NATIONAL PARK

"The wild shore of an inland sea," Pukaskwa National Park calls itself. The only wilderness national park in Ontario, the 725-square-mile refuge, opened to the public in 1983, hugs the northeast shore of Lake Superior 125 miles northwest of Sault Ste. Marie. It is shaped like a giant projectile point, aimed south.

Its name comes from the Ojibwa, but no one is certain of its meaning; "fish cleaning place" is most likely. The word is easier to pronounce than you might at first think: *PUCK-a-saw*. Ojibwa of the Pic River First Nation still have treaty rights inside the park—as do other members of the Robinson Superior Treaty Group—and about half the park's staff is made up of tribespeople.

Rugged and remote enough to have kept the loggers largely at bay—and lacking the significant mineral deposits that might have attracted miners—the park is one of central Ontario's last large areas of boreal forest mostly untouched by human development or industry. There is only one short road within the park, so forest succession has developed uninterrupted since the melting of the last of the glaciers 10,000 years ago. The park retains much of its pristine character even though mining and logging are in progress at its borders, and logging roads are now making once-remote backcountry more accessible.

You hike here on some of the oldest rock on the planet, the protruding edge of the Precambrian Canadian Shield. Erosion and glaciation sculpted the landscape, producing today's rocky grandeur. And clothing this ancient base is a northern boreal forest composed largely of black spruce, jack pine, and white birch. Along the park's western border stretch the rocky headlands, islands, coves, and sandy beaches of Lake Superior. Its waters average a chilly 39°F, which creates a cool coastline where alpine and arctic plants flourish. French explorer Étienne Brûlé visited Lake Superior in 1618 and wrote of "this body of water so large that one saw no land on either side."

Aboriginal Canadians built curious stone structures on the cobble beaches along the lake's north shore. Called Pukaskwa Pits by archaeologists, they may have been used as fire rings, food caches, shelters, lookouts, or places of sacred significance, but their exact use is unclear even today. At least a hundred have been found, often along ancient shorelines. They are ovals, three feet by six feet, or so, and are between three and five thousand years old. If you are lucky, you may spot one.

You will need to be even luckier to see a woodland caribou, for—though once numerous here—now perhaps as few as a dozen exist, and their continuing decline is the subject of research by park naturalists.

Just a hundred years ago, the two most important large mammals in the area were the wolf and the caribou, but with increased human

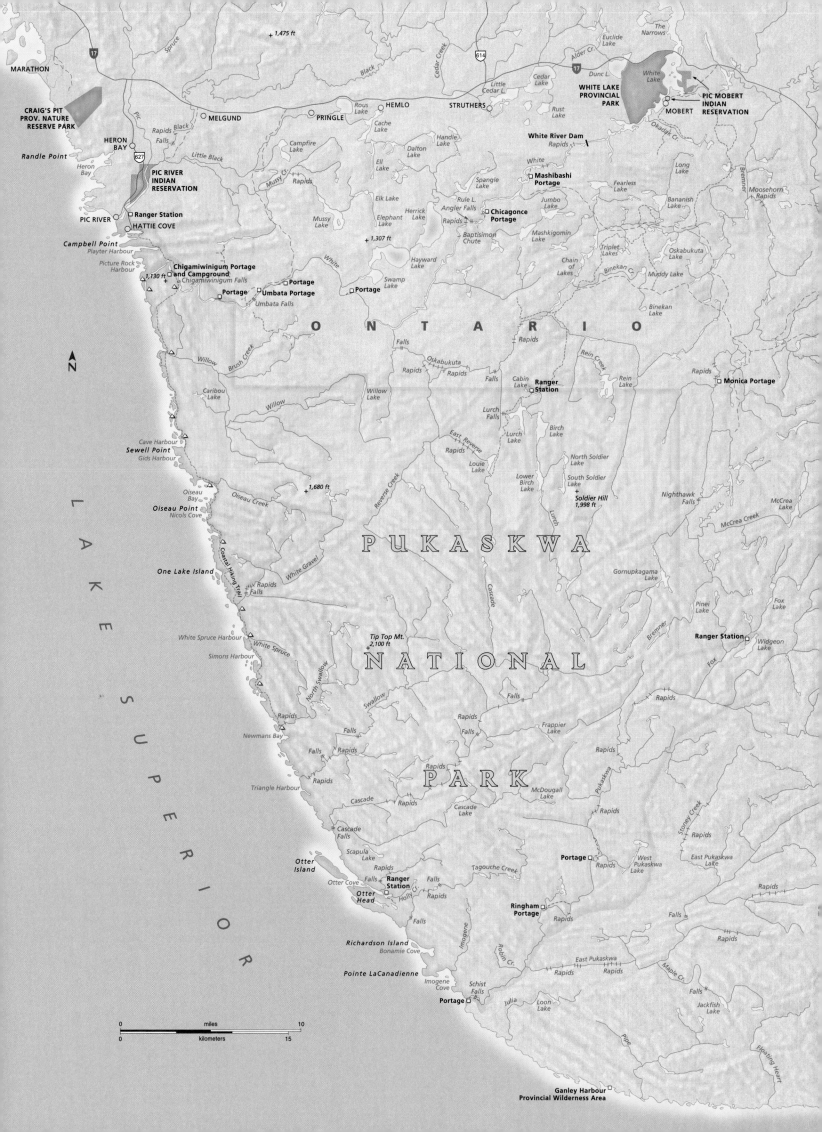

Massive outcrops of the Canadian Shield, among the oldest rock on Earth, shoulder breaking wavelets in Pukaskwa National Park, on the northeastern shore of Lake Superior in Ontario, Canada. Spruce, fir, and cedar forests cover the hilly interior of the 725-acre park.

activity in the adjacent ecosystem—especially logging—the balance changed. In logged areas, browse grew that attracted moose and a few white-tailed deer, which in turn drew more and more wolves to prey upon the caribou, which are less successful at defending themselves than moose. Now researchers conduct regular surveys to monitor the moose and caribou populations.

Fire is the dominant natural process within the park, and it controls the park ecosystem. The park has followed a program of suppressing all fires; however, it now considers a mix of alternatives: full suppression, partial suppression, and prescribed burns. Fire is a boon to white pine; it kills competing vegetation that shades its seedlings, thus slowing their growth. New generations of shrubbery, berries, wildflowers, mosses, and seedlings arise.

The rivers that run through Pukaskwa are short but powerful, dropping sometimes nearly 1,000 feet in under 40 miles. This makes for tumultuous falls and rapids and thrilling rafting and kayaking. The Pukaskwa River forms the southern boundary of the park and, especially from mid-May until early June, offers difficult but exciting paddling. In the upper river, riffles turn to rushing torrents, with ledges, boulder fields, and rock gardens whizzing past. Some rapids require portaging. Ringhams Gorge separates the novices from the pros with a five-foot drop. A run of the Pukaskwa takes between 8 and 14 days, depending on where you start. The White River offers a less difficult run, with all rapids marked with portages and a complete trip taking just 4 to 6 days. Note that the park does not regularly maintain portages.

Visitors more comfortable on dry land tread the many park trails, from short interpretive walking trails to longer treks. Several short trails begin near Hattie Cove, the easiest place to access the park at the terminus of

Highway 627. The Southern Headland Trail circles a rocky headland; the Beach Trail incorporates sand beaches and boreal forest; and the Halfway Lake Trail explores an aquatic ecosystem and a northern forest. These can be done in under four hours.

The Coastal Hiking trail is not for the faint hearted or the tender footed. Even some experienced backpackers call the trail tough, for in 40 miles it winds south along the coast from Hattie Cove over rough and broken terrain. Every half- to full-day hike brings you to a campsite with tent pads, fire grates, bear poles, and rustic toilets. Cairns rather than blazes mark the route. Many hikers arrange with local boat operators to pick them up at trail's end at the North Swallow River. You may want to time your visit to spring, before the bugs are out, or autumn, when birches and poplars burst into fall colors.

Paddlers not averse to risk-taking run the Coastal Canoe Route, an 8- to 14-day sea-kayak run along the coast of Lake Superior. Count on being wind-bound at least part of the time, and be prepared to face turbulent waters bred by rocky headlands and powerful winds; 25-foot waves are not uncommon, especially in late fall. The lake is not to be trifled with. It is said that even animals respect its fury; some migrating raptors prefer to fly around Lake Superior rather than across it.

LA MAURICIE NATIONAL PARK

La Mauricie National Park in southern Quebec sets itself the task of preserving a corner of the eastern slope of the Laurentian Mountains west of the St. Lawrence River.

The nomadic Attikamek people came and went here in prehistoric times. Much later, resource exploitation, tourism, and urban development gradually changed this part of the Laurentians—not necessarily for the better. The creation of the park in 1970 ended 150 years of commercial exploitation. Now some 200,000 visitors a year come to hike, canoe, and camp among lakes, forests, and rolling hills, all patterned with rivers, streams, and waterfalls. Sugar maple and yellow birch clothe sunny hillsides on thick, well-drained soils.

With the park open year-round, visitors hear spring peepers and see blossoming wildflowers in May; aquatic plants and orchids bloom from July to mid-August. Ruffed grouse drum in April and again in September. And cross-country skiing is popular in winter.

The loon, symbol of the park, is the most fragile of birds. Its long haunting call, plaintive and melancholy, thrills visitors as it echoes across the lakes. But only between 18 and 25 pairs inhabit the park, their numbers decreased and threatened by acid precipitation and visitors who—often inadvertently—disturb them during their nesting season.

The retreating glaciers left behind about 150 lakes of various sizes here, many of them arranged in strings along fractures in the Earth's crust. Largest is Lake Wapizagonke, 10 miles long and about 147 feet deep in places. It is one stop on a carefully mapped route that you can drive through the park. A handsome and useful guide published by the park, "Discovering La Mauricie National Park," will steer you to 15 or so other highlights—from the historic buildings of the Laurentian Club, a 19th-century fish and game club built and operated by wealthy sportsmen at Lac-à-la-Pêche, to the best spot for stargazing or moose-watching.

Birch trees glow gold in autumn in Quebec's La Mauricie National Park. More than 30 species of trees grow in the 207-square-mile park; forests cover 93 percent.

ISLANDS, DUNES, CLIFFS

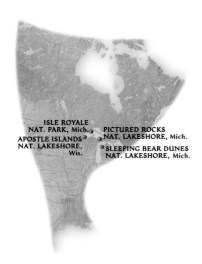

ISLE ROYALE
NAT. PARK, Mich.
APOSTLE ISLANDS
NAT. LAKESHORE,
Wis.

PICTURED ROCKS
NAT. LAKESHORE, Mich.

SLEEPING BEAR DUNES
NAT. LAKESHORE, Mich.

ISLE ROYALE NATIONAL PARK

"So far," wrote British naturalist Ewan Clarkson, "man has failed in his attempts to exterminate the wolf." Clarkson spent a season among the wolves and moose of Isle Royale, Michigan, in the 1970s. He called the wolf "a fellow traveler from the Pleistocene era." Of the moose, he wrote, "It is difficult to believe in a moose, even when you see one. It is as if all the leftovers of creation have been combined to make this creature with its long, stiltlike legs, the body of an ox, the neck of a horse, the head of a camel, and the ears of a mule."

The moose and the wolves both came late to Isle Royale, the moose swimming over sometime early in the 20th century; the wolves coming on foot across the ice during the exceptionally cold winter of 1948-49. Over the decades, their populations achieved a kind of balance—the moose feeding the wolves, the wolves keeping the moose herd in check. Today there are about 750 moose on the island and perhaps 25 wolves.

The wolf-and-moose-monitoring program on Isle Royale is the world's longest running wildlife research project, having completed its 42nd annual winter study. Researchers at first thought that decades of inbreeding might be harming the wolves' ability to reproduce, for their numbers fell during the early 1990s. Now biologists see no direct signs of genetic inbreeding problems and the numbers are recovering.

The wolves and the moose play out their complicated interdependence in spite of the presence of some 17,000 visitors to their island each year.

Isle Royale has long been recognized as a special and unique place, abounding in superlatives. Authorized by President Herbert Hoover in 1931 and established by Franklin Roosevelt in 1940, Isle Royale is 45 miles long and 9 miles wide at its widest and encompasses 850 square miles. About 98 percent of its area is officially designated wilderness. It was made an International Biosphere Reserve by the United Nations in 1981. A ridge-and-trough pattern runs parallel to Isle Royale's backbone, the Greenstone Ridge, as if the island had been raked from northeast to southwest.

Isle Royale sits in Lake Superior's northwestern corner; the nearest landfall is 15 miles away at Grand Portage, Minnesota. Travel on and around Isle Royale is by foot, floatplane, or boat. There are 165 miles of hiking trails on the island and numerous lakes. In fact, about 80 percent of the park is under water, either as ponds, streams, and rivers, or as the waters of the lake. Divers love to explore the many Lake Superior shipwrecks nearby.

The island is not pristine. It has had hard use over the generations, from earliest times. On one of the trails you may see three small pits, evidence of the prehistoric copper miners who worked here as much as 4,000 years ago. They stayed only in good weather, leaving for the winter, and may have mined the site for as long as a thousand years. Copper from these mines has been found by archaeologists as far away as

New York and Indiana. Modern copper mining flourished on the island in the second half of the 19th century, a period when large areas of the land were burned or logged and settlements developed.

French fur traders named the island for their king, Louis XIV, in the late 1600s, and the American Fur Trading Company began commercial fishing to feed its trappers in the late 1700s by netting lake trout, whitefish, and herring in the waters around the island. Now anglers fish for fun, taking trout, northern pike, walleye, and yellow perch.

There are some animals you might expect to find in the park, but won't. Caribou, coyote, lynx, and white-tailed deer, for instance, were once on the island but have not been sighted in decades. Other animals, like bears and porcupines, have never reached Isle Royale. Good swimmers can make it to the island in summer, and good walkers in winter. But bears do not swim long distances very well and are asleep in the coldest winter months when the ice is most solid. Porcupines are awake in winter but do not relish a 15-mile walk across nothing but ice. The yodel of the loon is heard here, as the northern lights play overhead.

The park is open from mid-April to the 31st of October. Visitors must make their own arrangements to get there, either by boat or floatplane. Rangers conduct interpretive programs and guided walks, and children aged 6 to 12 can become Junior Rangers.

Mushrooms sprout
from the forest floor
in Michigan's Isle Royale
National Park. The
island wilderness in the
northwestern corner
of Lake Superior covers
850 square miles.

Wildflowers and lichen
cling to massive boulders
on the islands at Rock
Harbor, on Isle Royale's
northeast end (left).

Accommodations are available only at Rock Harbor. Most trails are easy to follow, and the most dangerous thing you are likely to encounter is an insect: Black flies, mosquitoes, gnats, and other insects peak in June or July and, as in most places in the north woods, can be a severe nuisance. Campsites range from three-sided shelters that hold six people and tent sites for a maximum of three tents to sites for larger groups. Some 70 species of wildflowers and about 30 of orchids bloom on Isle Royale.

An artist-in-residence program brings painters, photographers, and poets here each year, artists whose works can be influenced by the north-woods wilderness. Each is given a rustic cabin and a canoe and is asked in return to conduct a program for visitors each week and give a finished work inspired by the island to the park. About 40 artists have so far completed a residency.

Its status as an island has helped to preserve Isle Royale as a wilderness haven—a roadless tract of fascinating animals, unspoiled forests, sparkling lakes, and the rugged and rocky shores of Lake Superior. Of all the superlatives the isle boasts, the park perhaps has the most fun with this one: Siskiwit Lake's Ryan Island is the largest island in the largest lake on the largest island in the largest freshwater lake in the world!

SLEEPING BEAR DUNES NATIONAL LAKESHORE

As the forest fire raged, the mother bear and her two cubs fled into the waters of Lake Michigan. The cubs swam valiantly but the water was too cold and the distance too great; they slipped beneath the waves. Reaching shore, the mother bear climbed a bluff and peered back helplessly, searching for her drowned cubs. The Great Spirit took pity on her, according to Ojibwa legend, and raised North and South Manitou Islands to mark the place where they drowned; the mother became a solitary dune overlooking the lake. She lies there still, a sleeping bear.

The shoreline and the two islands are now included in Sleeping Bear Dunes National Lakeshore, a 35-mile stretch of Lake Michigan's eastern coastline near the town of Empire, Michigan. It encompasses 70,000 acres of massive coastal dunes and bluffs, as well as beaches and forests of birch, pine, beech, and maple.

You can visit the two islands today, exploring among the abandoned homes of villagers on North Manitou or visiting the 100-foot lighthouse, active from 1871 to 1958, on South Manitou. It marked the location of the only natural harbor between there and Chicago. Old farm buildings, abandoned machinery, and a school and cemetery also recall the past on South Manitou. On North Manitou, low, sandy, open dune country on the southeast side of the island grades into high sand hills and blowout dunes on the southwest.

A bull moose and cow browse lush stands of forest and grasses on Isle Royale. About 750 moose, largest member of the deer family, live in the park.

Here, on the mainland, in addition to the dunes, you will find birch-lined rivers, dense beech-maple forests, and rugged bluffs towering near-ly 500 feet above Lake Michigan. Park activities peak in July and August, but October brings vibrant colors to the forests, and in winter cross-country skiers and snowshoers tour the park.

If you are feeling fit, tackle the Dune Climb, a strenuous but reward-ing hike, or follow a 2.8 mile loop to Sleeping Bear Point. Take a map, for it is easy to get lost, or to lose your children, in this expanse of sand. The restless dunes also are constantly on the move; sometimes they cover and kill trees, forming "ghost forests" like one on North Manitou Island.

And watch for the quick-stepping but endangered piping plover that you may find on the beaches.

PICTURED ROCKS NATIONAL LAKESHORE

Fans of Pictured Rocks National Lakeshore on Michigan's Upper Penin-sula disagree about the "best" time to visit, for each season offers some-thing special. Wildflowers herald the spring, summer brings warmth and abundant sunshine; fall colors spread a gaudy palette among the hard-wood forest, and winter snows clothe the bluffs in silence and fog.

The park is open year-round, although snow may close many of the roads in the region. Visitation is heaviest in July and August. Just five miles wide at its widest, Pictured Rocks National Lakeshore hugs Lake Superior for 42 miles. It was the first of the national lakeshores,

Deserted at dusk in the fall, a walkway in Michigan's Sleeping Bear Dunes National Lakeshore bridges acres of windblown sand. One area of coastal dunes is open for climbing 24 hours a day, year-round.

Thick forests crowd
sandstone cliffs
of Pictured Rocks
National Lakeshore,
where waterfalls
cascade into Lake
Superior on Michigan's
Upper Peninsula.

authorized in 1966. Park headquarters, which are shared with Hiawatha National Forest, are in Munising, Michigan.

You will get your best look at Pictured Rocks from a boat; trips can be arranged in Munising. Tours usually last three hours. Mineral-stained sandstone cliffs, rising dramatically from the lake, slide by, their forms shaped by wind, ice, and pounding waves. Iron tints them brown and tan, copper adds a greenish hue, and manganese colors them black.

Water attacks the cliffs from two directions—trickling down their faces or slamming in waves against their bases. People have been busy giving fanciful names to many of the eroded formations: for example, Miners Castle, Battleship Row, Indian Head, Lover's Leap.

Enabling legislation originally called for a scenic drive within the lakeshore; however, the drive not only has been deleted from planning but also has been legislatively prohibited. But you can walk. A 42-mile-long segment of the North Country National Scenic Trail, which when finished will run from the Adirondacks in New York to the lonely plains of North Dakota, passes through Pictured Rocks. Backcountry camp-sites and group sites are spaced every few miles along the trail.

Just to the east of Pictured Rocks is historic Grand Marais, Michigan—(big swamp or marsh, literally, although the French voyageurs of the 1600s intended its name to be "great harbor"). A touching memorial there honors commercial fishermen lost out of Grand Marais. A bronze mural shows scenes from the lives of the fishermen, and a plaque bears an inscription: "They have seen the works of the Lord and his wonders in the deep."

APOSTLE ISLANDS NATIONAL LAKESHORE

"At a distance of one to five miles in the lake lie a cluster of wooded islands…the Twelve Apostles. There appears to be fifteen or twenty in number, and they present a very beautiful and picturesque group." So wrote explorer Henry Schoolcraft in 1820, and visitors ever since have been similarly delighted with the "beautiful and picturesque" islands at the western end of Lake Superior.

Twenty-one of these islands and 12 miles of mainland today make up Wisconsin's Apostle Islands National Lakeshore, open all year for boating, sea kayaking, camping, hiking, diving, sportfishing, and cruising. They range in size from tiny 3-acre Gull Island to the 10,054-acre Stockton Island.

Wave action combined with freezing and thawing have carved caves along some of the islands' cliffs—delicate arches, vaulted chambers, and honeycombed passageways. In summer, outfitters in Bayfield guide kayak trips into them. Here, too, are what naturalists call sandscapes—a range of features from barren sandbars to dune habitats that support plant and animal communities. There are several types: Those that connect two islands to each other are called tombolos. American beach grass and beach pea trap wind-blown sand and organic matter to help anchor them.

The Ojibwa were here first, settling the islands in the 1400s. They regard Madeline Island as their ancestral home. Fur traders came next. Tourism began in the mid-1850s when excursion steamers, then railroads, brought tourists to Bayfield Peninsula hotels and the wealthy to lavish summer homes. Then quarrymen, beginning in 1869, mined the sandstone for urban midwestern buildings. Logs, fish, and even ice have been harvested from the islands and the waters nearby. But since the 1970s the land has been left pretty much alone, and denuded forests are slowly recovering.

Half a dozen lighthouses still stand on various islands. The Sand Island station is the only one built of locally quarried brownstone. Strong winds cause the lighthouse on remote Outer Island to sway; "Tower is shaking very bad," wrote the keeper in May 1916.

On Manitou Island, the Park Service has restored and preserved a fish camp from the days of commercial fishing. Fish boxes, clothing, nets, tools, and furnishings are arranged as if fishermen had just stepped away for a moment.

Beyond a rocky outcrop, moonglow spotlights Stockton, largest of 21 forested islands in Wisconsin's Apostle Islands National Lakeshore. Hardwood and evergreen forests meet in the reserve.

NORTHERN WOODS, PADDLER HEAVEN

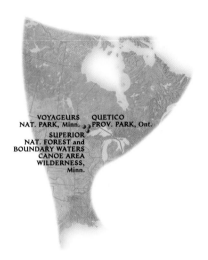

VOYAGEURS NAT. PARK, Minn. QUETICO PROV. PARK, Ont.
SUPERIOR NAT. FOREST and BOUNDARY WATERS CANOE AREA WILDERNESS, Minn.

SUPERIOR NATIONAL FOREST, BOUNDARY WATERS CANOE AREA WILDERNESS

"The Lord did well when he fitted the loon and his music into this lonesome land," wrote conservationist Aldo Leopold of the north woods. Today's Superior National Forest, 2,171,326 acres of land, water, rock, and trees, fits snugly into northeastern Minnesota's arrowhead. Theodore Roosevelt proclaimed it a national forest in 1909. Across 150 miles of border with Canada, it abuts Ontario's Quetico Provincial Park.

You will find Superior National Forest an area of diverse recreation possibilities, from camping and picnicking to boating and canoeing, fishing and backpacking. Especially boating and canoeing.

Some 446,000 acres are the surface waters of lakes and ponds, left behind by the retreating glaciers about 10,000 years ago; and 1,400 miles of canoeable streams flow within the boundaries of the forest. Drop a line over the back of your boat and you may catch walleye, northern pike, smallmouth bass, or lake, brook, rainbow, or brown trout.

Superior is at the southernmost edge of the boreal—or northern—forest, so pine, fir, birch, aspen, maple, and spruce rise around you. Deep in the forest the gray wolf prowls; this is its last stronghold in the lower 48 states. Shy and aloof, it is seldom seen by visitors, though perhaps 300 to 400 of the large carnivores live in the Superior forest—a population that accounts for some 15 percent of Minnesota's total population of about 2,500 of the animals.

European settlers in America began trying to extirpate wolves almost from the time they landed—and continued well into the 20th century. Weapons included poisoning, aerial hunting, control by state personnel, bounties, and a year-round open season on the animals. By the mid-1960s, the gray wolf was gone from the lower 48 states, except here in Minnesota where a few hundred survived.

In 1974, the Endangered Species Act gave protection to the wolf, and its numbers have bounced back, helped in part by a change in public attitudes—many people now recognize that the wolf is a legitimate part of the north-woods ecosystem—as well as a change in habitat: Widespread logging of the upper Midwest's conifers gave rise to extensive stands of aspen, which provide browse for the white-tailed deer that the wolves prey upon.

Although you are unlikely to see a wolf in Minnesota, you may, if you are lucky, hear one. They howl any time of year and any time of day or night.

"One thing is certain…," wrote Ewan Clarkson: "…wolves love to howl. Some more than others, perhaps, but for each…member of the pack, it becomes a joyous social occasion, with wolves gathering from all sides, anxious to make contact with each other, flank pressed close to flank…

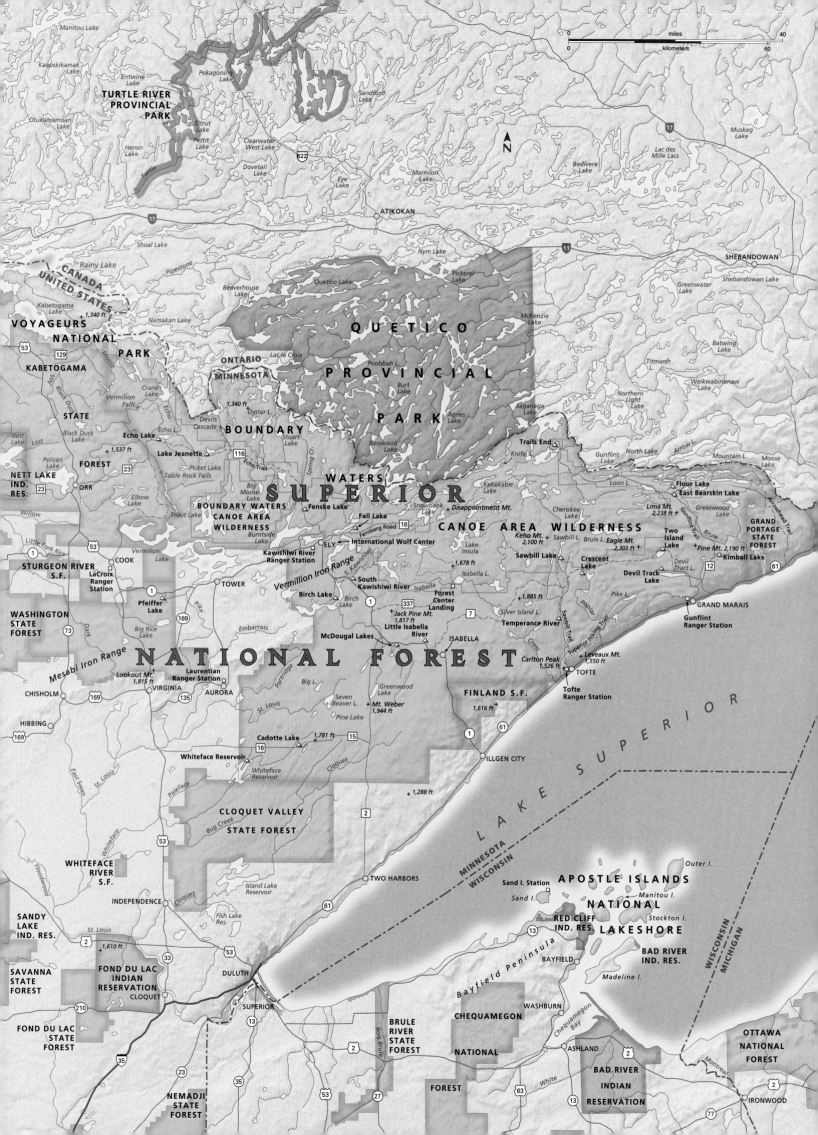

trembling, eager, bright-eyed, anxious not to miss a moment of the fun."

Paleo-Indians had a thriving culture here shortly after the glaciers retreated, leaving pictographs as evidence. From the region around Knife Lake, whose floor is a basalt pillow, they mined slate for making their knife and arrow tips. And—as in all this Great Lakes region—the French voyageurs passed through during the late 18th and early 19th centuries. By the time of World War I, much of the area had been either burned or logged.

During the height of the Great Depression in the 1930s there were 15 Civilian Conservation Corps (CCC) camps in Superior, each with a capacity of about 200 men, controlling erosion, planting trees, building trails, and improving roads. No doubt the same black flies and mosquitoes that torment us tormented them.

Generally, ice can be expected on the lakes any time after November 1, and they will not be open again until around the end of April. And about as soon as the ice is gone each year, paddlers take to the waters.

"The way of a canoe is the way of the wilderness and of a freedom almost forgotten," wrote Sigurd F. Olson, renowned Midwestern naturalist and author. "It is an antidote to insecurity, the open door to waterways of ages past and a way of life with profound and abiding satisfactions. When a man is part of his canoe, he is part of all that canoes have ever been."

"Like the kernel of a nut," Ewan Clarkson wrote, the Boundary Waters Canoe Area Wilderness nestles within Superior National Forest. Its 1,500 miles of canoe routes, 2,200 designated campsites, and approximately 1,000 lakes and streams sprawl across more than a million acres of forest; it is 150 miles wide from east to west and averages 16 miles from north to south. Established in 1964, today it is the most heavily used wilderness area in the country, visited by more than 200,000 people each year. In 1978 "wilderness" was added to the area's name.

Traditionally, Ely, Minnesota, is the starting place for a canoe trip into Boundary Waters, but there are some 60 entry points from which to choose. Permits are required and rationed, which increases your chance for solitude but decreases the number of permits available, so plan ahead. Portages are frequent and sometimes difficult, so be prepared for some heavy lifting.

Few experiences offer greater pleasures than a canoe trip into the heart of the Boundary Waters. Huge granite ledges offer sunny lunch stops. Waterfalls and rock cliffs invite exploring.

The area is also one of the largest bald eagle nesting areas in the lower 48, so you are likely to see one of these majestic birds perched in a treetop, surveying its domain, or even diving for fish. About 150 species of birds breed in Superior. The common loon is seen on nearly every lake, and the gray, or Canadian, jay will come right to your picnic table and snatch tidbits from your plate.

A rustling in the forest may turn out to be a tiny shrew, weighing less than an ounce—or a 1,200-pound bull moose.

At night, while the campfire flickers, the northern lights paint the horizon with first a misty green glow that sways gently, then forms rays, bands, and arcs, sometimes mixed with reds and blues. They are most vivid around the time of a new moon.

And even the sky above Boundary Waters is protected: Flying below 4,000 feet, except in emergencies, is prohibited.

Northern forest pierces mist gilded by sunrise in Minnesota's Superior National Forest. Spanning 150 miles along the U.S.-Canada border, the forest encompasses three million acres.

Mood indigo: Calm waters of Cherokee Lake, one of a thousand waterways in the Boundary Waters Canoe Area Wilderness (BWCAW) of Superior National Forest, reflect a sapphire sky. The BWCAW, with 1,400 miles of canoe routes, attracts 200,000 visitors each year.

QUETICO PROVINCIAL PARK

The Ojibwa word *quetico* is as beautiful as the countryside in Ontario it names, and as mysterious: Scholars cannot define it. With its mirror-smooth lakes, Quetico today is primarily a wilderness canoeing park. It sits on the southern edge of the Canadian Shield, the oldest and most stable rock mass on Earth. Clear, soft-water lakes, thin soils, and old rock characterize the shield.

Nearly two hundred years ago, explorer and geographer David Thompson passed through this country while mapping the U.S.-Canada border. In 34 years, he covered some 80,000 miles by foot, horseback, dogsled, snowshoe, and canoe and recorded his findings in 77 volumes of journals. He wrote of the northern lights he witnessed here: "The whole heavens were in a bright glow…and their brightness was often such that with only their light I could see to shoot an owl at twenty yards."

The Quetico has a history of protection going back nearly a hundred years to 1909, when the Quetico Forest Reserve was established. It was made a provincial park in 1913. Remote from Canada's large cities, Quetico has always been a more popular destination for Americans than for Canadians. Indeed, until 1954 there was no Canadian road access to it. It is open year-round but staffed fully only from the end of May to mid-September. Permits are required. Portages and campsites are slightly more primitive than those in Boundary Waters. The lakes and ponds are dotted with the shaggy dams and lodges of the country's most famous mammal, the beaver.

In *Plants of Quetico and the Ontario Shield,* long-time park naturalist Shannon Walshe, wrote of canoeing here: "As he paddles along, certain flowers stand out…. In July one cannot fail but see exquisite water lilies set against a background of dark water, the… shoreline fringes of snow-white meadow sweet, and gaudy yellow spikes of swamp candles."

VOYAGEURS NATIONAL PARK

When the American Revolution ended, the 1783 Treaty of Paris speci-fied that the boundary between the U.S. and Canada in this region fol-low the "customary waterway" that the voyageurs had used between Lake Superior and Lake of the Woods. Now Voyageurs National Park encompasses a 56-mile stretch of that route.

One early visitor called the region "a desert of rock, forest, and water." But it served the French-Canadian canoemen very well as they trapped and traded furs between Montreal and the Canadian Northwest in the late 18th and early 19th centuries. They were filling a demand that had decimated European sources of furs by the end of the Middle Ages. This region was a-crawl with French trappers while settlers were still huddled along the eastern seaboard.

Colorful characters, hardworking and resourceful, the voyageurs bat-tled rival fur companies, unfriendly Indians, and nature's forces. They scattered place-names behind them; although, interestingly, most are for water-related features. Even today, the ridges and hilltops are largely nameless. The round-trip for voyageurs from depots on Lake Superior to the interior of northwest Canada consumed four or five months.

The glaciers built the voyageurs' highway, and the birch bark canoe provided the transport. The Park Service calls this kind of canoe "a marvel of environmental adaptation," for it was constructed of birch bark, cedar boughs, and cedar or spruce root bindings, the whole thing sealed with pitch. Copied from the Indians, the canoes were light, easily navigable, and quickly repaired with materials always at hand.

The park was created in 1971, nearly 75 years after it was first pro-posed. It remains a place of unmarked paths, flooded trails, and stretches of trackless backcountry. Its waters are tangled with countless islands and channels where it is still possible to get turned around and even lost. "And that is perhaps the highest purpose of a national park," wrote Greg Breining, "to give us enough space that we can know…that we are in a land that is the way it was when human eyes first beheld it."

Ducks race the dawn in northern Minnesota's Voyageurs National Park. The reserve covers a 56-mile-stretch of the route French-Canadian fur traders canoed between the United States and Canada in the 18th and early 19th centuries.

Snake grass veils water lilies in a Voyageurs wetland (opposite). Bogs, swamps, beaver ponds, and lakes stud the rolling hills and islands of the park.

SCENIC RIVERWAY

ST. CROIX
NAT. SCENIC
RIVERWAY,
Minn., Wis.

ST. CROIX NATIONAL SCENIC RIVERWAY

The only river in the world protected along its entire length, the upper St. Croix, with the Namekagon, a tributary, was one of the eight original rivers included in the National Wild and Scenic Rivers Act of 1968.

The upper St. Croix, the lower St. Croix, and the shorter Namekagon make up the St. Croix National Scenic Riverway, stretching for about 252 miles from its source in northwestern Wisconsin to its junction with the Mississippi. For much of the riverway's length, it defines the border between Minnesota and Wisconsin.

Riffles and rapids mark the upper reaches, which are shallow and narrow. The lower stretches turn broad and slow between high bluffs.

A fort—Fort St. Croix—was here by 1688. It was possibly named either for a cross marking the grave of a French voyageur—or for the voyageur—near the town of Prescott, Wisconsin. During the course of the St. Croix's association with the human species, it has seen the usual parade of Indians, fur traders, and loggers passing along its banks. They all used its waters for sustenance, transportation, and commerce.

Following extensive logging of the primeval forest, today's younger tree cover—largely pines, brush, and hardwoods—attracts deer. In the occasional marshlands you may see ospreys or eagles patrolling the river for fish. Fishermen catch bass, muskellunge, and walleye in the St. Croix and trout in the Namekagon. The St. Croix contains the greatest diversity of mussel fauna in the upper Mississippi River system.

Both red and gray foxes stalk the banks. Farther downstream, where the river widens and slows, becoming Lake St. Claire, powerboats—and even houseboats—compete for the right-of-way with canoes.

The Park Service maintains seven trails along the riverbanks and on the bluffs, which are open year-round to hiking and, in winter, to cross-country skiing and snowshoeing. The St. Croix is one of the last undisturbed, large floodplain rivers in the U.S., and for this reason we can be grateful that its protection is assured under the National Wild and Scenic Rivers Act. About 90 percent of the river retains the feel of a truly free-flowing river, this in spite of several small dams and one large one. If you plan to canoe, be prepared to portage around them.

Landings, campsites, and the headquarters visitor center in St. Croix Falls are open year-round. As diversions from the natural world of the river and its immediate environs, the city hosts an arts-and-crafts fair in June and August, the Polk County Fair in July, and a wild river car show and swap meet, as well as a rodeo, in August.

And should you get tired of canoeing, hiking, fishing, and generally enjoying the natural glories of St. Croix, you are only a short drive from the famed Mall of America just southwest of the Minneapolis-St. Paul International Airport.

OZARK PLATEAU, PRAIRIE GRASSES

FLINT HILLS
NAT. WILDLIFE
REFUGE, Kansas

OZARK NAT. FOREST and
BUFFALO NAT. RIVER,
Arkansas

WICHITA MTS.
WILDLIFE REFUGE,
Oklahoma

OZARK NATIONAL FOREST, BUFFALO NATIONAL RIVER

The Ozark National Forest, more than a million acres, is scattered in chunks across northwestern Arkansas. It clothes the Ozark Plateau, plateaus uplifted as a unit and eroded by the swift rivers rising within them. The national forest was proclaimed March 6, 1908, by President Theodore Roosevelt.

Six nationally designated scenic byways, totaling about 183 miles, run through the Ozark National Forest and its companion St. Francis National Forest. In the Ozark National Forest, the drives will take you down narrow V-shaped valleys bordered by steep-sided slopes or sandstone and limestone bluffs. Clear, fast streams wind down the same valleys. Oak-hickory forest, with some scattered pine, turns to blazing oranges, reds, and yellows in fall, and in spring the dogwoods and redbuds blossom.

The Ozark is a working forest, so you may see evidence of logging or happen upon cattle grazing in open meadows. And hundreds of natural gas wells tap one of Arkansas's most plentiful resources.

Hunting and fishing, in season, are popular pastimes in the Ozarks. White-tailed deer, turkey, squirrel, and black bear are taken. And each year in June, "take-a-kid-fishing" derbies are held in honor of National Fishing Week.

Blanchard Springs Caverns, on Arkansas 14 southeast of Yellville, was called "the cave find of the century" when its huge upper level was discovered in 1963. Developed now, tours are offered daily except for selected holidays and some weekdays in the winter.

Five wilderness areas in the Ozark National Forest, totaling 65,826 acres, offer primitive camping, hiking, swimming, and a chance to commune quietly with nature. And from the steep and rugged terrain of one of them—the Upper Buffalo Wilderness—the Buffalo National River rises.

The Buffalo became the first National River, by act of Congress, in 1972. It is a unique administrative unit—of nearly 96,000 acres—having a broader corridor and tighter control than streams in the National Wild and Scenic Rivers System, so it enjoys even greater protection. For 147 miles from its source to its junction with the White River to the northeast, the Buffalo offers both swift and slow stretches as it descends some 2,000 feet. It passes through layers of sandstone and limestone, and the resulting bluffs rise as much as 500 feet alongside the river—the highest in the Ozarks.

"This river is too beautiful to die," said Supreme Court Justice William O. Douglas in 1962, protesting plans to dam the Buffalo. A decade of struggle—headed by the citizens who formed the Ozark Society—resulted in the dam's not ever being built.

The upper stretches of the river are usually too shallow and rough for canoeing, but hiking there, in the 14,200-acre Upper Buffalo Wilderness,

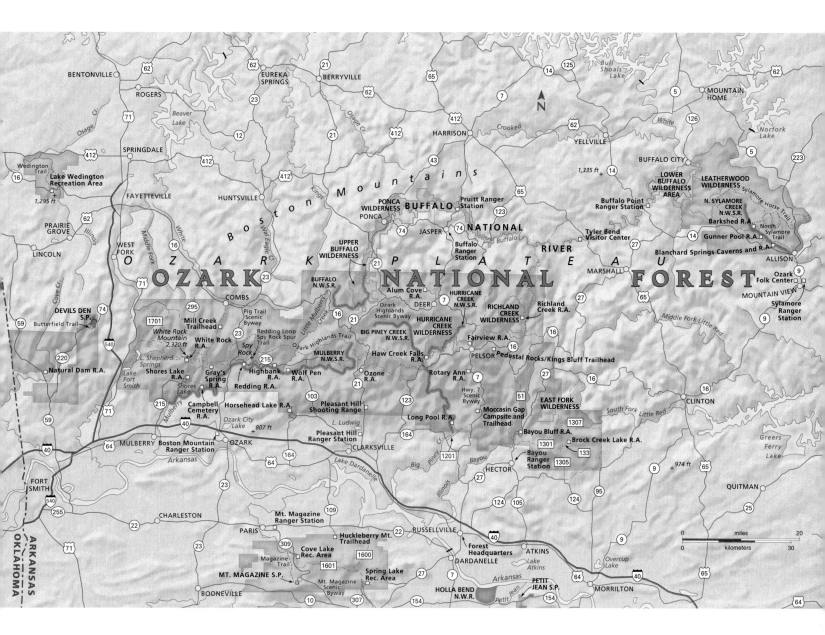

is prime. Far downstream, the final 30 miles of the river, slow and safe, pass through two wilderness areas—the Lower Buffalo and Leatherwood—some of Arkansas' wildest country, with only one takeout. With clear water gurgling beneath the bow of your canoe, you will pass lofty cliffs, overhanging hardwoods, and inviting gravel bars. You may see fishermen drifting along in flat-bottomed johnboats, angling for smallmouth, largemouth, and Ozark bass, catfish, and various panfish. If on the river during an "ample floating level," you will probably average about two miles an hour. Much of the river is safe for inexperienced boaters.

Both prehistoric and historic cultural sites are within easy hikes from where you beach your canoe. Some date back to the days of the Paleo-Indians more than 10,000 years ago, who occupied bluff shelters, and later peoples who built terrace villages here. In fact, "Ozark" is an Anglicized version of the French *aux arcs*, meaning "with bows," a reference to the Bow Indians, who lived in the region.

Some decades ago, archaeologists found thousands of small corncobs in Cob Cave, remnants of countless meals of Indians who lived in these parts before being pushed out in the early 1800s.

When Spanish and French explorers arrived in the mid-1700s, they competed with Osage Indians who were occupying seasonal hunting settlements between the White and Buffalo Rivers. Old homesteads remain.

Crystalline waterfalls curtain bluffs of Long Devils Fork Creek in northwestern Arkansas's Ozark National Forest. The stream, known for its limestone and sandstone bluffs and clear streams and cascades, runs through 11,800-acre Richland Creek Wilderness, one of five wilderness areas in Ozark National Forest.

Zinc miners were part of the parade, but their market collapsed in the 1920s, and CCC structures represent more recent Buffalo River history.

The passing seasons provide an ever changing panorama. Early spring brings fluffy white blossoms of the serviceberry, related to the rose family, and violet redbuds. Flowering dogwoods rise above wild iris, Dutchman's-breeches, and violets. Azaleas, daisies, and Indian paintbrush follow. Then, during autumn, goldenrod blooms on the riverbanks while overhead sweet gums, oaks, and locusts begin to show their fall colors.

As you drift along you may pass through actual clouds of fragrance

from pink clumps of wild azaleas clinging to a bluff. Algae-covered rocks on the streambed will appear to slide beneath as you pass, and water snakes may wriggle across the river, hoisting their heads out of the water. On the bank, willows gnawed off a few inches above the ground and sticks cleaned of their bark tell of beavers. You will seldom be without the sound of birdsong or the sight of a dozen tints of green in the forested hills. Minnows may go skimming near the surface with big black shadows right behind them. Snakes and turtles sun themselves along the banks, and bright red cardinals flit through the forest. Bobwhites call their names

Nestled in hills of southwestern Oklahoma, Wichita Mountains Wildlife Refuge protects a remnant of the mixed grass prairie that once blanketed the southern Great Plains. Originally established to protect dwindling American species such as bison and elk, the refuge ranks as the oldest managed wildlife preserve in the United States.

from the ridges. In the night, whippoorwills sing and bullfrogs bellow while coyotes howl. Fireflies mingle with the stars overhead.

Surprisingly, you may see an elk grazing alongside the river. A subspecies called eastern elk was once native to the Buffalo River, but they were gone by the 1840s. In the early to mid-1980s about 100 Rocky Mountain elk were released here; they are successfully breeding, and now number perhaps 450.

If you would rather drive than canoe, a scenic route between Yellville and Blanchard Springs Caverns offers antiques, arts and crafts, flea markets, B&B's, and home-style cooking in local restaurants. The extravagant country music shows of Branson, Missouri, are only about 40 miles from Harrison, site of the national river's headquarters.

WICHITA MOUNTAINS WILDLIFE REFUGE

Wild and weathered, the 59,020-acre Wichita Mountains Wildlife Refuge—92 square miles—lies entirely within Comanche County in southwestern Oklahoma. The mountains were named for another tribe, the Wichita, who were here when a Spanish expedition passed through in the 17th century.

President William McKinley established the area as a forest preserve July 4, 1901. Originally it was managed to protect wildlife species then in danger of extinction and to restore species that had been extirpated from the area. Animals that have been reintroduced include 15 bison, brought from the New York Zoo in 1907; 15 elk from Jackson Hole, Wyoming, in 1911-12; 30 Texas longhorn cattle from southern Texas in 1927; 11 pronghorns from Yellowstone Park in 1910-11; 13 wild turkeys from Missouri in 1912; and 7 bighorn sheep from a national park in Canada in 1929. Most of the species thrive today; however, the bighorn sheep and pronghorns did not succeed. Special management efforts are focused on saving the endangered black-capped vireo; the bird's greatest extent of suitable habitat in Oklahoma occurs here on the refuge. Refuge managers and volunteers trap and remove the brown-headed cowbirds that parasitize the vireos' nests and also use controlled fire to create stands of oak for their preferred nest sites.

Botanically, east meets west here in the center of the southern Great Plains. The Wichitas define a transition zone between the tallgrass prairies to the east and the short-grass prairies to the west. Buffalo and grama grasses of the western prairies thrive here, as well as big bluestem, Indian grass, and switchgrass of eastern regions. Even the so-called "cross timbers"—oak forests that feature a mosaic of patches of post and blackjack oak mixed with grassy meadows—represent a transition between east and west. Washington Irving, traveling here in 1832, said penetrating the wiry cross timbers scrub was "like struggling through forests of cast iron."

You will find photographing the wildlife a popular pastime here, as well as hiking, fishing, rock climbing, and camping among the lakes, streams, canyons, mountains, and grasslands. The refuge adjoins Fort Sill, an artillery training post for the U.S. Army.

FLINT HILLS NATIONAL WILDLIFE REFUGE

Migratory waterfowl find a haven at the Flint Hills National Wildlife Refuge in eastern Kansas. The 18,500-acre site, established in 1966, is bisected by the Neosho River just upstream from the John Redmond Reservoir, on land owned by the U.S. Army Corps of Engineers. Every spring and fall the skies darken with flocks of geese and ducks passing through, seeking a respite from travel; farmlands on the refuge are managed on a share basis, with the refuge's share providing food for the waterfowl.

A couple of trails will take you within easy photographing distance of wildlife, and boating, picnicking, camping, and fishing are also popular. And you can cut firewood, if you get a permit from the refuge manager. April and May are best for seeing songbirds and perching birds; November is best for catching the peak migration of waterfowl.

The refuge sits to the east of the Flint Hills of Kansas, a 50-mile-wide swath that runs north-south across the state. Nodules of flint are found in the limestone deposited by ancient seas more than 200 million years ago.

A sea of tallgrass here in mid-continent covered some 400,000 square miles, before farm, town, and road took nearly all of it. Dozens of different kinds of grasses grew eight feet tall on favored sites and were belt high in most places. As they rippled in the breeze, they flashed green and bronze and wine and gold. Too stony for plowing, the Flint Hills survived farming and remain the U.S.'s best example of virgin prairie.

Turtles and beavers carve V's in sleepy currents as you explore the refuge, and great blue herons lift off from dead trees in the middle of shallow ponds. Riverbanks are black mud and pale dead trees. Cicadas buzz. Turtles hear you coming and belly-flop into the dark water a second before you can spot them.

The Tallgrass Prairie National Preserve, one of the newest elements in the national park system, is a few miles to the west of the Flint Hills refuge. It will preserve, protect, and interpret for the public an 11,000-acre example of the now nearly vanished tallgrass prairie ecosystem.

Tallgrass prairie survives in the 50-mile-wide sweep of the Flint Hills in eastern Kansas.

SLOUGHS, PINES, PITCHER PLANTS

BIG THICKET
NAT. PRESERVE,
Texas

BIG THICKET NATIONAL PRESERVE

The Big Thicket National Preserve has been called a "biological cross-roads of North America." Once a huge area of three million acres sprawling across what is now the Coastal Plain of eastern Texas, Big Thicket is just a remnant, but a fascinating one, a mix of pine and cypress forest, hardwood forest, meadow, and black-water slough.

Blame it on the continental glaciers. When they pushed south, they herded species of both plants and animals before them; when they retreated, many of the species adapted to the changing conditions and stayed behind. An increase or decrease in elevation of just a few feet can produce a dramatic change in vegetation.

Today's preserve consists of 12 separate land units and 4 water corridors, all encompassing 86,000 acres, all that survive out of the three million acres of the original Big Thicket. The preserve was established in 1974 to protect this rich, biologically diverse region, and in 1981 it was designated an International Biosphere Reserve by UNESCO's Man and the Biosphere Program. Four biological influences bump against one another here: southeastern swamps, eastern forests, central plains, and southwestern deserts. Where such ecosystems meet—called ecotones—life-forms are most varied. According to the National Park Service, which administers the preserve, "Bogs sit near sandhills, and Eastern bluebirds nest near roadrunners."

Once this region was a wilderness of enormous trees and tangles of holly and leatherwood, interspersed with open savannas. Panthers, bears, and wolves prowled here, and it is one of the last places the ivory-billed woodpecker was spotted before it finally disappeared. On Pigeon Roost Prairie, they say, flocks of passenger pigeons were so enormous during migration that people miles away could hear tree branches cracking under their weight.

Caddo Indians from the north and Atakapas from the south knew the region as the Big Woods; later, Alabama and Coushatta Indians found shelter here before they were finally forced onto a reservation west of Woodville, which still exists. By the 1820s people were calling the region Big Thicket and avoiding its impenetrable tangle. It made an appealing hideout for various jayhawkers, moonshiners, and other assorted desperadoes. It was finally settled largely by pioneers from Appalachia; many moved deep into the thicket during the Civil War to avoid conscription. Lumbering on a small scale began around the same time and increased with the arrival of a narrow-gauge railroad in 1876. Oil strikes around the turn of the 20th century brought further change to the forest, and nearby rice farmers flooded some forest land.

Hiking and canoeing are popular ways of seeing Big Thicket. Several trails visit a variety of habitats and environments. In the Turkey Creek Unit, a 15-mile-long trail parallels Turkey Creek, with views of sandy

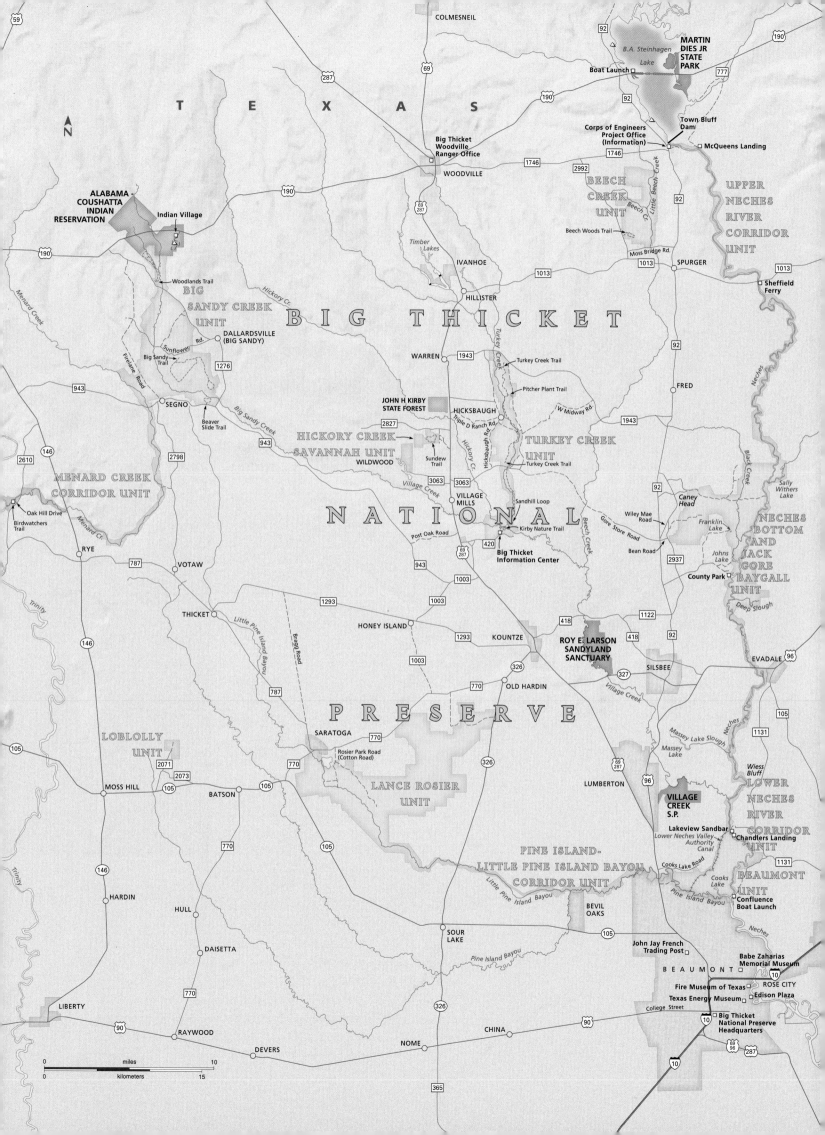

Long feathers crown a little blue heron in breeding plumage; its usually dull green legs have turned black. The birds inhabit coastal saltwater wetlands as well as freshwater ponds and marshes from Maryland through Texas.

Open-mouthed pitcher plants, one of four types of carnivorous plants that flourish in the Big Thicket National Preserve of Texas, invite insects to drop in. Four ecosystems—swamp, forest, plains, and desert—converge in the 86,000-acre refuge.

pine uplands, mixed forests, floodplains, and baygalls (boggy areas with stands of bay trees). The Pitcher Plant Trail on the northeast side of the Turkey Creek Unit has a boardwalk to lift you above the wetland and a viewing platform for observing the grasses, sedges, rushes, and wildflowers.

The trail's namesake pitcher plant is one of the four kinds of carnivorous plants found in the U.S. that grow here. The others are the bladderwort, the butterwort, and the sundew. The pitcher plant is the most common. Its long, narrow, funnel-shaped leaves, dotted with nectar glands, attract insects to the opening, then trap them inside with downward pointing hairs. Digestive enzymes and bacteria reduce the insects to nothing but tough exoskeletons and wings. The rest is absorbed into the plant. In spring and summer the preserve offers a program called "Insects for Lunch," which children especially find fascinating.

The Big Sandy Creek Trail, in the southeastern part of the Big Sandy Creek Unit, is 18 miles long and open to mountain bikes and horses. You cross through upland pine forests and beech-magnolia-loblolly pine slopes before entering a floodplain forest of basket oak, sweet gum, hornbeam, and holly. Bring your own horse or mountain bike, as there are no places for renting them.

The Beaumont Unit of the preserve boasts the easy Cooks Lake Canoe Trail. Two communities of flora blend here, the swamp forest—which is flooded year-round—and the floodplain forest—which floods only occasionally. Bald cypress and water tupelo predominate. Cypress, whose wood has often been used in boat building, bridgework, and as shingles, may live a thousand years; the water tupelo is a broadleaf, with dangling fruits that at least ten species of birds nibble on. Birding from a canoe on Cooks Lake is an especially good way of seeing herons, egrets, raptors, and swallows. Here you might even spot the rare ruddy turnstone or the even rarer tricolored heron.

This part of Texas gets hot in summer, so from early May through mid-September caution is advised. "Rain, heat, and humidity," says the Park Service, "are parts of the Big Thicket experience." The average high temperature climbs to above 90°F, and rainfall and humidity add to the discomfort. Spring, fall, and mild winter days are more suitable for a visit.

If you find yourself in the region of Big Thicket and it is too hot or

rainy to explore, visit Beaumont. It is a thriving city with a past dating back to early French and Spanish explorers snug against the banks of the Neches River just 30 miles upstream from the Gulf of Mexico. It began to expand from a settlement on the Neches in the 1830s as a lumber mill and trading center but really sprang to life on January 10, 1901, when the Lucas gusher blew in at the Spindletop salt dome just south of town. Beaumont became the cradle of the modern oil industry.

Today Beaumont refers to itself as the museum capital of Texas, for it has some 20 museums and galleries within its city limits.

WHITE SANDS, WHOOPING CRANES, SEA TURTLES

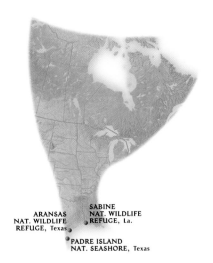

ARANSAS
NAT. WILDLIFE
REFUGE, Texas

SABINE
NAT. WILDLIFE
REFUGE, La.

PADRE ISLAND
NAT. SEASHORE, Texas

PADRE ISLAND NATIONAL SEASHORE

It was once called *Isla Blanca*—"the white island"—an appropriate name, for the white gulls, the white sands, and the seas that break into whiteness as they dissolve in foam on the beach; at night, a white moon silvers this quiet world. Padre Island stretches along the Texas Gulf Coast for 113 miles, the U.S.'s longest remaining undeveloped barrier island. And 70 of those miles are today the Padre Island National Seashore. About 800,000 people a year visit the seashore, to fish and windsurf, to bird and comb the beaches.

Early in the 19th century, Charles IV of Spain granted title of the island to Padre Nicolás Ballí, and it became named for him. It has been compared to a long, slender lizard, guarding the jagged mainland coast of southern Texas. Offshore, sand bars move constantly with the waves and the tides, making mapping impossible. Consequently, many ships have come to grief on the shoals here. As long ago as the early 1500s, Indians on the island combed the beach for flotsam from shipwrecks that had washed ashore.

For about 400 years, a parade of Spanish explorers, French voyageurs, English sea dogs, Indian warriors, friendly fishermen, black-robed padres, ship-wrecked conquistadors, Yankee traders, freed slaves, Mexican vaqueros, and adventurers of all nations passed along Padre Island. In 1553 the richest fleet ever to leave New Spain was driven onto the bar by a hurricane, and more than 300 men, women, and children survived the wreck only to fall victim to the island's Indians.

In 1847, John Singer, brother of Isaac of the sewing machine empire, was shipwrecked on Padre Island with his wife and son. They liked the island, bought some land on the southern end, and settled in. Children were born, and the family's headquarters grew to about 15 buildings. But because of their Union sympathies, they were ordered off the island by Confederates in 1861. Before hastily departing, Singer buried $80,000 in a jar near his home. When he returned to the island after the Civil War, he couldn't find it. So if you take a trip outside the refuge to South Padre, keep your eyes open.

Dynamic Padre's environments could be thought of as a system that changes constantly and where complex interactions of wind, land, and sea produce its unique features.

Most of the island is less than 20 feet above sea level, and active dunes move across it, destroying vegetation in their paths, leaving sandflats behind. It varies in width from about 1,000 yards to about 2.5 miles. Generally, if you move from the ocean to the lagoon behind the island, you pass across a sand beach; a stable ridge of dunes; vegetated flats with scattered but stable grass-covered dunes; barren, shifting sands of back-island dunes; fields; and featureless plains of wind-tidal flats.

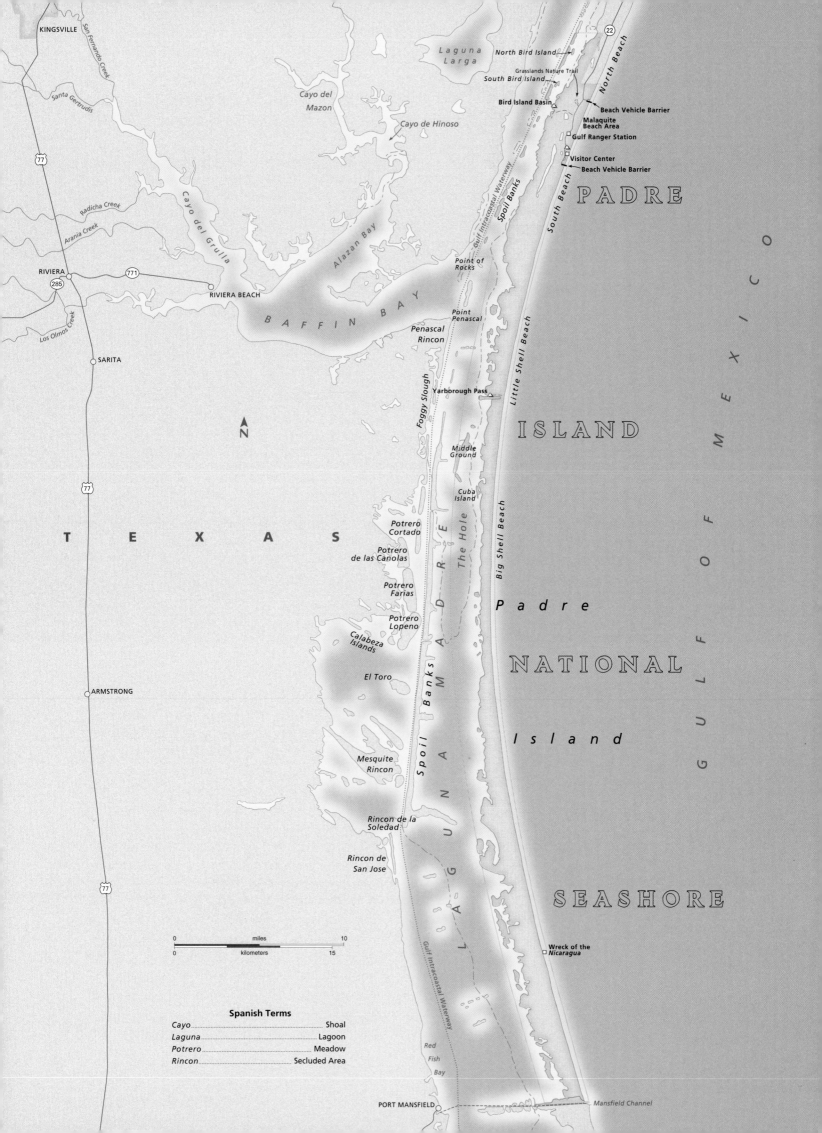

KINGSVILLE

San Fernando Creek

Santa Gertrudis

Cayo del Mazon

Laguna Larga

North Bird Island

Grasslands Nature Trail
South Bird Island

Cayo de Hinoso

Bird Island Basin

Beach Vehicle Barrier
Malaquite Beach Area

Gulf Ranger Station

North Beach

77

Radicha Creek

Arania Creek

Cayo del Grulla

Visitor Center
Beach Vehicle Barrier

PADRE

Spoil Banks

Gulf Intracoastal Waterway

Alazan Bay

RIVIERA

285

771

RIVIERA BEACH

Point of Rocks

South Beach

Los Olmos Creek

BAFFIN   BAY

Point Penascal

SARITA

Penascal Rincon

Little Shell Beach

Foggy Slough

Yarborough Pass

ISLAND

77

N

Middle Ground

Cuba Island

Potrero Cortado

Big Shell Beach

Padre

T E X A S

Potrero de las Canolas

Potrero Farias

Potrero Lopeno

NATIONAL

Calabeza Islands

ARMSTRONG

El Toro

Island

Spoil Banks

The Hole

L A G U N A   M A D R E

Mesquite Rincon

Rincon de la Soledad

SEASHORE

Rincon de San Jose

GULF OF MEXICO

G U L F   O F   M E X I C O

Wreck of the Nicaragua

miles		
0		10
0	kilometers	15

Gulf Intracoastal Waterway

Red Fish Bay

Spanish Terms

Cayo	Shoal
Laguna	Lagoon
Potrero	Meadow
Rincon	Secluded Area

PORT MANSFIELD

Mansfield Channel

22

Brackish ponds and ever shifting dunes represent only two of the many faces of Padre Island National Seashore. It protects 133,000 acres of barrier island off the southeast Texas coast.

A five-mile drive has been mapped by the Park Service to take you through each of these habitats, beginning at the entrance to the park and ending at the lagoon. You will pass the Grasslands Nature Trail, an interesting walk, also some artificially stabilized sand dunes; you will then navigate the Bird Island Basin Road, passing both freshwater and brackish ponds and marshes, and then end your drive at the back-island dunes.

Only one paved road leads visitors into the park, but you can drive along much of the beach—if you are careful. South Beach is open to your family car for the first five miles, but it is recommended that only four-wheel drive vehicles venture the next 55 miles to Mansfield Channel, which separates North Padre from South Padre. And take a good jack, shovel, spare tire, and boards or rags with you if you drive down island. It is against the law to drive into the dunes.

Plants and animals making up a unique biota adapted to the ever changing island. Sea oats, a pioneer species, grows in loose sand, intolerable to most other plants. By anchoring the sand, sea oats makes it possible for other plants to take hold; thus, the dunes grow, sometimes as high as 30 or 40 feet. They will stay put until something—a storm, or foot or vehicle traffic, for instance—kills the plants.

Birds are the predominate animals on Padre Island. Laughing gulls

circle overhead, and sandpipers skitter back and forth in the surf's froth, looking for crustaceans. Terns, herons, and egrets fly by, and in the shallows of the lagoon white pelicans hunt for fish. Killdeer, meadowlarks, and, in winter, sandhill cranes live farther inland on the dunes and grasslands. There are a few coyotes, black-tailed jackrabbits, lizards, and—watch your step!—Western diamondback rattlesnakes, also, on the island.

The Park Service is establishing a nesting colony of Kemp's ridley sea turtles on Padre. The most endangered of all sea turtles, these animals nest primarily near Rancho Nuevo, Mexico. For years, biologists collected eggs from there, incubated them at Padre Island, and released the yearlings into the waters of the Gulf. In 1996, two of the tagged turtles came ashore at Padre Island, members of the 1983 and 1986 "classes." Both laid viable eggs, and 111 hatchlings swam off into the Texas surf. Today the animals are surviving. Twelve nests have been found along the Texas coast, five of them within the seashore. You might see them from mid-April through August.

A visitor center, observation deck, a grocery and gift shop, showers, changing rooms, and campsites are at the Malaquite Beach complex, overlooking the Gulf. Summers here are long and hot; winters, short and mild. Humidity seldom drops below 70 percent. In the afternoon and

Wings that span four feet make the crested caracara a powerful hunter. The raptors, now rare in the United States, find refuge on Padre Island.

evening, sea breezes help moderate the high summer temperatures.

The park conducts a number of programs during the year, including beach walks, mini-talks, campfire programs, and a variety of programs and activities to interest children. There is no lodging in the park, but motels are available on the island. Windsurfing lessons for every level and rentals are available from an authorized concessionaire at Bird Island Basin. The park's only boat launching ramp is also there.

South Padre Island, not a part of the national seashore, is a popular spring break destination for college students. Mansfield Channel separates it from the park. Charter boats are available in Corpus Christi for deep-sea fishing. In 1954, a Park Service survey of the 3,700-mile U.S. coastline revealed that well under 10 percent was reserved for public recreation. To remedy this, Congress created three national seashores: at Point Reyes, California; at Cape Cod, Massachusetts; and here on the dazzling white sands of Padre Island.

ARANSAS NATIONAL WILDLIFE REFUGE

Just up the coast from Corpus Christi, Texas, and north of Padre Island is a refuge sacred to birders: the Aransas National Wildlife Refuge, established in 1937. It is a wintering ground for the endangered whooping crane, a majestic bird whose numbers dropped perilously close to extinction in the 20th century—as few as 21 birds existed in 1941—but whose numbers have recently risen to perhaps 400. About 200 of them now winter at Aransas. You can see them there from November to March, tall birds with red blazes on their crowns and startlingly black face masks. They stalk through the grasses with slow and deliberate dignity. They eat crabs, clams, crayfish, and small fish in the tidal marshes and sandflats and acorns and wild fruits in the refuge's uplands.

In late winter, as a prelude to mating, they dance, elaborate rituals of calling, wing flapping, head bowing, and tremendous leaps into the air. They mate for life, and, though accomplished dancers, they do not swim. It was not until 1954 that the birds' breeding grounds were found, 2,500 miles away in remote Wood Buffalo National Park in the Northwest Territories of Canada. Their bugling echoes across the 7,500 acres of tidal marshes and long, narrow sloughs of Aransas's 59,000-acres, which sprawl across most of the Blackjack Peninsula. Grasslands, live oaks, and redbay thickets cover deep, sandy soils. Aldo Leopold wrote of the whoopers' vocalizations: "When we hear this call we hear no mere bird. He is the symbol of our untamable past." More than merely beautiful, whoopers represent our fight to maintain vanishing animals.

Nearly 400 other species of birds can be seen at Aransas, including many that migrate; this part of the Texas coast is the lower end of an ancient funnel through which thousands of birds pass on their way to and from North and Central America.

There is a 16-mile, one-way driving tour through the refuge that will take you through grasslands, oak thickets, freshwater ponds, and marshland habitats; it provides excellent wildlife viewing opportunities. Perhaps the best way to see whoopers is by boat tour from the nearby town of Rockport; tour boats run between November 1 and April 15. Usually the birds depart for spring breeding in Canada between March 25 and April 1.

Whooping cranes execute complicated courtship dances each winter in Texas' Aransas National Wildlife Refuge. Some 200 of the birds, about half the known world population, winter in the preserve on the eastern Texas coast.

Gnarled live oaks anchor a shell-strewn beach at Aransas's Dagger Point (opposite). Saltwater marshes of the refuge provide clams and crabs that attract thousands of migrating birds.

Green algae coat the corrugated hide of an alligator in Louisiana's Sabine National Wildlife Refuge. Some thousand of the reptiles nest in Sabine's 124,511 acres of fresh- and saltwater marshes.

SABINE NATIONAL WILDLIFE REFUGE

The largest coastal marsh refuge on the Gulf Coast, the Sabine National Wildlife Refuge was established in 1937 to preserve a coastal wetlands area for wintering and migrating waterfowl. In southwest Louisiana, the refuge is just 30 miles southeast of Beaumont and Big Thicket. Migrating birds from both the Mississippi and Central flyways use the 124,511-acre refuge, which is also home to alligators and other reptiles, mammals, and numerous wading, water, and marsh birds. Fishermen line the banks of canals and bayous.

The Sabine refuge, a basin of wetlands, lies between the Gulf's beach cheniers—or oak ridges—and coastal prairies. Fresh waters and saline waters mix. Managers here burn, allow grazing, and manipulate both the water level and water quality to provide the best habitat for the animals.

The refuge is one of the most popular attractions in southwest Louisiana, with some 200,000 people visiting each year. As a casual visitor, the best way to experience Sabine is to walk its excellent Marsh Trail. Wading birds,

Roseate spoonbills
feed in Sabine's moonlit
shallows. Established
in 1937 to preserve
coastal wetlands for
migrating and
wintering waterfowl,
the refuge shelters
more than 250 different
kinds of birds.

marsh birds, waterfowl, songbirds, swamp rabbits, muskrats, nutria, water snakes, and the omnipresent alligators can be closely observed in almost any season. More than 250 kinds of birds are seen here. And about 40 species nest on the refuge. The most common grass you will see is the salt-meadow cordgrass growing alongside the trail; the most common bird, the moorhen. Ducks frequent the marsh all year but are more common during the fall, winter, and early spring.

Geese must have grit, so the refuge maintains a grit site where 300 tons of sand and bits of gravel are spread each year before wintering flocks arrive. It is a great place to observe the birds, and a photographic blind can be reserved for early morning shoots and close-ups.

Managers speculate that the refuge has more than a thousand alligator nests, so you are practically sure to see a 'gator. To estimate its size, guess at the distance in inches from the tip of its snout to a line across the base of the eyes; one inch is equivalent to one foot in length. "Do not," says the trail guide, "…attempt to move an alligator which may be blocking the trail"—advice that would seem to be superfluous!

BLACK HILLS AND BADLANDS

BLACK HILLS
NAT. FOREST,
S. Dak., Wyo.

BADLANDS
NAT. PARK,
S. Dak.

BLACK HILLS NATIONAL FOREST

A. B. Donaldson, a newspaper correspondent traveling with Gen. George A. Custer into the Black Hills in August 1874, wrote: "The lover of nature could here find his soul's delight; the invalid regain his health; the old, be rejuvenated; the weary find sweet repose and invigoration; and all who could come and spend the heated season here would find it the pleasantest summer home in America."

The Lakota first named this region: Their phrase *Paha Sapa* means "hills that are black." And, indeed, from a distance the summits rise like dark islands, their slopes clothed with ponderosa pine and white spruce, whose thick, dark-green needles blend from a distance, giving the hills their name.

The 1.2 million acres of the Black Hills National Forest today sprawl across western South Dakota and northeastern Wyoming. This is a land of rugged rock formations, canyons and gulches, open grasslands, tumbling streams, and deep blue lakes. It is also a region haunted by the Sioux, who, with other Plains Indians, rejected the government's offer to buy their lands after Custer's party confirmed gold. They fought losing battles for years and watched invasions by prospectors and settlers. They called Custer's route Thieves' Road. In 1875 they were ordered by the government to report for a head count; those who did not were termed hostile by the War Department, which authorized Gen. Philip H. Sheridan to round them up. Hostilities escalated, culminating in June 1876, in the Battle of Little Bighorn, where Custer's luck ran out.

The Indians won the battle but lost the war; the U.S. Army secured the Black Hills. Railroad building, mining, and lumbering commenced there in earnest, and the town of Deadwood was founded. It survives today as a lively tourist center, surrounded today on all sides by the Black Hills National Forest.

Devastating forest fires in 1893 precipitated concern for the forest, and in 1897 President Grover Cleveland established the Black Hills Forest Reserve, forerunner of today's national forest, which was designated in 1907. In 1898, the first commercial timber sale on federal land in the U.S. was authorized here.

Elevations of up to 7,000 feet give the Black Hills a comfortable summer temperature range and encourage conifer growth. The rocks of the area are among the oldest geologic formations in North America, dating back perhaps 2.5 billion years; the mountains containing them uplifted at about the same time as the Rockies—some 30 million years ago.

And, surrounded as they are on all sides by the Great Plains, the Black Hills have developed an extensive and unique biota. The overlapping of ranges of organisms has created a "whirlpool effect" of distributions involving many species, both plant and animal. "Many western forms reach the eastern limit of their range here and overlap with the westernmost

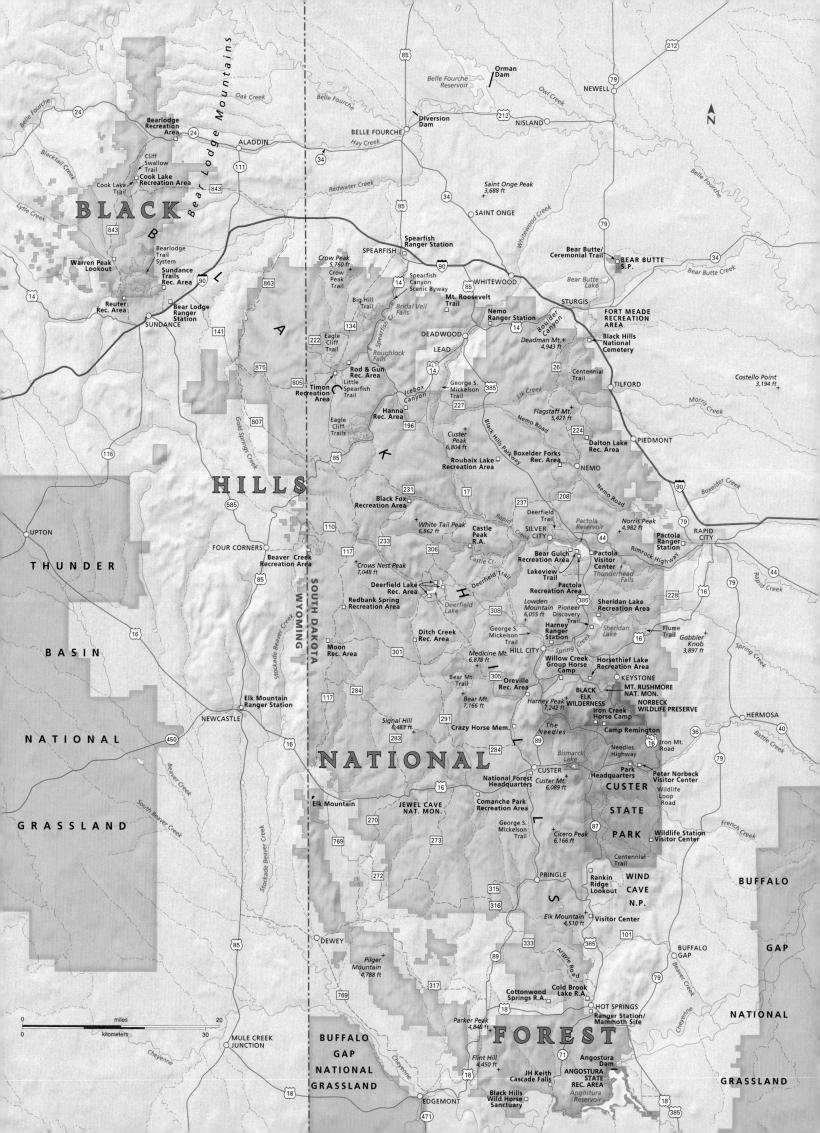

extension of eastern forms," biologists Sven Froiland and Ronald Weedon wrote. "Likewise many northern species reach the southern limit of their range here and overlap with central Great Plains forms."

Of the 1,585 plant species found in South Dakota, 1,260 are found in the Black Hills. White-tailed and mule deer are common; elk, less so. Mountain lions are present but difficult to spot, but coyotes' yipping frequently sounds through the night. Goshawks and ospreys nest in the forest, and bald eagles scavenge along streams in winter.

If you are looking for a scenic drive through Black Hills National Forest, two fine ones await your delight. The Spearfish Canyon Scenic Byway follows an old railroad right-of-way that was abandoned after flooding in 1933. You will wind along the bottom of a canyon with towering Paha Sapa limestone walls topped with patches of vegetation alongside. And the Peter Norbeck Scenic Byway, named for a former governor and senator from South Dakota, is 70 miles of hair-raising turns and outstanding scenery, including the Needles Highway, Iron Mountain Road, and Custer State Park. It also has hairpin curves and tunnels placed to frame the monumental features of Mount Rushmore. You will find the Forest Service visitor center on U.S. 385 at Pactola Dam, north of Hill City.

Many of the 600 miles of trails in the forest are designed for use not only by hikers but also by mountain bikers, horseback riders, and—in winter—cross-country skiers. There is a 300-mile network of trails for snowmobilers. The Harney Range Trail System offers loops through the Black Elk Wilderness Area—named for an Oglala Sioux holy man—which lies within the 35,000-acre Norbeck Wildlife Preserve. Harney Peak, the highest mountain east of the Rockies at 7,242 feet, is the centerpiece of the wilderness.

The Centennial Trail offers multi-day backpacking on a trip from Bear Butte Mountain in the north to Wind Cave National Park in the south. Namesake cliff swallows swoop and dart above the 3.8-mile Cliff Swallow Trail. The Flume Trail follows the Rockerville flume, built in 1880 to carry water to the gold mines. Old timbers and rock retaining walls used by the miners are still visible along the trail. You can collect small rocks or mineral specimens for personal use without a permit; gold panning is allowed in some areas, but check with the nearest ranger before you start. Similarly, for an eight-dollar permit, you can cut your own Christmas tree from the forest. White spruce, with short, sharp needles and a flat branching pattern that makes for a nice conical tree, is the most popular; Rocky Mountain juniper, the most aromatic tree in the forest, grows in dry and rocky areas in the southern sections; most abundant of the trees are the ponderosa pines.

The Black Hills "moonwalks," conducted by rangers on Fridays nearest the full moon, are unusual and popular. Although short, just a mile or two, they take a couple of hours. "Dress in layers," says the Forest Service, "wear comfortable shoes for walking, and bring a flashlight."

Other nearby attractions, in addition to Mount Rushmore, include Devils Tower National Monument in Wyoming and Wind Cave National Park and Jewel Cave National Monument in South Dakota. Custer State Park, which has fishing, hiking, rock climbing, boating, camping, and some interesting historic lodges, also shelters the largest bison herd in the United States.

Black Hills abstract: A climber threads the Needle's Eye, a granite monolith in South Dakota's Custer State Park with a weathered slit 4 feet wide and 40 feet high. Custer abuts the eastern edge of Black Hills National Forest.

BADLANDS NATIONAL PARK

"An indescribable sense of mysterious elsewhere—a distant architecture, ethereal." Such were the musings of architect Frank Lloyd Wright in 1935 when he visited the Dakota Badlands.

Designated a national monument four years later and a park since 1987, it consists of four separate units. The 244,000-acre park celebrated its 60th anniversary in 1999. About a million people a year visit now, but it still retains its mysterious quiet and loneliness—with a near absence of human noise.

Sharply eroded buttes, pinnacles, and spires blend with the largest protected mixed grass prairie in the U.S. Summer daytime high temperatures average about 87°F.

Humans have lived here for more than 11,000 years, and animals much longer. Researchers say the science of vertebrate paleontology in the U.S. had its roots in the White River Badlands formations. An array of extinct animals, ranging from tiny to enormous, once inhabited this region.

By the time of European contact, Lakota Sioux were living in the Badlands, and fur trappers, gold prospectors, and settlers encroached on

Sharply eroded pinnacles of Cathedral Spires jut from forested ridges and slopes in Custer. The park encompasses 73,000 acres and shelters 1,500 buffalo, one of the largest herds in the world.

their lands. The bloody Wounded Knee Massacre in 1890 sentenced the remaining Lakota to reservations.

One denizen, once feared extinct, is making a comeback. The black-footed ferret was among the rarest mammals on Earth. It depends on prairie dog towns for its habitat and on the prairie dogs themselves for its food. With the large-scale destruction of prairie dog towns, by 1985 only 18 ferrets survived. A determined program of captive breeding by

Like layers of a colorful cake, bands of sediment stripe the eroded cliffs of Badlands National Park in South Dakota. Gentle slopes of the Yellow Mounds area glow pink and green; beyond them the more durable rock formations of the Wall stretch a hundred miles across dry plains.

U.S. and Canadian biologists has resulted in the release of several animals and their successful breeding here in the park.

The park's North Unit includes a loop road with numerous scenic overlooks and trailheads, as well as the Ben Reifel Visitor Center, open year-round. To the south, the Stronghold and Palmer Creek Units are located within the Pine Ridge Indian Reservation. Both are jointly managed by the Park Service and the Oglala Lakota.

TUNDRA, DELTA, WHOOPERS, BISON

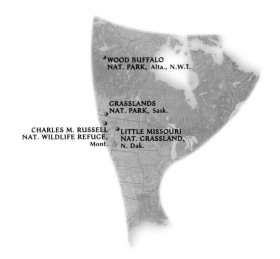

WOOD BUFFALO
NAT. PARK, Alta., N.W.T.

GRASSLANDS
NAT. PARK, Sask.

CHARLES M. RUSSELL
NAT. WILDLIFE REFUGE,
Mont.

LITTLE MISSOURI
NAT. GRASSLAND,
N. Dak.

WOOD BUFFALO NATIONAL PARK

When the whooping cranes that winter at Aransas National Wildlife Refuge on the Texas coast head north for their breeding grounds every spring, they cross east-central Texas, west-central Oklahoma, central Kansas and Nebraska, western South Dakota and North Dakota, northeastern Montana, and south-central Saskatchewan to arrive finally at the soggy marshes, lakes, and bogs of Wood Buffalo National Park. It is their last remaining natural nesting area. It is an epic journey, fraught with peril, but at last the business of nesting can begin.

Superlatives abound here. At approximately 17,300 square miles, Wood Buffalo is the largest of Canada's national parks and one of the largest in the world. It was established in 1922 to protect what is today the world's largest free-roaming and self-regulating herd of bison. Some of the plains bison brought in between 1924 and 1928 wandered south over the boundary and out of the park, so it was enlarged to its present size to accommodate them.

Not until 1954 were the whoopers' nesting grounds discovered in the remote north-central corner of the park. Until then, their summer whereabouts had been unknown. The key to saving the whoopers was found here, too: The birds generally lay two eggs each season but raise only one chick. For many years, biologists raided nests, removing one egg to hatch at various sites by sandhill cranes. This fostering effort was unsuccessful, however, so now scientists are learning more about whooping crane habitat and diet so that appropriate sites for relocation can be found.

Whooping cranes stick to ancestral breeding areas, migratory routes, and wintering grounds. Therefore, until more is known, there is little chance of establishing flocks in new regions. Thus the whoopers remain vulnerable to catastrophe—hurricane, oil spill, a red tide outbreak—especially in their wintering sites along the Texas coast.

Great rivers are here in Wood Buffalo as well. The Peace River flows through the park, and the Slave and Athabasca Rivers form its eastern border. Where the Peace and the Athabasca enter Lake Athabasca, one of the world's largest inland freshwater deltas sprawls. Migratory waterfowl from all four of North America's flyways pass through the delta in the spring and fall.

These two major sites—the whooper nesting area and the delta—have been given special recognition by the International Union for the Conservation of Nature for their importance in the protection of critical habitat for migratory birds. And in 1983 Wood Buffalo became the eighth site in Canada to be granted World Heritage status by UNESCO.

Karst geology of gypsum and unique salt plains dot a vast and undisturbed expanse of boreal wilderness in Wood Buffalo. The plains—flat and poorly drained, with elevations seldom more than a thousand feet

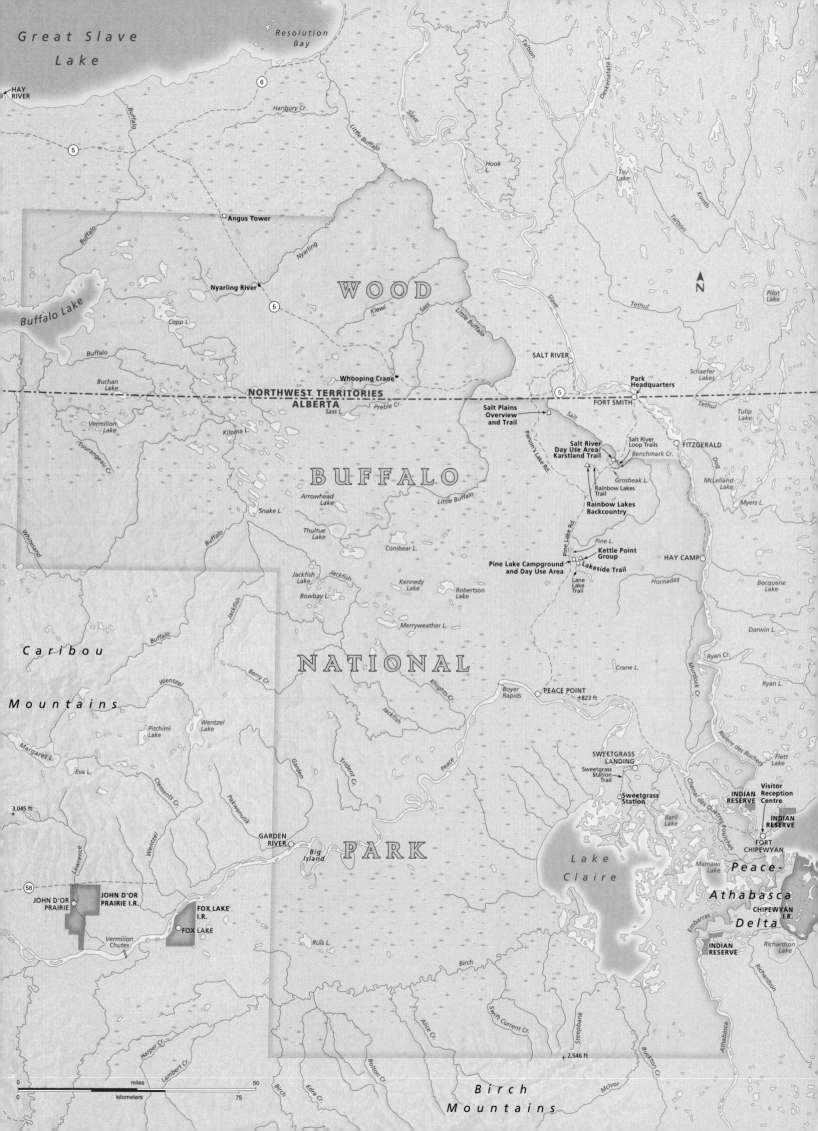

Great Slave
Lake

Resolution
Bay

HAY
RIVER

⑥

⑤

Buffalo

Hanbury Cr.

Little Buffalo

Slave

Taltson

Deskenatata L.

Hook
L.

Tsu
Lake

Konth

W O O D

Angus Tower

Nyarling

Nyarling River

⑤

Klewi

Sass

Little Buffalo

Tethul

Pilot
Lake

N

Buffalo Lake

Copp L.

Buffalo

Buchan
Lake

SALT RIVER

Slave

Schaefer
Lakes

Park
Headquarters

Whooping Crane

B U F F A L O

NORTHWEST TERRITORIES
ALBERTA

Sass L.

Preble Cr.

Vermilion
Lake

Kiloma L.

Salt Plains
Overview
and Trail

⑤

FORT SMITH

Tethul

Tulip
Lake

Salt

FITZGERALD

Touangeau Cr.

Salt River
Day Use Area/
Karstland Trail

Salt River
Loop Trails

Benchmark Cr.

Dog

McLelland
Lake

Arrowhead
Lake

Snake L.

Little Buffalo

Rainbow Lakes
Trail

Grosbeak L.

Myers L.

Whitesand

Buffalo

Thultue
Lake

Conibear L.

Rainbow Lakes
Backcountry

Pine Lake Rd.

Pine L.

Kettle Point
Group

HAY CAMP

Jackfish
Lake

Jackfish

Bowbay L.

Kennedy
Lake

Robertson
Lake

Pine Lake Campground
and Day Use Area

Lakeside Trail

Lane Lake
Trail

Hornaday

Bocquene
Lake

C a r i b o u

Wentzel

Berry Cr.

Merryweather L.

Darwin L.

N A T I O N A L

Ryan Cr.

Crane L.

Ryan L.

M o u n t a i n s

Pitchimi
Lake

Wentzel
Lake

Jackfish

Knights Cr.

Boyer
Rapids

PEACE POINT
+823 ft

Murdock Cr.

Margaret L.

Eva L.

Clements Cr.

Pakwanuiik

Garden

Trident Cr.

Peace

P A R K

Rivière des Rochers

Flett
Lake

3,045 ft
+

Lawrence

Wentzel

SWEETGRASS
LANDING

Sweetgrass
Station
Trail

Chenal des Quatre Fourches

Visitor
Reception
Centre

INDIAN
RESERVE

GARDEN
RIVER

Big
Island

Sweetgrass
Station

Baril
Lake

INDIAN
RESERVE

⑤⑧

JOHN D'OR
PRAIRIE

JOHN D'OR
PRAIRIE I.R.

FOX LAKE
I.R.

FOX LAKE

Lake
Claire

Mamawi
Lake

FORT
CHIPEWYAN

P e a c e -

A t h a b a s c a

Vermilion
Chutes

Harper Cr.

Lambert Cr.

Birch

Edra Cr.

Ruis L.

Bolton Cr.

Swift Current Cr.

Steepbank

+ 2,546 ft

Richardson
Lake

CHIPEWYAN
I.R.

D e l t a

INDIAN
RESERVE

Richardson

Embarras

miles   50
0
0
kilometers   75

Birch

McIvor

B i r c h
M o u n t a i n s

Athabasca

Buckton Cr.

above sea level—are a mosaic of muskeg, meandering streams, shallow lakes and bogs, and boreal forest, composed largely of white and black spruce, jack pine, balsam fir, aspen, and poplar.

The wildlife here is typical of the northern forest: black bears, wolves, moose, lynx, martens, wolverines, foxes, beavers, and snowshoe hares are abundant but elusive. Tracks and scat can be seen along hiking trails, but actual sightings depend largely on luck.

Ongoing management programs here include the study of fire ecology, karst topography, whooping cranes, wetlands ecology, restoration of timber berths—previously logged areas—and the biology and control of diseases in bison. The most northerly known hibernaculum of the red-sided garter snake is found at the Salt River Day-use Area in the park. Each spring, these small harmless snakes appear above-ground and mate before migrating to their summer feeding grounds.

As a vacation destination, Wood Buffalo is a long way from anywhere. The park's headquarters is in Fort Smith, Northwest Territories, which is accessible via the MacKenzie Highway and Route 5. As is the case with many highways here, portions of Route 5 are hard-packed all-weather gravel. Usually fewer than 3,000 people visit the park in a year. Supplies, services, and accommodations are available in Hay River and Fort Smith, just north of the park in the Northwest Territories.

A controversial road reopening—of a road closed in 1964—from Alberta through Wood Buffalo to Fort Smith is under consideration, opposed by conservationists and supported by the residents of Fort Smith; it would shorten their 814-mile drive to Edmonton by about 20 percent.

During some winters, if conditions are favorable, a winter road is open for about three months between Fort Smith and Fort Chipewyan and Fort McMurry inside the park. But distances are great and conditions are potentially dangerous, so plan carefully before making such a trip. Summertime visitors sometimes enter the park via canoe or other boat on the several major rivers.

A prime backcountry destination in the park is Sweetgrass Station south of the Peace River on the edge of vast meadows of the Peace-Athabasca Delta, which you can reach on the Peace River by canoe, float-plane, or motorboat. After hiking a few miles from Sweetgrass Landing, you will pass corrals built in the mid-1960s and used in the roundup of bison herds for anthrax vaccinations. You will be surrounded by marshlands that form a rich oasis for waterfowl, raptors, and other birds. Wolves are often present here, and you may, if you are lucky, observe the natural predator-prey relationship between them and the bison. If you go during June, July, or August, expect to be plagued by swarms of the legendary Canadian mosquitoes. Early to mid-September, when the weather tends to be cool, windy, and dry, is a better time to visit the park. A winter activity that is growing in popularity is viewing the aurora borealis, or northern lights.

Aboriginal people have inhabited the Wood Buffalo region for more than 8,000 years. When Europeans arrived in the early 1700s, they called the people they found here Beaver, Slavey, and Chipewyan. The Beaver moved west with the fur trade, and today the native inhabitants of communities around the park are mostly Cree, Chipewyan, and Métis. Traditional uses of certain park resources by local Indians—

Once master of the plains—its numbers reached 60 million—the American bison, or buffalo, now grazes protected grass and sedge meadows of Canada's Wood Buffalo National Park. It was established in 1922 to shelter the handful of buffalo that escaped slaughter as settlers swept through the plains in the late 19th century.

subsistence hunting, fishing, and trapping—continue and are considered an important part of the park's cultural history.

Subterranean streams emerge at salt plains in Wood Buffalo. The world's last flock of whooping cranes migrate from Aransas refuge in Texas each year to breed and nest in the 17,300-square-mile park.

LITTLE MISSOURI NATIONAL GRASSLAND

When the wind blows in the Great Plains, it blows everything not fastened down before it. So during the Dust Bowl of the 1930s, the skies were often dark with clouds of soil that had been loosened by plowing.

Grass is the anchor that holds the soil in place, and when homesteading disturbed the topsoil, the results were disastrous. In 1960, to begin repairing the damage, the national grasslands were born. Today there are 20 of them, managed by the U.S. Forest Service, encompassing some four million acres. The largest is the Little Missouri National Grassland in North Dakota, whose two chunks total more than a million acres. You will find here rolling prairies, dissected badlands buttes, riparian woods, floodplain forest, wooded draws, and mid- to shortgrass vegetation.

Ten thousand years ago, woolly mammoths and saber-toothed cats prowled here, pursued by Paleo-Indians, and in the 1800s Plains Indians rode after bison. Much later, ranching succeeded where farming failed, and today some 40,000 cattle graze on the Little Missouri. Oil and gas companies are pumping Williston Basin crude from the ground, and have built more than 3,000 miles of roads through the Little Missouri. So this is not untouched land.

But trophy mule deer, white-tailed deer, elk, antelope, and bighorn sheep thrive. Golden eagles are abundant, and sage and prairie grouse, pheasants, partridges, waterfowl, and turkeys can be seen. About 157,000

acres of badlands are being considered for the national wilderness system, and some sections of the Little Missouri River may be added to the National Wild and Scenic Rivers system.

If you visit, keep in mind that ownership of the land is a checkerboard, with private property abutting public; so get permission from landowners if you venture onto the backcountry roads and trails. A popular destination is Bullion Butte, one of the largest buttes in the badlands and, at 3,358 feet, one of the highest points in North Dakota. It is accessible only by foot, horseback, or four-wheel-drive vehicle.

The Little Missouri National Grassland surrounds the two units of Theodore Roosevelt National Park; the young Roosevelt ranched here in the 1880s.

GRASSLANDS NATIONAL PARK

"It is a country to breed mystical people, egocentric people, perhaps poetic people, but not humble ones." So wrote Wallace Stegner. Canada is still in the process of acquiring land for Grasslands National Park, which, when fully established, will encompass 350 square miles of prairie in two distinct blocks in southwestern Saskatchewan, near the border with

Montana. The western block, which straddles the Frenchman River, features deeply dissected plateaus, coulees, and 70 Mile Butte; the eastern block has layers of exposed strata in the Killdeer Badlands. Saskatchewan's first recorded dinosaur fossil was found here in 1874 by geologist and naturalist George Mercier Dawson, who was plotting the U.S.-Canada boundary. The park is also the only place in Canada where colonies of black-tailed prairie dogs can be found in their native habitat.

Grasslands is the heart of a huge region stretching south into Montana that experienced little human impact, though there are more than 3,000 inventoried aboriginal sites, including tepee rings, cairns, bison drive lanes, vision quest sites, and cobble effigies. It was here that Sitting Bull and his Sioux followers took refuge from the U.S. Army after the battle of Little Bighorn in 1876.

The goal of the park is to protect and preserve these sites, as well as this sample of the mixed prairie ecosystem. Settlement and ranching extirpated several species of animals, including bison, prairie wolf, plains grizzly, elk, wolverine, swift fox, black-footed ferret, greater prairie chicken, and—almost—the pronghorn.

Still, several endangered or threatened species survive here, including the burrowing owl, the mountain plover, the piping plover, and the sage thrasher. It is one of the few remaining places in Saskatchewan where prairie rattlesnakes and sage grouse can be found.

Val Marie, a village of fewer than 150 people, offers accommodations and services, as well as the park's visitor center. Birders have spotted 50 to 60 species in one day within walking distance of the town. Horse hitching rails are located throughout the village, so you can ride around on horseback to do your shopping.

CHARLES M. RUSSELL
NATIONAL WILDLIFE REFUGE

Though born in Missouri, Charles M. Russell—Charley to his friends—found in Montana his dream home. His paintings and sculptures of the countryside and its cowboys brought him fortune and fame—as well as the eponymous Charles M. Russell National Wildlife Refuge, second largest refuge in the lower 48 states.

It stretches up the Missouri River from Fort Peck Dam—the largest embankment dam in the U.S.—for about 125 miles, encompassing about 1,100,000 acres of land, of which 245,000 acres is surface water in the reservoir. There is native prairie here, as well as forested coulees, river bottoms, tabletop uplands, canyons, and the badlands so often portrayed by Charley Russell.

Lewis and Clark and their party passed up the river here, camping at several places now in the refuge. "The buffalo is scarce today, but the elk, dear and antelope are very numerous," they recorded in May 1805. Many of the myths and legends of the "old West" arose here, with their casts of colorful cattle barons, gold seekers, outlaws, cowboys, vigilantes, and horse thieves.

Both the summer and the winter can be brutal. Highs in July and August sometimes soar to 100°F. In winter the mercury can drop to an unofficial low of minus 50°F. Autumn is most comfortable. There is a popular 20-mile self-guided auto tour loop you may want to take on one of

Spring-blooming locoweed lights a slope near 70 Mile Butte in southwestern Canada's Grasslands National Park; beyond it mesas and eroded plateaus roll toward the Frenchman River. Grasslands, in an area once deemed the last frontier of the Canadian prairie west, consists of two blocks along the U.S.–Canada border and will cover 350 square miles.

the few graded and graveled roads. Traveling the other backcountry roads you will seldom see another person, except in hunting season. Services are nonexistent, so go prepared.

What you will find in plenty, however, is wildlife. Elk range freely here, and the extremely rare black-footed ferret is hanging on, dependent upon a decreasing supply of prairie dogs as prey. Bighorn sheep

Quiet envelops a canoeist in Charles M. Russell National Wildlife Refuge, in central Montana. Anglers cast for pike, trout, bass, and walleye in the Missouri River and Fort Peck Reservoir, largest lake in the state. The refuge stretches 125 miles up the Missouri River from Fort Peck Dam.

appear on the ledges and ridges of the higher ground in the Mickey-Brandon Buttes Area, and 236 species of birds have been identified. The refuge is one of the few places in the U.S. where the ritual mating dance of the sharp-tailed grouse occurs.

One of the first *Tyrannosaurus rex* fossils was discovered near Jordan in 1902, and the most complete one was unearthed here in 1990.

CANADA'S LARGEST, MOST REMOTE WILDLIFE REFUGE

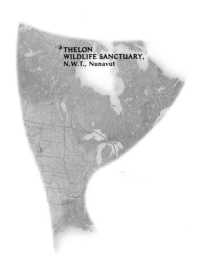

THELON
WILDLIFE SANCTUARY,
N.W.T., Nunavut

THELON WILDLIFE SANCTUARY

There are few places on Earth as untouched as the Thelon Wildlife Sanctuary on the border of Canada's Northwest and Nunavut Territories. It is part of one of the last, great, unaltered watersheds on Earth, covering 21,295 square miles. Thelon is the largest and most remote wildlife refuge in Canada.

Located equidistant between Hudson Bay and Great Slave Lake, the entire watershed of 54,966 square miles was never really settled, though Inuit to the east and the Dene Indian people to the west have hunted and fished everywhere in it for centuries. Surrounding the sanctuary is an area of 260,000 square miles—a territory the size of Texas—of tundra, rivers, and lakes, uncrossed by a road or a power line and without a single human community. It is the largest uninhabited area in continental North America. Here the tundra meets the boreal forest and forms the tree line.

The first people to live here arrived about 8,000 years ago, shortly after the continental glacier retreated. The Dorset culture, predating the Inuit, settled the Arctic coast about 4,000 years ago. Around A.D. 1000 Thule whale hunters moved eastward across the Arctic coast from Alaska, pursuing migrating bowhead whales. Later, their descendants, the Inuit, moved here from far-flung treeless corners of the far north—from Bathurst Inlet, the Back River/Chantrey Inlet, the Kazan River—in search of the source of valuable and extremely scarce driftwood brought by the Thelon and Dubawnt Rivers. The boreal forest that straddles the Thelon as it meanders across the tundra reaches in places some 125 miles north of tree line. In some of the languages of the north, in fact, *thelon* means "wooded river."

Early peoples left evidence of their presence: *inukshuks,* cairns standing on the landscape, marking water and land routes, caribou migratory paths, river crossings, fishing spots, campsites, lookouts, and food caches.

In 1899 English explorer David T. Hanbury came upon a group of Inuit from the Arctic coast on what is now known as the Thelon River. They "resort to this river to obtain wood for their sleighs," he wrote. "These natives had never set eyes upon a white man before, and had no articles of civilization whatsoever.... They were a jovial lot, and camped with us that night. In the evening they sang together, rather nicely, I thought."

If you visit the Thelon sanctuary, you will find yourself at the western edge of Canada's newest territory—Nunavut. Sixty percent of the Northwest Territories has become the official homeland of 27,000 people, 85 percent of them Inuit. The capital city is Iqaluit, population 4,500, on Baffin Island. Nunavut, meaning "our land," today is a territory like the Yukon or Northwest Territories, with its own locally elected parliament.

So now roughly two-thirds of the estimated 150,000 Inuit on Earth

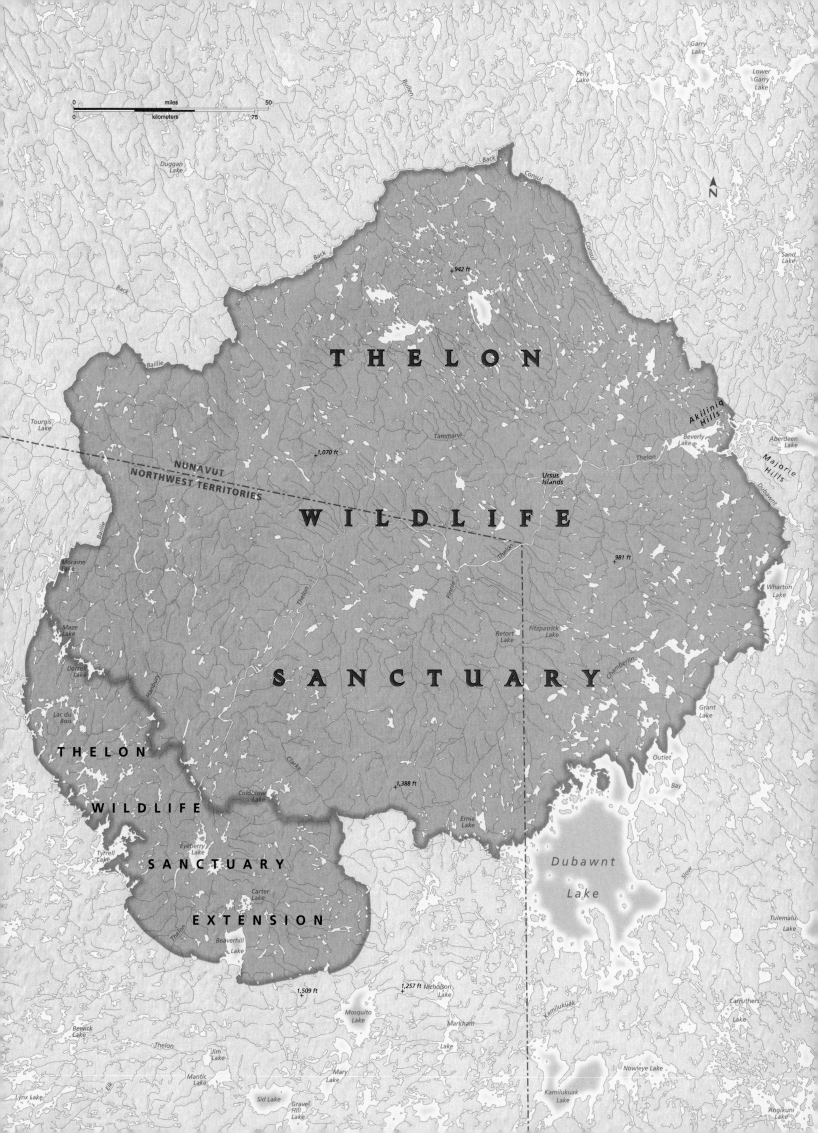

miles
0   50
0   75
kilometers

N

Garry
Lake

Lower
Garry
Lake

Duggan
Lake

Back

Consul

Bullen

Pelly
Lake

Sand
Lake

Back

Back

+ 942 ft

Baillie

T H E L O N

Akiliniq
Hills

Tourgis
Lake

Tammarvi

Beverly
Lake

Aberdeen
Lake

+ 1,070 ft

Thelon

Majorie
Hills

NUNAVUT
NORTHWEST TERRITORIES

W I L D L I F E

Ursus
Islands

Baillie

Dubawnt

Moraine
Lake

Thelon

+ 981 ft

Wharton
Lake

Maze
Lake

Thelon

Finnie

Fitzpatrick
Lake

Retort
Lake

Chamberlin

S A N C T U A R Y

Darrell
Lake

Hanbury

Grant
Lake

Lac du
Bois

Clarke

Outlet

Bay

T H E L O N

+ 1,388 ft

Coldblow
Lake

Ernie
Lake

W I L D L I F E

Eyeberry
Lake

Tyrrell
Lake

S A N C T U A R Y

Dubawnt

Carter
Lake

Lake

E X T E N S I O N

Thelon

Slow

Beaverhill
Lake

Tulemalu
Lake

+ 1,509 ft

+ 1,257 ft Nicholson
Lake

Bewick
Lake

Mosquito
Lake

Kamilukuak

Carruthers
Lake

Markham

Thelon

Jim
Lake

Lake

Mantic
Lake

Mary
Lake

Lynx Lake

Elk

Sid
Lake

Gravel
Hill
Lake

Kamilukuak
Lake

Nowleye Lake

Angikuni
Lake

have won some degree of self-determination. And they achieved it largely with a mixture of patience and compromise and little or no violence.

The first move toward self-government for Canada's Inuit came in 1976, and the law creating Nunavut was enacted in 1993 with the territory coming into being April 1, 1999. The new territory encompasses 770,000 square miles, roughly the size of Mexico, and faces enormous challenges; it has some of Canada's highest rates of unemployment, alcohol and substance abuse, and suicide. But the Inuit, with their traditional patience, are hopeful and determined.

One of the challenges they face is balancing their understandable desire for the amenities of modern life and a higher standard of living with the protection of their environment and their traditional lifestyle. Even now, diamond and gold are being explored and developed around the western fringes of the sanctuary.

The Thelon sanctuary began life in 1927 as a response by the Canadian government to the dwindling number of musk oxen, whose population was being reduced by the trade in their hides. So within the sanctuary there has been no hunting or — because the sanctuary was established before the arrival of modern roads and mining technology — mineral exploration for nearly 70 years. The ban on hunting has been respected by the Inuit, even though it has caused some hardship and ill-will.

Today, the greatest appeal of the sanctuary for visitors is the plentiful wildlife to be seen there. The musk-ox herd has reached perhaps 2,000, and nowhere else above tree line is there such a large population of wolves. Tundra swans breed in parts of the sanctuary, and molting Canada geese flock in huge numbers. One of the few inland colonies of lesser snow geese nests here, and it is also the breeding ground for peregrine and gyrfalcons and rough-legged hawks. Wolverines, arctic fox, and barren-ground grizzlies den here, preying on geese and their eggs in spring and summer. Most impressively, the Beverly caribou herd of some 500,000 migrates across the Thelon River twice a year en route to and from its calving grounds near the northeast corner of the sanctuary. Time your visit and you might get to see them.

The most practical way to visit the Thelon sanctuary is by canoe on the Thelon River, though the season is short — about eight to ten weeks, from late June to mid-August. About a hundred canoeists make the trip each year, though the upper reaches are hazardous and interrupted by strenuous portages. From the Hanbury-Thelon junction, however, the final 186 miles to Beverly Lake on this Canadian Heritage River are ideal, as you drift past boreal forest, sand flats, and tundra hills.

Where the river ends, you will find the tiny community of Baker Lake. It did not exist until the mid-1950s, when the Caribou Inuit began coming in off the land to settle in town. There is a dusty airport, the town's only other access. There are some hotels — including the Iglu Hotel — and outfitters, as well as galleries for Inuit arts and crafts and printmakers and a flea market where you may find some caribou mitts or parkas. There are scheduled flights into the airport, as well as charters. Geographically, Baker Lake lies practically dead center in the middle of Canada.

And, oddly enough, the community is famous for its square dances, which happen often and without warning, always at the Recreation Centre.

Ancient glaciers scoured the farthest northern reaches of western Canada, home of Thelon Wildlife Refuge. Largest and most remote refuge in Canada, it protects 21,295 square miles of tundra, rivers, and lakes in Canada's recently created territory of Nunavut.

Heavy horns shield the skull of a bull musk ox in Thelon (opposite). The refuge originated in 1927 as a preserve for the animals; the herd now numbers about 2,000.

The GREAT DIVIDE

CHAPTER III

ROCKY MOUNTAIN   WHITE RIVER   BLACK CANYON OF THE GUNNISON

GRAND TETON   YELLOWSTONE   BANFF   JASPER   YOHO   KOOTENAY

WATERTON-GLACIER   SAWTOOTH   HELLS CANYON   THE WILDERNESS CORE

Still waters of St. Mary Lake duplicate a dawn
in Glacier National Park, Montana.

BY THOMAS SCHMIDT

Stretching northwest from Colorado through Wyoming and Montana and along the Alberta-British Columbia boundary, this spectacular region of mountain, gorge, and glacier follows the Continental Divide along the spine of the Rocky Mountains for roughly a thousand straight-line miles. It takes in some of the most dramatic alpine scenery in the world and preserves irreplaceable biotic communities. Much of it is protected by a patchwork of public lands.

A bull elk eyes an intruder in Alberta's Banff National Park.

The Great Divide is the continent's primary watershed—dividing waters that flow west into the Pacific from those that flow south, east, or north into the the Gulf of Mexico or into the Atlantic or Arctic Oceans. It strongly influences the region's continental climate and helps to produce the tremendous variety of weather patterns that exist within the Rocky Mountain region. Latitude and abrupt changes in elevation also affect climate.

Taken together, these influences explain in large part why the region compresses such a broad spectrum of habitats into such a relatively small area. Here you will find prairie grasslands and misty red cedar groves, semiarid sagebrush flats, deserts, dense montane forests, and the treeless realm of the alpine tundra. A half-day's drive over some parts of the Divide leads through a variety of habitats equivalent to that encountered on a 3,100-mile voyage from south to north at sea level.

The Great Divide offers many valuable lessons in diverse biomes and ecosystems. Animals of the plains, such as pronghorn and bison, graze just a short distance from animals of the alpine tundra, such as mountain goats and pikas. Between the two extremes live grizzly bears, gray wolves, mountain goats, elk, two species of deer, black bears, moose, cougars, bobcats, wolverines, many rodents, several endangered fish species, and more than 250 species of birds.

The fascinating geology of the Great Divide is sometimes violent. Much of Yellowstone, for instance, erupted in a cataclysmic volcanic detonation 600,000 years ago, which left a crater 35 miles across.

While every site has its own unique creation story, the region as a whole shares a common geologic ancestry. It leads back roughly 500 million years to a slow but incredibly powerful collision between two of the Earth's tectonic plates. The western edge of the lighter North American continental plate overrode the Pacific oceanic plate.

The collision crumpled the western margin of the continent and caused the uplift that created the Colorado Rockies and the folding and faulting that raised the central, Canadian, and northern Rockies. Erosion stripped away overlying layers of rock. Volcanoes spewed lava and ash. And glacial ice carved the peaks and plowed out many valleys.

This chapter samples the best of the Great Divide region. It includes Colorado's Rocky Mountain National Park, with its sprawl of alpine tundra; Yellowstone, with its geothermal features and abundant wildlife; Idaho's Hells Canyon, the continent's deepest gorge; Alberta's Banff and Jasper National Parks, with their immense ice fields; and much, much more.

Color spots Yellowstone National Park, Wyoming.

Bistcho Lake

Hay

Chinchaga

Beatton

Peace

Smoky

Little Smoky

Utikuma Lake

Lesser Slave Lake

Athabasca

JASPER NATIONAL PARK

Mt. Robson +
12,972 ft

Fraser

Pembina

Brazeau

Mt. Columbia
+ 12,293 ft

N. Saskatchewan

R O C K Y

BRITISH COLUMBIA

ALBERTA

Columbia

Red Deer

YOHO NATIONAL PARK

BANFF NATIONAL PARK

Bow

KOOTENAY NATIONAL PARK

Kootenay

Selkirk Mountains

Upper Arrow Lake

Lower Arrow Lake

S. Saskatchewan

WATERTON-GLACIER INTERNATIONAL PEACE PARK
1 - Waterton Lakes National Park
2 - Glacier National Park

1

2

**CANADA
UNITED STATES**

Franklin D. Roosevelt Lake

Lake Pend Oreille

B I T T E R R O O T

Lake Elwell

Marias

Flathead Lake

WASHINGTON

St. Joe

R A N G E

Missouri

WILDERNESS CORE
Selway-Bitterroot Wilderness - 1
Gospel Hump Wilderness - 2
Frank Church-River of No Return - 3
Wilderness

1

Big Belt Mts.

M O N T A N A

Musselshell

HELLS CANYON NAT. REC. AREA

Hells Canyon

2

Salmon

Jefferson

Gallatin

Yellowstone

Granite Peak
+ 12,799 ft

Bighorn Mountains

OREGON

Snake

3

I D A H O

Red Rock

M O U N

Yellowstone Lake

Bighorn

SAWTOOTH NAT. REC. AREA

YELLOWSTONE NATIONAL PARK

Grand Teton
13,770 ft +

GRAND TETON NATIONAL PARK

Gannett Peak
+ 13,804 ft

Boysen Reservoir

Snake River Plain

Snake

American Falls Reservoir

Green

T A I N S

W Y O M I N G

Sweetwater

N. Platte

NEVADA

Bear Lake

GREAT SALT LAKE

Great Divide Basin

Flaming Gorge Reservoir

F r o n t

UTAH

Kings Peak
13,528 ft +

Uinta Mts.

ROCKY MOUNTAIN NATIONAL PARK

S. Platte

R a n g e

Longs Peak 14,255 ft +

White

WHIE RIVER NATIONAL FOREST

Colorado

C O L O R A D O

Big Sandy Cr.

Site discussed in chapter

Mt. Elbert
14,433 ft +

Pikes Peak
14,110 ft +

0   miles   400

Gunnison

Arkansas

KANS.

0   kilometers   500

BLACK CANYON OF THE GUNNISON NAT. PARK

Sangre de Cristo Mts.

San Juan Mts.

Rio Grande

Purgatoire

Cimarron

OKLAHOMA

NEW MEXICO

+ Wheeler Peak 13,161 ft

TEXAS

THE GREAT DIVIDE

141

ALPINE TUNDRA, CANYONS, GORGES

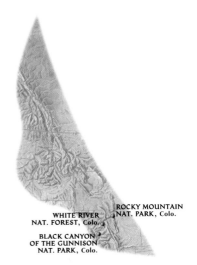

WHITE RIVER
NAT. FOREST, Colo.

ROCKY MOUNTAIN
NAT. PARK, Colo.

BLACK CANYON
OF THE GUNNISON
NAT. PARK, Colo.

ROCKY MOUNTAIN NATIONAL PARK

Famous for its high, glacially carved peaks and its marvelous expanse of alpine tundra, Rocky Mountain National Park straddles the Continental Divide northwest of Denver and takes in 415 square miles along the magnificent Front Range. It brags more than 100 named peaks over 10,000 feet, including Longs Peak, which, at 14,255 feet, is the highest in the park and the range's most famous summit north of Pikes Peak.

Approximately one-third of the park lies above tree line in the supremely fragile, weather-beaten life zone of the alpine tundra. Carpeted with an abundance of tiny but tenacious wildflowers, it is a vast, open, and gently rolling landscape. Panoramic vistas across a sea of peaks delight the eyes of visitors in all seasons.

The alpine tundra is what sets Rocky Mountain apart from the rest of the national parks in the lower 48 states. No other park preserves an alpine tundra zone so extensive and diverse. Fortunately for those who come here, the tundra is also easy to reach. A full 11 miles of the park's central highway—Trail Ridge Road—passes through the treeless realm, snaking along to reach its highest point of 12,183 feet.

As memorable as the tundra, and perhaps as characteristic of Rocky Mountain, are the extensive, savanna-like meadows of grass and ponderosa pine that stretch among the eastern foothills. Called parks, these enticing openings in the mountain forests also offer grandstand vistas—in this case, of glacially carved peaks and high ridges.

More than 150 lakes dot the glacial basins of Rocky Mountain's high country, many of them tucked beneath soaring cliffs a thousand feet high. Several important rivers, including the Colorado, have their headwaters within the park, and countless bone-chilling streams thread through the forests and wildflower meadows.

One of the most dependable sites in the Rockies for spotting elk and bighorn sheep, the park is also home to moose, mule deer, mountain lions, black bears, and river otters as well as a host of rodents, birds of prey, and songbirds. Gone, though, are the small herds of bison that settlers wrote about when they began arriving in Estes Park during the 1860s.

The park takes in a small portion of the Front Range, which cuts south from Wyoming all the way to Colorado Springs. The core of the range is composed mainly of Precambrian gneiss, schist, and granite—basement rocks, as they are sometimes called, the same type of rock that underlies the continents. At times over the past 300 million years, this particular mass of Precambrian rock lay under or along the shore of ancient shallow seas and accumulated a thick covering of sedimentary rock.

Then, roughly 65 million years ago, the Front Range began to rise slowly as a distinct block. Over the course of 20 million years or so, the range pushed upward 15,000 to 25,000 feet, but it never stood so

Like a pointing index finger, a granite spire stabs skyward on Longs Peak in Rocky Mountain National Park, Colorado. The 14,255-foot mountain, highest in the park, attracts thousands of climbers each summer. Some 50 have died on the mountain since explorer John Wesley Powell and his party scaled it in 1868.

high because it also eroded down to its Precambrian core. Later, the entire intermountain region was heaved upward again. In Colorado, the land rose about 6,000 feet, and streams and rivers cut into the mountains with renewed vigor.

This erosion was augmented by at least three major ice ages when massive glaciers flowed down from the crest of the range, broadening and straightening steep, stream-eroded valleys, piling up moraines, and carving out the spacious cirques that delight today's visitors.

No voice can take sole credit for suggesting the creation of Rocky Mountain National Park. But local innkeeper, climber, and conservationist Enos Mills was its most ardent and vocal partisan. A self-taught naturalist, natural history writer, and a contemporary of John Muir, Mills suggested the park in 1909, then traveled the nation for years, lobbying for its creation. In 1915, Rocky Mountain National Park was formally dedicated.

Most visitors to Rocky Mountain start with a day trip along Trail Ridge Road, a premier scenic road connecting Estes Park with the Kawuneeche Valley west of the Continental Divide. The road runs for 50 miles and takes in virtually all of the park's major life zones—grassy parkland meadows, vast evergreen forests, and breathtaking alpine tundra.

From Estes Park, you can follow U.S. 36 west to park headquarters, an unobtrusive stone building overlooking a classic parkland meadow. Inside, a short film offers an overview of the park. Continuing west to the Beaver Meadows Entrance Station, you will find yourself where Longs Peak and its companion mountains stand 6,000 to 7,000 feet above Beaver Meadow, with its prairie flowers, grass, and dry land shrubs. Often groups of elk are a bonus to this spot's appeal.

Farther along, the Mummy Range swings into view on the right as you approach Deer Ridge Junction and the official start of Trail Ridge Road. Before long, the road climbs into a deep forest of Englemann spruce, subalpine fir, and limber pine. A stop at Many Parks Curve, at 9,640 feet, pays off with its backward vista of several major parkland meadows; and at Rainbow Curve, 10,829 feet, one sees how the increasingly dry, frigid weather and blasting winds have dwarfed and deformed the surrounding trees.

Soon, the trees give out completely and the road crosses into the alpine tundra zone. At Forest Canyon Overlook, 11,716 feet, a short trail leads to one of the most spectacular sights in the park: a 20-mile rampart of glacially carved peaks and valley walls that plunge 2,500 feet from the observation platform.

Farther along, the road passes Rock Cut, at 12,110 feet, where a one-mile nature trail offers a primer on plant and animal life in the alpine tundra. You will find more information about the tundra at the Alpine Visitor Center, 11,796 feet, as well as an overlook of a broad, glacially carved basin frequented by elk. Then the road starts its long descent toward the Kawuneeche Valley, with interesting stops at Milner Pass, where it crosses the Continental Divide; Never Summer Ranch, a preserved 1920s dude ranch; and the Kawuneeche Visitor Center, which focuses on the ecosystems of the park's wetter, colder west side.

You might end your drive with a drink or a meal on the veranda of the historic Grand Lake Lodge, which overlooks two mountain lakes. If returning to Estes Park, you could consider turning north at Deer Ridge

Junction to follow U.S. 34 through Horseshoe Park, where visitors often spot bighorn sheep.

Elsewhere in the park, you might visit the Moraine Park Museum for its excellent geology exhibits, and the Bear Lake Area, for a myriad of splendid day hikes among magnificent glacial canyons.

WHITE RIVER NATIONAL FOREST

Sprawling across the magnificent peaks of west central Colorado, White River National Forest takes in some of the most intensely developed ski areas in the northern Rockies, including Aspen and Vail. At the same time, it protects all or part of eight small but crucial wilderness areas. This difficult and often controversial balancing act draws the keen interest of preservationists and developers alike.

The wilderness areas include Flat Tops, north of Glenwood Springs;

Summer thunderstorm boils above Iceberg Pass on Rocky Mountain's Trail Ridge Road. The reserve's central highway, Trail Ridge crosses a treeless realm of alpine tundra.

Eagles Nest, northeast of Vail; Holy Cross, southwest of Vail; and the Hunter Fryingpan, Collegiate Peaks, and Maroon Bells-Snowmass areas, which fan out around the town of Aspen.

The best known and most heavily used of them, Maroon Bells-Snowmass, lies just a few miles southwest of Aspen. Named for their color and shape, the Maroon Bells are massive 14,000-foot peaks that rise from the shore of a small glacial lake and loom over the surrounding forests, meadows, and a narrow canyon of vermilion mudstone. So popular is the day-hiking area out of Maroon Lake that during summer the access road is open only to nonmotorized traffic and shuttle buses from 9 to 5.

BLACK CANYON OF THE GUNNISON NATIONAL PARK

Located east of Montrose, the sheer-walled Black Canyon is the awesome gorge of Colorado's Gunnison River. This jagged gray rock cuts a gash across the semiarid lands of west-central Colorado for 53 miles, darkened by shadow and lined with steep walls of Precambrian gneiss, schist, and granite. No other canyon in America is at once so deep, so narrow, and so sheer. The 12 most spectacular miles lie within Black Canyon of the Gunnison National Park, where nearly vertical cliffs drop an average of roughly 2,000 feet from a landscape of grassy meadows and thickets of piñon pine and Gambel oak. Most of the remaining canyon stretches east to the adjoining Curecanti National Recreation Area.

Geologically, Black Canyon cuts down through an eastern extension of the great Colorado Plateau, which is a broad, high tableland that sprawls over much of the Southwest. The gorge was carved by the Gunnison River over a period of roughly two million years. Aided by landslides and side streams, the steep gradient of the river wore down through soft volcanic rock, then went to work on the much older, much harder crystalline rock of the present chasm.

Today, mule deer browse shrubs along the rim, and birds of prey, such as golden eagles and peregrine falcons, soar high above in search of rodents and small birds. Welling up from the void comes a constant hiss from the rapids of the Gunnison River, whose canyon stretch remains as one of the few unspoiled rivers in the country.

You may wish to start along the south rim at the visitor center, where exhibits touch on the canyon's geology, plants, animals, and history. Then as you drive the South Rim Road, take the time to stroll the footpaths that wind among the rocks to vertiginous overlooks. The path to Devils Lookout reaches the narrowest point in the canyon, where the distance between the rims squeezes to 1,150 feet. At Dragon Point, you can gaze across the canyon to Painted Wall, which drops 2,200 feet to the river. The North Rim Road, closed in winter, is harder to get to but also offers a fine drive and excellent trails along the brink of the canyon.

Curecanti National Recreation Area stretches along the eastern boundary (North Rim) of Black Canyon. This area takes in canyon walls, rolling desert hills, high mesas, and three reservoirs—Blue Mesa, Morrow Point, and Crystal—formed by dams. The two reservoirs within the canyon are long, narrow, and deep, with high cliffs rising directly from the water. The biggest—Blue Mesa Reservoir—floods the open country east of the gorge. All offer boating, fishing, waterskiing, and windsurfing.

Two million years in the making: The Gunnison River in west central Colorado carved a deep, steep, and narrow canyon. Twelve miles of the jagged gorge are protected in Black Canyon of the Gunnison National Park.

Like turrets of a Crusader's castle, rugged crags of Sievers Mountain float above mist edging Maroon Lake in Colorado's White River National Forest (opposite). Only a few hours west of Denver, the forest protects eight wilderness areas. Maroon Bells-Snowmass ranks as the most popular.

JAGGED PEAKS, SAGEBRUSH FLATS, GEOTHERMAL WONDERS

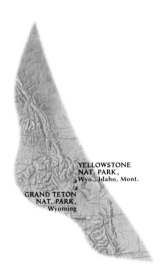

YELLOWSTONE
NAT. PARK,
Wyo., Idaho, Mont.

GRAND TETON
NAT. PARK,
Wyoming

GRAND TETON NATIONAL PARK

Established in 1929 to preserve one of northwest Wyoming's most dramatic alpine settings, Grand Teton National Park encompasses the eastern front of the Teton Range, which rises as an abrupt wall of sharp, bare rock peaks that tower 6,000 to 7,000 feet above the flat sagebrush floor of Jackson Hole. The mountains are the youngest in the Rockies and lack the usual vanguard of foothills that obscure vistas of other mountain ranges. Here, one gazes directly into the scenic heart of the range, which leaves an indelible impression on both mind and spirit.

Surprisingly diverse, the park also includes much of the semiarid valley floor, extensive wetlands, and a string of large morainal lakes that lie tight against the very base of the peaks. The Snake River, a seductive, trout-laden ribbon with cottonwood groves and cobblestone bars, cuts diagonally across the floor of the valley and runs the length of the park.

Roomy glacial canyons separate the peaks and cradle bone-chilling streams fed by melting snowfields and a scattering of tiny glaciers. The water slips through expansive wildflower meadows, pools in small alpine lakes, and plunges over the cliffs as waterfalls and eventually joins the Snake River.

Plant communities range from bands of streamside foliage to dry sagebrush flats, from mountain forests to the nearly treeless realm of the alpine zone. Grizzly bears and black bears roam the length of the Tetons. So do elk, deer, and bighorn sheep. Clusters of bison share the sagebrush flats with pronghorn, and moose browse willow thickets in wetland areas. Cougars hunt for deer, and wolves prey on elk wintering on the National Elk Refuge, which adjoins the park.

Though the Tetons are composed largely of rocks more than half as old as the planet, the range itself is quite young—the peaks began rising just nine million years ago. The mountains were uplifted along the Teton fault zone that skirts the base of the range. As they rose, the valley floor tilted westward and sank. Erosion stripped the central peaks of a thick overlying mantle of sedimentary rock, and the valley was filled in by all manner of geologic debris.

During the ice ages, glaciers formed along the Teton Range and joined together to carve the park's great U-shaped canyons. Today about a dozen small glaciers, formed long after the last ice age, cling to the peaks.

In the 1920s local residents joined Horace Albright, then superintendent of Yellowstone National Park, to lobby for preservation of the Tetons. In 1929, Congress established the park.

Meanwhile, John D. Rockefeller, Jr., who had visited the area with Albright in 1926, bought up large tracts of land and later donated them to the government. When added to the park in 1950, they more than tripled the park's area.

Travelers usually begin a trip through the park with a stop at one of

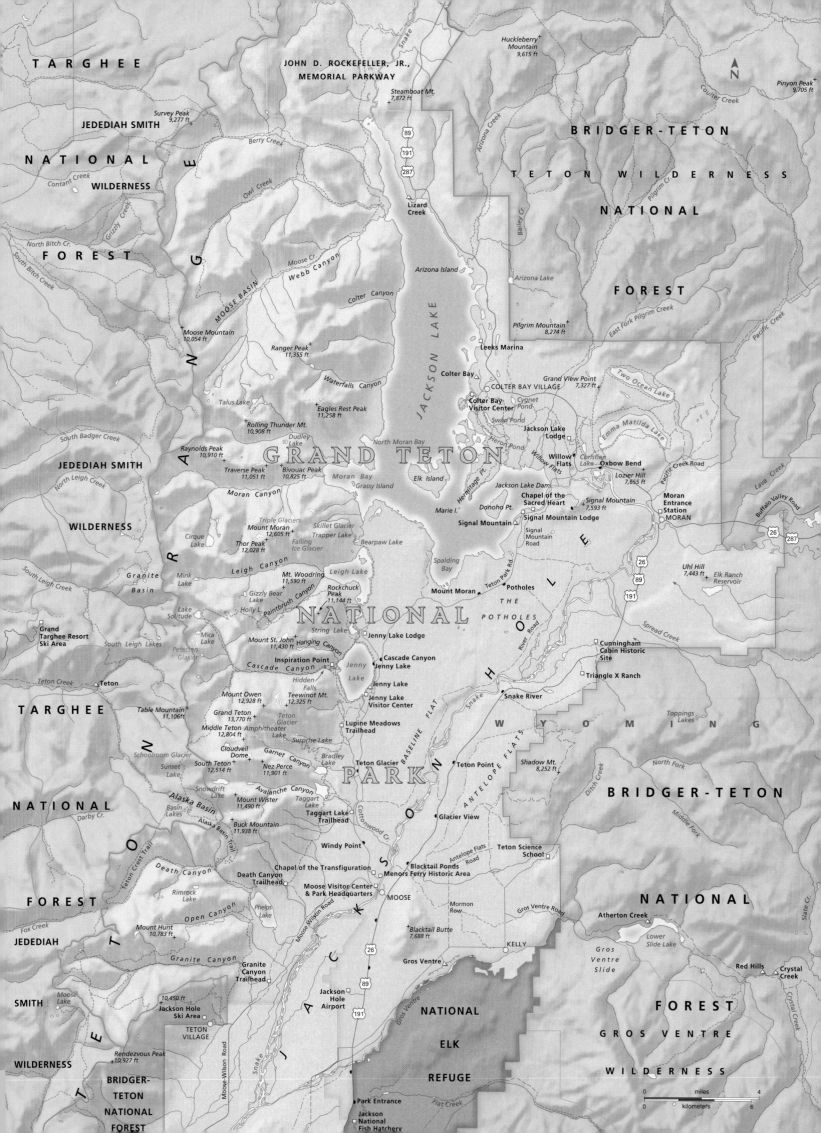

two major visitor centers: Colter Bay, in the north, with its fine Native American museum and 1.5-mile shoreline nature trail; or Moose, in the south, which lies along the Snake and offers excellent history exhibits at Menors Ferry. An information center at the north end of Jackson also offers good advice, maps, and fishing licenses.

The Teton Park Road and U.S. 191 form a convenient loop. The park road offers interesting exhibits at various turnouts and swings west for close-up views of the central peaks, including the imposing fang of the Grand Teton, elevation 13,770 feet. The highway furnishes more comprehensive vistas of the Tetons with the Snake River corridor as foreground.

Along the southeast shore of Jackson Lake, a winding road leads to the summit of Signal Mountain, which offers a grandstand view of the Tetons, Jackson Lake, and all of Jackson Hole with the Snake River

cutting through it. This is a good spot to get one's bearings and appreciate the geology of the place. At nearby Oxbow Bend, look for moose, otters, swans, and other waterfowl.

At South Jenny Lake Junction, a spur road curves toward the mountains and accesses a cluster of stunning lakes— Jenny, String, and Leigh. For a classic, but extremely popular, Teton excursion, take the shuttle boat for a small fee from the dock beyond Jenny Lake Visitor Center to the mouth of Cascade Canyon and hike to Hidden Falls (a half mile) and Inspiration Point (another half mile). A more secluded outing begins at the String Lake Trailhead and follows an easy, 2.2-mile trail through the woods to a marvelous beach on Leigh Lake, where views of Mount Moran, elevation 12,605 feet, are unequaled.

YELLOWSTONE NATIONAL PARK

The world's first national park, Yellowstone was established in 1872, just three years after the transcontinental railroad was completed and during an era when wild animals such as bison, wolves, bighorn sheep, and grizzly bears seemed to live in inexhaustible numbers.

Originally Yellowstone was set aside not to preserve habitat for these and other animals we now consider endangered but, rather, to protect its geothermal curiosities—geysers, hot springs, fumaroles, and mudpots. Those steaming oddities are still prime attractions, but Yellowstone now represents deeper values, too—values that its founders could scarcely have foreseen. Among other things, the park has contributed to our geologic understanding of the planet, and it has helped to prevent the extinction of important wildlife species such as bison, whooping cranes, trumpeter swans, peregrine falcons, and gray wolves.

Perhaps the most important consideration is that Yellowstone preserves a place where millions of city dwellers can establish a tangible connection with something increasingly rare and endangered in our day—the peace, beauty, and solitude of a wild and pristine natural landscape.

And what a landscape it is! Yellowstone Park's 2.2 million acres encompass vast lodgepole pine forests, intimate meadows, plunging canyons, expansive valleys, mountains, rivers, large wilderness lakes, and an abundance of waterfalls that range from stringlike veils to thundering cataracts.

Throughout the park roam a cornucopia of the West's most celebrated animals—grizzly bears, black bears, gray wolves, coyotes, cougars, wolverines, bison, mule deer, white-tailed deer, elk, bighorn sheep, mountain goats, pronghorn, golden eagles, bald eagles, osprey, peregrine falcons, trumpeter swans, whooping cranes, and many others. Thanks to the recent reintroduction of wolves, the park now includes every species known to have existed here in 1872.

The park's geology focuses on one dominant force: volcanism. A large body of magma known as the Yellowstone Hotspot resides several miles beneath

Silvery lupine springs from the pebbled banks of Spread Creek in northwestern Wyoming's Grand Teton National Park, which showcases the steep and rocky eastern face of the Teton Range.

Dawn fog shrouds the Snake River as it curves below snow-laden Teton peaks and meadows (opposite). Youngest range in the Rockies, the jagged crests contain some of the oldest rock in North America.

Emblem of the unspoiled
West, the Lower Falls
thunder 308 feet into the
river in the Grand Canyon
of the Yellowstone.
Oldest national park in
the world, 2.2-million-acre
Yellowstone was
established in 1872 to
preserve hot springs,
geysers, and other
geothermal features in
the northwestern corner
of what was then
Wyoming Territory.

the surface of the ground and is largely responsible for the park's geothermal wonders. The hotspot, a plume of molten rock from the Earth's mantle, melts overlying continental crust that then breaks through the surface. The hotspot may have had an influence in creating nearby mountain ranges, such as the Tetons, as well as much of Idaho's Snake River Plain.

But the most dramatic chapters in the geologic story are the sudden, cataclysmic explosions that shattered—indeed erased—vast swaths of Yellowstone three times during the past 2.1 million years. Caused by tremendous pressure that built up over the hotspot, these caldera-forming explosions were the biggest volcanic eruptions known to have occurred on Earth. They destroyed entire mountain ranges. By comparison, such famous eruptions as Etna, Krakatoa, and Mount St. Helens are reduced to popgun status.

Yellowstone's road system forms a figure eight with branches radiating to five entrance stations. The design makes it easy to enter from any direction and to visit the park's three major sectors—east, north, and west.

Walled off to the east by the mighty Absaroka Range, the park's eastern sector, entered from Cooke City and Silver Gate, Montana, is characterized by the rolling, open space of the Lamar Valley. Here, abundant

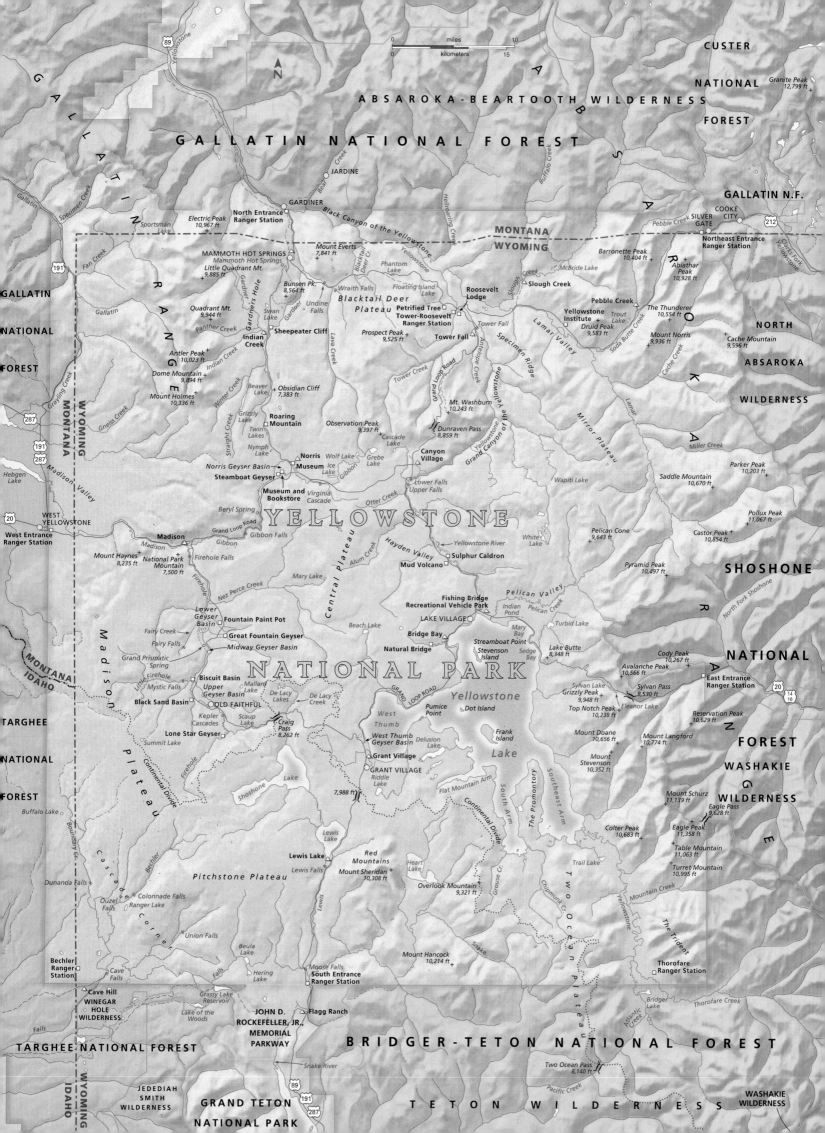

Frozen against a lightening sky, an elk cow and her calf bracket billowing steam and boiling water as Old Faithful erupts in Yellowstone's Upper Geyser Basin. The geyser, most famous of the park's wonders, attracts up to 25,000 visitors a day.

sagebrush and grasses cover the land, with pockets of aspen tucked among the hills and groves of cottonwoods along waterways. This area, drier than the rest of the park and at lower elevations, constitutes an important winter feeding ground for bison and elk.

If you choose to enter the northern sector of Yellowstone from Gardiner, Montana, you will pass through a grand stone arch (look for pronghorn) and will drive along the Gardner River (watch for bighorn sheep) to Mammoth Hot Springs (see elk and mule deer). There, steaming terraces of white travertine rise above the historic park headquarters buildings. Stop at the museum and Albright Visitor Center, then head for the terraces and take the boardwalk trail that leads to Jupiter, Minerva, and Canary hot springs.

At this juncture in your driving tour, you may choose to follow the top half of the figure-eight loop road south toward Steamboat Geyser or east past the Grand Canyon of the Yellowstone to Tower Junction. At Tower Junction, for a good view of the Yellowstone River rushing past cliffs of columnar basalt, stop at Calcite Springs overlook. Then, a bit farther south, take the short side trip to watch 132-foot Tower Fall spill between pinnacles of volcanic ash.

From Tower Junction, you may drive eastward into the Lamar Valley, a rumpled trough of grass and sedge frequented by elk and cradled by the Absaroka Range on one side and Specimen Ridge on the other. If you are lucky, you may even see gray wolves, reintroduced here beginning in 1995 with spectacular success.

On the other hand, if you drive south from Tower Junction, the main attraction will prove to be the Grand Canyon of the Yellowstone, where the river pours in quick succession over 109-foot Upper Falls and 308-foot Lower Falls. Take your time walking along the rims, then admire Lower Falls from two vantage points. Uncle Toms Trail leads from the south rim to a spot near the concussive face of the falls. Another trail offers switchbacks from the north rim down to the very brink of the falls.

Southward from the falls, the road follows the Yellowstone River into the wide-open spaces of Hayden Valley, where the vistas include herds of bison, elk, gleaming white tundra swans, and the occasional grizzly bear. The road will take you to Yellowstone Lake, America's largest lake at such a high elevation—7,735 feet. It measures roughly 14-by-20 miles, has 110 miles of shoreline, and occupies just a small portion of the caldera created during the last great volcanic eruption. The Yellowstone River flows into the lake's Southeast Arm, exits the north shore at Fishing Bridge, sweeps north through Hayden Valley, and plunges into its dramatic canyon.

If you continue driving southwest around the lake, the Grand Loop Road leads to Grant Village, on the shore of West Thumb, a wide bay created 150,000 years ago by yet another massive volcanic explosion. Be sure to check out the geothermal features of the West Thumb Geyser Basin.

From West Thumb, driving west will take you into the Upper Geyser Basin in Yellowstone's western sector. This basin boasts the world's most extraordinary concentration of geothermal features—more than 600 hot springs and steam vents and more than 70 geysers, including Old Faithful, a plume of steaming water that erupts at intervals of 45 to 80 minutes, reaches heights of 100 to 180 feet, and lasts two to five minutes. Many visitors start their forays into the marvels of geothermalism with this well-known geyser. Pick up a map at the visitor center and check out

Old Faithful's estimated times of eruption.

Other geysers and hot springs are scattered along the Firehole River northward for about 30 miles. An easy trail loop of roughly three miles takes in the main features on both sides of the Firehole River.

Driving north, pause at Midway Geyser Basin to see Excelsior Geyser, a lake-size pool of blue boiling water, and Grand Prismatic Hot Spring, another large pool but with a bed of brilliant, multicolored algae.

Farther north, the Lower Geyser Basin occupies a broad, sparsely forested plain that includes many thermal areas. The Firehole Lake Loop Drive is worth the detour to see Great Fountain Geyser, Pink Cone Geyser, and Firehole Lake. Nearby, the Fountain Paint Pots area is named for its bubbling mudpots, which are favorites with children.

Continue north to Madison Junction, where the Firehole and Gibbon Rivers join to form the Madison, and head northeast along the Gibbon River. Promising stops include 84-foot Gibbon Falls, Artist Paint Pots, and Gibbon Meadows, where you may spot elk and bison.

Soon you will arrive at Norris Geyser Basin, the hottest ground in the park and home to the world's largest active geyser, Steamboat. Bone up on geyser geology at the museum, then walk the Back Basin Trail loop to see Steamboat as well as other geysers and boiling pools.

Terraces of travertine, massive layers of calcium carbonate deposited by the water, edge Mammoth Hot Springs in northern Yellowstone. The park contains more hot springs and geysers than all the rest of the world.

ICE FIELDS, GLACIERS, MAJESTIC SNOWCAPPED PEAKS

JASPER NAT. PARK,
Alberta

BANFF NAT. PARK,
Alberta

YOHO NAT. PARK,
British Columbia   KOOTENAY NAT. PARK,
British Columbia

WATERTON-GLACIER
INTERNATIONAL
PEACE PARK,
Mont., Alberta

BANFF, JASPER, YOHO, AND KOOTENAY NATIONAL PARKS

Including the largest ice fields in the North American interior and bubbling with hot springs, this magnificent cluster of four national parks stretches along the crest of the Canadian Rockies and takes in a staggering 7,814 square miles of jaw-dropping alpine terrain. Brawny sedimentary peaks shoulder up out of vast evergreen forests and overlook spacious, glacially carved valleys. Beautiful mountain lakes nestle against the slopes, waterfalls pound over the cliffs, and powerful rivers course through the valley bottoms. Throughout this glorious tangle of peaks, chasms, glaciers, and forests roam most of the Rocky Mountains' celebrity mammals, including gray wolves, black bears and grizzlies, moose, elk, deer, mountain goats, and bighorn sheep.

Taken together, the four parks form one of the largest mountain preserves in the world. Banff, in Alberta, Canada's first national park, was established in 1885 and extends northwest along the Continental Divide for roughly 130 miles to Sunwapta Pass. From there, Jasper carries on for another 120 miles. Yoho and Kootenay, in British Columbia, adjoin Banff's southern half and spill west from the divide.

Aside from the area's sheer scale and wild beauty, ice is what sets this place apart from other national parks in the Rocky Mountains. Many active glaciers and several major ice fields drape the crest of the range and gnaw patiently away at the peaks, adding their own embellishments to the spectacular carvings left by ice age glaciers. Of the more than ten named ice fields within or along the borders of the parks, the Columbia is by far the largest and most easily reached. At the juncture of Banff and Jasper Parks, it covers 125 square miles, reaches a depth of 1,200 feet, and ranks as the largest body of ice in the continent's interior.

Meltwater from the ice fields, glaciers, and winter snow accumulation feeds some of North America's most important rivers and eventually finds its way to three oceans: the Pacific, by way of the Columbia River; the Arctic, via the Athabasca as a tributary of the Mackenzie; and the Atlantic via the North Saskatchewan and Nelson Rivers through Hudson Bay.

Fortunately for visitors, the parks are tied together by the single most spectacular road network anywhere in the Rockies. Trans-Canada 1 crosses the range from east to west, bridging Banff and Yoho, crossing between Calgary, Alberta, and Golden, British Columbia. Provincial Route 93 winds northeast through Kootenay, crosses the divide, and then parallels the crest of the range through Banff and Jasper. In addition, myriad excellent trails offer hiking experiences that range from casual interpretive walks to expeditionary treks.

Start in the town of Banff, which lies along the swift blue waters of the Bow River in a broad valley ringed by forested peaks. Worthwhile

Rugged peaks of the
Canadian Rockies
cup azure lakes and
pristine snowfields in
Banff National Park,
Alberta. Banff, Canada's
oldest park, forms the
heart of a cluster of
four preserves that
encompass 7,814
square miles of
alpine wilderness.

stops include the Whyte Museum of the Canadian Rockies, the Banff Park
Museum, and the historic administration building with its terraced gardens. Cave and Basin National Historic Site, a compelling hot springs
site, is the birthplace of Canada's national park system. Elsewhere in Banff,
soak at Upper Hot Springs, ride the Sulphur Mountain Gondola, drop
by Bow Falls, and visit the 1888 Banff Springs Hotel, a colossal native-
stone palace perched above the valley.

From Banff, head north on the Bow Valley Parkway, which offers better views of the mountains than the Trans-Canada and far better chances
of seeing wildlife. Stop at Johnston Canyon for an invigorating 1.6-mile
hike up the narrow limestone chasm to two explosive waterfalls.

Then, on to Lake Louise, a pale, milky green body of water that stretches off between high, knobby peaks and dead ends against the steep walls
of Mount Victoria, which soars 5,695 feet above the lake. An easy trail
leads from picturesque Chateau Lake Louise to the end of the lake, a
2.5-mile round trip. In the town of Lake Louise, the park's visitor center

offers a summary geology of the Canadian Rockies and acts as trailhead for the Bow River Trail, a 4.4-mile interpretive loop.

North of Lake Louise stretches a grand swath of mountain terrain accessed by Canada's highest road, the Icefields Parkway (Provincial Highway 93), which was named for the more than a hundred glaciers visible along its 143-mile route.

Stop at Bow Lake for a good look at Crowfoot Glacier and a distant view of Bow Glacier Falls—a violent plume of white water that drops nearly 500 feet. At Bow Summit, elevation 6,787 feet, a spur road cuts west to Peyto Lake Viewpoint, a rewarding overlook of a creamy blue glacial lake. Beyond Saskatchewan River Crossing, the road climbs steadily toward the treeless alpine zone. Along the way, consider hiking Parker Ridge Trail, a 1.5-mile ascent to an view of the Saskatchewan Glacier bending from the edge of the Columbia Icefield. Soon, the parkway crosses into Jasper National Park and descends to the Athabasca Glacier, which lies between Mount Athabasca (left) and Snow Dome.

Continuing north, look for mountain goats at the Athabasca River Viewpoint, then turn onto Provincial Highway 93A and stroll to Athabasca Falls, a frothy plume of white water that pours from a narrow chasm. The detour to the base of Mount Edith Cavell is worth the slow, nine-mile drive to see this vast wall of dark gray rock that rockets upward nearly one vertical mile from the parking area. Angel Glacier spills from the cliffs.

The town of Jasper lies along the Athabasca River within sight of four mountain ranges. Here you will find small lakes scattered across the valley floor, a network of hiking and biking trails, and the Jasper Tramway, which offers stunning views of the Whistlers (a mountain named for its colony of marmots), the Columbia Icefield, and the valley itself. Southeast of town, Maligne Lake stands out as a beauty spot even in a region of exceptional alpine scenery.

British Columbia's nearby national parks Yoho and Kootenay—both smaller than Banff and Jasper—warrant additional time spent in the area. In fact, "Yoho" comes from a Cree word meaning "awe," which befits this alluring tract of wild land. Here, Trans-Canada 1 breaks through the glaciated crest of the Bow Range and drops into the valley of the Kicking Horse River. It is a great drive, but the most compelling spots, such as the classic alpine setting of Lake O'Hara, lie hidden in side valleys.

Along the highway, look for Lower Spiral Tunnel Viewpoint, with its view of Yoho Valley pressed between the peaks. A side trip leads to Meeting-of-the-Waters, where the clear waters of the Kicking Horse blend with the silt-laden current of the Yoho. Within the valley, stop at Takakkaw Falls—with a fall of 833 feet, it is one of the highest waterfalls in Canada and plunges yet another 1,248 feet over glaciated limestone cliffs.

Kootenay National Park lies to the south of Yoho and takes in two deep, glaciated valleys surrounded by broad, sedimentary mountain masses typical of the Canadian Rockies. Highway 94 penetrates the mountain wall at Radium Hot Springs, leading through the narrow, red rock gap of Sinclair Canyon and then breaking out far above the Kootenay River.

Farther along, pull over at Hector Gorge Viewpoint to watch the Vermilion River rush between the Mitchell and Vermilion Ranges and to look for mountain goats on the slopes of Mount Wardle (above the highway on

Massive horns of a Rocky Mountain bighorn ram spiral backward from its heavy brow; they grow for the life of the animal—like the rings of a tree, an indicator of its age. Some 3,000 bighorns roam the wilds of Alberta's Jasper National Park.

Winter snow softens hard rock ridges at Athabasca Falls in Jasper. Athabasca lies within easy viewing range of the 143-mile Icefields Parkway, Canada's highest road, which follows below the crest of the Rockies through Jasper and Banff.

the north). Paint Pots Nature Trail leads to three cold springs surrounded by colorful oxidized clay.

Do not miss Marble Canyon, a narrow chasm filled with the tumbling water of Tokumm Creek. Ahead lie Vermilion Pass and Banff National Park.

WATERTON-GLACIER INTERNATIONAL PEACE PARK

Glacier National Park rises from the rolling plains of northwestern Montana and rambles westward over the Continental Divide as a glorious sprawl of mountain, canyon, forest, and lake.

The conservationist John Muir, no stranger to beautiful places, described Glacier as some of "the best care-killing scenery on the continent."

Glacier lies at the heart of an immense tract of wild lands that include the adjoining Canadian national park of Waterton Lakes, in Alberta, as well as two national forests and a vast wilderness complex. Taken together, these protected areas encompass roughly 6,400 square miles. It is a magnificent landscape of knife-edge ridges and soaring cliffs that plunge thousands of feet into roomy, U-shaped valleys covered with thick evergreen forests. Remote rivers cut through deep canyons, and hundreds of creeks and waterfalls spill down from the mountains into long, fjord-like lakes.

A first-class wildlife preserve, Glacier and the surrounding wild lands offer visitors excellent opportunities for spotting grizzly bears, black bears, mountain goats, bighorn sheep, deer, elk, moose, even bison. More elusive are the wolves of Glacier's remote North Fork Valley.

Glacier was established in 1910 and Waterton Lakes in 1895, thanks in large part to the conservation efforts of writers such as naturalist George Bird Grinnell and F. W. Godsal. Waterton was named for its string of breathtaking mountain lakes, while Glacier stands as a testament to the awesome power of ice age glaciers.

To the south of Glacier is the Great Bear Wilderness, and then the Bob Marshall Wilderness Area, which was named for a founder of the Wilderness Society. It joins with a second wilderness area, the Scapegoat, to the south, to form a 1.5-million acre core of roadless lands within the Flathead and Lewis and Clark National Forests.

As befits a large wilderness area, the Bob Marshall complex is difficult to penetrate, arduous to visit. The parks are another matter. Though they are rugged, vast, and wild, Glacier and Waterton are easy to visit. Major highways skirt their boundaries, and excellent roads climb far into some of their glorious mountain valleys. Historic lodges overlook some of the finest terrain, and excellent trail networks open up the backcountry.

Most visitors to Glacier begin with a trip over Logan Pass on Going-to-the-Sun Road, a spectacular mountain drive that samples all of the major life zones and landscapes within the park. It starts on the east side of the park, along the shore of St. Mary Lake, climbs through deep forest, and tops out above tree line in an expansive realm of vibrant wildflower meadows, spindly peaks, and plunging cliffs. Consider taking the rewarding, 1.5-mile hike from the Logan Pass Visitor Center to Hidden Lake Overlook.

At the pass, the road crosses the Continental Divide and begins its descent into the wetter, warmer climate of the McDonald Valley. Stop at Red Rock Point to watch the sapphire waters of McDonald Creek zig-zag between blocks of vermilion mudstone, and stroll the Trail of the Cedars (one mile, trailhead across the road from Avalanche Creek parking lot), which leads through a mossy climax forest of giant cedar, hemlock, and black cottonwood. Then it is on to Lake McDonald, with its beautiful pebble beach.

Another major destination, Many Glacier lies in the park's northeast sector where three magnificent glacial basins converge within sight of the Swiss-style Many Glacier Hotel, built in 1914-15. Famous for its splendid hiking terrain, the area is also a great bear-watching site in late summer and autumn.

Eroded limestone of Cathedral Crags glows gold at evening in British Columbia's Yoho National Park. It preserves 507 square miles of towering rock walls, thundering waterfalls, and 28 mountain peaks more than 11,000 feet high.

In Alberta's Waterton Lakes National Park, the main valley encloses
a string of four lakes, beginning with the smallest and northernmost —
Maskinonge — and Lower, Middle, and Upper Waterton, which is a long,
narrow body of water ringed by spectacular peaks.

Take time to stroll through the historic Prince of Wales Hotel, which

Scarves of snow drape greening slopes beyond a solitary mountain goat in northwestern Montana's Glacier National Park. The preserve, center of one of the largest and most intact ecosystems on the continent, adjoins Canada's Waterton Lakes National Park.

overlooks the lakes, and consider a cruise to Goat Haunt, at the south end of the lake, where an easy one-mile trail leads to Rainbow Falls. Elsewhere in the park, roads wander through beautiful valleys to Cameron Lake, nestled beneath a cirque of high peaks, and to Red Rock Canyon, a lovely chasm of pink stone frequented by bighorn sheep.

RAZORBACK RIDGES, RIVERS, V-SHAPED CANYONS

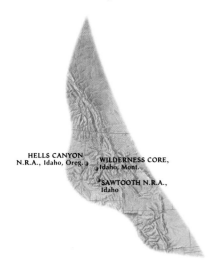

HELLS CANYON
N.R.A., Idaho, Oreg.

WILDERNESS CORE,
Idaho, Mont.

SAWTOOTH N.R.A.,
Idaho

SAWTOOTH NATIONAL RECREATION AREA

Located in central Idaho north of Ketchum, the Sawtooth Recreation Area takes in nearly 1,200 square miles of jagged granite peaks, spacious valleys, pristine mountain lakes, a handsome river chasm, and dozens of natural hot springs. Though the area includes four separate mountain ranges, the peaks that tend to linger long in memory are the Sawtooths—an abrupt rampart of splintering bare rock crags, razorback ridges, cirques, and towers that run north and south and are west of the town of Stanley for roughly 30 miles. They form the western wall of the spacious Sawtooth Valley, the cradle of the Salmon River and the site of crucial spawning grounds for endangered salmon.

The core of the range is made up of pink granite that welled up through the Earth's crust 50 million years ago and intruded into the surface of an older mass of granite. Later, these rocks rose slowly into place, uplifted along a fault line while the valley floor slipped downward. More recently, ice age glaciers carved the peaks into the shapes we enjoy today.

The Sawtooth Wilderness Area follows the spine of the range, accounts for more than a quarter of the recreation area, and offers hikers an intricate landscape of plummeting cliffs, crumbling peaks, tiny alpine lakes, and numbing streams. It is a popular area, where distances are short, and the views are gratifying.

Across the valley stand the White Cloud Peaks, made up of limestone and some granite but obscured from the valley floor by foothills. The Salmon River flows north between the ranges, then veers east near Stanley and tumbles down a stony canyon dotted with hot spring pools.

The south end of the Sawtooth Valley is walled off by two more mountain ranges: the Smoky Mountains, to the west, and the Boulder Mountains, with summits reaching 11,000 feet, to the east. Between them, the Big Wood River flows south through the recreation area's second major valley. Mountain goats and bighorn sheep graze among the high summits and colorful wildflower meadows. Deer, elk, and black bears move in and out of the dense evergreen forests, and various birds of prey hunt the meadows and open prairie floors of the valleys.

Unfortunately, not all forms of wildlife thrive here. Annual spawning runs of sockeye and chinook salmon have been decimated in recent decades. Years ago, great numbers of fish made the 900-mile journey from the Pacific up the Columbia, Snake, and Salmon Rivers. Today, very few return to the Sawtooth Valley. Some spawning seasons have passed when not a single sockeye returned. Fisheries biologists blame this catastrophe on a series of hydroelectric dams downstream on the Columbia and Snake Rivers. A captive breeding program offers a slim ray of hope that the salmon runs might be restored to some degree.

Start your visit with a drive south from Stanley along Idaho State

75. Just south of town, drop by the Stanley Ranger Station of the Sawtooth National Forest for maps and advice about the many off-road trails and destinations among the Sawtooths.

Farther south, take the turnoff for Redfish Lake, where lodgepole pine forests ring a long, narrow body of turquoise water that ends abruptly beneath two immense peaks: Heyburn Mountain and Grand Mogul. Redfish Lake Visitor Center offers a panoramic vista. Excursion boats cruise from nearby Redfish Lake Lodge to a wilderness trailhead at the foot of Heyburn and Grand Mogul.

Back on Idaho State 75, stop at the Sawtooth Hatchery, where exhibits survey the long-term decline of chinook and sockeye salmon populations and summarize efforts to revive their numbers. From the hatchery, continue south on Idaho 75 to the Galena Overlook for its full-length vista of the Sawtooth Range, then cross over Galena Summit and follow the Big Wood River Valley down to the Ketchum area.

Next, head back to Stanley and follow Idaho 75 east into a narrow, forested gorge of the Salmon River. The turbulent river drops 15 feet to the mile and rushes past several hot springs. The largest and easiest to find is Sunbeam Hot Springs, which bubbles into the river from a high embankment 11 miles east of Stanley.

Muted in misted waters of Stanley Lake, 9,860-foot McGown Peak glows rose at first light in central Idaho's Sawtooth National Recreation Area. Glaciers carved the sharp outlines of the pink granite Sawtooths, one of four mountain ranges in the 756,000-acre recreation area.

HELLS CANYON NATIONAL RECREATION AREA

The deepest gorge in North America, Hells Canyon plummets 7,500 vertical feet from a ring of jagged mountain peaks to the brawling surface of the Snake River. It runs along Idaho's border with Oregon for more than a hundred miles, cutting through a remote and extremely rugged landscape of parched desert chasms, precipitous lava cliffs, and shady ridgetop forests. Much of it lies within Hells Canyon National Recreation Area, which stretches south on the Idaho-Oregon border from the Washington border, includes a long stretch of Oregon's Imnaha River, and takes in some of the wildest portions of the Wallowa-Whitman, Payette, and Nez Perce National Forests.

Within the canyon, the Snake flows freely for nearly 70 miles as a protected Wild and Scenic River. When combined with tributary streams in surrounding protected lands, the Hells Canyon stretch of the Snake makes up one of the largest wilderness watercourses in the coterminus United States.

The eastern wall of Hells Canyon is formed by a mountain divide that separates it by just a dozen miles or so from the continent's second

Roiling rapids of the
Snake River—serene
from a distant overlook—
sliced through volcanic
rock to gouge Hells
Canyon, at 7,500 feet
the deepest gorge on
the North American
continent. Much of the
canyon lies within
652,488-acre Hells
Canyon National
Recreation Area, whose
territory falls within both
Oregon and Idaho.

White water of the Selway
River boils through a
deep, V-shaped canyon in
Idaho's Selway-Bitterroot
Wilderness (opposite).
Among three Wild and
Scenic Rivers that lace
a 1.3-million-acre
wilderness in western
Idaho, the Selway offers
one of the best rafting
wilderness trips
in North America.

deepest gorge, the Salmon River Canyon. That canyon reaches a maximum depth of roughly 7,500 feet and converges with Hells Canyon northwest of Riggins. The dividing ridge culminates in a ring of crags called the Seven Devils Mountains.

Extreme elevation differences in the canyons compress widely diverse habitats into relatively small areas, making it possible for disparate wildlife species to live in close proximity. Within the Hells Canyon National Recreation Area live cougars and deer, bighorn sheep, mountain goats, lynx, black bear, a large herd of elk, and a wide variety of birds of prey.

Geologically, Hells Canyon offers some of the most intriguing stories in the Great Divide region. For roughly 700 million years, the area it now occupies lay along the west coast of North America and faced open ocean. Then, roughly 150 million years ago, the whole continent began to inch westward—as a result of the rifting that was forming the Atlantic Ocean— and to slide over the floor of the Pacific Ocean.

Gradually, bits and pieces of land that once lay far out to sea appeared on the horizon and approached the coast as if on a giant conveyor belt. Tropical volcanic islands, coral reefs, stray masses of continental crust, even micro-continents, broke off the oceanic plate and were eventually grafted onto the continent. Long after this same tectonic plate collision helped build the Rocky Mountains, magma welled up from the Earth's mantle and spilled across much of Oregon, Washington, and western Idaho. These lava flows started 16 to 17 million years ago, continued intermittently for millions of years, and built up extensive flows of basalt now called the Columbia Plateau. Hells Canyon and the Salmon River Canyon cut across the plateau's eastern margin.

Visiting Hells Canyon is demanding. Roads are narrow, rough, steep, and usually unpaved. Trails are generally difficult. But the rewards are great for those who can spend some time.

From the Riggins area, Forest Road 517 climbs 6,500 feet in 19 miles to an outstanding vista at Heavens Gate in the Seven Devils area. The view takes in a broad sweep of the gorge and Oregon's Wallowa Mountains. Nearby, Heavens Gate Scenic Trail leads a half mile to Heaven's Gate Lookout, where you can see both Hells Canyon and Salmon River Canyon converge 50 miles to the northwest.

North of Riggins, consider following Forest Road 493 west over the dividing ridge. After 17 jouncing miles, it dead-ends at Pittsburg Landing along the banks of the Snake in the desert heart of the gorge. Idaho 71 accesses the southern end of the recreation area from Cambridge, Idaho, and ends at Hells Canyon Dam. Along the way, at Oxbow Crossing, Oregon 86 climbs out of the gorge and intersects with Forest Road 39 (paved), which winds north along the rim and leads to a paved spur road (FR 3965) running three miles to spectacular Hells Canyon Overlook. Forest Road 39 also connects with roads following Oregon's Imnaha River.

THE WILDERNESS CORE

East of Hells Canyon and north of the Sawtooth Range stretches a vast wilderness complex that takes in nearly four million acres of deep river canyons, dense evergreen forests, high craggy peaks, and some of the finest white water in America. This core of virtually continuous pristine land is protected by three adjoining wilderness areas—the Frank Church-River of No Return, the Selway-Bitterroot, and the Gospel Hump. In addition, all sides of the wilderness hub are buffered by eight national forests.

Encompassing 2.3 million acres, the Frank Church alone ranks as the largest designated wilderness area outside of Alaska and sprawls over a region slightly larger than Yellowstone National Park. To the north lies the 1.3 million-acre Selway-Bitterroot; to the northwest, the 206,000-acre Gospel Hump.

Three Wild and Scenic River corridors cut through this glorious tangle of rugged, lonely lands. The Salmon River barrels nearly due west across the heart of the country, eventually carving out the second-deepest gorge in North America. The Middle Fork Salmon River flows into it from the south, while the Selway starts just seven miles from the Salmon's banks and then bends far off to the northwest.

All of the rivers rush through deep V-shaped canyons whose walls plummet from high forested ridges. The canyon bottoms are narrow, the walls made up of gray granite that stands as smooth slabs or steep talus slopes studded with craggy outcrops.

Considering the sheer breadth of protected territory and the extreme differences in elevation, it should come as no surprise that the wilderness areas include a wide variety of habitats. Desert-like canyon bottoms along the western reaches of the Salmon River give way as elevation increases to the expansive forests of lodgepole pine and Douglas fir that cover most of the Frank Church Wilderness. The moist high country harbors subalpine fir and Englemann spruce, while to the north the Selway-Bitterroot Wilderness adds misty forests of old-growth western red cedar and hemlock, as well as the rarefied realm of the alpine zone along the crest of the Bitterroot Mountains. Throughout roam deer, elk, bighorn sheep, mountain goats, black bears, moose, mountain lions, and (recently reintroduced) wolves.

Travel through the wilderness complex is difficult and time-consuming—unless you book a cushy raft trip with one of the many outfitters who run the rivers. Dead-end spur roads ring the wilderness, penetrate its fringes, and make for delightful car-camping trips as long as you expect to travel no more than 50 miles a day.

The SOUTHWEST

CHAPTER IV

GRAND CANYON   PETRIFIED FOREST   PARIA CANYON-VERMILION CLIFFS

COCONINO   SAGUARO   CABEZA PRIETA   CARLSBAD CAVERNS   GUADALUPE MOUNTAINS

BIG BEND   CANYONLANDS   BRYCE CANYON   ZION

ARCHES   GREAT BASIN   DEATH VALLEY   JOSHUA TREE   INYO

Oak Creek rushes over boulders below Cathedral Rock
in Arizona's Coconino National Forest.

BY JEREMY SCHMIDT

The desert Southwest of the U.S. featured in this atlas—regions of Arizona, New Mexico, Texas, Utah, California, and Nevada—offers a range of landscapes, climates, and scenic wonders unmatched anywhere else on the continent. Here you will find deep canyons, layered mesas, towering buttes, dunes, and ragged, sun-blasted mountains. You will also find green forests, alpine lakes, powerful rivers, broad valleys, rows of snowcapped peaks, and seemingly endless open space. But desert is the primary theme of this region.

A collared lizard suns itself in
Petrified Forest National Park, Arizona.

The Great Basin Desert stretches across most of Nevada and Utah. The Mojave occupies southern Nevada and parts of southern California. The Sonoran marches from central Arizona into Mexico. New Mexico and Texas claim a large chunk of Chihuahuan Desert, and the Painted Desert (a desert based on geology rather than on elevation and climate) sprawls roughly from the Grand Canyon to Petrified National Forest. These deserts' contrasting climate, flora, and fauna are represented in national parks, monuments, and forests, as well as in wildlife refuges.

Strange things live in this Southwest desert region—saguaros, Joshua trees, gila monsters, jumping cholla, pupfish, ocotillo, sidewinders, kangaroo rats, and vampire bats—in addition to many species found elsewhere on the continent. In parts of the Southwest, snow is rare. In others, like the North Rim of the Grand Canyon, it may lie deep for months each year. The bottom of Death Valley is the hottest place on the continent. Less than 300 miles away a glacier exists on Wheeler Peak in Nevada.

Geologically, the story is a complex one. The Colorado Plateau, home of Arches, Canyonlands, Bryce, and Zion National Parks, is a province of sedimentary formations deposited 500 to 70 million years ago. The plateau is a comparatively stable region, and the thousands of feet of sedimentary strata laid down over hundreds of millions of years are still relatively horizontal. In places the layers have faulted or folded, and magma from deep within the Earth has seeped out or erupted from volcanoes, covering areas with lava. Streams have cut through the mostly horizontal formations, and differential weathering and erosion have resulted in bold escarpments, broad benches, and beautifully shaped formations.

The geology of the Basin and Range physiographic region—a region sharing similar landforms—includes Great Basin, Death Valley, Joshua Tree, Saguaro, Carlsbad, and Big Bend National Parks. This region's history is different from that of the Colorado Plateau. Around 17 million years ago, while the period of compression that uplifted the Rocky Mountains continued, tensional faulting on the Colorado Plateau and Great Basin stretched and broke the region into parallel blocks to form uplifted mountain ranges with alternating down-dropped basins. These tilted to form a corrugated landscape of parallel mountain ranges separated by low-slung valleys.

That pattern changes in the southern part of the desert Southwest, where Saguaro, Big Bend, and Carlsbad Caverns National Parks have their own distinct natural histories.

Yet, as a whole, the Southwest holds in common dramatic landscapes and unusual life-forms, all of which evoke awe and wonder.

Prickly pears thrive in
Arizona's Saguaro National Park.

THE
SOUTHWEST

Site discussed in chapter

| miles | | 400 |
| kilometers | | 500 |

Santa Rosa Range

Humboldt

11,388 ft +

GREAT SALT
LAKE

Great Salt
Lake Desert

Shoshone Mts.
Toquima Range
Monitor Range
Shell Creek Range
Egan Range
Ruby Mts.

Utah
Lake

UTAH

**GREAT BASIN
NATIONAL
PARK**

G R E A T

B A S I N

Sevier

Green

ARCHES
NATIONAL PARK

NEVADA

Boundary Peak
+ 13,143 ft

INYO NATIONAL FOREST
(EAST SECTION)

**ZION
NATIONAL
PARK**

CANYONLANDS
NATIONAL PARK

BRYCE CANYON
NATIONAL PARK

Colorado

C O L O R A D O

Lake
Powell

Monument
Valley

San Juan

**DEATH VALLEY
NATIONAL PARK**

**PARIA CANYON-
VERMILION CLIFFS
WILDERNESS**

P L A T E A U

*Chuska
Mts.*

San Juan
Mts.

Wheeler +
Peak
13,161 ft

*Sangre de
Cristo Mts.*

M o j a v e

-282 ft
• Lowest point in
North America

Death Valley

Lake
Mead

**GRAND
CANYON
NATIONAL PARK**

Painted Desert

Colorado

Little Colorado

R O C K Y

Conchas
Lake

Canadian

Pecos

Prairie Dog Town Fork Red

D e s e r t

CALIFORNIA

Lake
Havasu

**COCONINO
NATIONAL FOREST**

+ Humphreys Peak
12,633 ft

**PETRIFIED FOREST
NATIONAL PARK**

Cap Rock Escarpment

A R I Z O N A

Mogollon Rim

Baldy Peak
+ 11,404 ft

N E W   M E X I C O

4,754 ft
+

*L l a n o
E s t a c a d o*
(Staked Plain)

Palomar Mt.
6,138 ft +

**JOSHUA TREE
NATIONAL PARK**

Salton Sea

S o n o r a n

Salt

Gila

San Carlos
Reservoir

San Andres Mts.

Rio Grande

M
O
U
N
T
A
I
N
S

+ 11,971 ft

T E X A S

PACIFIC
OCEAN

Imperial
Valley

D e s e r t

Gila

**CABEZA PRIETA
NATIONAL
WILDLIFE
REFUGE**

*Black
Range*

Gila

**SAGUARO
NATIONAL PARK**

Sacramento Mts.

*Guadalupe
Mts.*

**CARLSBAD CAVERNS
NATIONAL PARK**

Colorado

UNITED STATES

MEXICO

+ **GUADALUPE MOUNTAINS NATIONAL PARK**

Guadalupe Peak
8,749 ft

Pecos

E d w a r d s

2,487 ft
+

P l a t e a u

*Davis
Mts.*

Amistad
Reservoir

Hill Country

**BIG BEND
NATIONAL
PARK**

Rio Grande

Nueces

173

BUTTES, CANYONS, MESAS, PLATEAUS

GRAND CANYON
NAT. PARK, Arizona

PETRIFIED FOREST
NAT. PARK, Arizona

GRAND CANYON NATIONAL PARK

The Grand Canyon in Arizona has inspired waves of purple prose from writers and poets, yet when you first stand on its rim, especially in the rich light of sunset or sunrise, you might decide that the gushiest of language is an understatement. The only appropriate comment seems to be none at all. Indeed, people often fall silent as they approach the edge. It takes them a few minutes to regain their breath—and their wits.

Perhaps it has to do with the suddenness of the encounter. There is no gradual approach. You walk on flat ground to the abrupt edge of a cliff, and if that were not enough, there is another one below it, and another, and another into the red glowing depths. Your sense of scale warps. It is hard to grasp the distances involved, and raw numbers help only a little. Measured along the Colorado River from Lees Ferry to the Grand Wash Cliffs, the canyon is 277 miles long. At Grand Canyon Village, about a third of the way along, where it cuts through the heart of the Kaibab Plateau, it is roughly a mile deep, and its rims stand about 10 miles apart.

The canyon seems to have existed forever but, in fact, is relatively young. An important part of the proof lies at its western, downstream end, where lakebed deposits—datable by isotopic techniques—show that five to six million years ago, no Colorado River was flowing through a Grand Canyon in its present location. Geologists theorize that, when the lower Colorado began to flow into the Gulf of California, the river caused erosion upstream, until it met the ancestral Colorado River on the Kaibab Plateau, thus beginning the erosion that created the canyon we know today.

The canyon might be young, but the rocks forming its walls are truly ancient, beginning with the hard, black two-billion-year-old Vishnu schist found at its bottom and stepping up through long ages of deposition. The great bulk of layers are sediments deposited during the Paleozoic era, a time of about 300 million years, beginning about 550 million years ago. Other, younger layers were deposited on top of them, but these have mostly vanished from the canyon, carried off by erosion. (The younger layers

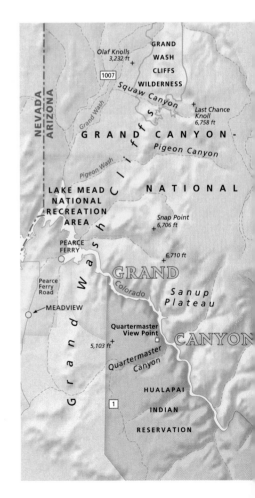

outcrop miles to the north in a series of high cliffs called the Grand Staircase, which includes the Vermilion Cliffs north of the park.) The old layers, stacked neatly one on top of the other, record a large portion of the Earth's history. Geologists find evidence of continental collisions, the births and deaths of mountain ranges, the eruptions of volcanoes, the rise and fall of oceans, and changes of climate through the ages.

As for plants and animals, the canyon offers a one-stop assortment of habitats. Chuckwallas and roadrunners lay claim to its hot lower reaches, while elk, occasionally cougars, and rarely black bears prowl the cool forests of the North Rim. A hike from the river to the rim is equivalent, in climatic terms, of traveling from southern Arizona to Canada. Between the two lies a stunning range of landscapes and biota: desert, to be sure, and numerous prickly, tough-skinned, even poisonous creatures; but also pockets of moisture and delicate water-loving creatures—tree frogs, maidenhair ferns, orchids, beavers, and kingfishers.

People have lived in the canyon for at least 4,000 years, going back to hunters who placed split-twig figurines resembling deer and bighorn sheep in caves, continuing through other cultures to Ancestral Puebloans and the current residents, the Havasupai and Hualapai, whose homes are in the western end of the canyon. Miners and other exploitive adventurers explored the canyon in the late 1800s, continuing their activity into the 1900s. In 1903, President Theodore Roosevelt visited the canyon and delivered a famous speech, saying "Leave it as it is. You cannot improve on it. The ages have been at work on it, and man can only mar it." In 1908 he established Grand Canyon National Monument. Since then, despite

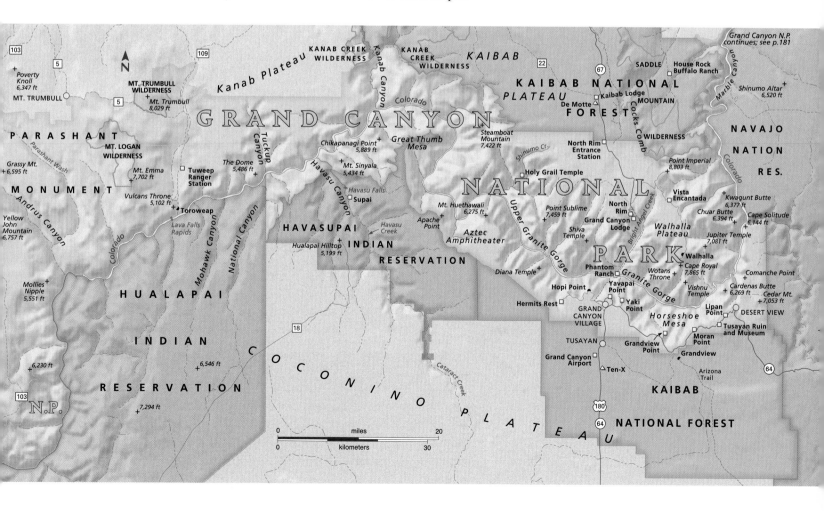

Lit by a setting sun, a rainstorm passes Cape Royal, on the North Rim of the Grand Canyon. Below the overlook, steep ridges stair-step down a mile to the Colorado River. President Theodore Roosevelt created Grand Canyon National Monument, forerunner of the national park, in 1908. Its majestic panoramas attract more than four million visitors each year.

repeated enlargement and national park status granted in 1919, the park has faced a barrage of challenges to its ecological integrity. Environmental concerns include air quality, which can get bad enough to diminish the view, and the river corridor, heavily impacted by the Glen Canyon Dam, completed in 1966, which lies immediately upstream.

Most people — more than four million annually — visit the South Rim.

On the South Rim, from Grand Canyon Village, the Hermit Road (closed to private vehicles during high season; free shuttle buses operate) hugs the canyon brink eight miles to its end at Hermits Rest. Desert View Drive heads east, leaving the park on its way to Cameron. Stunning viewpoints abound, each one offering a different perspective and a new assortment of buttes, mesas, and side canyons. From any of them,

Colorful crystals gleam in stone logs of the Crystal Forest in northeastern Arizona's Petrified Forest National Park. Tourists dynamited many of the petrified trees to gather souvenirs before the park was established in 1962.

note the Tonto Platform, a broad sandstone shelf that lies above the hard metamorphic rock of the inner gorge. The river is visible in places; with binoculars you might see rafts running rapids.

River trips are a splendid—perhaps the best—way to see the canyon. So is hiking. The South Kaibab or Bright Angel Trails are good choices, if only for a walk of several hours. (Warning: Canyon trails are more strenuous than they look; be prudent, carry water and some salty food, and remember that coming back up is harder than going down.) The first 1.5 miles of the South Kaibab drops a thousand vertical feet to Cedar Ridge through the top canyon strata: the gray Kaibab limestone and Toroweap formation, white Coconino sandstone, and the red Hermit shale. If you would rather avoid the stiff climb back up, stroll the Rim Trail where piñon and juniper trees provide shade and the canyon is never out of sight. Look for (but do not take!) fossils in the Kaibab limestone.

The North Rim, about a thousand feet higher than the South Rim, supports a mixed forest of ponderosa pine, spruce, fir, and aspen. From here, views of the canyon are different from those from the other rim, and the atmosphere is alpine. Start with the short walk to Bright Angel Point, a narrow promontory with stomach-tightening views into Bright Angel Canyon. Then drive 23 miles to Cape Royal via the Walhalla Plateau. Offering perhaps the most expansive rim vista of all, Cape Royal overlooks the bend where the southward flowing Colorado River turns west and cuts through the high Kaibab Plateau.

PETRIFIED FOREST NATIONAL PARK

Just over a hundred miles east of Flagstaff, in the bright expanse of sculpted hills called the Painted Desert, Petrified Forest National Park preserves the remnants of an ancient landscape far different from what exists now.

More than 200 million years ago, this was a broad floodplain washed by rivers flowing down from forested uplands. The rivers carried loads of sediment along with forest debris, including large numbers of trees. Deposits of silt, mud, and volcanic ash buried the trees and with time and groundwater carrying silicon dioxide, they became petrified. Today, huge stone trunks, exposed by erosion, lie scattered across the land.

The park began as a national monument in 1906 and became a national park in 1962. It was set aside on the initiative of local people who feared losing the petrified wood to souvenir hunters and commercial collectors. At the Crystal Forest site, logs were reduced to stone chips before the park was established. Even now, the theft of petrified wood continues.

Although best known for its stone "forests," the park also offers pueblo archaeological sites, petroglyphs, fossils from some of the earliest dinosaurs, and a variety of animals and plants. Located on a transition zone between desert and shortgrass prairie, it displays elements of both. Pronghorn share space with black-tailed jackrabbits, prairie dogs, collared lizards, western rattlesnakes, kangaroo rats, coyotes, ravens, raptors, occasional elk, and even the odd black bear. In the spring, mariposa lilies, Indian paintbrush, and evening primrose bloom among the snakeweed, rabbitbush, and buckwheat.

Travelers headed west on Interstate 40, which cuts across the park, should begin at the Painted Desert Visitor Center. From there, a paved road wanders along the rim of the Painted Desert, pausing at viewpoints overlooking the brightly colored clay hills. The colors come from reddish iron oxides, dark carbon and manganese compounds, and other natural pigments. Walk the Painted Desert Rim Trail (0.6 of a mile) for close-up views of juniper woodland and its creatures—among them desert cottontails and white-tailed antelope squirrels.

Ironically, more people lived here 800 years ago than today, as evidenced by the stabilized site of the 100-room Puerco Pueblo, a community of about 200 until around 1350. Its builders etched petroglyphs on nearby Newspaper Rock and left us with a solar calendar at Puerco Pueblo that still tracks the circle of the seasons.

The best wood concentrations are near the south entrance off U.S. 180. Long Logs Trail features an abundance of trees piled across one another in a log jam. The longest exposed trunk is 116 feet long. Giant Logs Trail, which begins at the Rainbow Forest Museum, loops past "Old Faithful," the park's largest log, measuring 9 feet around the base.

Banded clay hills of the Painted Desert abut an ancient floodplain littered with stone logs in Jasper Forest. In its 93,533 acres, Petrified Forest National Park preserves one of the world's largest concentrations of petrified wood.

RED ROCK COUNTRY, VOLCANIC CINDER CONES

PARIA CANYON-
VERMILION CLIFFS
WILDERNESS, Ariz., Utah

COCONINO
NAT. FOREST, Arizona

PARIA CANYON-VERMILION CLIFFS WILDERNESS

The Paria Canyon-Vermilion Cliffs Wilderness, on the north-central Arizona-Utah border, combines some of the most exposed landscape in the Southwest with some of the most hidden. The reddish Vermilion Cliffs rise 3,000 vertical feet in a long, impressive rampart—an arc of cliffs topped by wind-deposited Navajo sandstone. The wilderness area is the narrow strip between the top of the cliffs and U.S. 89A, which runs parallel to their base, and the lower Paria Canyon, beginning in Utah to the vicinity of Lees Ferry in Arizona. To fully appreciate the cliffs, a long view is easily obtained from U.S. 89 across the valley where it climbs Echo Cliffs on its way to Page. From this point, it becomes clear that the Vermilion Cliffs march in from the west; Echo Cliffs march in from the south. They meet at an apex, at Lees Ferry, through which flows the Colorado River, freshly emerged from the Glen Canyon Dam.

In the large triangle between the two lines of cliffs stretches a broad flat shelf of Kaibab limestone—the same rock layer that forms part of the Grand Canyon rims; indeed, the abrupt shadowy gash cutting through the middle of that shelf is Marble Canyon, upper end of the Grand Canyon. The Vermilion Cliffs have eroded far back from the river because their top layers are Navajo sandstone and because they stand on the soft silt-stone and shale of the Chinle formation. Obviously, this dry open land-scape is prime habitat for jackrabbits, lizards, blackbrush, prickly pear, and birds, including those with the biggest wingspan in America. Vermilion Cliffs is one of several release points in the effort to recover wild populations of endangered California condors. By late 1999, 16 of the great scavengers were ranging far from the cliffs in search of carrion.

The 38-mile-long Paria Canyon, in contrast to the open cliffs, is so deep and narrow that in places not even a condor can see to its bottom. Carved by seasonal flash floods, it is a secret world beneath the desert surface—a not altogether pleasant world. Although softened in places by gardens of riparian plants including cottonwoods, columbines, monkeyflowers, maidenhair ferns, and primroses, and filled with the song of canyon wrens, Paria is better known as a slot canyon, characterized by its deep shade, quicksand, pools of stagnant, muddy water, and piles of flood debris.

Flash floods are a life-threatening possibility that requires careful planning on the part of hikers. Yet despite distinct drawbacks, the canyon and its tributaries—notably the very narrow slot of Buckskin Gulch and the even narrower Wire Pass—are fascinating and strangely beautiful places. They are so improbably attractive that the Bureau of Land Management (BLM) enforces a limited permit system for overnight use. Hikers apply far in advance for a chance to walk the 38.4 miles from the White House Trailhead to Lees Ferry on the Colorado River.

COCONINO NATIONAL FOREST

Occupying the high plateau and mountain country of northern Arizona, the higher elevations of Coconino National Forest are a delightful respite from summer heat. In July, for example, when the lower deserts swelter, cool breezes whisper here through long-needled ponderosa pines. Huge thunderheads rise above San Francisco Mountain, rains drench the forest, then the thunderheads fade away with sunset. Water from those storms, plus meltwater from winter snows, cools the land, keeps it green, and runs off through a network of exquisite red-rock canyons.

The most popular portion of the forest is to the north, on San Francisco Mountain, known locally as San Francisco Peaks, a cluster of volcanoes sacred to the Navajo, Hopi, and other area tribes. The Coconino's southern boundary, a fault-zone escarpment called the Mogollon Rim, is no less dramatic. As much as 2,000 feet high, this natural battlement separates the cactus-studded upper Sonoran Desert from the realm of pines. On its northern edge, the forest slopes gradually to the radiant open spaces of the Painted Desert to the northeast, and north to sage grasslands leading to Grand Canyon.

The Coconino rests on a foundation of Paleozoic sediments—the same brightly colored sandstone, limestone, and shale found in the Grand Canyon. But here, those layers lie for the most part hidden beneath dark lava flows, cinder fields, and volcanic mountains. They come into view around the edges of the forest, or where canyons have sliced deep enough to expose them. One prime example is Oak Creek Canyon, whose famous red rocks stand beneath a six- to eight-million year old cap of basalt. Some of the volcanic activity occurred in historic times. Although San Francisco Mountain last erupted between 400,000 and 600,000 years ago, it presides over a huge field of smaller and younger volcanic cones. Among these, Sunset Crater began a series of eruptions in A.D. 1064, as established by tree-ring dating, spewing ash over 800 square miles and

True to their name, the 3,000-foot Vermilion Cliffs rise red beyond a shadowed rock face near Lees Ferry, in the 112,000-acre Paria Canyon-Vermilion Cliffs Wilderness on the Arizona-Utah border.

Sheer walls squeeze the Paria River in a 38-mile-long canyon carved by seasonal flash floods (opposite). Overnight backpackers register six months in advance to trek through the defile.

Autumn sunlight warms walnut and sycamore trees in Oak Creek Canyon, north of Sedona, Arizona. One of the most popular attractions in Coconino National Forest, the gorge winds through limestone, shale, and crimson sandstone exposed by millennia of erosion.

Like powdered sugar, winter's first snow dusts San Francisco Mountain, in Coconino (right). The mountain's three summits, the highest being Humphreys Peak, ring the crater of a dormant volcano. At 12,633 feet, Humphreys ranks as the highest peak in Arizona.

sending area residents scrambling for safety.

Few places in America can boast such a range of elevation—almost 10,000 vertical feet from the warm Verde River Valley on the southwest edge of the forest, north to the 12,633-foot top of Humphreys Peak, one of three peaks making up San Francisco Mountain. This translates to a rich variety of climates and topography. It was here, camped on the mountain slopes in 1889, that biologist C. Hart Merriam conducted research leading to his landmark theory of life zones and their relationship to latitude and elevation. Merriam noticed that traveling up the mountain slope took him through habitat changes similar to what he would experience traveling north to Canada. The summit of the San Francisco Mountain supports Arizona's only alpine life zone. Not far below, quaking aspens put on brilliant displays every autumn. Tall, columnar ponderosa pines dominate the middle elevations. Piñon pines and junipers form a partnership—the PJ forest or "pygmy" forest—at lower elevations where conditions are too warm and dry for larger trees. Broadleaf trees and shrubs, including Gambel oak, sycamore, and cottonwood, favor canyons blessed with year-round streams.

The wildlife list reflects the diversity of habitats. At its top: elk, mule deer, white-tailed deer, pronghorn, black-tailed jackrabbits, mountain lions, bobcats, coyotes, and black bears. Visitors often remark on the Abert's squirrels, with their striking tasseled ears. Wild turkeys scurry along the forest floor. Falcons cruise the canyon rims while bald eagles and osprey are attracted by riparian areas shared with raccoons, beavers, songbirds, and aquatic insects.

People have been drawn to the forest for thousands of years, as evidenced by numerous archaeological sites, including petroglyph panels and cliff dwellings. Some of the most important ones are protected by four national monuments, also of interest for biologic and geologic reasons. Northeast of Flagstaff are two national monuments: Sunset Crater features a symmetrical, thousand-foot-high cone surrounded by lava flows and fields of black cinders. At Wupatki, abandoned structures representing several cultural groups dot the landscape. East of Flagstaff, Walnut Canyon preserves ancient alcove dwellings in a compact woodland canyon. On the edge of the Verde Valley, the two units of Montezuma Castle protect a large alcove dwelling and a sunken lake fed by a huge spring.

Among the forest's beauty spots, Oak Creek Canyon and the town of Sedona are famous. People are drawn to the spectacular red rocks and cascading stream. For a wilder, more rugged canyon experience, consider hiking in Sycamore Canyon, Wet Beaver, or West Clear Creek Wilderness Areas. How different are these riparian canyons from the snow-twisted aspen forests of the high peaks, the eerie Japanese-garden landscape of the cinder cones northeast of Flagstaff, or the open ponderosa parklands so pleasant to explore on forest backroads.

LONG-ARMED CACTUSES, LAVA-CAPPED PEAKS

CABEZA PRIETA
NAT. WILDLIFE
REFUGE, Arizona

SAGUARO
NAT. PARK, Arizona

SAGUARO NATIONAL PARK

They have starred in more Western movies than John Wayne. Throwing long shadows across celluloid horizons, saguaro cactuses have come to symbolize the American Southwest. But in fact, these elegant long-limbed plants live only in a limited portion of the Sonoran Desert, including southwestern Arizona and adjacent areas of northern Mexico.

Their home is one of the hottest, driest, and botanically most interesting parts of the continent. Summer daytime temperatures rise well above 100°F for weeks at a time. Annual rainfall averages only 12 unreliable inches—in many places less. A good portion of that comes during summer thunderstorms that pour down too suddenly for the thin, rocky soil to absorb much water. You might expect few living things to survive in such a difficult place, yet the Sonoran Desert is a rich environment blessed with more than 2,700 plant species placed neatly across the desert. It is a veritable sculpture garden of eccentric flora. The various species of cactuses get top billing; besides saguaro there are barrel cactus, fishhook cactus, hedgehog cactus, teddybear and staghorn cholla, prickly pear, and others. Also prominent are the shrubs and low trees: paloverde, mesquite, creosote bush, ocotillo, and many more.

In spring, if winter rains have been sufficient, the desert erupts in dense carpets of orange poppy, blue lupine, globemallow, scorpion weed, primrose, and brittlebush. The air fills with an intoxicating blend of floral perfume and birdsong, and it is hard ever again to think of the desert as a barren place.

Saguaro National Park protects prime patches of saguaro habitat in two separate units on the outskirts of Tucson, Arizona. The east unit, which climbs into the pine forest of the Rincon Mountains, was declared a national monument by President Herbert Hoover in 1933. The west unit, set among rocky slopes of the Tucson Mountains on the other side of the city, was added by President John F. Kennedy in 1961. National park status was conferred by Congress in 1994.

The saguaro begins life as a tiny green bud sheltered by a paloverde, mesquite, or creosote bush. At 25 years, it may reach two feet in height. At about age 75, it puts out its first branch. It might live more than 200 years, stand as much as 50 feet tall with numerous twisting arms, and weigh 15,000 pounds. When moisture is available, it absorbs it through a shallow but widespread root system. Its pleated sides expand to accommodate up to 200 gallons of water stored in its spongy flesh. It has no water-squandering leaves; photosynthesis occurs in its green, waxy skin. If necessary, it can survive a year with no additional rain.

As it grows, a saguaro becomes the center of a small community. Nesting holes excavated and later abandoned by gila woodpeckers and gilded flickers become homes to elf owls, screech owls, kestrels, cactus wrens, and other birds—even honeybees. Red-tailed and Harris's hawks build

Cactus bouquet: In
spring vibrant flowers
line the thick pad of
a prickly pear in the
Sonoran Desert outside
Tucson, Arizona.
Two units of Saguaro
National Park protect
91,944 acres of a fragile
and complex ecosystem
shaped by intense
heat, overwhelming
dryness, and seasonal
rainy cycles.

Symbols of the arid
Southwest, giant
saguaros reach for the
sky amid a scattering
of prickly pears in
Saguaro National
Park (right).

nests on the outstretched limbs. Every spring, large white flowers appear
at the ends of the saguaro's arms. Each flower lasts only a day, but new
ones appear every night for several weeks. The blossoms attract long-
nosed bats at night, white-winged doves, honeybees, and other pollina-
tors during the day. Fruits, which ripen in summer, feed javelinas, foxes,

coyotes, rodents, and birds. They are also gathered by Tohono O'odham Indians, who make them into jam, syrup, and candy.

Some things saguaros cannot survive. Sustained cold kills even mature ones, which helps explain why they prefer rocky south-facing slopes—hot in summer but sun-warmed in winter. Other threats include

Barren boulders cup rainwater that reflects a rock face and burnished crags in southwestern Arizona's Cabeza Prieta National Wildlife Refuge. Rain that collects in natural stone basins, called *tinajas,* and one intermittent seep provides the only water in 860,010-acre Cabeza Prieta, third largest refuge in the lower 48 states.

livestock grazing, vandalism, and outright theft for landscaping purposes. Grazing no longer occurs in the national park.

Most visitors drive the scenic roads, stopping for short hikes, bird-watching, or flower gazing. For an easy introduction to Sonoran plants and animals, stroll the Cactus Garden Trail or the Desert Discovery Nature Trail, both near the visitor center in Saguaro West. In the east unit, the Tanque Verde Ridge Trail climbs from the Javelina Picnic Area more than 15 miles into the woodlands of the Rincon Mountains; even a short section of the trail is rewarding, and other easy walks beckon.

No one should miss the Arizona-Sonora Desert Museum, a living concentration of desert biota. Here you can safely come eye-to-eye with rattlesnakes, scorpions, and tarantulas; watch river otters and beavers through underwater windows; stand in a jeweled cloud of hummingbirds; and peer into the dens of nocturnal creatures, including—yes—vampire bats. After all, the allure of the desert lies in its juxtaposition of harsh reality with seemingly impossible delicacy.

CABEZA PRIETA NATIONAL WILDLIFE REFUGE

Whereas Saguaro National Park, being so close to Tucson, can appear tame like a city park, such is not the case with the wild sun-scorched terrain of Cabeza Prieta National Wildlife Refuge a hundred miles due west. Cabeza Prieta, or "Dark Head," is the Spanish name for a lava-capped peak in the southwest corner of this 860,010-acre, unwatered, unpeopled, and—in some eyes—desolate expanse. Almost any desert is softened by occasional springs and canyon-bottom riparian zones, but Cabeza Prieta is about as dry as they come. The refuge claims only one intermittent seep and scattered *tinajas,* natural rock basins that collect rainwater. In general, the roughly 400 species of plants and 337 species of vertebrate animals that live here rely on scanty precipitation that ranges from three inches per year in the west to a whopping nine inches in the east. Most of the animals survive by sheltering underground during the day. Many also conserve water through remarkable physical adaptations. Some rodents can actually produce their own water metabolically.

Many of the familiar Sonoran plants live on the refuge: saguaro, ocotillo, creosote bush, paloverde, and desert ironwood. Desert bighorn sheep live in the mountains; endangered Sonoran pronghorn roam the open country. To see a pronghorn is a lucky occurrence. The same is true for sensitive species like desert tortoises, willow flycatchers, peregrine falcons, and cactus ferruginous pygmy-owls.

Spring, fall, and winter are the best times to visit. Summer, because of the heat, can be dangerous. In any season, carry ample water and plenty of other supplies; there are no services. One road, the Charlie Bell west of Ajo, is passable by high-clearance two-wheel-drive vehicles. The other route requires four-wheel drive; it bumps along just north of the Sonora, Mexico, border following the desperate path of El Camino del Diablo (Devil's Highway). For many years until about 1870, when the railroad reached Yuma, this was actually a preferred route to California from Mexico—a relative shortcut, but a risky one, especially in summer. Piles of stones mark the graves of those who miscalculated. Any visit must begin at the refuge headquarters and visitor center in Ajo, where you can pick up an entry permit. Cabeza Prieta is an experience of rare solitude.

CAVERNS, CHIHUAHUAN DESERT, LIMESTONE REEFS

CARLSBAD CAVERNS
NAT. PARK, N. Mex.

GUADALUPE
MOUNTAINS
NAT. PARK, Texas

CARLSBAD CAVERNS NATIONAL PARK

Some of the finest wonders on Earth lie hidden from view. We discover them by chance and marvel at the richness of nature that can seemingly squander such beauty in utter darkness. The first lights ever known to illuminate the deep corridors and chambers of Carlsbad Caverns were candles and lanterns carried by local settlers, drawn to the natural entrance by what looked like smoke rising from the ground. It was not smoke but clouds of bats leaving the cave on their nightly feeding excursions.

The cave's reputation grew as visitors—many of them guided by local cowboy Jim White—emerged with fantastic stories of vast underground spaces. In 1923, the Department of the Interior took an interest, and sent inspector Robert Holly to have a look. He was stunned by what he saw, and soon after his visit, President Calvin Coolidge declared the cave a national monument. The next year, the National Geographic Society with the U.S. Geological Survey sent geologist Willis T. Lee to lead an exploring expedition in the cave. He and his team worked for six months; their report, published in NATIONAL GEOGRAPHIC magazine, brought the cave into the light of public renown. The area became a national park in 1930.

The caverns' geologic history begins about 250 million years ago in a Permian ocean, with the lives of countless marine organisms whose shells, rich in calcium carbonate, piled up to form limestone reefs thousands of feet thick. Over time, the ocean retreated, and the reefs were uplifted. Today we see them—the Capitan Reef—as the high peaks and wooded canyons of the Guadalupe Mountains that rise so dramatically above the desert of West Texas.

The caverns developed through a combination of factors common to limestone-solution caves around the world. Rainwater, made slightly acidic by mixing with carbon dioxide, seeps through cracks in the bedrock. By dissolving and carrying off the limestone solution, it slowly forms underground passages. Later, when the water table drops, the passages drain, and a depositional phase begins. As calcite-laden water percolates into the cavern, the carbon dioxide escapes. The water loses its dissolving power, and the calcite crystalizes again into new and wonderfully fluid shapes—cave formations called speleothems, such as stalactites, stalagmites, columns, flowstone, and soda straws.

At Carlsbad, the dissolution process was augmented by hydrogen sulfide gas rising from deposits of oil and gas beneath the reef; mixed with water, the gas produced sulfuric acid. Also, the collapse of ceiling rock enlarged some rooms, including the 14-acre Big Room—highlight of the basic cave tour, a one-mile trail. To get there, most people ride an elevator 755 vertical feet beneath the visitor center. The self-guiding trail leads through well-lit forests of speleothems and features with names like Bottomless Pit, Crystal Spring Dome, and Painted Grotto.

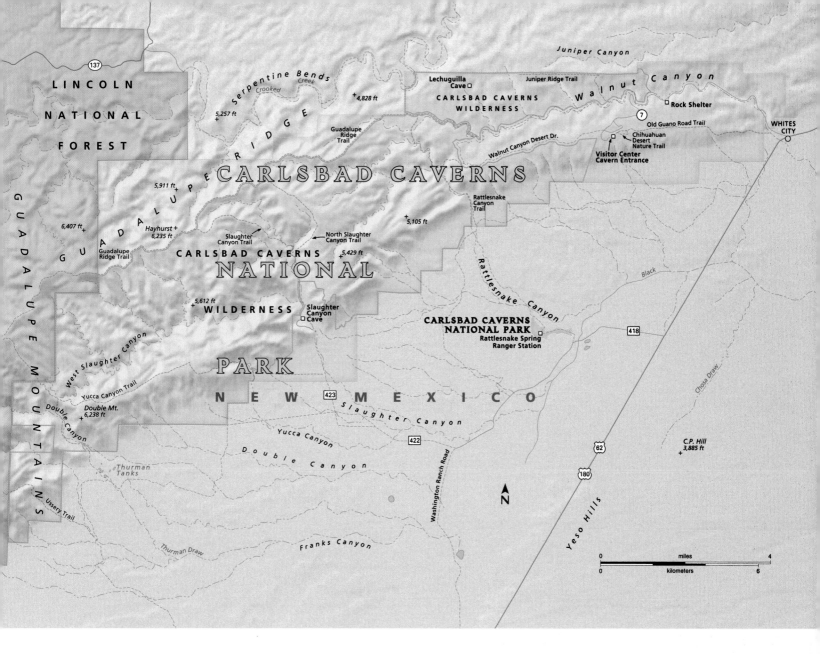

Other options include the Natural Entrance Route, a one-mile path that descends into the gaping natural cave mouth and follows a large passageway down to the Big Room. You can join a ranger for a tour of the Kings Palace or select from a menu of wilder, more adventurous trips into undeveloped areas (additional fees required).

Carlsbad is by no means the only cave in the park. A total of 85 are known, including enormous Lechuguilla Cave. Explored to a depth of 1,567 feet, it ranks as the deepest in the United States and the fifth longest in the world. Unusually rich in rare and fragile speleothems, Lechuguilla is reserved for research and exploration, but the park offers wild-cave tours in two other undeveloped caves—Slaughter Canyon Cave and Spider Cave. Carrying your light source, sometimes having to crawl or squeeze through tight spaces, you can get an explorer's view of the underground.

Although most visitors come for the cave, the rugged and scenic surface of Carlsbad is worthy of attention. The 9.5-mile Walnut Canyon Desert Drive offers a leisurely self-guided introduction to plants and animals of the northern Chihuahuan Desert. Plants such as agave, sotol, ocotillo, various cactuses, mesquite, and creosote bush are common. Rattlesnake Springs, the park's water source, is a good birding spot. Of chief interest among all surface phenomena is the bat flight. Those same clouds of bats that drew Native Americans and settlers to the cave entrance—

hundreds of thousands of bats, seven species but mainly Mexican free-tailed bats — emerge each evening from early May through October. A visible tornado of wings, they head for feeding grounds in the Pecos and Black River Valleys. Early in the morning, their bellies full of insects, they return. With folded wings, as if celebrating the extravagant generosity of nature, they plunge like stones back to their underground roosts.

GUADALUPE MOUNTAINS NATIONAL PARK

Some ten miles southwest of Carlsbad Caverns, along the same great Permian reefs, the Guadalupe Mountains in Texas come to a dramatic and sudden end in a series of limestone summits overlooking the desert plains. Among the peaks is 8,749-foot Guadalupe Peak, the highest point in Texas. This lofty white escarpment is the focal point of Guadalupe Mountains National Park.

The high country supports Douglas fir, ponderosa pine, and southwest white pine, forests that are home to elk, mule deer, black bears, bobcats, and mountain lions, as well as chickadees, wild turkeys, Steller's jays, and pygmy nuthatches. At lower elevations lizards, rattlesnakes, meadowlarks, cactus wrens, kestrels, and Swainson's hawks thrive in shrubby grasslands sprinkled with agave, prickly pear, sotol, and cholla.

The key is elevation. More than 5,000 vertical feet stand between the park's high and low points. This is enough to create splendid scenery and a strong contrast in climate and vegetation. Sliced into the mountains, rugged canyons, including renowned McKittrick Canyon, provide an intermediate zone where elements of high forest, desert, and riparian woodland come together.

Once the homeland — and for a time the last stronghold — of the Nde, or Mescalero Apache, the mountains and the national park are now largely designated as wilderness. History lives in the form of ranch buildings and old cabins. Frijole Ranch with its 1870s house is now a museum evoking life on the Texas frontier. Near park headquarters, you can walk among the remains of the Pinery, a stop on the 1858 Butterfield Overland Mail Stage route. A four-wheel-drive vehicle will take you along the western side of the range to Williams Ranch.

More than human history has changed over the past century. Current observations indicate a shift in biota. There was more grass, fewer shrubs, and far more wild animals. Grizzly bears and jaguars might have roamed the mountains; bighorn sheep, bison, wolves, and native elk (as opposed to the reintroduced elk found here now) surely did. Overgrazing is one culprit. Decreasing rainfall is also a likely factor.

In general, the backcountry is both rugged and dry. Foot and horse trails lead through the interior, up Guadalupe Peak, and around El Capitan,

Underground art: The cave formations — or speleothems — in New Mexico's Carlsbad Caverns National Park include columns, chandeliers, soda straws, and cave pearls formed by the deposition of calcium carbonate-laden water over the ages. The lowest part of Lechuguilla, the nation's deepest limestone cave, lies 1,567 feet below the ground.

the 8,085-foot point of the great promontory. By far the most popular trail is in McKittrick Canyon, watered by an intermittent stream that pours out of the high country and crowded with broadleaf trees, shrubs, and birds. A petroleum geologist named Wallace Pratt, struck by the canyon's outstanding beauty, bought land there in the 1930s and, beginning in the 1950s, ultimately donated 5,000 acres to the National Park Service. Autumn foliage draws so many visitors that, on some days, the park limits—based on parking space—the number of hikers permitted to enter. It is a testament to the value of conservation.

Wind ripples gypsum dunes in Guadalupe Mountains National Park. Beneath the limestone peaks, remnants of ancient fossil reefs, water's powers of dissolution created the hidden wonders of Carlsbad Caverns.

CHISOS MOUNTAINS, DESERT, THE RIO GRANDE

BIG BEND NAT. PARK,
Texas

BIG BEND NATIONAL PARK

The Earth never rests. Oceans come and go. Continents drift and collide majestically into each other. Mountains rise and weather tears them down. These events, recorded in the rocks and landforms of the Earth's crust, tell wonderful stories, if only we can read them.

Geologists can read enough about the wild Basin and Range Province of southwest Texas to know that Big Bend National Park is a complicated patch of ground. Held in the embrace of a broad curve of the Rio Grande, the park is an 800,000-acre expanse of rugged mountain, open desert, and river canyon. Its oldest rocks are 500 million years old. Deep canyons and high cliffs of limestone speak of a shallow sea that deposited calcium carbonate-rich sediments from eroded uplands. When the warm, shallow sea retreated, it left behind fossils of turtles, dinosaurs, huge crocodiles, and the giant flying reptile, *Quetzelcoatlus northropi*, a pterodactyl whose featherless wings spanned 36 feet or more.

Big Bend was uplifted when the Rocky Mountains rose some 70 million years ago. But its rugged heart, the Chisos Mountains, was built by volcanic eruptions and igneous intrusions that happened about 40 to 24 million years ago, about the same time that tensional faulting dropped the central portion of the park several thousand feet, so that this region, like the mountains and valleys in Nevada, is part of the Basin and Range. Lava bombs, ash flows, displaced strata, and recent earthquakes are some of the more obvious signs that the Earth continues to change.

Big Bend divides into three worlds—desert, mountains, and river. Paved roads visit all three; in addition, 157 miles of unpaved four-wheel-drive backroads wind through remote sections of the park to areas of natural and historic interest. These include springs, canyons, river bottoms, desert hills, cactus-studded flats, an abandoned mercury mine—Mariscal Mine—and scattered ranch buildings. Big Bend is full of history. Human occupation goes back some 10,000 years to a time when nomadic hunters lived among woodlands after the last ice age.

The desert of Big Bend is classic Chihuahuan: sotol, yucca, ocotillo, creosote bush, lechuguilla, and a variety of small cactuses; also roadrunners, coyotes, kangaroo rats, jackrabbits, lizards, rattlesnakes, javelinas, and falcons. Rising above the desert, the Chisos Mountains are an island of relative coolness and moisture where pines, junipers, oaks, Douglas firs, aspens, madrones, and other temperate plants—survivors from the ice age—make their last stand. If the climate cools again, they could expand downward; but if the climate continues to warm, they will fade away, and desert creatures will take their place.

One paved road penetrates the Basin, climbing over 5,770-foot Panther Pass, then dropping into the basin. Near the pass, the Lost Mine Trail climbs 2.4 miles to one of the area's best views. The Basin is loaded with

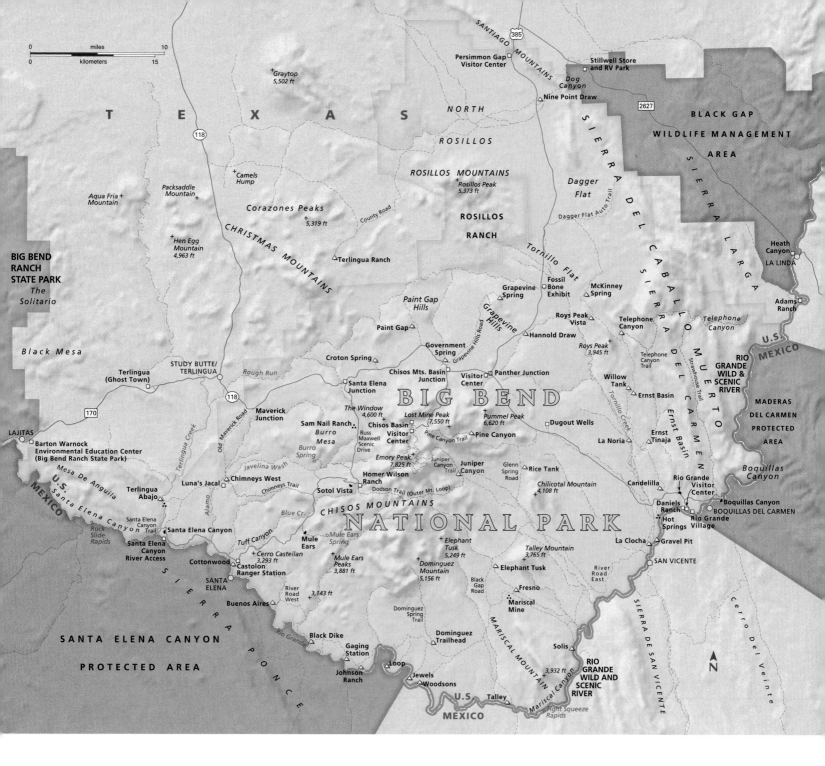

walking options. No one should forgo the short Window View Trail. Strong hikers might choose the 13-mile round-trip to the 7,400-foot South Rim vista, bagging the 7,825-foot summit of Emory Peak along the way.

The Rio Grande is the park's green belt, meandering for 118 miles along the southern boundary. Herons, kingfishers, turtles, beavers, catfish, and other aquatic creatures live in this lushly vegetated oasis. On the other side is Mexico, where the Chihuahuan Desert is included in two areas recently designated for protection: Maderas del Carmen in Coahuila and Cañon de Santa Elena in Chihuahua. Between the countries, the river has carved three deep canyons through three sequential limestone uplands. Seeing them by boat (day trips or longer) is a treat, but you can also peer into them from land. The Ross Maxwell Scenic Drive leads south from Santa Elena Junction through volcanic country to Castolon Historic District and beyond to the Santa Elena Canyon Overlook. Another road goes to Boquillas Canyon Overlook near Rio Grande Village,

Black against a brightening
sky stands an ocotillo
that has shed its leaves
during the dry season in
Big Bend National Park.
Chihuahuan Desert covers
97 percent of the southwest
Texas preserve, home
to more than a thousand
species of plants.

Shadows play across
the 1,500-foot-high walls
of Santa Elena Canyon,
one of three major gorges
along the Rio Grande
in Big Bend (right).

a renowned birding spot. Big Bend may have more bird species—446
noted—than any other American national park. Among residents is one
endangered species: the black-capped vireo.

Before Big Bend became a park in 1944, the land suffered from extensive overgrazing and loss of native plants, resulting in severe erosion.
Today, grasses and other plants, some started from seed in greenhouses
outside the park, are slowly reclaiming damaged areas. At the same time,
park staff and volunteers work to remove tamarisk, a nonnative tree that

can suck small water sources dry. The park now has an estimated population of about 20 adult bears. Killed off by the mid-1940s, bears hung on in the neighboring Mexican mountain ranges. In the late 1980s they came back, naturally recolonizing the Chisos Mountains. Another change: In the Chisos high country, Carmen Mountains white-tailed deer seem to be yielding territory to desert mule deer, a species better adapted to arid living. If true, it is a natural event tied to expanding desert conditions and a lesson in the changing nature of our planet.

SANDSTONE ARCHES, PINNACLES, HOODOOS

ARCHES
NAT. PARK, Utah
CANYONLANDS
NAT. PARK, Utah
BRYCE CANYON
NAT. PARK, Utah
ZION
NAT. PARK,
Utah

CANYONLANDS NATIONAL PARK

No wonder geologists love the Colorado Plateau, that vast expanse of colorful rock centered in much of Utah, western Colorado, northern Arizona, and northern New Mexico. First, they have no trouble seeing the rocks they want to study. Desert soils are thin; vegetation is sparse; erosion, by slicing and carving the landscape, has revealed its inner structure. Furthermore, the plateau is a zone of relative stability in a sea of geologic upheaval. Immediately to the west, tensional faulting has torn the Basin and Range physiographic region into hundreds of parallel blocks, causing them to tilt, rise, sink, and be buried under erosional and volcanic debris. To the east, the Rocky Mountains are a confusing battle zone of uplift, erosion, glaciation, and volcanic eruption. Meanwhile, the Colorado Plateau's limestone sediments, laid down over hundreds of millions of years, have remained neatly in place. They have been cracked, uplifted, warped, folded, and covered with lava on a local scale, but in general the plateau retains its original structure to a remarkable degree. This makes it an unusually good recorder of geologic history.

Occupying 527 square miles of the plateau, Canyonlands National Park embodies a sweeping range of geologic special effects. Sprinkled through its deep canyons and high windswept mesas are sandstone arches, hoodoos, pinnacles, domes, and fins. Sheer cliffs stand thousands of feet above lush river bottoms. Tiny streams echo in enormous overhanging alcoves. The bedrock itself takes on so many shapes that it seems almost fluid.

The park divides neatly into three districts separated from each other by the Colorado River on the east and the Green River on the west, which flow together to form a rough Y. At the top of the Y, a high mesa called Island in the Sky offers some of the finest, most expansive views in canyon country—a hundred miles or more of tangled rockscape, flat-topped mesas, and distant mountain ranges. Twisting along the edges of it, the two rivers flow in canyons lined with bright green vegetation. Having taken in the grand view, you may want to also visit one of the oddest of geologic oddities: Upheaval Dome, a great rounded blister of rock. Was it caused by an expanding salt deposit or a meteorite?

The Needles District takes its name from an extensive array of red-and-white banded pinnacles jammed together with arches and narrow canyons and hidden grassy meadows. An intimate three-dimensional landscape loaded with birds and wildflowers, it is ideal for day hiking to places like Devils Kitchen, Chesler Park, and Druid Arch.

Across the Colorado River, the Maze District is an even more convoluted system of tight canyons, sandstone fins, pinnacles, and perched platforms. You can drive any high-clearance vehicle to Hans Flat, where the views are huge. Beyond there, you will need four-wheel drive or a mountain bike to reach the Dolls House, a cluster of knobby spires;

Water, persisting over time through periods of uplift and faulting, shaped the twists and turns of the White Rim below Grandview Point in Utah's Canyonlands National Park. Here, the Colorado and its tributaries eroded sedimentary sandstones into canyons, mesas, and buttes— a landscape 19th-century explorer John Wesley Powell called "a wilderness of rock."

or the Land of Standing Rocks, with its rows of high parallel fins. The Maze is a tangle of interlocking canyons that challenges the strongest hiker; this is no place for the unprepared.

Rocks are of prime interest at Canyonlands, but piñon and juniper trees cover the high promontories. Grass, wildflowers, and shrubs shelter in little gardens among the rocks. Yucca, prickly pear, and claret cup cactus bloom in the spring, joined by the bright red of Indian paintbrush, the flamboyant yellow of cliff rose, and the pale orange of globemallow.

An excellent way to see the park is by river. Stillwater Canyon on the Green and Meander Canyon on the Colorado are gentle floats, but you must arrange a shuttle back upriver or face the big white water of Cataract Canyon (permits necessary), which begins at the confluence.

BRYCE CANYON NATIONAL PARK

If erosion means wearing down or destruction, there has to be a better word for the process that made Bryce Canyon National Park. It is true that wind, water, and gravity have carried away great quantities of rock, but the fantasy of color and form that remains can only be seen as an act of creation. Bryce Canyon occupies the top step of the Grand Staircase, a procession of rock layers that begins at the rim of the Grand Canyon and climbs northward over cliff bands named for their colors: Chocolate, Vermilion, White, Gray, and Pink. Traveling the region, you repeatedly cross the formations of different compositions that formed in different environments. Zion National Park is carved into the Navajo sandstone

of the White Cliffs. Bryce is in the Pink Cliffs—rich in iron and calcium carbonate, laid down 63 to 40 million years ago in freshwater lakes. Uplifted and exposed to the creative sculpting of erosion, the old sediments have become a fiery-colored maze of ridges, fins, spires, and hoodoos.

Touring the park is simple. The 18-mile main road winds along the wooded top of the cliffs on the Paunsaugunt Plateau, stopping often at vista points. Virtually everyone stops first at Sunrise Point, and if you have limited time, there is little reason to go farther. Better to walk the Rim Trail, which skirts the cliff edge on the east from Fairyland Point to Bryce Point. The views are tremendous. On clear days, you can see a hundred miles or more to the south and east—that is, if you can take your eyes off the brilliant scene at your feet. The ground drops away to the east some 2,000 vertical feet to the Paria River Valley. Go at dawn, when warm sunlight ignites the red- and yellow-banded landscape.

If you feel the lure of a closer look, a few trails drop beneath the rim into the glowing landscape; these connect with the Under-the-Rim Trail which zigs and zags 22 miles from Rainbow Point to Bryce Point. Even a short hike can put you in the heart of the hoodoos. The 1.5-mile Navajo Loop Trail passes a landmark spire called Thor's Hammer and passes through Wall Street, a narrow gorge where tall Douglas firs stretch skyward. The 1.8-mile Queen's Garden Trail, which begins at Sunrise Point, is the least difficult of the below-rim routes. The "garden" is a cluster of hoodoos near a formation said to resemble Queen Victoria, which takes some imagination to picture. Yet there are many true gardens—natural ones tucked among the spires with juniper, piñon pine, Gambel oak, maple, mountain mahogany, yucca, sagebrush, and wildflowers perfectly arranged. Songbirds, hawks, jays, canyon wrens, and woodpeckers enliven the scene in summer. Jackrabbits, coyotes, foxes, mule deer, ground squirrels, ringtails, and black bears also make their homes here and leave their tracks in the soft clay.

ZION NATIONAL PARK

The monumental scale of the formations in Zion National Park inspired a local Methodist minister to think of heaven's glory and to name the features accordingly. The Great White Throne, the Three Patriarchs, the Sentinel, the Watchman, the East Temple, Mount Majestic, and other monoliths tower thousands of feet above narrow Zion Canyon. At its bottom, the North Fork of the Virgin River slides over boulders and rock ledges in the shade of venerable cottonwood trees, its gentle music mingling with birdsong. In spring, wildflowers scent the air, and the loud chirps of canyon tree frogs echo from ponds and dripping springs.

The lowest and oldest stone formation in the park is Kaibab limestone, which also forms the rimrock of the Grand Canyon; it is seen only in the Kolob Canyons district of Zion. Above it is the Moenkopi formation, 1,800 vertical feet of mixed sandstone, limestone, shale, and gypsum. Above that come the soft purplish Chinle, the orange Moenave, the red Kayenta, and then the leading star of Colorado Plateau rock, the white-and-red Navajo sandstone. Originating as dunes during the Jurassic period, the Navajo still shows the crossbedded layers deposited by ancient winds. In the upper reaches of Zion—seen along Utah Highway 9 to Mount Carmel—it takes the form of domes and billowing hills (note: vehicles

Airborne duelists, male Utah prairie dogs marked for scientific study fight for territory in Bryce. Some 130 of the animals, which once numbered about 95,000, now survive in the park.

Sunrise, centered behind a rock spire called Thor's Hammer, brushes limestone pinnacles in Utah's Bryce Canyon National Park (opposite). Water that, with uplifts and faulting, carved the landscape in Bryce continues to whittle away rock towers known as hoodoos.

over 7 feet 10 inches wide or 11 feet 4 inches high require an escort through the narrow Zion-Mount Carmel Tunnel, for an extra fee). But where streams have cut deeply into it or through it, the Navajo forms sheer, sometimes overhanging, large cliffs; the Navajo is more than 2,000 feet thick in Zion.

Most visitors spend their time along the Virgin River in the dramatic central canyon. Trails lead along the river and up the canyon sides. The strenuous five-mile trail to Angels Landing is not for anyone who fears heights, but it provides a splendid view. Gentler trails lead to Emerald Pools and Weeping Rock. The 16-mile Virgin River Narrows hike, where the vertical canyon walls come to within yards of each other, is a popular but rugged trip that takes one or two days and special permits. Anyone who does not mind getting wet feet can sample the Narrows from below, with one major condition: Stay away during thunderstorm season from late June through mid-September. The Virgin River has not carved this magnificent canyon with its normally clear and gentle current; flash floods, when they come, can be powerfully destructive.

ARCHES NATIONAL PARK

The naming of Arches National Park was no challenge. What else could you call a place with one of the world's largest concentrations of natural sandstone arches? Elsewhere a rare landform, here are more than 2,000 in a variety of shapes and sizes. Landscape Arch, improbably slender, stretches 306 feet from one end to the other. Delicate Arch, a symbol for the state of Utah, stands on the edge of a precipice with the La Sal Mountains rising behind. Double Arch describes itself, but the name gives no hint of its huge size.

The arches resulted from several factors. First, the Entrada sandstone is an ideal sculpting material—uniform in composition and relatively soft. Second, far beneath the Entrada lies a thick deposit of salt from ancient seas. The salt is a plastic foundation; that is, it changes shape under the influence of pressure, deforming enough to crack the more rigid rock layers that lie above it. In the case of Arches, the Entrada broke into long parallel blocks. When exposed to weathering, these blocks erode into rows of narrow stone fins standing side by side like pews in a church. Further action by wind, water, and frost then erodes the fins, creating openings that eventually develop stable curved shapes.

All stages of the process can be seen at Arches, from jointed bedrock to rows of fins, to the first tiny openings of new arches and the large gaps where old arches weakened and fell in the past. All around them exists a delightful garden of rock shapes—balanced rocks, narrow chasms, hummocky buttes, and box canyons. The 24-mile park road traces a scenic path among them, but only by walking can you fully appreciate the intricacies of the landscape. The two-mile trail in the Devils Garden leads through whimsical stone playgrounds of up and down and through and under.

Among the surprises to anyone who expects the desert to be a harsh and lifeless place is the richness of plants and animals. True, there are cactuses

Rushing water speeds the Virgin River through Zion Canyon in spring in Zion National Park. Piñon pines, junipers, cottonwoods, and willows on the canyon floor yield to walls of red and white sandstone.

and lizards and scorpions and various snakes here, but also soft and delicate creatures: hummingbirds, tree frogs, columbines, and ferns.

One entity that all desert travelers should understand is the dark knobby crust that covers undisturbed ground. Called cryptobiotic soil, it is a living combination of algae, fungus, bacteria, and moss that despite its humble appearance plays an important role in desert life—stabilizing the ground, retaining moisture, adding nitrogen: providing a base for the entire biological community of the high desert. It is a big job for something so fragile that a footstep can cause decades of damage.

Arches owes its fame in part to conservationist and writer Edward Abbey, whose book *Desert Solitaire* told the story of a season spent in the park. His writing encouraged an appreciation for a landscape too often viewed as prickly, scaly, poisonous, insufferably hot, undesirable, and nearly worthless. Arches is prickly, all right, but far from worthless, as the growing popularity of this natural treasure proves.

Framing a red sandstone world, North Window looks onto Turret Arch in Arches National Park. The 76,519-acre rock garden in the high desert of eastern Utah contains one of the world's largest concentrations of natural arches.

COLD DESERTS, HOT DESERTS

INYO
NAT. FOREST
(east section),
Calif., Nev.

GREAT BASIN
NAT. PARK, Nevada

DEATH VALLEY
NAT. PARK,
Calif., Nev.

JOSHUA TREE
NAT. PARK, Calif.

GREAT BASIN NATIONAL PARK

The Great Basin, in the Basin and Range physiographic province, is a vast bowl with no outlet, and because it is in the rain shadow of the Sierra Nevada, it is a desert. Within its borders, which cover most of Nevada and parts of neighboring states, not a single river escapes to the ocean. The outstanding geologic feature of the region is its repeated theme of alternating basins and mountain ranges—a corrugated topography that grew out of tensional faulting beginning some 17 million years ago. In the simplest terms, the Earth's crust was stretched and broken into numerous elongated blocks. These in turn tilted so that one side rose and the other side moved downward.

Great Basin National Park, in eastern Nevada, sprawls across the southern portion of the Snake Range, one of the more prominent tilted blocks. Because it sank toward the east, its steeper side faces west. Entering the park, visitors drive up that long eastern slope from the sage-covered valley. The visitor center stands beside Lehman Caves, named for pioneer Absalom Lehman, who is credited with discovering the caves in 1885. President Warren G. Harding declared them a national monument in 1922, and it was the seed of the current national park. Many supporters worked for the park's establishment, but its most persistent champion was local newspaper editor Darwin Lambert, who wrote and lobbied for 33 years until the park was created in 1986.

Lehman Caves is one of the best decorated caverns in America. Of particular interest along the half-mile underground trail are the unusual shield formations: twin stone disks, often draped with stalactites and other flowstone shapes, that grow outward from cave walls like clam shells. The two halves are separated by tiny cracks. Why do they not grow together? What accounts for their round shapes? The formation of shields is an intriguing mystery. The cave also has fine displays of soda straws, fluted columns, helictites, gypsum flowers, drapery, aragonite, cave popcorn, and more.

The Wheeler Peak Scenic Drive climbs steeply upward from the cave, rising through piñon-juniper woodland to a forest of aspen and mixed conifers. Nearly 5,000 vertical feet above the valley floor, the road ends at a high alpine basin. Icy lakes glitter beneath 13,063-foot Wheeler Peak, the highest point in Nevada. In the shadow of its dramatic east face exists a small patch of climate cold enough to support a small glacier. If you make the trip on a hot summer day, you get a firsthand experience of the relationship between elevation and habitat. The high forest, with Douglas firs, limber pines, bighorn sheep, mountain lions, elk, deer, marmots, and alpine wildflowers, is essentially an island of cool air and moisture surrounded by a dry sea of sagebrush.

The high basin is a day-use area. Easy trails wind past Stella and Teresa Lakes; a more challenging 4.3-mile round-trip trek climbs 2,900

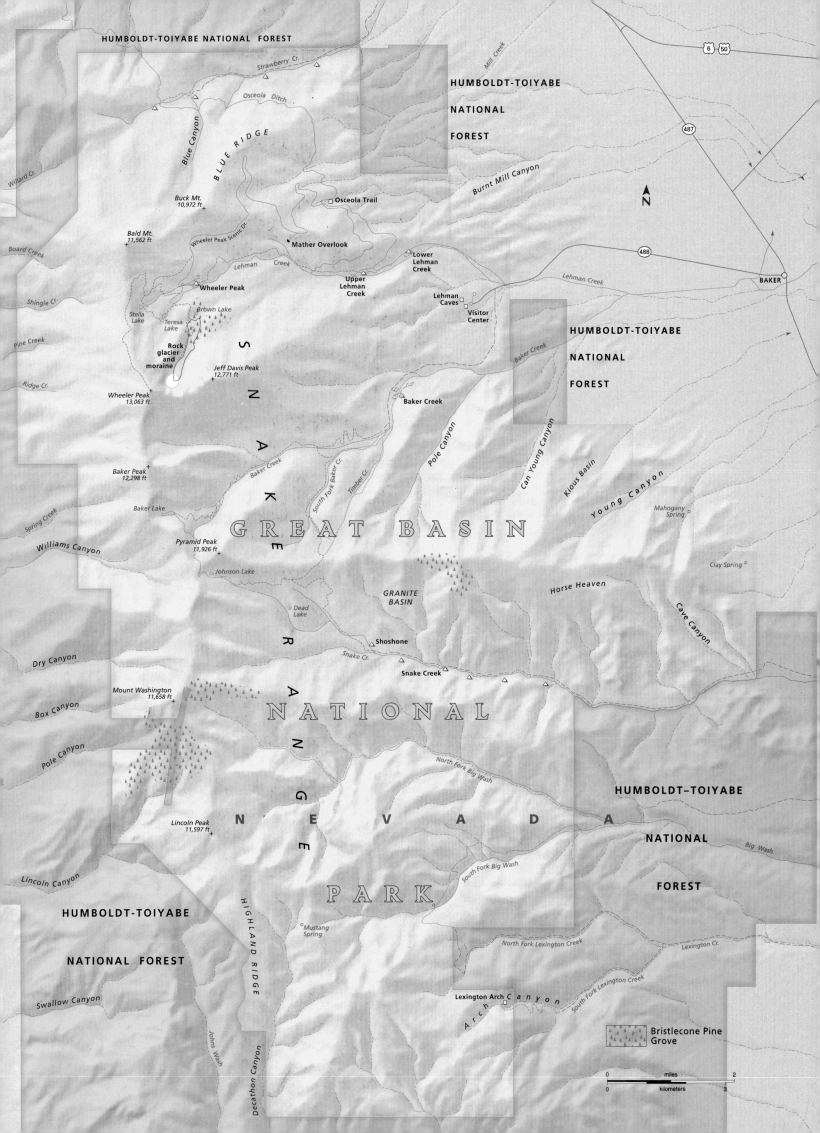

HUMBOLDT-TOIYABE NATIONAL FOREST

Strawberry Cr.

Osceola Ditch

Willard Cr.

HUMBOLDT-TOIYABE

NATIONAL

FOREST

Mill Creek

6 50

487

BLUE CANYON

BLUE RIDGE

Buck Mt.
10,972 ft

Osceola Trail

Burnt Mill Canyon

N

Board Creek

Bald Mt.
11,562 ft

Wheeler Peak Scenic Dr.

Mather Overlook

Lehman   Creek

488

Lower
Lehman
Creek

Lehman Creek

BAKER

Shingle Cr.

Wheeler Peak

Upper
Lehman
Creek

Lehman
Caves

Visitor
Center

Pine Creek

Stella Lake

Teresa
Lake

Brown Lake

Baker Creek

HUMBOLDT-TOIYABE

NATIONAL

FOREST

Ridge Cr.

Rock
glacier
and
moraine

Jeff Davis Peak
12,771 ft

S
N
A
K
E

Baker Creek

Pole Canyon

Can Young Canyon

Kious Basin

Young Canyon

Wheeler Peak
13,063 ft

Baker Peak
12,298 ft

Baker Creek

South Fork Baker Cr.

Timber Cr.

Mahogany
Spring

Spring Creek

Baker Lake

G R E A T   B A S I N

Clay Spring

Williams Canyon

Pyramid Peak
11,926 ft

R
A
N
G
E

Johnson Lake

Granite
Basin

Horse Heaven

Cave Canyon

Dry Canyon

Dead
Lake

Shoshone

Snake Cr.

Snake Creek

Mount Washington
11,658 ft

N A T I O N A L

HUMBOLDT–TOIYABE

Box Canyon

North Fork Big Wash

NATIONAL

Pole Canyon

N   E   V   A   D   A

FOREST

Lincoln Peak
11,597 ft

N
G
E

Big Wash

Lincoln Canyon

South Fork Big Wash

P A R K

HUMBOLDT-TOIYABE

HIGHLAND RIDGE

Mustang
Spring

NATIONAL   FOREST

North Fork Lexington Creek

Lexington Cr.

Swallow Canyon

Johns Wash

Decathon Canyon

Lexington Arch

Arch

Canyon

South Fork Lexington Creek

Bristlecone Pine
Grove

0   miles   2

0   kilometers   3

Survivors from an ancient age, bristlecone pines in eastern Nevada's Great Basin National Park date back to more than 3,000 years ago, when pharaohs ruled Egypt. The Great Basin, of which the national park encompasses 77,180 acres, is a cold desert of pitched peaks and broad valleys. It shelters more than 400 species of plants.

vertical feet to the windy summit of Wheeler Peak. The gnarled bristlecone pines seem to grow out of solid rock. More than 4,000 years old, these are some of the oldest creatures on Earth. Ironically, the harsh conditions of high elevation encourage longevity; bristlecones that take root in more comfortable circumstances grow much bigger but live only a few hundred years.

Near the visitor center, a gravel road leads south to Baker Creek and the trailhead for Baker Lake, an all-day 12-mile round-trip hike or a backpacking trip through meadows and stands of mountain mahogany, manzanita, aspen, and pine.

A 12-mile unimproved dirt road, approached from Utah, visits the south end of the park, ending at Lexington Arch, a limestone structure whose opening might once have been a cave tunnel. Few visitors get this far. Fewer still make it into the North or South Forks of Big Wash, where conditions are wild and solitude is virtually certain.

DEATH VALLEY NATIONAL PARK

Although Death Valley National Park has some respectable mountains, including 11,049-foot Telescope Peak, attention here focuses on the park's low point: the Badwater Basin salt pan, 282 feet below sea level, lowest plot of ground in the Western Hemisphere, and one of the hottest, driest, most forbidding places on Earth.

The valley itself is a trough stretching 120 miles between two fault-block mountain ranges—the Panamint and the Amargosa—on the western side of the Great Basin. The valley's dryness and heat come partly from being in the rain shadow of the Sierra Nevada and partly as a result of the valley's own microclimate. It was first called Death Valley by a group crossing it in 1849. Hoping to find a shortcut to the California goldfields, they almost lost their lives. Years later miners returned, lured by gold, silver, and other minerals. The most famous mines produced borax, hauled from the valley floor in 20-mule-team wagons. Ghost towns and mine workings are now part of the historic scene.

For thousands of years, Native Americans have lived in this Mojave Desert valley. Ancient cultures left scattered stone artifacts, petroglyphs, and unusual circles and wavy lines made of carefully selected cobbles; their meaning is a mystery. Current native residents, the Timbisha Shoshone, call the valley and its surroundings *tüpippüh,* or "our homeland." Like many other tribes, they lost their land as the U.S. expanded and, with it, important parts of their culture. In a cooperative project, the National Park Service and the Timbisha are working to restore some of what has been lost, including traditional use of some park land.

In 1994, the California Desert Protection Act upgraded the Death Valley National Monument to a national park and expanded it to 3.3 million acres—a huge sweep of desert stretching far beyond the valley itself.

Like corrugated cardboard, eroded mudstone—once the bed of a prehistoric lake—creases California's Death Valley National Park from Zabriskie Point. Hottest, driest, and lowest spot in North America, the 120-mile-long valley formed when a section of Earth's crust sank.

Among park landmarks, the salt flats of Badwater Basin prove at close range to be miniature badlands of jagged pinnacles. Dunes cover 14 square miles near Stovepipe Wells, attracting hikers and etched by the tracks of kangaroo rats, kit foxes, and other nocturnal creatures. At the Racetrack, rocks leave snail-like trails as they move across a wet mud-flat, presumably pushed by the wind when the surface is slicked by water. Visit Dantes View for a grand panorama from 5,000 feet above the valley. Zabriskie Point is famous for sunset views of its colored hills.

Although temperatures above 120°F are not uncommon on the valley floor during summer (the record is 134°F) the park is a pleasant place during spring and fall—and can get downright cold in winter. Nor is it barren of life, as early reports once described it. Salt Creek is home to a desert pupfish; and killdeers, snipes, and herons frequent its grassy banks. Cottonwoods shade natural springs. Pickleweed and saltgrass survive on salty ground that would kill most plants. Mesquite, creosote bush, desert holly, cholla, and beehive cactus are common above the salty valley floor. Going higher, there are Joshua trees, piñon pines, junipers, mountain mahoganies, and even maples. These and all the many creatures that live among them belie the forbidding name of this intriguing place.

JOSHUA TREE NATIONAL PARK

They look like something Dr. Seuss might have thought up—fanciful, eccentric, unlikely, and delightful to children of all ages. Growing 30 to 40 feet high, with thick upward-curving branches, Joshua trees resemble saguaro cactuses gone furry. Neither cactuses nor trees, they are giant yucca, and their bottle-brush clumps of leaves are not the least bit soft.

The park named for these unusual plants began as a national monument in 1936. The 1994 California Desert Protection Act expanded and upgraded the monument to a national park covering 794,000 acres and spanning parts of two great deserts. The eastern side, below 3,000 feet elevation, lies in the Colorado Desert (part of the Sonoran) which is characterized by paloverde, chuparosa, ocotillo, jumping cholla, and ironwood. The higher western side is Mojave Desert—a bit cooler and moister—and is home to the Joshua tree. On the wildlife list: mule deer, bighorn sheep, desert tortoises, roadrunners, mountain lions, coyotes, yucca night lizards, chuckwallas, and sidewinder rattlesnakes.

The park receives little rain, but it is not all dusty dry. Desert fan palms grow up to 75 feet tall in several verdant oases. One of these, Cottonwood Spring near the south boundary of the park, has been an important water source for centuries, valued by Cahuilla Indians, gold miners, and travelers. Artifacts of that long history are scattered about the oasis. There is good hiking in the area and excellent birding. Watch for hooded orioles, which build hanging nests beneath the palm leaves. Two other oases, Forty Nine Palms, in the north, and Lost Palms, in the south, are reached only by hiking and offer similar pleasures.

The smooth granite outcrops at places like Jumbo Rocks and Wonderland of Rocks appear to have been exposed to the weathering effects of the desert for eons; yet most of their shaping occurred during wetter times when they were buried beneath the ground. The rock is monzogranite, a molten intrusion some 100 million years old. After crystalizing at depth, it cracked into rectangular blocks when it was uplifted. Overlying rock eroded away, and groundwater trickled through the cracks, prying the rock apart into rounded boulders. The blocks remained buried in their own debris until the climate turned dry, at which point the land lost its protective cover of dense vegetation. Then erosion stripped away the softer material and left the boulders exposed to view.

Many visitors look forward eagerly for the spring wildflower bloom, which can begin in February at lower elevations, then it advances to higher elevations through March and April. Because annuals germinate in autumn, the bloom depends on early rains; a wet spring cannot make up for a dry fall.

Among conservation concerns is the recent invasion of exotic grasses. By filling in the spaces between Joshua trees and other desert plants, grass becomes a fire hazard. Before the invasion, fires were infrequent and burned only small patches of desert. The dried grass, however, causes more frequent fires that can spread farther and burn hotter. The increased frequency of fires is destroying the mature woodland habitants of piñon, juniper, and oak. The grasses recover quickly; however, the woodlands cannot sustain repeated burning.

Spiny crowns and twisted trunks of a Joshua tree stand out in sharp relief at sunset in southern California's Joshua Tree National Park. The giant tree yuccas grow above 3,000 feet in the Mojave Desert, which covers the western part of the park.

Salty towers of tufa, a porous form of calcium carbonate, loom 40 feet above Mono Lake in Inyo National Forest. Mono, a vast inland sea twice as salty as the Pacific, has no outlets. Water leaves the lake only through evaporation; minerals and salts remain.

INYO NATIONAL FOREST

The Basin and Range Province ends at the Sierra Nevada in a craggy rampart topped by 14,494-foot Mount Whitney. The highest peak in the lower 48 states, it stands less than a hundred miles from the salty bottom of Death Valley. That long east-facing rampart overlooks the Owens Valley and, beyond it, the White Mountains. Together, they make up the westernmost basin and the westernmost range in the province.

These are the lands of Inyo National Forest, in California and Nevada—rugged on a grand scale, scarred by volcanoes and shaken by earthquakes. In the rain shadow of the Sierra, it is dry country, but there is enough water for an assortment of plants, including Jeffrey pine, lodgepole pine, red fir, and aspen. Among the high peaks, heavy snowfalls support streams

and lakes. A list of wildlife would include Sierra Nevada bighorn sheep, black bears, cougars, eagles, bobcats, and coyotes.

The forest's premier natural reserves are the John Muir Wilderness Area, tucked up against Sequoia-Kings Canyon National Parks, and the Ansel Adams Wilderness, next to Yosemite National Park. Both offer superb hiking through country that conservation pioneer John Muir loved and described so well. At 10,000 feet in the White Mountains stand groves of ancient bristlecone pines, accessible by road. Mono Lake is a rare and fascinating body of water. One of the continent's oldest lakes, its briny shores are marked by strange tufa towers. Too salty for fish, the lake supports vast numbers of brine shrimp and alkali flies, which in turn attract millions of migrating birds.

The

CHAPTER V

FAR WEST

CHANNEL ISLANDS YOSEMITE SEQUOIA-KINGS CANYON REDWOOD HART MOUNTAIN ANTELOPE REFUGE

KLAMATH BASIN CRATER LAKE NORTH CASCADES MOUNT BAKER-SNOQUALMIE

MOUNT RAINIER MOUNT HOOD OLYMPIC PARK OLYMPIC FOREST PACIFIC RIM NAHANNI

GLACIER BAY TONGASS WRANGELL-ST. ELIAS KLUANE DENALI YUKON DELTA

Braking with powerful wings, a bald eagle comes in for an iceberg
landing in Alaska's Tongass National Forest.

BY BARBARA SZERLIP AND MARK MILLER

This great arc of territory encompasses much of North America's west, commencing in California as far south as the Channel Islands and following the northwest-bending Pacific shore north along the Canadian coast to the Yukon Delta of western Alaska. The Far West's topography includes many mountain ranges, including the Cascade Range and the Coast Mountains. These volcanic peaks were rough-cast during a fiery, eruptive era beginning sometime between 25 and 10 million years ago and continuing to this day. They were sculpted into their present appearance about 3 million years ago — a geologic blink of an eye — during the Pleistocene epoch, when much of the Pacific Northwest, including its tallest peaks, was buried beneath great accumulations of snow and ice. From these flowed massive glaciers that over eons advanced and retreated like colossal rasps, bullying the land beneath them into high ridges, grinding mountains down to gently contoured hills, and plowing deep trough-like valleys, leaving kettle lakes, ocean straits, and 2,000-foot-deep fjords.

Moss cloaks maple trees in Mount Rainier
National Park, Washington.

The enormous scale and diversity of Far West landscapes — from Mount McKinley of the Alaska Range, whose vertical rise surpasses the highest in the Himalaya and can be seen 200 miles away; a waterfall that plummets 14.5 times farther than Niagara; thundering wild rivers; vast soggy plains of tundra; ice fields so large they generate their own weather; and North America's largest collection of fitfully sleeping volcanoes — makes this a region apart, a Brobdingnagian kingdom that tends, by comparison, to make most other North American landscapes seem almost Lilliputian.

Like its terrain, the Far West's wildlife is frequently oversized. Its biggest bears weigh in at 1,500 pounds and stand more than nine feet tall. Its wilderness ponds are browsed by 1,300-pound moose with antlers extending six feet across. Some of its oldest trees were growing when pharaohs ruled Egypt.

Were it not for a succession of determined and articulate conservationists who dedicated their lives to the public protection of hundreds of millions of acres of forests, coastlines, and mountains, the Far West would be far less than it is today. The conservation movement acquired a manifesto in 1901 with the publication of *Our National Parks*, John Muir's rhapsodic and compelling description of the West's natural treasures. The book's stinging criticism of the shortsighted forestry practices of his day spurred the establishment of the National Park Service, an epochal and precedent-setting event in which the federal government accepted chief responsibility for the stewardship of wilderness, which Muir considered a spiritual "necessity."

The 21 places visited in this chapter testify to the astonishing diversity and splendor of the legacy Muir and his fellow visionaries bequeathed to all North Americans — indeed to people everywhere — and define the scope of the responsibilities that come with it — most of all our moral obligation to pass it along, undiminished.

Bering Str.
Little Diomede I.
Cape Prince of Wales
Seward
Peninsula
St. Lawrence
Island
Norton
Sound
ARCTIC CIRCLE
Koyukuk   +4,236 ft
limit of
Wooded
Country
Ray Mts.
Yukon
White Mts.
NORTHWEST
TERRITORIES
Smith Arm of
Great Bear Lake

St. Matthew I.
Yukon
Delta
Kaiyuh Mts.
YUKON
Ogilvie Mts.
+7,749 ft
Mackenzie
Franklin Mts.

YUKON
DELTA
NATIONAL
WILDLIFE
REFUGE
+2,904 ft
DENALI NAT. PARK
AND PRESERVE
Mt. McKinley (Denali)
20,320 ft Highest point in
North America
ALASKA   RANGE
U.S.
CANADA
TERRITORY
PLATEAU
Selwyn Mts.
MACKENZIE MOUNTAINS
Mackenzie
Nahanni
NAHANNI
NAT. PARK
RESERVE

Cape Mohican
Hazen Bay
Nunivak
Island
+3,579 ft
Kuskokwim Mts.
Killbuck Mts.
Mts.
Susitna
Wrangell Mts.
Copper
WRANGELL–ST. ELIAS
NAT. PARK AND PRESERVE
KLUANE
NAT. PARK RESERVE
Mt. Roosevelt
9,751 ft

Cape Newenham
Iliamna L.
Kenai
Pen.
Cook Inlet
Prince
William
Sound
St. Elias Mts.
+Mt. St. Elias 18,008 ft
TONGASS
Cassiar Mountains
BRITISH

Nushagak Pen.
Bristol Bay
Becharof L.
+Mt. Katmai 6,716 ft
Afognak I.
Malaspina Glacier
(largest glacier in
North America)
+Mt. Fairweather
15,300 ft
COLUMBIA
Williston
Lake

SEA
Umnak I.
Unalaska I.
Unimak I.
ALASKA PENINSULA
Shelikof Str.
Kodiak I.
Trinity Is.
GULF
OF
ALASKA
GLACIER BAY
NAT. PARK AND
PRESERVE
Chichagof I.
Kruzof I.
Baranof I.
NATIONAL
Admiralty I.
Kupreanof I.
Revillagigedo I.
COAST
Fraser
Plateau
Cariboo Mts.
Fraser

NDS
FOREST
Kuiu I.
Prince of
Wales I.
Dall I.
Dixon Entrance
Graham I.
QUEEN
CHARLOTTE
ISLANDS
Moresby I.
ALEXANDER   ARCHIPELAGO
Hecate Str.
Queen
Charlotte
Sound
Mt. Waddington
13,176 ft
MOUNTAINS

PACIFIC
THE
FAR
WEST
VANCOUVER ISLAND
CAN.
U.S.
Cape Flattery
PACIFIC RIM
NAT. PARK RESERVE
OLYMPIC NAT. PARK
AND OLYMPIC NAT. FOREST
MT. RAINIER NAT. PARK
NORTH CASCADES
NAT. PARK
MT. BAKER–
SNOQUALMIE
NAT. FOREST
WASH.
Mt. Rainier 14,410 ft
Columbia
CASCADE
MT. HOOD NAT. FOREST
Mt. Hood 11,239 ft
HART
MOUNTAIN
NATIONAL
ANTELOPE
REFUGE

OCEAN
Cape Blanco
COAST
RANGE
OREGON
RANGE
CRATER LAKE NAT. PARK
KLAMATH BASIN
NAT. WILDLIFE REFUGES
1 - Klamath Marsh Refuge
2 - Upper Klamath Refuge
3 - Bear Valley Refuge
4 - Lower Klamath Refuge
5 - Tule Lake Refuge
6 - Clear Lake Refuge

REDWOOD
NAT. PARK
Cape Mendocino
Mt. Shasta
14,162 ft
CALIF.
Sacramento Valley
Tahoe
NEV.
Mono Lake

YOSEMITE NAT. PARK
KINGS CANYON NAT. PARK
SEQUOIA NAT. PARK
Monterey Bay
San
Joaquin
San
Joaquin
Valley
SIERRA   NEVADA
+Mt. Whitney
14,494 ft Highest
point in 48
contiguous U.S.

Point Conception
Channel Is.
CHANNEL ISLANDS
NAT. PARK

Site discussed in chapter

0   miles   500
0   kilometers   500

CLEAR WATER, KELP FORESTS, WHALES

CHANNEL ISLANDS
NAT. PARK,
Calif.

CHANNEL ISLANDS NATIONAL PARK

Even on clear days, the five isles of this quarter-million-acre preserve off the southern California coast are often veiled by haze or fog, creating the aura of a world apart. Which, indeed, they are — of more than 2,000 plant and animal species thriving on Anacapa, Santa Barbara, San Miguel, Santa Rosa, and Santa Cruz, 145 are either unique or have evolved over time to differ (in size, shape, or color) from their mainland relatives.

The islands within the Channel Islands National Park extend from the Santa Barbara Channel south to the San Pedro Channel off Laguna Beach just north of Los Angeles. The park headquarters and the Robert J. Lagomarsino Visitor Center are located in the city of Ventura. It was during the presidency of Jimmy Carter that the islands attained national park status. In addition, 1,658 square miles of ocean surrounding them were designated as a national marine sanctuary.

Some biologists have gone so far as to dub this windswept collection of grasslands, marshes, cliffs, beaches, tide pool shelves, and 200-odd sea caves the North American Galápagos.

The white-footed deer mouse and its nemesis, the house-cat-size island fox, are found nowhere else in the world — nor are the isles' spotted skunk and the Santa Cruz Island scrub-jay. Santa Rosa Island harbors one of only two known stands of Torrey pine, one of the rarest North American pines, a hardy tree contorted and made gaunt by wind and salty soil.

The tenacious, salt-tolerant ice plant that covers much of Santa Barbara Island with a thick greenish brown mat was brought here by people from South Africa sometime before 1900. Perhaps the most conspicuous evidence that nature has gone its own way here is the coreopsis, a tree sunflower that can grow to ten feet in height, its yellow blossoms so large and vivid that they can be seen from the California mainland 11 miles away.

Half of the park's 250,000 acres — and much of its extraordinary biological diversity — lies beneath the waves. Indeed, three times as many people voyage here to explore the waters around the islands as ever set foot on their shores. Cool-water systems, such as those found around the Channel Islands, are shaped by cold ocean currents. These nutrient-rich waters nourish large populations of small fish and crustaceans, which in turn feed larger fish and marine mammals.

Lovers of sea life will find everything from tide pool worlds of anemones, sea urchins, starfish, black abalones, crabs, and barnacles to nearly a thousand species of fish and plants in the Channel Islands National Marine Sanctuary, which extends six nautical miles around each island.

Many of these creatures, such as California's state marine fish, the garibaldi, are found in giant kelp forests — those around Anacapa are

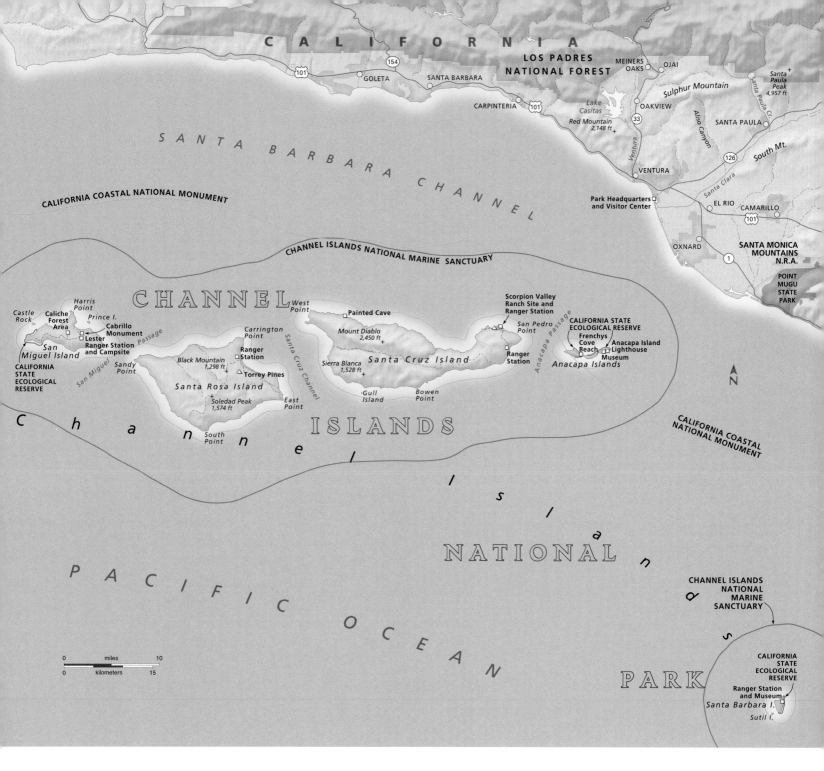

a favorite destination for divers and underwater photographers—
which conceal them from great white sharks. These fearsome predators inhabit the islands' open waters with migrating gray, humpback,
pygmy sperm, and blue whales.

Whale-watching trips to the Channel Islands advertise that pas-
sengers may be lucky enough to see the great blues, the largest marine
mammals still living on Earth. These awesome mammals may reach a
hundred feet in length, live to be a hundred years of age, and consume
hundreds of tons of food each year.

White-sided dolphins cavort in the wake of fast-moving boats, sharing the chilly shallows with six species of seals and sea lions, most of
which mate and give birth on the beaches of San Miguel that boasts
the largest breeding colony of its kind in the U.S.

Above the often choppy Pacific, Brandt's cormorants, black

oystercatchers, noisy western gulls, and black storm-petrels circle relentlessly, each species in its own pattern and rhythm, in a never ending quest for food. Among the most graceful are brown pelicans, nearly extinct in the 1970s, whose awkward gait on land belies their remarkable agility in flight.

The fossilized remains of dwarf mammoths have been found and dated to the ice age, when lower sea levels bared land to form Santarosae, a single island. Hundreds of archaeological sites, some dating back 13,000 years, confirm a long history of human habitation. The Chumash lived on the islands when the first Europeans sailed up the California coast in 1542. Eventually Spanish settlers who laid claim to the area relocated the Chumash to mainland Franciscan missions.

The Nature Conservancy owns the western portion of 60,645-acre Santa Cruz, the largest island in the park. Permits are required to visit the Nature Conservancy's portion, but the part of the island managed by the Park Service requires none. Campers, hikers, bird-watchers, boaters, sea kayakers, snorkelers, and scuba divers have the memorable privilege of experiencing a pristine natural world of uncommon rarity.

Underwater acrobat, a sea lion swivels past giant kelp in Channel Islands National Park, off the coast of southern California. The five islands and surrounding waters of the reserve shelter six species of seals and sea lions.

Wildflowers compete with lichen on the steep shores of San Miguel Island (opposite). Heavy fogs at San Miguel, farthest west of the Channel Islands, foster spectacular blossoms in spring.

MONOLITHS, SEQUOIAS, U-SHAPED GLACIAL VALLEYS

YOSEMITE NAT. PARK, Calif.
SEQUOIA-KINGS CANYON
NAT. PARKS,
Calif.

YOSEMITE NATIONAL PARK

Until 1833, Yosemite's spectacularly deep glacial valley in the Sierra Nevada of California and its thundering waterfalls were known only to the Miwok people who summered there. In 1868, 30-year-old John Muir, whose recovery from temporary blindness following an accident deepened his innate spirituality and his appreciation of natural beauty, walked through waist-high wildflowers into the Sierra Nevada high country for the first time. It marked the beginning of his lifelong dedication to the preservation of California's lofty wilds. "Thousands of tired, nerve-shaken, over-civilized people are beginning to find out that wilderness is a necessity," he wrote presciently, "that mountain parks...are useful not only as fountains of timber and irrigating rivers but as fountains of life."

The Scottish immigrant's 1901 book, *Our National Parks,* was a poetic tribute and a plea for increased protection. One reader was President Theodore Roosevelt, who traveled to the West to see for himself and spent his first night in Yosemite camped under the stars with Muir in a grove of sequoias. The giant evergreens' "majestic trunks," the Rough Rider later reflected, "beautiful in color and in symmetry, rose round us like the pillars of a mightier cathedral than ever was conceived even by the fervor of the Middle Ages." The two outdoorsmen laid the foundations for a federal conservation crusade that would result in the inclusion of Yosemite Valley and Mariposa Grove into Yosemite National Park, established in 1890. In six years Roosevelt established 5 national parks, 55 wildlife reserves, 150 national forests, and 18 national monuments.

Descriptions of Yosemite's dramatic beauty attracted landscape painters like Albert Bierstadt in 1860 and Thomas Hill and Harry Cassie Best, whose daughter would marry photographer Ansel Adams, the park's photographer-laureate. Their images introduced Americans to the U-shaped glacial trough whose vertical walls, once objects of veneration from the Valley floor, have become celebrated as one of the world's supreme rock climbing challenges. The most daring and skilled come here to climb free solo—scaling cliffs alone, without a partner, and without the protection of ropes or other climbing equipment. The premier challenge is the sheer face of El Capitan (The Captain), the largest single granite rock on Earth, which rises 3,593 feet above the Valley floor. Another especially regarded among climbers is 13,114-foot Mount Lyell, Yosemite's highest granite peak.

Waterfalls abound, many descending in one massive sheet, without the interruption of ledges or outcroppings. The longest plunges are the three falls that make up Yosemite Falls (14.5 times higher than Niagara Falls): Sentinel, Ribbon, and Silver Strand. The trail from the Valley floor that follows Bridalveil Creek up to the translucent pool at the foot of 620-foot Bridalveil Fall is one of the park's most popular strolls. Supplied by the melting of perennially heavy high-country snowpack, the

Ribbons of morning mist lace ponderosa pines in Yosemite National Park, California. Naturalist John Muir's advocacy led to Yosemite's designation as a national park in 1890 and to the inclusion of Yosemite Valley and Mariposa Grove in 1906.

falls usually reach their peak flows in early April and May. During winter, the cascades become draperies of ice; at the base of Upper Yosemite Falls, a cone of ice once built up to some 300 feet high.

The park's 1,189 square miles are etched with more than 800 miles of hiking and horseback trails. (Horses may be rented at White Wolf on the way to Tuolumne Meadows or in the Valley.) Among favored destinations is Tenaya Lake, popular with swimmers, windsurfers, and sailboaters. In winter, thousands of downhill and cross-country skiers converge at nearby Badger Pass, along with snowshoe hikers and ice skaters. Most of those who make the drive up to Glacier Point in summer come for the experience of looking straight down 3,200 feet to the Valley floor; a few, however, arrive with hang gliders atop their cars. A long hike, using cables as a handrail, will take you to the precipice of Half Dome, Yosemite's most distinctive geologic feature. Resembling a colossal boulder neatly cleaved in two—its other half was ground away by the glaciers that gouged the Valley—its massive, famously photographed vertical face often takes on a rosy hue as sunset nears. The Valley's scenic rival is Tuolumne Meadows, the park's most popular hiking destination, with a 330-site campground. A high-country basin framed by soaring crags and glacier-shaped peaks, it was once an important deer hunting ground of the Mono Indians.

The remoteness of Yosemite Valley discouraged logging and spared its renowned sequoias, some of them perhaps 3,000 years old. The largest grove is Mariposa (Spanish for "butterfly"), where one tree known as the Grizzly Giant extends a branch more than six feet in diameter—a girth greater than the trunks of the largest trees found east of the Mississippi. A natural arboretum, the park supports 36 other tree species, including the ubiquitous California black oak and ponderosa pine, and the white-bark pine, whose pale trunks grace some of Ansel Adams's most beautiful Yosemite photographs. It is a perfumed garden as well; some liken the scent of crushed Jeffrey pine twigs to vanilla, while others mention pineapple. Dogwoods and azaleas bloom in May, followed by several months of black-eyed Susans, cow parsnip, lupine, goldenrod, and other wildflowers, which debut in the foothills and later burst open at higher elevations.

Despite heavy human traffic, Yosemite Valley still abounds in wildlife. (At the turn of the last century, Muir reported seeing panthers here.) Most famous—some would say notorious—are black bears, pesky nuisances to campers who neglect to keep foodstuffs out of their reach. Numerous too are the mule deer, coyotes (whose distinctive yelps echo through the evening stillness), and yellow-bellied marmots. Bighorn sheep were reintroduced in 1986 and now thrive. The census of the park's bird population lists more than 240 species, among which the great gray owl and the golden eagle provide visitors with perhaps the most dramatic sightings. Another notable is the peregrine falcon, the dive-bombing raptor whose presence here was bolstered by the successful rearing of captive-born chicks introduced into nests on El Capitan in 1981.

Since 1927, the park has boasted one of America's most distinctive hotels. Reminiscent of a grand hunting lodge, combining both native and art deco motifs, the Ahwahnee—the Miwok name for Yosemite Valley—was designated a national historic landmark in 1987. Every Christmas season, the hotel presents the Bracebridge Dinner, a multicourse feast complete with Renaissance costumes, music, and theatrics. The event is

226

so popular that reservations must be made at least a year in advance. In January, the Ahwahnee hosts Yosemite Chefs' Holidays, a series of weekend-long cooking classes presented by many of California's most celebrated culinary stars.

Most visitors, however, still come seeking restorative communion with nature. A reservation system now handles ever increasing requests for campsites, and shuttle buses have replaced campers' vehicles as the primary mode of transport within the Valley and other popular destinations. The result is a model for ensuring that Muir's "tired, nerve-shaken" legions will always experience a refreshing respite in this, his most-beloved wilderness "fountain of life."

SEQUOIA–KINGS CANYON NATIONAL PARKS

Of all the things on Earth that exhibit some form of what we call life, one of the largest is the sequoia tree, perhaps named after the Cherokee who devised an alphabet for his tribe. Thirty-six groves of this member of the redwood family cluster in these parks, including seven of the tallest and broadest trees known to exist. Sequoias have grown as tall as 26-story buildings and have achieved a girth at their base of 113 feet. Nineteenth-century loggers sometimes labored more than a week to fell

Moonrise bronzes the weathered face of 7,569-foot El Capitan north of the Merced River. On the south side of Yosemite Valley, snow dusts the ragged granite of Cathedral Rocks.

just one sequoia. In 1876, a section of one mammoth was shipped to Philadelphia for exhibition, where astonished viewers took it for a hoax.

"Perhaps more than half of all the Big Trees have been sold," wrote their most articulate protector in 1901, "and are now in the hands of speculators and mill men." Evidence of John Muir's sad estimate endures at Big Stump Basin, once the site of the world's largest stand and now a sobering cemetery of colossal stumps. Among the survivors here are trees that some botanists date back to the dynasties of ancient Egypt. Among the most imposing are those at Grant Grove, including the 275-foot-tall General Sherman, with a circumference of 102.6 feet, flanked by a trio of burly giants—General Grant, Washington, and Lincoln—ranging between 267 and 246 feet tall, with circumferences from 98.3 to 101 feet, and still growing.

Sequoia's 404,909 acres and Kings Canyon's 458,832 acres—more than 1,350 square miles combined—include some of the most inspiring wilderness in the Sierra Nevada. The topography, wonderfully diverse, is a hiker's mecca: snowcapped granite cliffs, mile-deep glacial canyons, nearly a thousand alpine lakes, waterfalls, and three stretches of Wild and Scenic white-water rivers. Switchback trails in the uptilted Mineral King Wilderness are well-known for their stunning views. Eight hundred miles of trails cover the backcountry, enabling backpackers and horseback riders to retreat far from roads.

The parks' valleys, often crowded with incense cedar, ponderosa pine, black and live oaks, and sugar pine, are seldom without the chatter of chickarees, pinecone-clipping Douglas squirrels, and myriad species of birds. Wildflowers brighten the landscape with sparks of color in spring.

Among park wonders is Crystal Cave, discovered in 1918, a showcase of elaborate marble—not limestone—stalactites and draperies. A twisting nine-mile road leads to the one-hour tour. Over everything looms 14,494-foot Mount Whitney, the highest point in the lower 48 states, known to film buffs as the backdrop for Humphrey Bogart's demise in the 1941 adventure classic *High Sierra*.

King of this country is the black bear, which can also be brown, cinnamon, or blond, and roams the foothills and high country, living mostly on grasses, berries, acorns, and insects. Another ubiquitous local is the marmot, notorious for gnawing through the radiator hoses and wires of visitors' vehicles. With the exception of snowshoe walks, most naturalist-led activities take place in summer.

Archaeological evidence, including rock paintings, suggests that Native Americans settled here as early as A.D. 1350 and enjoyed an uncontested domain for nearly 500 years, until the California Gold Rush. Sequoia National Park was established in 1890 and was initially administered by the U.S. Cavalry to put muscle behind the government's determination to stop the felling of sequoias and to halt the intensive sheep grazing.

Adjoining Kings Canyon was designated a park in 1940, and since then it and Sequoia have been administered together. Public awareness of their exceptional qualities has generated enduring grass-roots conservationist sentiment that would gratify John Muir.

In the year 2000, President Bill Clinton designated 328,000 acres of the Sierra Nevada as the Giant Sequoia National Monument, which will further federal protection of the trees and the land around them.

Conifers climb jagged granite ridges of Kings Canyon in California's Sequoia-Kings Canyon National Parks. The preserves on the western slopes of the Sierra Nevada protect the most extensive groves of sequoias in the world.

Lichen-encrusted snags fence a giant sequoia in Sequoia-Kings Canyon (opposite). The evergreens, largest living things on Earth, live more than 2,000 years; some measure 36 feet in diameter.

COAST REDWOODS, BLUFFS, BEACHES

REDWOOD NAT. PARK, Calif.

REDWOOD NATIONAL PARK

"God has cared for these trees," wrote John Muir of sequoias a century ago, "saved them from drought, disease, avalanches and a thousand straining, leveling tempests and floods. But he cannot save them from fools."

These works of the ages, as they have been called, must once have seemed an inexhaustible presence. When European mariners first reconnoitered North America's West Coast in the 1500s, redwoods grew widely. It is believed that perhaps four species claimed some two million acres, their shady groves carpeted, then as now, with rhododendron, woodland iris, huckleberry, clumps of shamrock-shaped sorrel, and groves of sword ferns whose saw-toothed fronds can grow taller than a man.

Today, North America knows but two survivors of the redwood family: the coast redwood, which grows along the Pacific from just south of California's Monterey Peninsula north to southwestern Oregon at elevations from sea level to 3,000 feet, and the giant sequoia, which thrives inland between about 3,000 and 7,500 feet.

Had Muir's like-minded allies not founded the Save-the-Redwoods League in 1918 to champion the establishment of national and state parks in California, it is almost certain that his beloved giants would have been logged to extinction.

Although the names "redwood" and "sequoia" are often used interchangeably, they refer to different trees. The confusion arises in part from their botanical classifications: Both were originally classified by the genus *Sequoia*—the coast redwood as *Sequoia sempervirens*, ("trees giant, evergreen"); the giant sequoia, at first, as *Sequoia gigantea*. The tendency of coast redwoods to outgrow giant sequoias in height by about 50 feet leads many to assume that the former, and not its stocky sibling, is the "giant" of the pair. The distinction is further blurred by the fact that the Golden State's official tree, the "California Redwood," includes both, making no distinction between the two.

Both, indeed, inspire awe. The park's tallest coast redwood—also believed to be the world's tallest tree—is the National Geographic tree, a 365.5-footer estimated at more than 600 years of age. Amply watered by coastal fogs that produce rainlike dripping from the trees' needled boughs, *Sequoia sempervirens* can grow to diameters of 22 feet and support as much as 1.6 million pounds—three times the weight of a steam locomotive. North America's fastest growing conifer (or cone-bearing tree), it is virtually impervious to disease and boring insects, insulated by a thick bark from all but the most intense fires and able to withstand lightning strikes—among the reasons some have endured 2,000 years.

The giant sequoia is shorter and stockier than its statuesque relative—the tallest example known rises 307 feet—but its massive trunk has been known to reach 41 feet across, supporting more than 2.5 million pounds

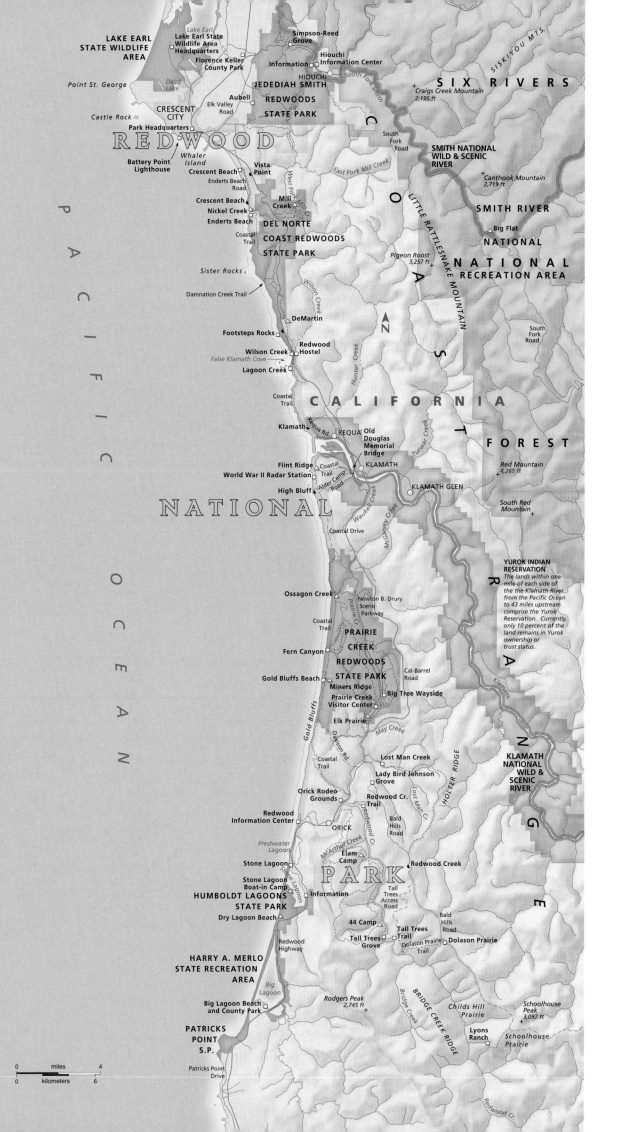

LAKE EARL
STATE WILDLIFE
AREA

Lake Earl

Lake Earl State
Wildlife Area
Headquarters

Florence Keller
County Park

Point St. George

Dead
Lake

Information

Simpson-Reed
Grove

Hiouchi
Information Center

HIOUCHI

South Fork Smith

SIX RIVERS

Craigs Creek Mountain
2,195 ft

SISKIYOU MTS.

Castle Rock

CRESCENT
CITY

Aubell
Elk Valley
Road

JEDEDIAH SMITH
REDWOODS
STATE PARK

South
Fork
Road

SMITH NATIONAL
WILD & SCENIC
RIVER

Canthook Mountain
2,719 ft

Park Headquarters

REDWOOD

Battery Point
Lighthouse

Whaler
Island

Crescent Beach

Vista
Point

SMITH RIVER

NATIONAL

Enderts Beach
Road

East Fork Mill Creek

Mill
Creek

West Fork Mill Creek

Big Flat

Crescent Beach

Nickel Creek

Enderts Beach

DEL NORTE
COAST REDWOODS
STATE PARK

Coastal
Trail

Pigeon Roost
3,257 ft

NATIONAL
RECREATION AREA

Sister Rocks

Wilson Creek

Damnation Creek Trail

DeMartin

Footsteps Rocks

Wilson Creek

False Klamath Cove

Redwood
Hostel

Lagoon Creek

Hunter Creek

CALIFORNIA

Coastal
Trail

Requa Rd.

Klamath

REQUA

Old
Douglas
Memorial
Bridge

FOREST

Red Mountain
4,265 ft

Flint Ridge

World War II Radar Station

Coastal
Trail

Alder Camp
Road

KLAMATH

Turwar Creek

High Bluff

KLAMATH GLEN

South Red
Mountain

NATIONAL

Waukell Creek

McGarvey Creek

Coastal Drive

YUROK INDIAN
RESERVATION
The lands within one
mile of each side of
the Klamath River
from the Pacific Ocean
to 43 miles upstream
comprise the Yurok
Reservation. Currently,
only 10 percent of the
land remains in Yurok
ownership or
trust status.

Ossagon Creek

Newton B. Drury
Scenic
Parkway

Prairie Cr.

Coastal
Trail

PRAIRIE
CREEK
REDWOODS
STATE PARK

Cal-Barrel
Road

Fern Canyon

Klamath

Gold Bluffs Beach

Miners Ridge

Prairie Creek
Visitor Center

Big Tree Wayside

Gold Bluffs

Elk Prairie

May Creek

KLAMATH
NATIONAL
WILD &
SCENIC
RIVER

Davison Rd.

Coastal
Trail

Lost Man Creek

HOLTER RIDGE

Lost Man Cr.

Lady Bird Johnson
Grove

Orick Rodeo
Grounds

Redwood Cr.
Trail

Redwood
Information Center

ORICK

Redwood Cr.

Bald
Hills
Road

PACIFIC OCEAN

Freshwater
Lagoon

McArthur Creek

Elam
Camp

PARK

Stone Lagoon

Redwood Creek

Stone Lagoon
Boat-in Camp

Stone Lagoon

HUMBOLDT LAGOONS
STATE PARK

Information

Tall Trees
Access
Road

Dry Lagoon Beach

44 Camp

Tall Trees
Trail

Bald
Hills
Road

Tall Trees
Grove

Dolason Prairie
Trail

Dolason Prairie

Redwood
Highway

HARRY A. MERLO
STATE RECREATION
AREA

Big
Lagoon

Rodgers Peak
2,745 ft

BRIDGE CREEK

Childs Hill
Prairie

Schoolhouse
Peak
3,097 ft

Big Lagoon Beach
and County Park

BRIDGE CREEK RIDGE

Lyons
Ranch

Schoolhouse
Prairie

PATRICKS
POINT
S.P.

Patricks Point
Drive

Redwood Cr.

0   miles   4

0   kilometers   6

LITTLE RATTLESNAKE MOUNTAIN

of wood. *Sequoiadendron giganteum* (as it is now known) also lives longer. In 1919 a botanist examined the stump of a behemoth felled by loggers and counted 3,220 annual growth rings; when the Romans founded London, the tree was halfway through its 14th century.

Western America's primordial redwoods remained inviolate until the mid-1800s, when fortune hunters lured by California's Gold Rush saw in the shaggy coastal monarchs a fortune far more accessible than placer gold: termite and fire-resistant lumber. (The giant sequoias were initially considered too brittle for commercial exploitation.)

Today, only 45 percent of that forest remains—roughly 144,000 acres. Of that remnant, however, some 6,000 acres are privately owned and, to the dismay of preservationists, are subject to logging. Fortunately, redwoods are exceptionally tenacious, sending up shoots from their stumps and roots that, left alone, will grow tall and strong within a few decades. California's state parks are home to thousands of acres of second-growth *sempervirens*, some already quite large, intermixed with Douglas fir, western hemlock, oak, madrone (with its distinctive, peeling orange bark), and bay laurel.

Ancillary benefits of Muir's legacy are wildlife habitats so fecund that they can support sportfishing and hunting while ensuring species survival. Anglers come to Redwood National Park for rainbow and cutthroat trout, as well as silver and king salmon.

Prairie Creek Redwoods State Park is known for its herd of Roosevelt elk, including thousand-pound bulls that carry magnificent racks of antlers from spring to fall. An abundance of fauna supports a lively traffic in jet-boat sightseeing tours along the Klamath River year-round.

As this region straddles one of North America's four major flyways—routes flown in spring and fall by millions of migratory birds and waterfowl representing some 370 species—the park is a nesting place for cormorants, murres, mallards, puffins, blue herons, and spotted owls, among many others. Seasonal migrations occur offshore as well, attracting thousands of whale-watchers to the marine mammals' coast-hugging December-January southerly swims and their March-April return to Alaskan feeding grounds. Between sightings, visitors content themselves with the sheer beauty of the broken, rocky coastline, probably the result of sliding tectonic plates that collided here, uplifting strata from beneath the sea. This ancient upheaval left a rockhound's treasury; knowledgeable scavengers especially prize green serpentine and stones flecked with gold.

For many, though, the most appropriate wilderness experience in Redwood is a backcountry hike, particularly along the beautiful Coastal Trail, which raises the possibility of glimpsing black bear and black-tailed deer. (Mountain lions inhabit this region as well but are generally wary of humans.) The trail following Redwood Creek, whose sandbars make excellent campsites, wanders through Tall Trees Grove. The Fern Canyon Trail leads to a lush emerald grotto where a half dozen species of ferns cling to 50-foot-high vertical walls.

Some visitors find the frequent rain and fog that nurture these forests a nuisance, and poison oak can engender painful allergic rashes. During storms, the great trees may shed large lower branches, known as widow-makers. But most who wander even a short way into the park's ancient groves embrace a broader perspective, as they behold the primordial Earth, abiding in all its perfect chaos.

Sunshine sifts through coast redwoods in Lady Bird Johnson Grove of California's Redwood National Park (opposite). It was established to protect old-growth coast redwoods; the world's tallest trees, they take 400 years to mature and reach heights of 300 feet.

Twilight paints the Pacific off Del Norte Coast Redwoods State Park, one of three California preserves within the national park's boundaries. Waves pound cliffs and sea stacks along eight miles of wild coast in Del Norte.

PRONGHORN, WATERFOWL, BIGHORN SHEEP

HART MOUNTAIN
NAT. ANTELOPE
REFUGE, Oreg.

KLAMATH BASIN
NAT. WILDLIFE REFUGES,
Oreg., Calif.

HART MOUNTAIN NATIONAL ANTELOPE REFUGE

The graceful pronghorn is the last surviving member of a family that traces back some 20 million years and exists on no other continent. Though known as "American antelope goat," it is actually neither of the two. It is, however, the only animal in the world with branched, lyre-shaped horns—they are not antlers—and the only one that sheds its horns as if they were antlers. The fastest animal in North America, it can sprint up to 50 miles an hour. Its speed, combined with protruding eyes that enable it to discern small moving objects four miles away, makes it one of the most elusive game animals known—an advantage here, as hunting is one of Hart Mountain National Antelope Refuge's attractions.

The 275,000-acre high-desert refuge northeast of Lakeview in southern Oregon—its elevations range from 4,500 to 8,065 feet—supports about 1,800 pronghorn, 800 mule deer, and 500 California bighorn sheep (reintroduced in 1956), along with coyotes, bobcats, badgers, quail, partridges, and regally plumed sage grouse, known for their oft-filmed foot-stamping, wing-flapping courtship dances. Hart Mountain is a massive fault-block ridge rising like a section of broken sidewalk, its west side 3,600 feet above the Warner Valley. Its low vegetation is tufted by 12 species of sagebrush and juniper trees surrounded by wild gooseberry and native bunch grasses. Aspen, willow, and ponderosa pine flourish in canyons and along the broken rock rims, where songbirds serenade horseback riders, hikers, and overnight backpackers.

Above, bald eagles ride thermals, night hawks circle, and peregrine falcons dive in a never ending hunt for food. (Starvation is a leading cause of death among raptors.) Redband trout and threatened Lahontan cutthroat trout dart like swift shadows in the refuge's pellucid streams.

In the early 19th century, there were an estimated 40 million pronghorn roaming the continent—nearly as many as there were American bison. Commercial hunters killed them by the thousands, however, for use as bait to poison wolves and coyotes, a slaughter that by the 1920s had reduced the number of pronghorn to about 20,000. A citizen outcry ensued; in 1936 President Franklin D. Roosevelt created this refuge, the summer range where pronghorn bear their young, from public lands.

Hart Mountain works in tandem with the 575,000-acre Sheldon Antelope Range across the Nevada border, where the animals winter. In the early 1900s, in an effort to reverse more than a century of damage to streambeds, vegetation, and the wildlife they sustain, cattle grazing on Hart Mountain refuge lands was discontinued until the year 2009.

Remote and wild, with unpaved roads, unmaintained trails, and only rudimentary campgrounds, Hart Mountain holds rich rewards of solitude and wildlife viewing for those willing to brave primitive conditions.

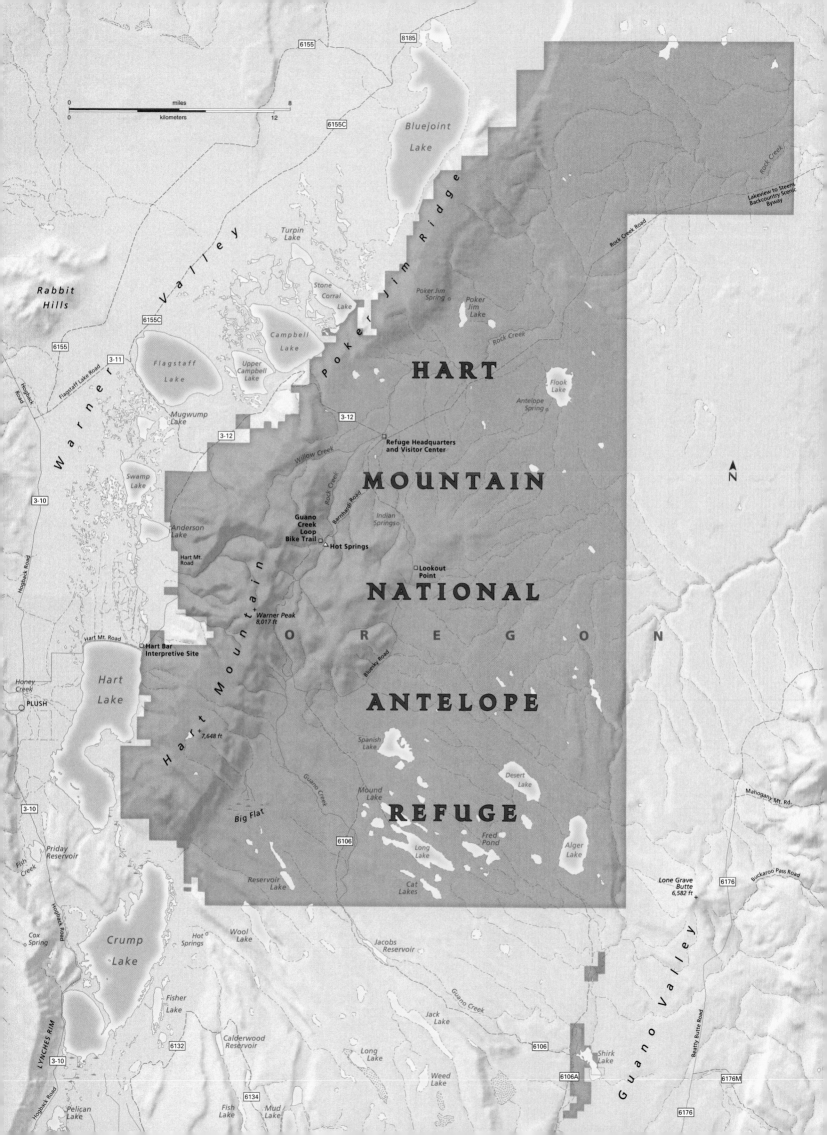

Tundra swans feed in sun-stained shallows of Klamath Basin National Wildlife Refuges. The birds, which migrate from the Arctic fringes of the continent, winter by the thousands on the shallow ponds, lakes, and marshes of Klamath. The complex embraces six wildlife refuges on the Oregon-California border.

KLAMATH BASIN NATIONAL WILDLIFE REFUGES

Embracing 192,000 acres in northern California and southern Oregon, six refuges in the Klamath Basin support the largest seasonal concentration of waterfowl on the continent—433 species of resident and migratory wildlife. The arrival of migrants to its extensive marshlands includes an abundance of ducks and geese that draw hunters from around the nation.

In autumn, the population of birds here peaks at over a million, a remarkably dramatic visual phenomenon that hints of what this place was during autumns a century past when perhaps six million gathered. After 1905, however, dams, ditches, and other alterations built as part of the Klamath Reclamation Project on what was then Klamath and Tule Lakes diminished wetland areas and consequently reduced the number of waterfowl they could support. The refuges' habitats, however, still reflect the original range of environments—freshwater marsh, grassy meadow, coniferous forest, sagebrush, and juniper grassland. Precipitous rocky defiles and cliffs provide a safe haven for mule deer and coyotes.

During spring migration, at its height in early March, white pelicans and honking Canada geese come here to nest. By summer, young birds proliferate, with downy grebe hatchlings riding on their parents' backs. The refuges' most dramatic spectacle, which some early witnesses likened to a biblical Eden, begins in autumn with the arrival of northern pintails, mallards, widgeons, black brants, greater white-fronted geese, and snow

geese by the hundreds of thousands. Snowy and great egrets, osprey, double-crested cormorants, white-faced ibises, and great blue herons depart by late October and are soon replaced by nearly a million mallards, green-winged and cinnamon teals, sandhill cranes, and tundra swans, which darken the sky as they fly en masse against the white backdrop of snow-mantled Mount Shasta. Raptors rule from September through February, when as many as a thousand bald (meaning white-headed) eagles, the largest number in the lower 48, come to winter. The perimeter of Bear Valley Refuge in Oregon is known as a site for viewing the bald eagles' sunrise "fly out," when perhaps a hundred or more leave their roosts in search of prey. The nation's symbol shares its habitat with golden eagles, eight species of hawks, and eight kinds of owls.

Although automobile touring of this waterfowl haven complex is possible—there are two ten-mile-long routes in the adjacent Tule Lake and Lower Klamath Refuges—the best way to explore is by boat. The most extensive and diverse of several canoe trails is on the Upper Klamath Refuge in Oregon; seven blinds offer superb photography opportunities.

Despite President Theodore Roosevelt's establishment in 1908 of the Lower Klamath Refuge as the nation's first waterfowl refuge, fully 80 percent of Oregon's and California's historic wetlands—about 185,000 acres of lakes and marshes—were lost to development. The enclave that remains protects the self-renewing growth of red goosefoot, smartweed, hardstem bulrush, and sago pondweed that sustains the diverse bird population.

CASCADE LAKES, MOUNTAINS, WATERFALLS

MT. BAKER-SNOQUALMIE NAT. FOREST, Wash.
NORTH CASCADES NAT. PARK, Wash.
MT. RAINIER NAT. PARK, Wash.
MT. HOOD NAT. FOREST, Oreg.
CRATER LAKE NAT. PARK, Oreg.

CRATER LAKE NATIONAL PARK

About 7,700 years ago, an 11,000-foot-high volcano erupted in the Cascade Range of what is now southern Oregon. The blast was unimaginably violent, perhaps a hundred times more powerful than the 1980 explosion of Mount St. Helens, propelling a colossal amount of pumice and hot ash into the air. The gray fallout buried landscapes for miles around and was blown north to Canada. In the eruption's aftermath, the top 5,000 feet of Mount Mazama collapsed into its fiery magma chamber, forming a caldera with a rim measuring some 33 miles around. From the caldera's depths, two cinder cones erupted and flows formed a central platform. Over a period of centuries, the caldera filled with 4.6 trillion gallons of rainfall and snowmelt, creating 1,932-foot-deep Crater Lake—one of the world's deepest—and turning its highest volcanic cone into Wizard Island. The lake's exceptional beauty derives in part from its vivid blue color, a phenomenon resulting from the water's depth and extreme purity. (Little organic matter or mineral content interferes with the penetration and scattering of the sun's blue spectrum wavelengths.)

Ancestors of Klamath and Modoc Indians witnessed this pyrotechnic cataclysm—one of the greatest geologic explosions in human history. Traditional lore of the Klamath people on this subject parallels geologic events. According to that lore, the eruption was a battle between Skell, the god of the Upper World and Llao, god of a Below World. Native Americans regarded the exquisite sapphire lake as a sacred and mysterious place. Not until 1853 did the first white men, a group of gold prospectors, climb to the rim of this hollowed-out mountain and peer down in astonishment at its azure lake a thousand feet below.

"All ingenuity of nature seems to have been exerted to the fullest capacity to build a grand awe-inspiring temple, the likes of which the world has never seen before," wrote William Gladstone Steel who, in 1902, saw his dream realized with the establishment of a 183,244-acre national park here. How a Kansas schoolboy came to champion a lake hidden in a remote part of Oregon is a story of serendipity. In 1870, the young Steel read a description of Crater Lake in a newspaper that had been wrapped around his school lunch; it made an indelible impression. He and his family moved to Oregon 2 years later, but 13 years would pass before he finally stood on the caldera's edge, taking in firsthand the six-mile expanse of water. The panorama affected him so much that for the next 17 years, he used most of his personal assets to bring Crater Lake under federal stewardship—lecturing and lobbying, and at one point stocking the lake with baby rainbow trout, which he carried down from the rim by the bucketful.

Collared by conifer forests slanting down steep 2,000-foot inclines, Crater Lake attracts half a million visitors each year, most during the Cascades' short summer season, when traffic on the 33-mile Rim Drive

and its more than 20 scenic overlooks can be heavy. Many with time to stay spend it at one of Lost Creek Campground's 16 tent sites, or in Mazama Campground, which has 217 sites. Wizard Island and Cleetwood Cove are perennially good trout and kokanee salmon fishing grounds. Between the Fourth of July and Labor Day, hiking traffic peaks on backcountry trails, particularly the park's 33-mile share of the famed Pacific Crest Trail, which wends its way from Mexico to Canada, and the trails ascending Mount Scott, Garfield Peak, and Crater Peak.

Ranger-led walks, offered in summer and winter, focus on natural history. If you opt for winter, be prepared to use snowshoes—snowfall here

Still waters do run deep in Crater Lake. The caldera of an ancient volcano in southern Oregon, it filled with snow, rain, and springwater to a depth of 1,932 feet— deepest lake in the United States. Wizard Island, a volcanic cone, pokes above the surface near the western shore.

averages 533 inches annually, some of the heaviest in the country, and drifts can linger through July. Many of the park's facilities close down in winter, but cross-country skiers of every level flock to Crater Lake to backcountry ski or use several of the marked but ungroomed trails, patrolled by ski volunteers on weekends.

Almost 600 plant species have established themselves here since Mount Mazama's explosive decapitation. This is evergreen country, and in the lower elevations there are ponderosa pines and lodgepole pines with sugar pines and white firs. Higher up—most of the park ranges from 5,000 feet and higher—Shasta red firs and mountain hemlocks flourish and on the rim are the gnarled, contorted shapes of whitebark pines, twisted by their never ending battle with the wind and snow. In July and August, meadows come alive with a tapestry of phlox, shooting star, paintbrush, lupine, columbine, five kinds of monkeyflower, and other wildflowers.

Most of the park's 60 mammal species are elusive and seldom seen by motorists; however, backcountry hikers stand a good chance of glimpsing black bears, Rocky Mountain and Roosevelt elk, mule deer, yellow-bellied marmots, pine martens, porcupines, and snowshoe hares.

Oregon's long high-country winters send all but the hardiest birds flying south; the winter population includes Clark's nutcracker, Steller's jays, and ruffed grouse. Come spring, horned larks, spotted owls, hawks, and black-backed and three-toed woodpeckers return in force. A rare but riveting sight is that of a golden or bald eagle soaring above the caldera, riding its updrafts on wings spanning seven feet.

NORTH CASCADES NATIONAL PARK COMPLEX

The essence of the 504,781-acre North Cascades National Park and the Ross Lake and Lake Chelan Recreation Areas is water—melting off glaciers and surging down boulder-filled streams, filling sapphire lakes, feeding rivers, and plunging from great heights in wind-blown plumes. The sheer number of waterfalls in this part of Washington gave the Cascades its name. Among the prettiest, say many, are Ladder Creek, which is fronted by a suspension bridge, 242-foot Gorge Creek Falls on the North Cascades Highway, and feathery Rainbow Falls, which plummets 312 feet in the Lake Chelan area.

Meltwater from some 700 alpine glaciers in the northern Cascades is crucial to the region's ecology. The largest, including Boston, Redoubt, Challenger, and Inspiration, scour and gouge the landscape while influencing vegetation, delivering minerals to the ecosystem, and keeping streams running fast even during summer dry spells.

Archaeologists believe that ancestors of the present-day Coast Salish and other local tribes inhabited the North Cascades, at least in summer, for some 10,000 years. Henry Custer was the first European to describe what came to be known as "the North American Alps," declaring in 1859: "Nowhere do the mountain masses and peaks present such strange, fantastic, dauntless and startling outlines as here."

Within ten years, recreational climbers were taking on their challenges. Many major summits, including Dome, Bonanza, Goode, Formidable, and Magic were not climbed until the 1930s, and the difficulties of other peaks reflect in the names given to Mount Terror, Mount Despair, and Damnation Peak.

North Cascades has two unpaved roads for internal access. The North Cascades Highway, Highway 20, starts at Lake Ross and crosses to Winthrop on the east side. It must be closed in winter for about five months. Solitude and peace, however, are what appeal most to the backpackers and horseback riders who roam the park's more than 350-mile network of trails. Winding through evergreen timberland to backcountry campsites and fly-fishing streams and lakes, some—in the Stehekin Valley—are marked in winter for cross-country skiers. Snowmobilers use Highway 20. Winter or summer, arguably the best way to experience the peace prevailing within the shaggy evergreen depths of this sprawling preserve is to trek through

Glacier-draped sentinel, 9,131-foot Mount Shuksan guards the western reaches of North Cascades National Park in western Washington. Only two unpaved roads lead into the park. Its wild and rugged peaks lure hikers, backpackers, and mountaineers.

old-growth forests that sprouted five or six centuries ago—stands of grand-fatherly Douglas fir or millennium-old western red cedars—towering above younger, shade-tolerant hemlocks and, at higher elevations, sparser forests of Pacific silver fir. Flowering plants flourish—more than 1,000 species coexist with a myriad of other plants so numerous they have not yet been completely inventoried. The list of year-round birds is about 30 species, with 76 species breeding here, and another 100 or so sojourning seasonally. Besides the falling of water and the sigh of wind, the only natural noise in the forests is theirs—particularly the chattering of gray jays, the tapping of woodpeckers, and the delicate piping of black-capped chickadees. At the higher elevations white-tailed ptarmigans may explode from the brush when anyone approaches, and the dipper, or water ouzel, dives into the park's bone-chilling rivers and streams to stalk the bottom in search of aquatic insects.

Although the reservoir at Ross Lake permits boating, so much of the rugged park is beyond the convenient reach of casual visitors that their curiosity supports a small industry in scenic flights by aircraft. Other out-fitters profit from the park's superb white-water rafting streams.

Few visitors, however they may arrive, are fortunate enough to even glimpse the mammals at the top of the North Cascades food chain: the gray wolf and the mountain lion (also called cougar). Black bears like-wise keep their distance, and standoffish mountain goats are likely to be seen only as distant daubs of white against gray mountain faces, a reminder that one need not venture far into this enclave to encounter the unmarked boundary of what 19th-century writers called the Great Wild.

Incandescent shrubs
light Heather Meadows
in late September in
Washington's Mount
Baker-Snoqualmie
National Forest.
On the western slopes
of the North Cascades,
the forest is heavily used
by Seattle-area residents.
A trail off Mount Baker
Scenic Byway leads hikers
to Heather Meadows.

MOUNT BAKER-SNOQUALMIE NATIONAL FOREST

Some have compared the North Cascades to the European Alps, and although Europe's famed mountains are not volcanic, there are striking similarities, including dramatically precipitous inclines and lushly flowered mountain meadows. The Mount Baker-Snoqualmie National Forest's 1.7 million acres embrace some 140 miles of the western slopes of the Cascade Range, ramping up steeply from sea level to summits nearly two miles high, from the northwestern corner of the state south to Mount Rainier National Park. More than a hundred active glaciers continue the geologic sculpting that initiated these rugged contours during the last ice age.

About half of the forest's timber is old growth. Douglas fir, western hemlock, and red cedar of remarkable girth and stature blanket the slopes to about 3,000 feet. The next 2,000 feet bristle with Pacific silver fir and grand fir. At lower elevations, a lush and exuberant variety of ferns thrives alongside trailing blackberry, salmonberry, devil's club, rhododendron, some wild ginger, vanilla leaf, and the rare cascara. In late spring, meadows burst into color as heather, glacier lilies, shooting stars, queen's cup, honeysuckle, bleeding heart, and dozens of other wildflowers bloom.

Though but a short drive from downtown Seattle—part of the forest is within King County—this is unusually wild terrain. Eight sections of the forest (about 42 percent of its area) are designated wildernesses, where motor vehicles and mechanized equipment are not allowed.

Surrounding the wildernesses are vast tracts of forestland just as rugged and to all appearances just as pristine, latticed by a 1,500-mile network of trails. Most trails outside wilderness areas are from three

to five miles long; within the wild zones, they typically follow (and occasionally ford) rivers and streams and link primitive campsites. One advantage of high-elevation camping here is the absence of poisonous snakes, although backpackers are likely to meet giant or long-toed salamanders and will almost certainly receive nocturnal visits from foraging field mice and marmots.

For mountaineers, Mount Baker (at 10,778 feet the tallest challenge), Glacier Peak, Sloan Peak, and 6,852-foot Whitehorse Mountain (the lowest) offer ascents ranging in difficulty from easy to extreme—particularly in late summer when snowbridges over crevasses melt away.

As the season tilts toward autumn, hunters arrive in search of deer, Roosevelt elk, black bears, mountain goats, and grouse, which share the dense forest groves and thickets with bobcats, cougars, and rabbits. Of some 150 bird species identified here, the two most visitors hope to glimpse are the golden eagle and the bald eagle.

Washington's heavy snows and rainfall keep seven major rivers flowing through the forest year-round, none prettier than the stretches of the Skagit River and its tributaries—158 miles in all—designated Wild and Scenic. Come spring, white-water enthusiasts take to canoes, kayaks, and rafts to shoot rapids and speedy stretches whose flow is accelerated by snowmelt from upcountry watersheds. Overnighting in campgrounds or rustic lodges, many travelers by watercraft pause en route for interludes of fishing for rainbow, cutthroat, and steelhead trout and salmon.

And, as its name implies, the 365,000-acre Alpine Lakes Wilderness, shared with Wenatchee National Forest, sparkles with nearly 700 lakes and ponds.

It is possible to explore the forest by car and with no exertion whatsoever. The dizzying switchbacks of the two-lane 24-mile-long Mount Baker Scenic Byway from Glacier to Artist Point on Mount Baker reward motorists with eagle-eye views of Mount Shuksan and the Nooksack Valley. The 35-mile Stevens Pass Scenic Byway crosses the crest of the range from a historic district steeped in railroad history to Leavenworth.

At the southern end of the forest, Mather Memorial Parkway's 75 miles feature views of old-growth forests, grazing elk, and Mount Rainier's immense, perpetually snowy summit. In midsummer, drivers often stop to pick huckleberries, wild blackberries, and thimbleberries. In autumn, particularly after rains, mushroom aficionados poke about the forest floor to gather chanterelles, boletes, and corals.

Winter arrives in early November, blanketing the forest's four downhill ski areas with snowpack that can measure as deep as 20 feet and last into May. Downhill skiers favor Mount Baker's runs (where Olympians have trained). For those who prefer solitude and wilderness scenery to high-speed exhilaration, there are snowshoeing and cross-country skiing on groomed trails.

For those who push through these deeply silent forests in winter, the modern world slips temporarily away, in a snowscape that appears as it must have in centuries past to the two dozen or so Native American tribes who made their homes here. The Yakama Nation and 16 other tribes remain active in the forest's management, their tribal leaders making decisions about wildlife habitat, watershed administration, and timber rights, preserving this legacy for all.

Shimmering snow crystals echo a lavender layer of fog below the Tatoosh Range in Mount Rainier National Park, Washington. Glaciers carved the sawtooth mountains from ancient lava flows.

MOUNT RAINIER NATIONAL PARK

"Your plan to climb Takhoma is all foolishness," the guide warned. The year was 1870, and General Hazard Stevens and Philemon B. Van Trump were determined to be the first white men to reach the summit of a peak so grand that it could be seen 200 miles away. "If you reach the great snowy dome," the Indian continued, "then a bitterly cold and furious tempest will sweep you into space like a withered leaf."

The Yakama, among several other tribes, had inhabited the foothills surrounding the 14,410-foot volcano for thousands of years, but Stevens, a Civil War hero, was not to be dissuaded. As he and his climbing partner neared the mountaintop, night was coming on. As the guide had predicted, a freezing storm descended. Facing certain death from exposure, the pair caught the smell of sulfur coming from a steam vent in the icy peak. They followed the scent to a fissure and crawled down into it, finding warmth inside a cave. The following day they emerged into clement weather, and before long they stood triumphant on Takhoma's summit.

To Stevens, however, the peak's name was Rainier—in 1792 George Vancouver proclaimed it so to honor a countryman—although Royal Navy Rear Admiral Peter Rainier was never to set eyes on his towering namesake. In 1899, President William McKinley designated the mountain and the densely forested wilderness surrounding it, now an area of 235,625 acres, America's fifth national park.

The landscape merited the honor. Twenty-six major glaciers—including Carbon, at the lowest elevation, and Emmons, the largest in the lower 48 states—and some 50 minor ice rivers slide over some 38 square miles of the park. Rainier's allure (in rosy afternoon light, it often resembles an enormous mound of melting peach ice cream) inspires whimsy as well as heroism. In 1921, a 16-member wedding party managed to replicate Stevens's feat and celebrate a marriage atop Mount Rainier. Forty years later, the mountain was deemed an appropriate training ground for the first successful American ascent of Mount Everest, in 1963. Every year, about 10,000 people set out to reach the summit; roughly half succeed.

There is considerably more to this national park, however, than its imposing centerpiece. Elsewhere in the Pacific Northwest, except in the

Olympic Peninsula's national parklands, timber harvesting has trimmed old-growth Douglas fir forests to about 15 percent of their original area. Within Rainier, however, cathedral-like groves of centuries-old western hemlocks and red cedars rise in the lowland forest, at 2,000 feet, in the Grove of the Patriarchs, their branches providing perches for hunting hawks and owls and their serene grandeur hinting of primordial Earth. Higher, Alaskan yellow cedars thrive, their massive bases garlanded by huckleberry bushes and, in spring, delicate calypso orchids. Higher still, subalpine firs reproduce by sending down roots where their drooping boughs touch the ground, sharing this chill and windy zone with white-bark pines that may be shaped into krummholz, "crooked wood" twisted and stunted by winter winds and heavy snowfall. By midsummer, however, surrounding meadows are blooming exuberantly, vibrantly colored by dozens of wildflowers—avalanche lilies, lupine, marsh marigolds, partridgefoot, magenta paintbrush being among the most vivid.

One of Mount Rainier's early advocates was the naturalist John Muir, the Sierra Club co-founder who once noted the contrast between mankind's desire "to establish a narrow line between ourselves and the feathery zeros we dare call angels" and the contrary human tendency to erect "a partition barrier of infinite width to show the rest of creation its proper place."

But within Mount Rainier's boundaries, no barriers impede the wanderings of wildlife—black bears, mountain lions, elk, wolves, mountain goats, raccoons, porcupines, and mischievous hoary marmots. Black-tailed deer have their fawns—usually twins—in June and are frequently spotted with them in early evening, grazing in the meadows. Many of the 50-odd species of mammals found here, however, are nocturnal, thus elusive and rarely seen. Birders have identified more than 125 species, including the white-tailed ptarmigan that lives at high elevations and is noted for its remarkable and rapid change of color—from dark summer feathers to snow-white winter camouflage.

The park is hugely popular and heavily visited; most of the two million people who enter arrive between the Fourth of July and Labor Day. To help them make the most of their visit, rangers and naturalists lead daily walks and illustrated campfire talks. Anglers are welcome, but Rainier's streams and rivers are not stocked, and their populations of fish (mostly trout) are relatively thin. For hikers and backcountry campers, the park's 250 miles of trails offer an extraordinary variety of challenges. The 93-mile Wonderland Trail completely encircles Mount Rainier and can take up to two weeks to hike. The five-mile (round-trip) Skyline Trail from Paradise to 6,800-foot-high Panorama Point rewards the exertion of high-country devotees with 360-degree views that remind some of alpine vistas in Austria and Switzerland. Horses are allowed on designated trails, and four backcountry camps are designed for riders and their mounts.

High snowfields and steep terrain combine to create dozens of thundering waterfalls, many of them reachable by automobile. The Sunrise Overlook, at 6,400 feet, is the loftiest in the park accessible to motorists, who line up to reconnoiter glaciers using free telescopes installed there. The Stevens Pass Road winds past Reflection Lakes. When placid, the water reflects Rainier so perfectly that in photographs it is difficult to distinguish the peak from its mirror image.

Much of the park is shuttered in winter, when snowfalls average

Fire and ice forge 14,410-foot Mount Rainier; 26 glaciers stripe the dormant volcano. Tallest peak in the Cascade Range, it forms the core of the fifth oldest national park in the United States. Hikers and backpackers enjoy 250 miles of trails across snowfields and through forests and meadows.

30 to 50 feet. (An astonishing 93 feet, a world record, fell in 1971-72.) The snow makes for excellent cross-country skiing and snowboarding. For many, Mount Rainier is loveliest when a blanket of snow softens its contours.

"Of all the fire-mountains which, like beacons, once blazed along the Pacific Coast," wrote Muir, who especially admired Rainier's forests and flowers, it was also "the noblest in form." Geologists predict it will blaze again within the next five centuries. Its serene sloped-shoulder silhouette conceals a fiery heart. After the dust settles, the ancient processes by which forests and flowers sprout from rock and lava will begin here anew.

MOUNT HOOD NATIONAL FOREST

A bit of vintage Northwest legend holds that the fabled giant logger Paul Bunyan encamped one summer evening long ago east of Oregon's Willamette River. To build a fire, he uprooted an entire forest of firs with his bare hands and at sunup covered the enormous pile of embers with rocks and soil, adding a sprinkling of snow as a final artistic touch. His creation, it is said, is perennially snowcapped Mount Hood, a volcano rising 11,239 feet.

Named after a British naval officer in 1792, the peak is surrounded by a million-acre forest that embraces six wilderness areas; one of the last stands of dense, old-growth Douglas fir and western hemlock trees in western Oregon; the dramatically deep and wide Columbia River Gorge; and two rustic retreats. One of them—Timberline Lodge—is a national historic landmark, and the other—Multnomah Lodge—has been designated a national historic building.

Dedicated anglers probably know the forest as well as many rangers, for running through it are some 500 miles of trout streams (bolstered by many trout-stocked lakes) and 227 miles of salmon and steelhead streams. Many find their way to the Clackamas, a National Wild and Scenic River, whose tumultuous white water tests rafters' skill and nerve. Perhaps even more intrepid are those who trek into the wilderness surrounding 10,497-foot Mount Jefferson with its five glaciers. Mount Jefferson is one of the steepest and most difficult climbs among Oregon's high summits.

Beneath the canopy of silver fir, red cedar, and lodgepole and ponderosa pine is a thousand-mile network of hiking trails. There are 107 campgrounds with more than 2,000 sites. A 40-mile leg of the 2,650-mile Pacific Crest Trail between Mexico and Canada links this forest with several dozen other national forests, parks, and wildernesses.

In spring, meadows burst into color with blooming dogwood, red currant, and mock orange. And great swaths of wildflowers (including 14 species found nowhere else) stipple trailsides that overlook the Columbia River's winding curves in the Columbia River Gorge National Scenic Area. There, huckleberry harvesting is a favorite summer pastime at Larch Mountain, Indian Springs, and Rainy Lake.

In winter, when downhill skiers and snowboarders flock to Mount Hood, the footpaths become cross-country ski trails. At day's end, many snow-sport fans—those with enough energy left over to hike the 1.2-mile trail—repair to Bagby Hot Springs where also, long ago, members of the Columbia River Wascos tribe and the Deschutes River Walla Walla tribe eased their weary muscles.

Within the forest live six kinds of owls—most notably the rare northern

Frost ices wild strawberry leaves near the Columbia River Gorge on the Washington-Oregon border. From the river, Mount Hood National Forest extends south more than 60 miles. Many visitors come in summer to pick berries and mushrooms.

spotted owl, a habitué of old-growth Pacific Northwest forests and thus a symbol of environmentalists' efforts to ban logging where endangered creatures breed. Above the trees, red-tailed hawks circle, while bald and golden eagles ride updrafts over mountains.

Bluebirds sing from tree limbs, while ruffed grouse and ringnecked pheasants find shelter in the underbrush below, amid the world of black bears, mountain lions, bobcats, elk, black-tailed deer, wild turkeys, and mule deer.

Motorists and bicyclists touring the Columbia River Gorge National Scenic Area pass dozens of waterfalls. The grandest of the falls, and the gorge's most popular scenic attraction, is Multnomah Falls two miles west of Oneonta, whose 620-foot dive is Oregon's highest cascade and the second highest year-round waterfall in the United States. A 0.2-mile trail—closed indefinitely because of rockfall—zigzags up a series of arduous switchbacks to a viewpoint where the waterfall tumbles into space. The easterly view up the Columbia River Gorge makes it clear how early explorers could have supposed it to be the fabled Northwest Passage across the continent. The great waterway fell short of that mark, but the vast forest running south from it has yet to disappoint anyone.

Silver fountains cascade 120 feet over basalt columns at Ramona Falls in the Mount Hood Wilderness Area of the national forest. The falls is a popular side trip off the Pacific Crest Trail, which winds 2,650 miles from Mexico to Canada.

TEMPERATE RAIN FORESTS
TIDE POOLS, ORCAS

PACIFIC RIM
NAT. PARK
RESERVE, B.C.

OLYMPIC
NAT. PARK AND
OLYMPIC NAT. FOREST,
Wash.

OLYMPIC NATIONAL PARK

"If that not be the home where dwell the Gods," wrote an 18th-century British naval captain of the peak he named Mount Olympus, "it is beautiful enough to be." So too are the other mountains standing shoulder to shoulder with the 7,965-footer, the tallest among the craggy peaks forming the mountain core of Washington's Olympic Peninsula. They overlook one of the most unspoiled ecosystems in the contiguous United States—95 percent of the park is designated wilderness—including the largest old-growth rain forests in the Northwest.

Nineteenth-century maps often depicted a blank at the heart of the peninsula, where the tight, circular cluster of the Olympics looms over Puget Sound and the Pacific Ocean. A rugged glaciated hub spoked by 13 rivers and hundreds of smaller streams, its interior was not penetrated by white men until 1878. In 1889, five men came out of the wilderness having demonstrated what a newspaper extolled as "an abundance of grit and manly vim." A number of peaks—Meany, Dana, and Lawson, among others—commemorate the publishers and editors of the *Seattle Press* who financed that expedition, which took five and a half months.

The untrammeled wilderness that those explorers beheld still exists, still decorated by numerous species of wildflowers, 1,200 other plant species, 70 species of mammals, and 300 species of birds. Eight types of wildflowers exist here and nowhere else and 20 types of animals, including among them slugs, insects, fish, a salamander, and the Olympic marmot. Had it not been for a conservation campaign waged over nearly half a century, however, they, along with much of the peninsula, might have fallen prey to the teeth of chain saws.

Salvation commenced in 1887, when President Grover Cleveland created a forest reserve of 1.5 million acres. In 1909, President Theodore Roosevelt withdrew 615,000 acres of the forest reserve where logging was allowed to establish Mount Olympus National Monument. (He acted in part to protect the habitat of a dwindling population of Roosevelt elk, a species named for him.) Meanwhile the nation's consumption of paper was rapidly increasing, and within a decade President Woodrow Wilson bowed to pressure from business interests and reduced the monument's area by about half.

Large trees were valuable commercially. To protect them, environmentalists proposed in 1935 to restore some 400,000 acres to the national monument and upgrade it to national park status. Pulp and paper manufacturers objected, warning of irreparable damage to the local economy, dependent upon logging since the 1860s. A contentious three-year tug-of-war ended with the establishment of a park that today encompasses 922,651 million acres. The rightness of their campaign was confirmed in 1981, when Olympic National Park was designated a World Heritage

site, a recognition of priceless environmental value accorded to such places as Australia's Great Barrier Reef and Yosemite in California.

The park's U-shaped valleys and knife-edge summits exhibit the telltale footprint of glaciers. One of the most active is Blue Glacier, which, even though it has been retreating for the past century, can flow—in places—as much as 180 feet in a year.

Abundant precipitation—hundreds of inches of rain and snow per year—and rich soil have produced some of the largest evergreens yet found in this temperate rain forest. The tallest Douglas fir yet found in the park rises 298 feet, the loftiest grand fir stands 251 feet, and a western hemlock tops 241. Many who encounter the oldest groves of these stately behemoths, which include towering western red cedar and Alaska cedar, remark at their cathedral-like ability to draw the gaze upward.

They coexist with bigleaf maple, red alder, black cottonwood trees, and—at higher elevations—silver fir, Alaska cedar, mountain hemlock,

and subalpine fir, creating habitats for a diverse community of mammals, ranging from black bears, mountain lions, and Columbia black-tailed deer to bobcats, marmots, skunks, and mice. As elsewhere in the Pacific Northwest where shelter, abundant water, and isolation combine, birds congregate here to mate and nest.

There are no uncharted regions remaining in the Olympics; the topographic maps hikers use to find their way to primitive wilderness camps depict a 600-mile-long trail system that covers the park like a net. Come winter, visitors travel by ski and snowshoe, the best means of moving on foot across the deep snow that accumulates here.

A separate unit of the park lies along the Pacific Ocean. It is one of the longest stretches of uninterrupted wilderness coastline in the lower 48 states. Stretching more than 60 miles—a wave-battered shore visited by harbor seals, sea lions, sea otters, gray whales, and orcas—its rocky tide-pool shelves bristle with multicolored sea anemones, sea urchins, and starfish. Just beyond the breakers sea otters seem to toil endlessly, using stones on their chests to crack open clams and mussels gripped in their nimble forepaws. Soaring gulls produce the same result by dropping bivalves onto rocks. This is the natural world as it should be—wild, rough, chaotic, and beautiful—a living pageant of the world before time.

OLYMPIC NATIONAL FOREST

Unlike the national park its timbered foothills surround, about 84 percent of this 632,324-acre federal holding is subject to "multiple use," a term provocative to preservationists because it permits not only recreation but also logging, cattle grazing, and mining. There are, some argue, recreational advantages to this, such as an extensive system of roads enabling scenic backcountry drives by car, motorcycle, or mountain bike, vehicle-friendly camping in undeveloped areas, the option to hike with dogs, to hunt, or to traverse trails on horseback.

Stricter rules apply within the 88,265 unsullied acres of the forest's five wilderness areas—Buckhorn, Wonder Mountain, Mount Skokomish, Colonel Bob, and The Brothers. "Zero impact" camping is encouraged; such things as campfires above 3,500 feet, the use of wheeled vehicles or motorized equipment, and groups exceeding 12 are prohibited.

Climbing opportunities abound on peaks like Mount Fricaba, rising to 7,010 feet. Included in the forest's 201-mile network of footpaths and interpretive walks is Mount Mueller Trail, an equestrian-friendly 13-mile loop featuring splendid views of the Olympic Mountains, Lake Crescent, and the Strait of Juan de Fuca, as well as seasonal wildflower extravaganzas. Between April and October, anglers vie for Pacific salmon and several varieties of trout in the Gray Wolf, Dungeness, and Big Quilcene Rivers, while other people, in rubber boots, roam beaches and estuaries to dig for razor, geoduck (pronounced "gooey duck"), and steamer clams and oysters. High-country fishing starts in July, as the high lakes don't thaw before mid-June.

Come autumn, hunters arrive, licensed to stalk Columbian black-tailed deer, black bears, Rocky Mountain goats, snowshoe hares, and Roosevelt elk. (The peninsula's elk population, estimated at between 5,000 and 7,000, is the world's largest.) Fall is also berry picking season. And as the holidays approach, forest visitors can obtain permits to harvest Christ-

mas trees from among the forest's youngsters. If you come, be prepared for weather that is cold, wet, and windy.

Though long gone is the era when lumberjacks prided themselves on felling ancient giants and striking poses on their massive stumps—one vintage photograph shows 28 people crowded atop a decapitated Douglas fir—the forest still produces about ten million board feet annually. Logging proponents note that timber is a renewable resource, but environmentalists fear that, as western red cedar is downed and replaced with higher-yielding Douglas fir, naturally diverse timberlands will become single-species tree farms, followed by an inevitable decline in the quality of wildlife—not only within this forest but also in the park it embraces. To the extent that Olympic achieves a balance between humans and nature, it may point the way toward resolving the decades-old dispute between preservationist sentiments and commercial imperatives.

PACIFIC RIM NATIONAL PARK RESERVE

Facing the Pacific with all of Canada at its back, this 123,406-acre reserve on Vancouver Island offers long beaches and remote islands ideal for fishing, camping, and kayaking. Diverse marine life and some 50 submerged shipwrecks combine to make this one of the finest scuba diving destinations on the continent. And though the ocean can be treacherous

Even the light glows green in the Elwha River Valley of Olympic National Park. Air plants sprout from a bigleaf maple; licorice ferns crowd its base. Sustained by more than 12 feet of rain annually, plants cover nearly every inch of the Olympic rain forest. Ninety-five percent of the park is designated wilderness.

for small craft, an assortment of coves, inlets, bays, lakes, and streams offer some of the most scenic paddling in North America.

Shaped by glaciers, the landscape is at the edge of the Pacific, Juan de Fuca, and North American tectonic plates. It is seismically active and characterized by faulting and wave-cut cliffs. Heavy precipitation—a dry year brings 12 feet, a wet one over 22—waters rain forests dominated by Sitka spruce (some approaching 300 feet in height), western hemlock, and western red cedar (prized by Native American dugout carvers and 19th-century shipwrights). Black-tailed deer, Vancouver Island wolves, black bears, cougars, minks, and martens wander the terrain, and some 250 species of birds—mostly migrants—have been counted. Residents include ducks and song sparrows; common goldeneyes and trumpeter swans are migrants. Red-throated loons, cormorants, great blue herons, bald eagles, Steller's jays, and tufted puffins all nest here. Seals, sea lions, and sea otters cavort in the chilly Pacific with elusive giant Pacific leatherback turtles, all wary of orcas—killer whales that wear their black-and-white coloring like glistening tuxedos as they breach and submerge with a ponderous grace. Anglers will find trout and four freshwater species of salmon in the lakes and streams, and offshore waters teem with perch, herring, cod, sole, halibut, and many fancifully named rockfish.

Each March, the villages of Tofino (a popular deep-sea sportfishing port) and Ucluelet join in hosting the Pacific Rim Whale Festival, a three-week celebration of the gray whale's northern spring migration. Two generations ago this great marine mammal faced extinction, its population (like the sea otter's) decimated by overhunting, but international protection in 1947 came soon enough to reverse the gray whale's decline. Today, the reserve offers ringside seats for the passage of some 19,000 grays as they make their annual 4,960-mile shuttle between Mexico's Baja California (where they breed and calve) and the Bering Sea (where they feed in summer). Gray whales pass this way again in late September and early October during their return trip south. The reserve's nutrient-rich waters and many sheltered bays serve as way stations, making this a superb place—one of the world's best—from which to observe the whales as they cruise by at a stately two to four knots, their exhalations blasting steamy plumes into the air between dives.

The rugged, 47-mile-long West Coast Trail, connecting Bamfield and Port Renfrew, offers some of Canada's most photogenic coastal and rain forest scenery. Most readily traversed between June and September, it requires between six and ten days to complete. Originally constructed to enable shipwrecked mariners to walk to safety (this shoreline claimed so many lives that it was once dubbed the graveyard of the Pacific), the trail follows an old telegraph route that once connected lighthouses and breezy hamlets perched on headlands. The shoreline is still untamed. Hikers must ford rivers by rope or cross them on suspension bridges or by ferry, climb and descend cliffs by ladder, and slog over bogs and through deep gullies—often in less-than-clement weather. The trek, however, rewards the adventurous with seldom-visited beaches, some as wild as any in North America, and a green riot of life under rain forest canopies, where waterfalls cascade over mossy precipices. And every now and then, hikers will come upon coastline overlooks that remain as pristine as when they greeted the forebears of the Nuu-chah-nulth First Nations people, who assert ancestral rights to the reserve based on the nearly 300 native archaeological sites identified so far. (Until their claims are resolved, Pacific Rim—managed as a national park—remains a park reserve.)

Life on the edge: A receding tide in Barkley Sound bares waving seaweed and a tiny crab amid shattered shells in the Broken Group Islands of Canada's Pacific Rim National Park Reserve (opposite). Pacific breakers pound the more than a hundred wooded islets off the southwestern edge of Vancouver Island, British Columbia.

Dense fog dims a morning sun in Pacific Rim. Fog and heavy rainfall feed a rain forest of western red cedars and hemlocks, Sitka spruces, Pacific silver firs, lichens, and mosses in the 193-square-mile reserve.

WILD RIVER, KARST, TRUMPETER SWANS

NAHANNI
NAT. PARK
RESERVE,
N.W.T.

NAHANNI NATIONAL PARK RESERVE

Nahanni's 1,840 square miles enclose a wild stretch of land in the southern Mackenzie Mountains of Canada's Northwest Territories—a rugged backcountry of river gorges, massive waterfalls, alpine tundra, limestone caves, and boreal forest still so remote that no roads lead into it. Access by visitors is possible only by helicopter or floatplane. In 1978, UNESCO designated the park its first World Heritage site, proclaiming its principal waterway, the Nahanni, "one of the most spectacular wild rivers in North America." The river, named after the Naha—"People of the West," is an ancient one, believed to predate most of the mountains it cuts through. The Naha are considered to have been what is now the Northwest Territories' earliest inhabitants, and the Dene, their descendants, live in the area today. Parks Canada, which established the reserve in 1972, is so determined to preserve the river's ecological integrity that only two dozen visitors are admitted per day—half accompanied by guides, the rest on their own.

Fort Simpson, about 90 miles east and dating back to 1804 when the North West Company established fur trading posts along the Mackenzie River, is the jumping-off place for most wilderness forays, where high season is July and August. To roam on one's own requires considerable experience—there are no lodges, facilities, or telephones inside the reserve—and even seasoned canoeists, kayakers, and hikers may find it more practical to join an outfitter's guided tour.

Among the more popular group expeditions are canoe trips commencing from Rabbitkettle Lake and raft trips down the South Nahanni and its tributary, the Flat River, whose white-water runs are rated among North America's most challenging and scenic. Winding and turbulent, shot through with eddies, whirlpools, rapids, and boils, the South Nahanni cuts through valleys thick with white spruce and poplar, wildlife, and four spectacular, progressively deeper steep-walled canyons, the last nearly 4,000 feet deep. It is customary for river visitors to carve a miniature paddle and leave it at the Deadmen Valley, an old forestry cabin, as proof they have been there.

Undisturbed wildlife habitats are home to an extraordinary variety of creatures—13 species of fish, including arctic grayling and Dolly Varden trout—and more than 120 species of birds, the best known being golden and bald eagles, peregrine falcons, and trumpeter swans. Among the 40 species of mammals are grizzlies and black bears, gray wolves, woodland caribou, Dall sheep, mountain goats, and beavers.

One of the park's most impressive natural features is Virginia Falls, a thundering 410-foot-high wall of water—more than twice the height of Niagara Falls—cascading around a central rock spire. The site is made even more Edenlike in spring, when wild orchids bloom beside patches

of snow. Another destination is Rabbitkettle Hotsprings, whose waters rise from more than a mile below the surface and gush out at a comfortable 68°F. Geologists estimate that it took the mineral-rich fountain some 10,000 years to form its "tufa mounds," a succession of soft rock terraces nearly 90 feet high. To protect these fragile formations, only five visitors—accompanied by park staff—are allowed to traverse them at any given time, and all must be barefoot. Also unique to Nahanni are wind-eroded sandstone shapes called the Sand Blowouts and the labyrinth of sinkholes, caves, ravines, and underground streams—karst landscape—that cuts lacelike beneath the reserve's limestone plateaus. North of the reserve's boundary is the Cirque of the Unclimbables, a collection of granite towers that includes the elegant 2,200-foot Lotus Flower Tower. The only risk of injury here is to rock climbers who dare defy its name.

The town of Yellowknife, 310 miles to the east and perched on the north shore of Great Slave Lake, is a favorite gathering place for observing the aurora borealis in all its eerie silent splendor.

Two hundred years ago, the Mackenzie River's watershed supported a large indigenous population. Many descendants of those people living now in Fort Liard, Nahanni Butte, and Jean Marie River are awaiting the resolution of their aboriginal land claims and other issues that address alleged historical inequities. Until these are settled, Nahanni will remain a reserve, rather than a full-fledged national park.

DEEP FJORDS, GLACIERS, PRIMEVAL FORESTS

WRANGELL-ST. ELIAS
NAT. PARK AND
PRESERVE, Alaska

KLUANE NAT. PARK
RESERVE, Yukon Territory

GLACIER BAY
NAT. PARK AND
PRESERVE, Alaska

TONGASS
NAT. FOREST, Alaska

GLACIER BAY NATIONAL PARK AND PRESERVE

Covering more than 3.3 million acres on the Gulf of Alaska in southeast Alaska, dramatic and remote, Glacier Bay can be reached only by air and sea. The size of Connecticut, Glacier Bay is North America's largest water-area park. It is a wilderness of extreme contrasts, including lofty peaks, ponderous tidewater glaciers, bogs, and alpine tundra, fjords, beaches recessed in sheltered coves, freshwater lakes, and dense coastal rain forests.

In 1794, English explorer George Vancouver described what little he could see of the area as "solid mountains of ice rising perpendicularly from the water's edge." When naturalist John Muir arrived, less than a century later, tidewater glaciers had pulled back some 50 miles, uncovering a vast bay. "Back in their cold solitudes," he wrote, glaciers work "unwearied through unmeasured ages," only to "melt into streams and go singing back home to the sea."

They vary in color. Some glaciers whose ice holds trapped air bubbles are white or pale; those glaciers with ice compressed by their own weight range from blue to greenish black. Others that carry rock and earth have moraines of brown or black.

A glacier's journey can be a long one. Fairweather Glacier begins on the slopes of 15,320-foot Mount Fairweather. Others—remnants of the little ice age that began about 4,000 years ago, such as those at John Hopkins Inlet—descend steeply over short distances, dropping from mountains that rise to 6,520 feet from sea level in as few as four miles. From time to time, sharp gunfire-like cracks rend the stillness, as a slab weighing hundreds of tons breaks off from one of these enormous ice tongues and crashes into the sea to form an iceberg. How high a berg floats depends on its size and mass. As an iceberg melts, its center of gravity shifts, which can cause it to suddenly roll over or rise up like a breaching whale and fall back into the water, creating potentially deadly hazards for small boats and kayaks.

The glaciers' ebb and flow creates a living laboratory where botanists study how plants establish themselves on raw ground in a process known as plant succession. About 13,000 years ago, the ice covering all of this region except its tallest summits began to retreat, exposing landscapes that had not seen the sun in eons. Wind and birds carried seeds and spores to them, and soon life asserted itself in the form of lichens, algae, and mosses greening rock crevices and loose gravel. Tundra and pine-alder scrub came next, followed by cottonwoods and willows, and then spruce and hemlock.

In less than two centuries, what had been covered by ice in George Vancouver's day has evolved into a rain forest crowded with huge Sitka

spruce trees. The explosion of life continues; today Glacier Bay is home to 420 plant species that include blueberry, devil's club, soapberry, and skunk cabbage in its forests, all sustained by annual rainfall averaging 75 inches, most of which falls in September and October.

Brown bears, black bears, and mountain goats have roamed here for thousands of years between glacial epochs, as have coyotes, moose, deer, lynx, wolves, wolverines, marmots, shrews, voles, and porcupines. Birds, such as the American peregrine falcon, the marbled murrelet, the bald eagle, and the spectacled eider, find shelter here alongside kingfishers, red-necked phalaropes, mergansers, and tufted puffins.

At the top of the marine mammal food chain is the orca, which shares the offshore waters with harbor porpoises, Steller sea lions and huge colonies of harbor seals. Schools of halibut and salmon, dietary staples of Glacier Bay's sea otters, minks, and eagles, attract anglers. In the past,

Icebergs melt below a tidewater glacier, one of a dozen, in southern Alaska's Glacier Bay National Park. The giant rivers of ice carve deep and narrow fjords best explored by boat or kayak. The park contains more than a hundred glaciers.

commercial fishermen also harvested this region's populations of salmon, herring, ling cod, skate, rock cod, flounder, and crabs.

Whales frequent the rich feeding grounds of Icy Strait, a popular location for whale-watching in summer, when the prize is to witness a humpback breaching—30 to 40 tons of whale catapulting into the air for unknown reasons. (Some believe they breach simply for the fun of it.)

Humpbacks are also known for their haunting "songs"—atonal but oddly musical squeaks, groans, wails, and moans—which can last for half an hour and may be a form of communication, group identification, and even navigation.

The best way to see Glacier Bay is from the water. Most visitors take the 65-mile boat trip from Bartlett Cove to the tidewater glaciers, a highlight of its ranger-led excursions. At Bartlett Cove, the Forest Loop Trail, a mile-long loop through spruce and hemlock, includes a relatively easy stroll to the beach. The Bartlett River Trail, a 4-mile round-trip, ending at the waterfowl estuary, requires two to three hours; and the Bartlett Lake Trail, a 6-mile round-trip through a rain forest, about four hours.

Among Glacier Bay's most intriguing features are its wilderness coves, which are best explored by sea kayak or on foot after arriving there by water. (Camping—with a permit—is allowed.) For those without the time or equipment, the *Spirit of Adventure* tour boat from Bartlett Cove offers transportation to several inlets where a few steps onto the stony shore transport you from modern times to timelessness.

TONGASS NATIONAL FOREST

Three times larger than any other national forest in the United States, southeastern Alaska's Tongass is the ultimate example of a northern-latitude rain forest. Its fecundity and its surpassingly wild beauty will be its salvation, for that has generated a groundswell of opposition to on-going harvests of its remaining old-growth timber, as well as support for the designation, so far, of 21 wilderness areas within its 17 million acres.

Its topography is distinguished by an unusual immensity of scale—perennially snowcapped peaks, deep glacial valleys exhibiting their characteristic U-shape, broad major rivers, and nearly 11,000 miles of shoreline so pristine in places a footprint seems a desecration. Glaciers abound; the Stikine Icefields near Petersburg stretches for 120 miles, and mammoth Mendenhall Glacier, near Juneau, measures a mile and a half wide.

Much of Tongass remains relatively untrodden, and here are the habitats crucial to its most familiar native creatures, which include mountain goats, moose, foxes, flying squirrels, coyotes, wolverines, and porcupines. Elsewhere, however, the forest hosts a considerable traffic in backcountry explorers. (Mendenhall is such a popular destination that the glacier has a visitor center and campground.) Dozens of scenic trails wind through Tongass's cool and humid forests, and more than a thousand miles of logging roads are open to mountain bikers.

The burgeoning popularity of sea kayaking and canoeing in the Pacific Northwest is due in large part to the Inside Passage's enticing, usually placid labyrinth of waterways—most notably those within the 2.3-million-acre Misty Fiords National Monument, known for steep glacial fjords, coastal ecosystem, and abundant populations of salmon and trout. Outfitters rent kayaks and provide instruction and guidance; kayaks and canoes may be carried aboard ferries from Bellingham, Washington, or Prince Rupert, British Columbia. Taking to the sea offers a unique and dramatic opportunity for observing marine life close-up—these waters teem with humpback and killer whales, sea lions, sea otters, seals, and porpoises. The broken geography creates a lattice of waterways and hundreds of verdant islands, many cradling crystal-clear lakes. Separated by narrow straits and channels, often accessible only by floatplane, many have Forest Service log cabins on their wooded shores, which may be rented for $25 per night. Sojourning on one of these little isles for several days is to experience what locals proclaim as "the real Alaska."

Within the cluster of the Alexander Archipelago is Prince of Wales, the third largest island in the United States. Although its spruce-hemlock forests have been heavily logged by native corporations, the roads cut through them by loggers have made it especially popular among mountain bikers, fishermen, and hunters in search of black bears and Sitka black-tailed deer. Sinkholes and caves pock some 700 square miles of the island's limestone and marble bedrock. Two short and easy trails, El Capitan and Cavern Lake, lead to caves offering safe on-your-own exploration.

To the Tlingit people, Admiralty Island was *Kootznoowoo,* or "Bear Fortress," aptly named, as some 1,500 grizzlies still thrash and root

Beyond a field of blooming fireweed in Brotherhood Park, outside Juneau, Alaska, the Mendenhall Glacier sweeps down from the Coast Mountains in Tongass National Forest. Largest national forest in the U.S., Tongass encompasses 17 million acres.

Rock art: Iron deposits,
built up from minerals
in the water that washed
them, mottle stones and
pebbles in Alaska's
Wrangell-St. Elias National
Park and Preserve.
The park east of Anchorage,
six times the size of
Yellowstone, sprawls
across more than 13
million acres—80 percent
of it snow, rock, and ice.

through its forests. A national monument, Admirality Island experiences heavy precipitation that creates a rain forest environment at lower elevations and a semi-permanent ice field among its peaks. Martens, minks, beavers, and nesting bald eagles share Admiralty with trumpeter swans and Vancouver Canada geese.

The small but thoughtfully designed Tongass Historical Museum in downtown Ketchikan provides an insightful overview of the region's commercial fishing industry and also its Native American pageant, the latter a complex heritage of unusual artistic sophistication evident in the totem pole outside the city library, which depicts a traditional myth called Raven Stealing the Sun.

WRANGELL-ST. ELIAS NATIONAL PARK AND PRESERVE

The edge of America's largest national park—at 13.2-million acres, six times the area of Yellowstone—is an easy day's drive from Anchorage via the scenic Glenn (Alaska 1) Highway. The usual superlatives accorded Alaska fall short of conveying the stupendous scale of the topography here. Named for two of its mountain ranges, Wrangell-St. Elias contains the continent's largest assemblage of glaciers—including the Malaspina, whose area exceeds the state of Rhode Island's. (It carries so much silt that trees and other plants grow to maturity during their lurching transport downhill, only to topple over at the glacier's terminus as the ice beneath them crumbles or melts.) The glaciers rasp minerals from the terrain they scour and serve as salt licks and mineral sources for the animals living in the open terrain that flanks them.

Annual snowfalls reaching 20 feet back-load Nabesna and Hubbard Glaciers, gargantuan frozen rivers that have plowed and bulldozed the landscapes beneath them for the last 11,000 years. (In 1986, Hubbard—now receding—advanced more than a mile, sealing off a major fjord and acquiring the nickname "galloping glacier.") The ice that reaches the ocean's edge breaks off and falls into it, producing icebergs in a process known as calving. Three major mountain ranges—Chugach , in addition to Wrangell and St. Elias—converge within the park and contain 9 of the 16 highest peaks in the United States, including four topping 16,000 feet. Cratered Mount Wrangell is one of North America's largest active volcanoes, having last erupted in 1900. Bagley Icefield stretches across 80 miles.

About 80 percent of Wrangell-St. Elias is high country, some of it still unexplored, and most of it inhospitable. (The easiest way to survey it quickly is from the air; outfitters offer tours by plane.) Left untrammeled, its interior supports a remarkable variety of creatures. Visitors hope to sight Dall sheep, distinguished by their massive, curling horns, as they forage precipitous ridges above the tree line. Moose graze in lake shallows and willow bogs. In the autumn, grizzly bears congregate along salmon spawning streams for an annual feast that complements their mostly vegetarian diet. The park's preserve section is open to sport hunters, many of whom come from abroad. They prize rare—only one has been taken so far—quarry such as "glacier bears," a gunmetal blue color phase of black bears. Other game include caribou and lynx. Foxes, beavers, and porcupines are left alone, as are members of the park's two herds of transplanted bison.

Despite environmentalists' interest in the territory enclosed by Wrangell-St. Elias, until the late 1980s the park's interior was largely overlooked by backpackers, campers, and hikers, most of whom headed for points north. There are no maintained trails here, although primitive roads lead deep into the park and serve as jumping-off points for those able to navigate using topographic maps, which are essential.

This is a genuinely remote wilderness with mercurial weather, requiring visitors to carry at a minimum a topographic map, a compass, some food, drinking water, warm clothing, a flashlight, waterproof matches, sunglasses, sunscreen, a hat, first aid kit, and a folding knife.

On subalpine slopes, trekkers encounter mountain goats grazing in meadows that in spring sparkle with vivid blue lupine, Jacob's ladder, purple monkshood, pink firewood, and yellow paintbrush.

At higher elevations they stand a good chance of observing bald and golden eagles riding updrafts in search of prey to feed their young — the chicks of bald eagles would be ensconced in rough twig-and-stick nests built in the highest branches of tall trees; those of golden eagles would be on cliffs.

Seasoned mountain climbers rate Drum, Sanford, Wrangell, Blackburn, Bona, and St. Elias as among the most interesting or challenging ascents. In winter, cross-country skiers confront temperatures as low as minus 50°F but have virtually all of the park to themselves.

In milder seasons fishermen angle for salmon, lake and rainbow trout, graylings, steelhead, Dolly Varden, and burbot. Other visitors cruise coastlines to observe harbor seals, sea lions, sea otters, and porpoises—possibly even glimpsing a beluga whale.

In late spring and summer, the Chitina, Bremner, and Copper Rivers run high and fast, attracting white-water kayakers, canoeists, and rafters, who are ferried to put-in points on the first two streams by air taxi. Besides the challenges of Class II-IV rapids, river runners pass through wetland regions teeming with migratory waterfowl, including trumpeter swans, ducks, loons, and geese, whose raucous seasonal visits evoke visions of the continent before Europeans arrived.

The Copper River's name reflects the mining industry that flourished here between 1911 and 1938. Bankrolled by J. P. Morgan and the Guggenheim family, the operation included a 196-mile-long railroad for hauling away copper ore (and some 300 million dollars in silver) dug from the green cliffs east of the Kennicott Glacier, one of the richest veins yet discovered. The mines' extensive and often photographed ruins are a national historic landmark.

In 1913 the discovery of gold in Chisana (pronounced Shoo-shana) triggered Alaska's last great gold rush, enticing thousands into making the difficult overland journey from the port of Valdez to what became known as "the largest log cabin town in the world." The boom was brief; however, small-scale mining for gold, copper, and zinc continues on private landholdings within the park, most of them the property of Ahtna Indians, whose ancestors were known for producing finely-wrought copper tools.

KLUANE NATIONAL PARK RESERVE

In 1979 this great tract of wild landscapes—Kluane National Park Reserve in the Yukon Territory's mountainous southeast corner, together with Alaska's Wrangell-St. Elias and later Tatshenshini-Alsek Wilderness and Glacier Bay—was inscribed as a joint Canadian/American site on UNESCO's World Heritage List, creating the largest protected wilderness area on Earth.

Kluane's enormous sprawl—nearly 5,440,000 acres—ranges in elevation from just under 2,000 feet to well above 19,000, creating a wide range of life zones inhabited by a diverse hierarchy of creatures. It is a territory of superlatives: 19,524-foot Mount Logan is Canada's highest peak and the second highest in North America.

The stunning St. Elias Mountains are the Western Hemisphere's second highest coastal range after the Andes. The Bagley Icefield, which dates back to the last ice age and is one of largest nonpolar ice fields on Earth, is so vast that it creates its own climate. (All of its average monthly temperatures are below freezing.)

Glaciers—thousands of them—are the preeminent natural force in the park's loftiest elevations, where annual snowfall reaches 60 feet. In the late 1960s, Steele Glacier advanced more than 11 miles in four months—about 500 feet per day. The surges of 40-mile-long Lowell (or Naludi) Glacier are similarly aggressive, occasionally blocking the Alsek River with a dam of ice and creating temporary glacial lakes. Their ponderous

"White thunder," as the Tlingit Indians called it, echoes across Disenchantment Bay when ice sheers off Hubbard Glacier in Wrangell-St. Elias. In 1890 members of the first National Geographic expedition discovered the 70-mile-long glacier, one of more than 150 in the park, and named it after the Society's president—Gardiner Greene Hubbard.

sliding is accompanied by a muffled crunching and crackling as their colossal weight crushes boulders beneath them.

Flourishing at lower elevations, the moist subarctic conifer forests known as taiga commence where the tundra ends. For thousands of years they have been the territory of the Southern Tutchone First Nations people, whose ability to thrive in the region's rugged terrain, despite harsh winters, derived from their intimate familiarity with its animals, plants, and weather, and with the vagaries of its lakes, streams, and rivers—knowledge transmitted from antiquity to the present day by means of a still vital tradition of oral history and lore.

They hunted in montane forests striped with white spruce, balsam poplar, and trembling aspen, and on the alpine tundra, which in summer blooms with more than 200 different plants. Dall sheep are Kluane's most numerous large mammal (estimated to number at about 4,000), seen foraging year-round on the slopes of Sheep Mountain.

The park's most familiar creatures include moose, caribou, mountain goats, wolverines, minks, red foxes, lynx, snowshoe hares, black and brown bears, and a transient population of gray wolves.

Nearly 200 species of birds have been sighted here, and 118 species nest in Kluane—mountain bluebirds, ptarmigans, arctic terns, yellow-rumped warblers, peregrine falcons, and golden eagles being among the most photogenic.

The park's cadre of brown bears is believed to be Canada's greatest concentration of the stout, shaggy quadrupeds, dubbed "grizzlies" because of the silver-tipped hairs seen on older bears. Some male grizzlies mature to 1,500 pounds, about twice the weight of the largest male black bears. To maintain their great bulk, which sustains them during long periods of deep winter sleep, they root and forage relentlessly, daily consuming more than 80 pounds of berries, flowers, herbs, roots, and insects—and during salmon runs gorging themselves on the fish.

Within Kluane, wildlife protection takes priority over recreation. Despite the popularity of the Alsek River's Class III and IV rapids among white water runners, a 28-mile stretch of the stream has been declared a preserve to save grizzly bear habitats and a number of fragile valley plant species, and rafting trips are now limited to one per day.

Hiking trails—the most reliable routes to wildlife sightings—range in difficulty from short easy strolls to arduous routes requiring rock climbing, fording chilly streams, and several days' time. Kathleen Lake Campground, with 41 sites as well as ample firewood and well water, is a favorite destination, open from mid-June through mid-September, and permits backcountry idylls lasting up to two weeks.

Preservationists strongly encourage catch-and-release fishing, which means using hooks with barbs crimped flat and immediately returning one's catch to the water. This practice ensures a large population of rainbow trout, northern pike, arctic grayling, and freshwater sockeye salmon whose experience-sharpened instincts require ever greater skill by subsequent anglers.

Many of the reserve's trails are ancient footpaths that the Tutchone walk today. They alone trod them until the discovery of gold in 1903 brought in hordes of environmentally reckless miners. That rush, followed by the construction of the Alaska Highway during World War II, spurred

Like a ghostly banner, an aurora borealis—or the northern lights—streaks the night sky above Kluane National Park Reserve in the southeastern corner of Canada's Yukon Territory. Auroras, seen primarily in high latitudes of both hemispheres, occur about 25 times each year. Kluane, which lies north of the 60th parallel, abuts Wrangell-St. Elias.

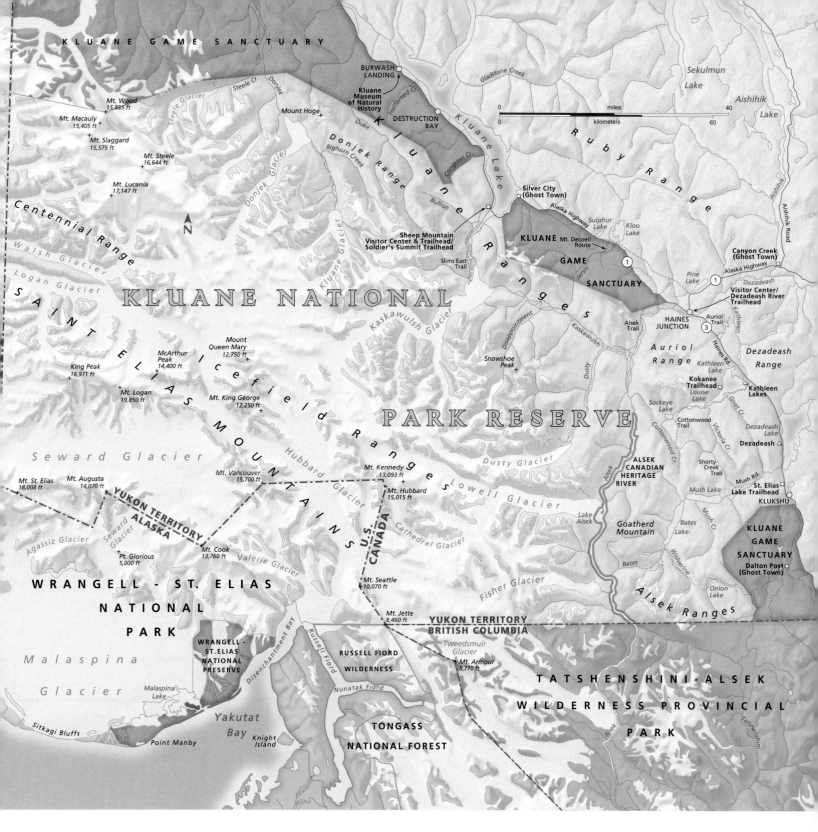

conservationists to lobby for a game reserve, established here in 1943.

Kluane's "reserve" designation acknowledges ongoing negotiations of Yukon native land claims asserted by the Southern Tutchone, Kluane, and others. Meanwhile they, along with members of the Champagne and Aishihik First Nations, whose domain once flanked the 260-mile-long Alsek River, exercise aboriginal rights to hunt and fish reserve land while participating in its management.

Native tradition is celebrated every year in July when the Southern Tutchone convene their Gathering. Open to the public, the week-long event includes craft demonstrations, games, traditional music, and dance.

Another annual celebration of the region is the Yukon Sourdough

Rendezvous Festival with its pioneer saga theme, held in nearby White-horse, the Yukon's capital. A couple of the favorite events are the sled dog races and the air show.

Few events hereabouts, however, generate more interest than the autumn salmon runs through this territory. In August, viewing platforms overlooking the Whitehorse Rapids Dam and Fish Ladder are crowded

ATLAS OF NATURAL AMERICA

Twin arms of Kaskawulsh Glacier unite below peaks of the St. Elias Mountains in Kluane. As glaciers plow downward, the slow-moving rivers of ice scrape and push up rocks ahead of them, creating glacial ridges of rocky debris called moraines.

with people as the longest chinook (or king) migration on Earth occurs.

Thousands of fish swimming mightily against the current leap from the water to ascend the terraced steplike "ladder" that allows them to bypass the dam and reach spawning grounds. The spectacular phenomenon is a dramatic demonstration of only one of the reasons why Kluane's wilderness is a World Heritage site.

MOUNT McKINLEY, SPIRES, TUNDRA

DENALI
NAT. PARK AND
PRESERVE, Alaska

DENALI NATIONAL PARK AND PRESERVE

At 4.7 million acres, Denali's huge area corresponds to everything else about it. Things here are big. Every vista is deep, and everything appears on a scale so vast that the eye is often fooled—a valley appearing several miles wide may span 30 miles. Crowned by 20,320-foot-high Mount McKinley, which dominates the area, the park's most distinctive features were sculpted by ice age glaciers: deep U-shaped valleys and the truly spectacular peaks of the Alaska Range. Their sawtooth spires and knife-edge ridges oversee snowfields, blue glacial pools, and a vast plateau of tundra and boreal forest. To Athapascans, Mount McKinley is Denali, meaning "the high one." It is so high that it makes its own weather and has treacherously powerful storms.

A granite heart clothed in ice hundreds of feet thick in places, this mountain was first climbed successfully in 1913 by an Episcopal missionary with the memorable name of Hudson Stuck—but that was in summer. A winter climb did not succeed until 1967; the climbers in that attempt battled windchill temperature measuring minus 148°F. To climb McKinley, clear a month on your calendar (not in winter), and keep in mind that only about half of those attempting this mountain actually reach its summit.

The park was originally established in 1917 as a game refuge to protect the local wildlife from commercial hunters, who supplied the protein in Alaska Railroad workers' diets. With the completion of the railroad in 1923, a trickle of tourism began. (Visitors were ferried from the platform to the park hotel by horse-drawn carriage.)

For the next half century, however, Denali remained remote. Today, it is Alaska's most popular national park, attracting some 370,000 visitors annually. In 1976 it became an International Biosphere, and in 1980 the park area was expanded and a preserve was added, where hunting is allowed.

Denali encompasses a complete subarctic ecosystem. Bleak to some, captivating to others is the taiga (Russian for "land of the little sticks"), a vast stubble of spruce, aspens, birch, and balsam poplar, softened by alders and dense shrubs. Tundra dominates, however, with its humbler flora of fireweed, bush cranberries, and blueberries. Late August transforms it into a pointillist's canvas of red, blue, and orange leaves, and the smell of fermenting berries reminds some of wine. Picking is allowed, but visitors must beat the park's bears to this sweet harvest.

Naturalists keep track of 37 mammal species here, the best known and largest being the grizzly, caribou, wolf, Dall sheep, and moose. Denali's creatures make this a generally peaceable kingdom by keeping their distance from one another. In summer, moose stand in placid lakes,

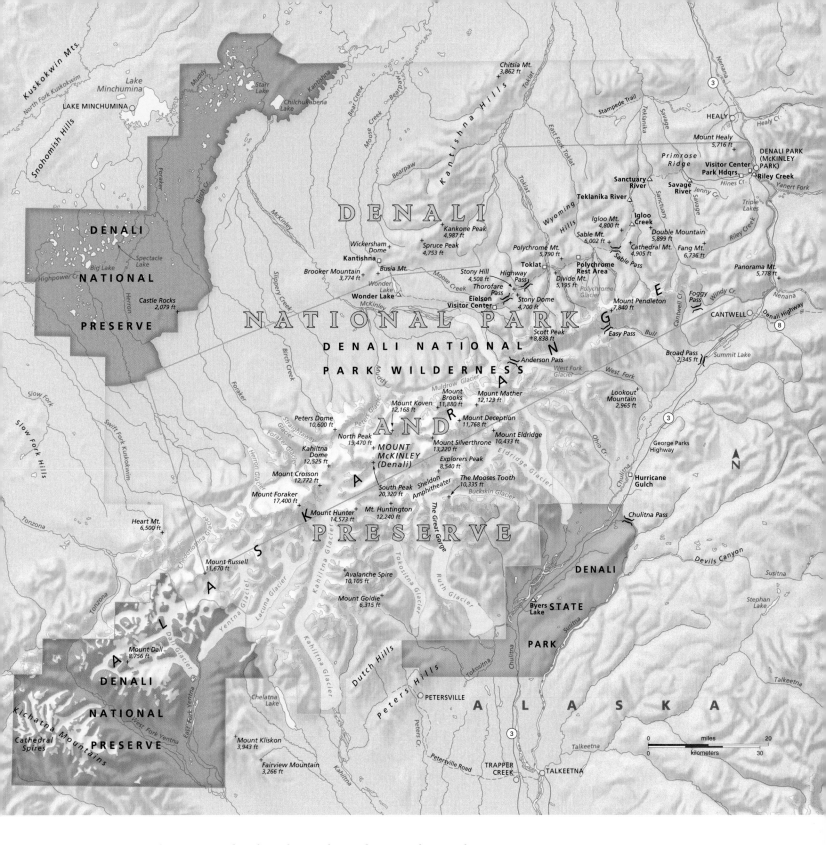

emerging with water cascading from their antlers and aquatic plants trailing from their mouths. Come fall, however, the huge bulls fight over harems of cows. Dall sheep prefer rocky mountainsides. Bright white, they travel in bands of about 60, and the males sport big, curling horns. Denali's wolves, instinctively wary, are seen far less often than are their tracks, which in the case of adults can be as wide as a fist.

Denali's caribou herd, some 20,000 strong in the 1940s, has diminished to a mere 2,200. (Their hoofs, reminiscent of elegant women's high heels, despite their delicate appearance give the caribou an advantage when negotiating snow and tundra.)

Lest Denali's grizzlies suffer a similar decimation—fewer than

Red-leafed in early September, blueberry bushes lure a female grizzly in Alaska's Denali National Park and Preserve. It was established in 1917 to protect North America's largest mammals: grizzly bears, moose, caribou, Dall sheep, and wolves.

Dawn fog veils Wonder Lake; beyond it snow softens the knife-edge ridges of 20,320-foot-high Mount McKinley (right). Athapascans called it Denali—"the high one." Climbers doing the West Buttress route from the Kahiltna Glacier, starting at around 7,000 feet, have to climb about 13,000 feet over 12 miles.

a thousand of the bears survive in the 50 states—biologists here use radio telemetry and other nonintrusive methods to identify and protect the habitats essential to their existence. Acknowledging the fierce reputation of these great brown bears, which can run up to 40 miles an hour and weigh as much as 450 pounds, John Muir called them "not companions of men but children of God," adding: "His charity is broad enough for both."

Fortunately, Denali is also large enough for both, for this is hiker and backpacker heaven, with an added bonus of 16 to 20 hours of daylight in spring and summer. Insect repellent, rain gear, and a warm sweater are essentials for day hikes. Take binoculars and a camera, as this is one of North America's premier outdoor photography destinations.

One 89-mile road cuts into the park's center from park headquarters to Wonder Lake (mountain bikes are allowed), but most of the land is accessible only on foot or, in winter, with snowshoes, on cross-country skis, or by dogsled. Autumn colors usually peak by late August, and winter follows quickly; snows often close off parts of the Park Road between mid-September and early June.

Ranger-led walks and guided off-road discovery hikes are available,

as are wildlife-oriented bus tours, which last from six to seven hours. Dog-sled demonstrations take place three times a day at the kennels; in winter, the dogs earn their keep pulling rangers on patrol. If you plan to arrive by car, the drive from Anchorage (about five hours) or Fairbanks (about three) affords good stream fishing opportunities and handsome wilderness views.

In winter, the roads are often snow packed, so bring along emergency supplies and anything else you cannot do without for 24 hours. There is no scheduled plane service, but charters are available. Alaska Railroad trains with sight-seeing cars providing 360-degree views make daily runs past Denali, stopping every day in summer and once a weekend in winter en route to Anchorage or Fairbanks.

Just beyond the park's borders, concessionaires offer horseback riding, white-water rafting (on the Class IV Nenana River), and helicopter or fixed-wing aerial tours. If you are in the area for the summer solstice (June 21), consider joining the local citizenry as they celebrate with midnight footraces, barbecues, and all-night softball games. Perpetual twilight, like the near darkness that comes in December, is just one more of the unique charms of this multifaceted park.

RIVER DELTAS, MARSHES, TUNDRA

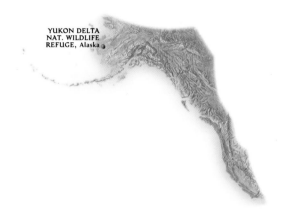

YUKON DELTA
NAT. WILDLIFE
REFUGE, Alaska

YUKON DELTA NATIONAL WILDLIFE REFUGE

A treeless wetland plain with a long coastline on the Bering Sea and one of world's largest river deltas, the Yukon Delta National Wildlife Refuge is named for one of its great watercourses.

Access to the refuge—low tundra, a shoreline broken by 13 bays and 22 large river mouths, intertidal flats, fresh and saltwater marshes, lakes, ponds, bogs, and grass meadows—is largely limited to boat or floatplane. In 1980, as part of the Alaska National Interest Lands Act, a 26-million-acre expanse of this watery Ohio-size wilderness was declared an official haven for wildlife: the Yukon Delta National Wildlife Refuge.

A compelling rationale for that official action was the annual exodus of waterbirds that fly here from six continents to breed and nest, a spectacular phenomenon that involves more than 2,000,000 ducks, 750,000 tundra swans and geese, and as many as 100,000 godwits.

An additional fly-in brings an estimated 1,000,000 shorebirds to the deltas of the Yukon and Kuskokwim Rivers, the most important shorebird nesting area in the U.S. These seasonal migrations are reflected in the region's Yup'ik Eskimo people's aboriginal names for April (*tinmirrat tatqiat*—month of the geese), May (*kayangut anutiit*—month of egg-laying), July (*ingun*—month of molting), and August (*tengun*—month of flight).

From *tinmirrat tatqiat* to *tengun,* the refuge is noisy with the chatter of nesting birds, the black turnstone, black-bellied plover, and the bristle-thighed curlew, among others. Of particular interest to ornithologists is the red-necked phalarope, whose females take the lead in courtship, then leave their mates to incubate their eggs while they go off in search of other males to entice. Biologists roam the upland tundra hoping to sight golden plovers, whimbrels, and Hudsonian godwits; slog through bogs where yellowlegs and short-billed dowitchers breed; and walk alpine and subalpine banks with an eye out for the wandering tattler. In known areas, it is likely that they will glimpse emperor geese and threatened spectacled eiders.

Reindeer and musk oxen thrive where they have been introduced into the refuge's 1.1-million-acre Nunivak Island, in the Bering Sea. Hill country and mountains in the refuge support native populations of moose, caribou, grizzly and black bears, wolves, and red foxes; and its mazelike waterways are replete with beaver and mink. Game species are plentiful enough so that hunting is permitted, although those in pursuit of waterfowl must use shotgun shells containing nontoxic steel pellets. The abundance of trout, char, and grayling in mountain streams, along with pike, whitefish, and burbot in lowland waters, once sustained a cottage industry of guides who took anglers into the backcountry.

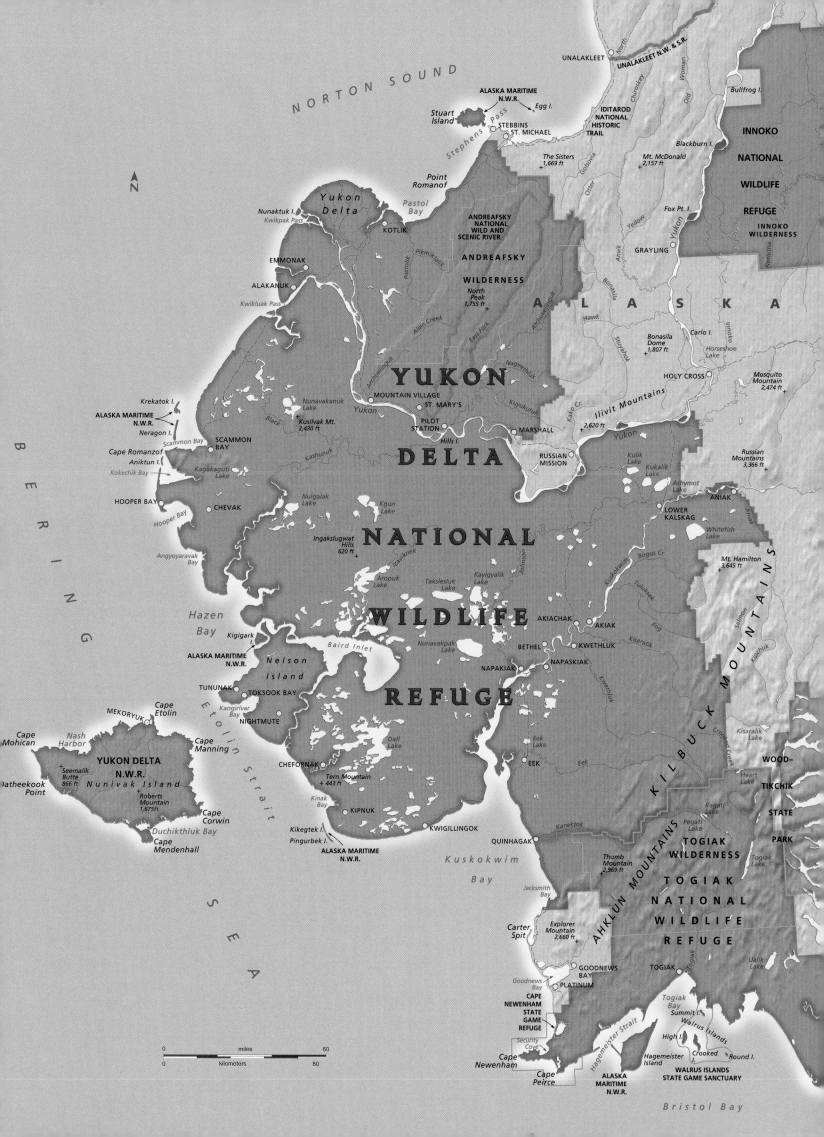

NORTON SOUND

Yukon Delta

UNALAKLEET

UNALAKLEET N.W. & S.R.

North

Chiroskey

Woman

Old

Bullfrog I.

IDITAROD
NATIONAL
HISTORIC
TRAIL

INNOKO

NATIONAL

WILDLIFE

REFUGE

Golsovia

Blackburn I.

ALASKA MARITIME
N.W.R.   Egg I.

Stuart
Island

Stephens Pass

STEBBINS
ST. MICHAEL

The Sisters
1,669 ft

Mt. McDonald
2,157 ft

Otter

Yellow

Fox Pt. I.

INNOKO
WILDERNESS

Point
Romanof

*Pastol
Bay*

Anvik

Hawk

Yukon

GRAYLING

Nunaktuk I.
Kwikpak Pass

KOTLIK

ANDREAFSKY
NATIONAL
WILD AND
SCENIC RIVER

ANDREAFSKY

A L A S K A

Bonasila

Carlo I.

Archuelinguk

Bonasila
Dome
1,807 ft

EMMONAK

WILDERNESS

Stuyahok

Horseshoe
Lake

ALAKANUK

North
Peak
1,755 ft

Allen Creek

East Fork

Archuelinguk

HOLY CROSS

Mosquito
Mountain
2,474 ft

Kwikluak Pass

YUKON

Hawk

Kuyukutuk

Nageethluk

Kako Cr.

Ilivit Mountains

2,620 ft

Yukon

Russian
Mountains
3,366 ft

MOUNTAIN VILLAGE

ST. MARY'S

Yukon

*Nunavakanuk
Lake*

Kusilvak Mt.
2,430 ft

Black

PILOT
STATION

Hills I.

MARSHALL

Kulik
Lake

Kukalik
Lake

Krekatok I.

ALASKA MARITIME
N.W.R.

Neragon I.

Cape Romanzof
Aniktun I.

Kokechik Bay

SCAMMON
BAY

Scammon Bay

Kashunuk

*Kagakaguti
Lake*

RUSSIAN
MISSION

*Arhymot
Lake*

ANIAK

Russian
Mountains
3,366 ft

HOOPER BAY

CHEVAK

*Nuigalak
Lake*

*Kgun
Lake*

LOWER
KALSKAG

*Whitefish
Lake*

Hooper Bay

Johnson

Kuskokwim

Bogus Cr.

Mt. Hamilton
3,645 ft

*Angyoyaravak
Bay*

Ingakslugwat
Hills
620 ft

Izaviknek

*Aropuk
Lake*

*Taksleluk
Lake*

*Kayigyalik
Lake*

Tuluksak

Salmon

*Hazen
Bay*

*Nunavakpak
Lake*

AKIACHAK

AKIAK

Fog

K I L B U C K   M O U N T A I N S

*Kigigark
I.*

ALASKA MARITIME
N.W.R.

*Nelson
Island*

Baird Inlet

BETHEL

KWETHLUK

Kwethluk

Kisaralik

*Kisaralik
Lake*

TUNUNAK

TOKSOOK BAY

NAPAKIAK

NAPASKIAK

WOOD–

MEKORYUK

Cape
Etolin

NIGHTMUTE

*Kangirlvar
Bay*

*Dall
Lake*

*Eek
Lake*

EEK

Eek

Crooked Creek

*Heart
Lake*

TIK'CHIK

Cape
Mohican

*Nash
Harbor*

Cape
Manning

CHEFORNAK

Tern Mountain
443 ft

*Kisaralik
Lake*

STATE

YUKON DELTA
N.W.R.
Nunivak Island

Seemalik
Butte
866 ft

Etolin Strait

*Kinak
Bay*

KIPNUK

PARK

*Datheekook
Point*

Roberts
Mountain
1,675 ft

Cape
Corwin

Kanektok

*Pegati
Lake*

*Kagati
Lake*

TOGIAK
WILDERNESS

Duchikthluk Bay

Cape
Mendenhall

Kikegtek I.
Pingurbek I.

ALASKA MARITIME
N.W.R.

KWIGILLINGOK

QUINHAGAK

Thumb
Mountain
2,969 ft

TOGIAK

*Togiak
Lake*

A H K L U N   M O U N T A I N S

NATIONAL

B E R I N G

*Kuskokwim
Bay*

WILDLIFE

S E A

Jacksmith Bay

Carter
Spit

Explorer
Mountain
2,660 ft

REFUGE

*Ualik
Lake*

GOODNEWS
BAY

*Togiak
Bay*

Summit I.

Walrus Islands

*Goodnews
Bay*

PLATINUM

TOGIAK

CAPE
NEWENHAM
STATE
GAME
REFUGE

*Security
Cove*

Cape
Newenham

Cape
Peirce

ALASKA
MARITIME
N.W.R.

Hagemeister Strait

High I.

Hagemeister
Island

Crooked
I.

Round I.

WALRUS ISLANDS
STATE GAME SANCTUARY

Bristol Bay

YUKON

DELTA

NATIONAL

WILDLIFE

REFUGE

*Hazen
Bay*

miles   60
0

kilometers
0   80

Tucked into the refuge's center is Bethel, a town of about 5,000 that is raised on stilts to prevent its buildings from thawing the permafrost layer beneath the topsoil and sinking into self-created quagmires. Each January, the lonely but tight-knit community hosts the Kuskokwim-300 Sled Dog Race, a three-day mad dash that attracts the fastest teams in this far northwest corner of the continent. The event also celebrates the region's centuries-old Yup'ik culture: The delta encompasses 42 Eskimo villages in which traditional hunter-gatherer lifestyles are still practiced. (The nightly

Maze of marshlands (left),
the deltas of the Yukon
and Kuskokwim Rivers
in western Alaska support
more than a hundred
million nesting and breeding
waterfowl each year.
Yukon Delta National
Wildlife Refuge, largest
in the refuge system, covers
26 million acres, much
of it treeless wetland plain.

Hunted for hides and meat,
the musk ox disappeared
from Alaska by 1865.
An introduced herd thrives
on the Nunivak Island
portion of the Yukon Delta
refuge, providing stock
for other preserves.

National Public Radio broadcast from Bethel is in both English and Yup'ik.)
About seven million refuge acres belong to Native American corporations.
Many Yup'ik depend on the taking of polar bears, walruses, sea otters, and
five species of salmon for food, clothing, handicrafts, and income—subsistence harvesting rights recognized and protected by the United States, Rus-
sia, and Canada. This people's resourceful stewardship of refuge land
demonstrates that it is possible for humans to live in balance with even the
most delicate of natural environments.

The ARCTIC NORTH

CHAPTER VI

ARCTIC NATIONAL WILDLIFE REFUGE IVVAVIK VUNTUT AUYUITTUQ

BYLOT ISLAND BIRD SANCTUARY QUTTINIRPAAQ

High Arctic wilderness enfolds a visitor to Quttinirpaaq,
Canada's northernmost park.

BY BARBARA SZERLIP AND MARK MILLER

The broad swath of North America's highest latitudes—running from the Arctic Circle up to the top of the world, the North Pole—is embraced in this chapter on the Arctic North. Within this domain lie the uppermost portions of Alaska, the Yukon, the Northwest Territories (with their many islands), and Nunavut. It is a dazzling region of coastal plains, rivers, ice fields, and glacier-sculpted cliffs, an ocean some parts of which are perpetually frozen, and land held in an icy grip for up to ten months of the year.

The Arctic North has proved itself a testing ground for imaginative adaptation, a place where all life-forms, to survive, have been forced to exhibit extraordinary flexibility, stamina, and even artistry. For example, polar bears evolved from brown-furred forest-dwelling vegetarians into snowy white carnivores more at home on ice floes than on land. Numerous bird species learned to migrate enormous distances—in the case of the bandit-masked arctic tern, halfway around the world—to take advantage of the region's brief summer. Few places on Earth can match for sheer scale the Arctic's avian colonies, many of which are now protected within more than a dozen bird sanctuaries. Since tundra conditions have existed for only a few million years, botanists say that true Arctic plant species have not had time to evolve. But what does grow here—like glacier crowfoot, which can photosynthesize at temperatures below zero—have found ingenious ways to amplify the sun's meager warmth and withstand repeated freezing.

Over many thousands of years, the Inuit developed survival methods too—using the kayak and the harpoon for hunting, training *qimmiit* (huskies) to pull *qamutiit* (wooden sleds), learning to make domed snow houses, edging parka hoods with wolverine fur (which doesn't collect painful ice crystals), preserving meats, fashioning medicines from perennial flowers, rendering oil from seal fat, and twisting lamp wicks from dried moss and arctic cotton (a type of flower head).

For the most part, the region was scarcely disturbed until the 1960s. By 1980 more than $800 million had been invested in Arctic oil and gas exploration. When discoveries on Alaska's North Slope and in the Beaufort Sea spurred further proposals for megaprojects, it became apparent to the region's aboriginal tribes that self-determination was imperative if their traditional homelands and cultural heritages were to be protected. This led to land-grant agreements, the establishment of several national parks in which the Inuit and Gwitch'in share responsibility, and, on April 1, 1999, the creation of an Inuit-controlled political entity, Nunavut (Our Land), 747,340 square miles staked out in the Northwest Territories. Claiming a fifth of Canada's land mass, Nunavut is a vast, forestless expanse where caribou outnumber the 27,000 human inhabitants, many of whom live by hunting and fishing in remote communities. This most recently created territory, like all the Far North, is a spectacular kingdom of flora, fauna, and aboriginal cultures.

Arctic terns nest and breed each
summer in Quttinirpaaq.

THE
ARCTIC NORTH

Site discussed in chapter

0   miles   500
0   kilometers   700

G R E E N L A N D   S E A

Crown
Prince
Christian
Land

Peary
Land

King
Frederik VIII
Land

King Wilhelm Land

7,037 ft

King
Christian X
Land

QUTTINIRPAAQ
(ELLESMERE ISLAND)
NAT. PARK

Lincoln Sea

Challenger Mts.
U.S. Ra.

Barbeau Peak
8,543 ft

Nansen Sd.

Nyeboe
Land

Hall Basin

Kennedy Chan.

Knud Rasmussen Land

9,300 ft

G R E E N L A N D
(DENMARK)

Gunnbjørn
12,139 ft

Denmark Strait

Axel
Heiberg
Island

Greely Fd.

Kane Basin

Hayes
Peninsula

Smith Sd.

10,728 ft
Ice Thickness
11,188 ft

King Christian IX Land

Mont Forel
11,024 ft

Borden
Island

Peary Chan.

Prince Gustaf Adolf Sea

Ballantyne Str.

Ellef
Ringnes
Island

Mackenzie
King I.

Melville
Bay

Ice Thickness
9,728 ft

Prince Patrick
Island

Hazen Str.

Norwegian
Bay

Q U E E N   E L I Z A B E T H   I S L A N D S

Ellesmere Island

B A F F I N

B A Y

Uummannaq Kangerlua

Arctic Circle

Ice
Thickness
7,020 ft

King Frederik VI Coast

M'Clure Str.

P A R R Y   I S L A N D S

Melville Island

Grinnell
Pen.

Bathurst
Island

Jones Sd.

Devon Island

Cornwallis
Island

Viscount Melville Sound

Barrow Str.

Lancaster Sd.

Cape Byam Martin

DAVIS STRAIT

Qeqertasuup Tunua

King

...nd

...ince Albert
...eninsula

Stefansson
Island

Somerset
Island

Brodeur
Pen.

Prince Regent Inlet

6,400 ft

BYLOT ISLAND BIRD SANCTUARY
Bylot Island

Borden
Pen.

Buchan Gulf

Scott Inlet

Eglinton Fjord

Clyde Inlet

Frederik IX
Land

7,185 ft

...aston Pen.

V i c t o r i a

I s l a n d

Prince
of Wales
Island

M'Clintock Channel

B a f f i n

N U N A V U T

I s l a n d

Henry Kater Pen.

Home Bay

Collinson
Peninsula

Boothia
Pen.

Victoria Str.

Gulf of Boothia

AUYUITTUQ
NAT. PARK

8,500 ft

Cumberland
Peninsula

Cape Dyer

Exeter Sd.

King
William
I.

Pelly
Bay

Simpson
Pen.

Melville
Peninsula

Prince
Charles
I.

Foxe

Nettilling
Lake

Hoare Bay

Cape Mercy

...oronation
...ulf

Queen Maud
Gulf

Bathurst
Inlet

Chantrey
Inlet

Committee
Bay

Rae
Isthmus

Basin

Amadjuak
Lake

Cumberland Sd.

8,238 ft

Cape
Farewell

ARCTIC CIRCLE

O C E A N

283

CARIBOU, TUNDRA, MIGRATING BIRDS

ARCTIC
NAT. WILDLIFE
REFUGE, Alaska   IVVAVIK NAT. PARK,
Yukon Terr.
VUNTUT NAT. PARK,
Yukon Terr.

ARCTIC NATIONAL WILDLIFE REFUGE

Each year, 130,000 Porcupine caribou migrate more than 700 miles to and from their traditional calving grounds far north of the Arctic Circle. For thousands of years, generation after generation of these caribou—named for the Porcupine River that cuts through their winter range—have repeated this arduous trek, which includes swimming across fast-flowing rivers swollen by melting snowpack.

On Alaska's North Slope, the northeastern coastal plain is the herd's northernmost reach. Although this swath of tundra—bordered by the Beaufort Sea to the north, the U.S.-Canada border to the east, and the Canning River to the west—makes up only 10 percent of the Arctic National Wildlife Refuge's nearly 20 million acres, it is considered the refuge's biological heart.

By early June, 40,000 to 50,000 pregnant females arrive at the coastal plain, in advance of the bulls and juveniles. In most years between one-half and three-quarters of the herd's calves are born here, most of them during the same week every year. Soon, hundreds of nursing cows graze peacefully amid willows and grasses, the air filled with the distinctive bleats of wheat-colored, wobbly-legged newborns whose antler buds are covered with grayish velvet. (Cousins to reindeer, caribou are the only members of the deer family of which both sexes grow antlers.) Following an evolutionary pattern, the calving period coincides with the snowmelt and the plain's subsequent greening.

But there's more to this vast portion of Alaska's North Slope than caribou. The Arctic National Wildlife Refuge includes barrier islands, marshy tundra, rolling hills, 18 major rivers, glaciated peaks of the eastern end of the Brooks Range topping 8,000 feet, and vast spruce forests. At a latitude where temperatures can drop to minus 70°F in winter, Arctic plants have evolved adaptations for survival. Some species develop a thick, insulating layer of fuzz. Others grow in protective cushions or mats, have dark hairs that absorb solar heat, or angle their cup-shaped petals toward the sun, concentrating warm rays onto seed heads.

With a diverse assemblage of wildlife and habitats unequalled anywhere in the U.S., the Arctic National Wildlife Refuge has been called America's Serengeti. The inventory of mammals includes grizzly bears, arctic foxes, solitary wolverines, highly social gray wolves, moose, Dall sheep, and musk oxen. And, of course, the inventory would not be complete without polar bears, classified as marine mammals because they spend much of their lives roaming the ice pack, stalking seals or diving for an occasional walrus pup.

Within the refuge's boundaries lies one of the most important polar bear denning habitats in the U.S. Mating takes place in spring and early summer. But a remarkable process called delayed implantation keeps the embryos in a suspended state for about six months, until autumn, when the

Nomads of the north: Members of the Porcupine caribou herd ford the Kongakut River on their annual trek to calving grounds in northeastern Alaska's Arctic National Wildlife Refuge. Some 130,000 Porcupine caribou migrate north more than 700 miles each spring to the Arctic coastal plain, then backtrack in summer to southern fall and wintering areas.

pregnant females dig dens in deep snowbanks on land or in crevasses, and the embryo (sometimes twins) resumes its development.

With the advent of the area's brief summer, the refuge's habitats teem with life. Millions of migratory birds, representing about 180 different species—including golden eagles and peregrine falcons—arrive from as far away as Southeast Asia, Africa, South America, and Antarctica, a majority to nest and raise their young.

A remote wilderness, the refuge is accessible primarily by boat or plane from Fort Yukon, Kaktovik, or Deadhorse. The range of Arctic wildlife can be enjoyed while backpacking (there are no developed facilities or trails), boating, or hunting. The Sheenjek and Ivishak Rivers are fabled among experienced rafters and kayakers.

IVVAVIK NATIONAL PARK

The migration of the Porcupine caribou herd is the longest and most perilous of any land animal on Earth and is especially dangerous for calves. It is not uncommon for juveniles to be abandoned at one of the many hazardous river crossings or to meet their fate as the prey of a grizzly bear or wolf. But by the steely statistical balance of nature, enough newborn calves manage to survive the trek to ensure the herd's continuation.

Unaware of international borders, Porcupine caribou also calve to the east of Alaska's coastal plain in Ivvavik National Park, a Canadian park

in Yukon Territory to the east of the Arctic National Wildlife Refuge and to the north of Vuntut National Park. The landscape is mostly open and treeless with rounded hills and occasional rock outcrops, called tors, that have been shaped by thousands of years of erosion by wind, water, and frost. Ivvavik is dominated by the British Mountains, which were part of the vast, ice-free land bridge called Beringia that once connected North America to Asia. Kettles, formed long ago when chunks of glacial ice melted, pockmark the Buckland Hills to the northeast, and channels that once contained glacial meltwater distinguish Ivvavik's coastal plain.

Created in 1984 as Northern Yukon National Park, this 3,926-square-mile expanse was the result of a land settlement between the Inuvialuit (the Inuit of the western Arctic) and the Canadian government. In 1992 the name of the park was changed to "Ivvavik," which in the Inuvialuit language means "a place for bearing and raising young; a nursery."

Musk oxen, ponderous and shaggy ice age survivors, graze on the coastal plain, while moose forage the valley bottoms. Forest-dwelling martens and porcupines venture as far north as the tree line, and wolves range wherever they must to find prey. Contributing to this intricate web of wildlife are red and arctic foxes, grizzly bears, and Dall sheep, here at their northernmost range. In summer, more than 135 species of migrating birds are drawn to Ivvavik's lakes, rich deltas, and brackish lagoons, some from as far south as South America's Patagonia (the golden plover

and the northern phalarope) and the Antarctic (the arctic tern). By early September, snow geese descend by the thousands, replacing the avian flyers who have headed south. A few hardy species, like the ptarmigan and the diurnal snowy owl, reside here year-round.

Between mid-June and mid-August the tundra transforms into a garden carpeted with vast stretches of wildflowers. This short summer season—followed by an abrupt and exuberantly colorful autumn with occasional winterlike conditions and heavy fogs—is the best time to take advantage of Ivvavik's excellent backpacking opportunities. There are no designated trails.

Visitors are urged (indeed, cautioned) to research their wilderness routes beforehand—topographic maps and aerial photos are available. And before setting out, they are required to file a detailed description of their route with the park warden in Inuvik, about 125 miles east in Northwest Territories.

Ivvavik was established with the understanding that it would ensure a future not only for wilderness recreation and indigenous wildlife but also for the land's aboriginal heritage. The six Inuvialuit communities retain the exclusive right to harvest caribou, musk oxen, ducks, geese, seals, and beluga whales. Snowmobiles and rifles complement dogsleds and harpoons.

VUNTUT NATIONAL PARK

Established in 1995, Vuntut, extends the protected area of the Porcupine caribou's migration route an additional 1,677 square miles into their fall and wintering range.

Vuntut, Ivvavik, and Alaska's Arctic National Wildlife Refuge embrace close to 37,000 square miles. As with Ivvavik to the north, Vuntut is the product of an aboriginal land settlement—in this case, between the Vuntut Gwitch'in ("people of the lakes") and the government of Canada. The two parties share equal management responsibility. Like the Yukon Inuvialuit and the Gwitch'in of Alaska, the Vuntut Gwitch'in have deep cultural ties to the caribou and retain the right to trap, fish, and hunt within the park.

In summer, the Old Crow Flats wetlands—a vast plain of 2,000 shallow lakes resting on a substratum of permafrost south of Vuntut National Park and north of the Porcupine River—warm quickly in 24-hour sunlight, producing a rich food supply for half a million nesting tundra swans, red-necked grebes (which piggyback their young), and other migrant waterfowl.

The flats also provide habitat for moose (which migrate here from the Arctic National Wildlife Refuge), grizzly bears, and numerous plant-eating muskrats and their enemy, the mink.

Old Crow Hills is a popular hiking challenge, and travel on the Old Crow and Porcupine Rivers is a major park attraction. Untouched by glaciers during the last ice age, the Old Crow Flats served as a refuge for woolly mammoths, large-horned bison, 450-pound beavers, and other long-extinct creatures. Camels, which originated in the Americas before migrating to Asia via Beringia, also roamed here. As a result, this is one of the richest sites in all of North America for Pleistocene fossils.

Close encounter of the Arctic kind: Porcupines forage as far north as the tree line in Canada's Ivvavik National Park. Although the 3,926-square-mile reserve in the northeast corner of Yukon Territory was established to protect caribou calving grounds, it shelters many other animals, among them moose, musk oxen, wolverines, and martens.

Forever frozen, ice sheets called *aufeis* squeeze Wolf Creek in Ivvavik (opposite). Average monthly temperatures in the park rise above freezing only three months of the year.

GLACIERS, FJORDS CIRQUES, STUNNING TOWERS

BYLOT ISLAND
BIRD SANCTUARY,
Nunavut

AUYUITTUQ
NAT. PARK,
Nunavut

AUYUITTUQ NATIONAL PARK

Jutting out toward Greenland on Baffin Island's breathtaking Cumberland Peninsula, Auyuittuq National Park encompasses 7,607 square miles of deep glacier-gouged mountain valleys, steep-walled ocean fjords, ancient rivers of ice, and spiky peaks. Set aside in 1972, Auyuittuq (pronounced "ow-YOU-ee-tuk," it means "the land that never melts") was the first national park established north of the Arctic Circle.

The park is an exhibit of glaciology, with horns, cirques, and polished pinnacles sculpted from the Canadian Shield, and massive boulders (called erratics) balanced or perched in unusual positions. Mount Thor, at 5,485 feet, draws climbers from around the globe.

The most popular destination, however, is Akshayuk Pass, a spectacularly scenic 60-mile-long glacial valley carpeted with lush tundra — dwarf birch, willow, heather, and blueberries — that bisects the peninsula's mountain ramparts. In spring and summer, hikers, backpackers, and climbers traverse the pass's dramatic and challenging terrain, particularly between Overlord Mountain and Summit Lake along the Weasel River, their recreation enhanced by 18 hours of sunlight daily. The valley's snowpack remains firm into early June, making for excellent spring skiing. Depending on the season, local outfitters will ferry visitors to Auyuittuq's southern entrance at Overlord by snowmobile or boat; between mid-June and mid-July, icy conditions allow access only on foot, a two-day walk from the town of Pangnirtung.

A unique opportunity in this part of the world is to cross-country ski on frozen ocean. In May, 62-inch-thick ice limns the coastline and fills in bays and fjords — creating a singularly memorable experience for skiers. For the experienced, there is white-water kayaking on the Sylvia Grinnell River, south of the park near Iqaluit, Nunavut's capital.

The remote north side of Auyuittuq, with its glaciers and fjords (some reaching depths of 3,000 feet or more), presents a stark comparison to Akshayuk Pass. Penny Ice Cap, named after 19th-century explorer William Penny, dominates the skyline. This vestige of the ice age covers some 1,969 square miles and rises 6,890 feet, its ice nearly a thousand feet deep in places. A focal point for several scientific studies about climatic change and global warming, the Penny Ice Cap works the levers of local weather by cooling winds that pass over it, increasing their velocity as they descend through nearby mountain passes.

Most accessible in spring, northern Auyuittuq is a superb and popular vantage point for viewing wildlife, which include musk oxen, caribou, grizzlies, wolves, wolverines, polar bears, and even walruses. Lingering snows and difficult terrain make guided snowmobile or dogsled trips a convenient and fascinating option for taking in both the landscape and its diverse inhabitants. (Exploring this section of the park on foot is only

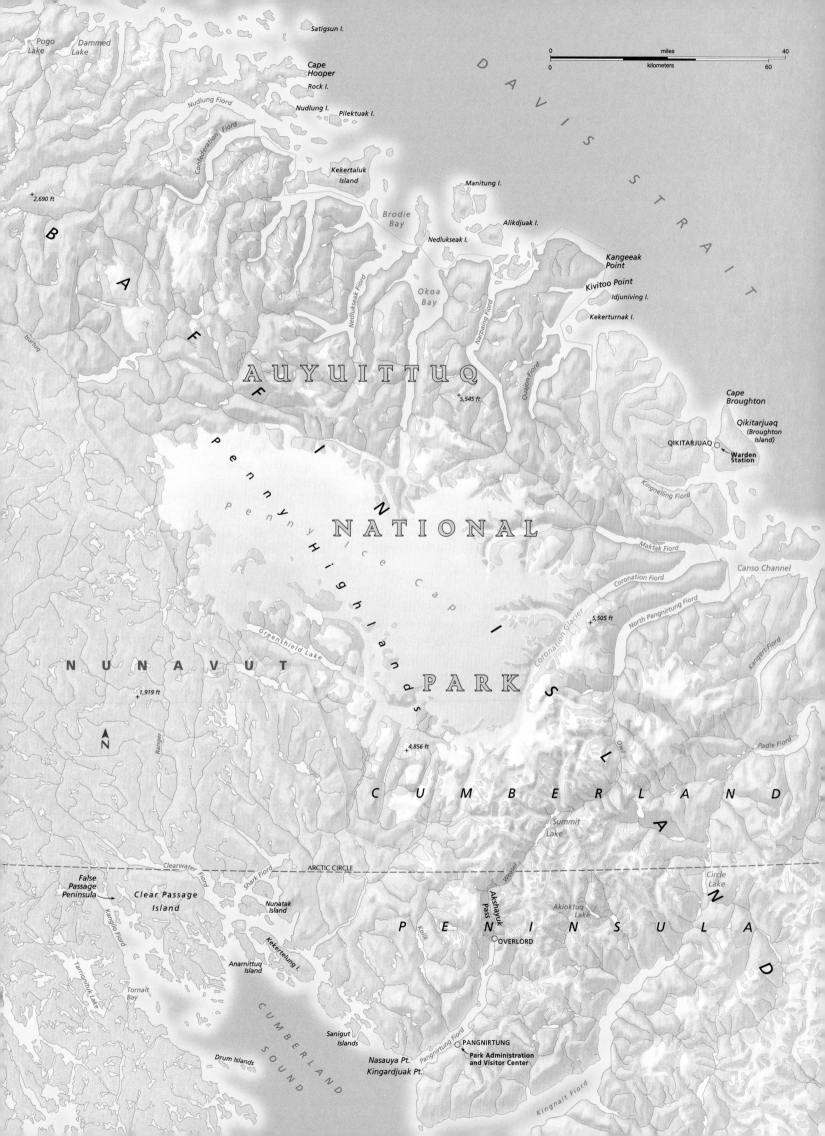

for seasoned backcountry travelers experienced in Arctic terrain.) Unlike in the park's south section, outfitters for the north side negotiate their own fees, which can run as high as $200 per person to enter the park.

For all its inviting grandeur, this remains a glacial wilderness, and with glacial activity comes inherent dangers. Backpackers should be aware of potential rockfall when hiking in narrow valleys and should plan to cross Auyuittuq's streams in the early morning, before they swell dramatically with glacial meltwater. Flash flooding can occur during heavy rainstorms, and strong winds carrying sand have been known to strip the paint from buildings and machinery.

River estuaries on Cumberland Sound reward summer anglers with arctic char, a determined fighter considered one of the world's most challenging game fish. Wherever there is snow or mud, tracks betray the frequent comings and goings of lemmings, ermine, red foxes, white wolves, and arctic hares. Peregrine falcons skim the tundra, in search of fledgling black guillemots and passerines, sharing the vivid skies with snow buntings, red-throated loons, and Canada geese.

As with other Arctic parks, Auyuittuq was established as the result of an agreement between the Canadian government and an aboriginal group with ancient ties to the land, in this case the Inuit — one of the few hunter-gatherer cultures remaining in the world. In an ice-scape of subtle pastels—blues, greens, lavenders, grays, and blinding whites—where long stretches of darkness alternate with months of perpetual light, the Inuit see their world as proof that time is without borders and without end.

BYLOT ISLAND BIRD SANCTUARY

Set in the watery wedge between Baffin Island's Borden Peninsula and Eclipse Sound, Bylot Island in Sirmilik National Park, Nunavut, is a desolately striking place of sandy beaches, ice fields, and glacier-draped mountains towering 6,233 feet above sea level.

Between May and September this seemingly uninhabitable triangle of land is invaded by multitudes of marine and land animals and an estimated 52 species of birds. In 1965, the island, along with all marine waters within two miles of shore, was officially designated a Canadian bird sanctuary—one of 14 bird sanctuaries (5 are pending) and national wildlife areas scattered throughout Nunavut that run the alphabetical gamut from Akimiski to Utkuhiksalik.

Perhaps the most impressive assemblage of Bylot's avian migrants are the 50,000 black-legged kittiwakes and 320,000 thick-billed murres that nest on the cliffs of Cape Hay and Cape Graham Moore, filling the air with great bands of rustling wings. Kittiwakes are small gulls that forage over marine waters in search of small surface organisms. Related to puffins and the now extinct great auk, murres can dive 300 feet or more underwater in search of prey. Instead of building nests, they lay their eggs on steep rock ledges—nature, in its wisdom and whimsy, having given them pear-shaped eggs that do not roll easily.

Cape Hay alone formerly saw roughly a million murres summering there, but the population of Bylot Island's colony has been much reduced by overhunting on their winter grounds, fishing-net deaths, and marine pollution. The murres leave Bylot Island in September to spend the rest of the year on the offshore and coastal waters of the North Atlantic.

Pastel clouds wreath Mount Asgard as it glows red at dawn above Turner Glacier in Canada's Auyuittuq National Park. Featured in the James Bond movie *The Spy Who Loved Me,* Asgard's two truncated peaks tower more than 6,500 feet above surrounding glaciers in the southern section of the Baffin Island park.

Ivory gulls soar along the floe edge — the place where currents meet land-fast ice, off Pond Inlet, a settlement at the north end of Baffin Island. In August, Pond Inlet is a popular destination among experienced Arctic kayakers, who enjoy the challenges of quickly moving drifting floes, occasionally severe winds, and whales appearing unexpectedly from under the ice.

Between mid-May and July, Pond Inlet is also the place to pick up floe-edge tours, a memorable way to observe seals, seabirds, walruses, belugas, orcas, and narwhals at close range. The tours typically last seven to nine days; many include travel through exquisite scenery across the frozen ocean and tundra to the floe edge, seated in a *qamutiik* (dogsled) pulled by a snowmobile or huskies.

Inuit have occupied the Pond Inlet area for thousands of years; the kayak is one of their traditional modes of travel. The first recorded visit by Europeans was that of the eponymous Robert Bylot and William Baffin in 1616; Pond Inlet was named for a British astronomer.

The southwest corner of Bylot Island is a rolling plain of lush wetlands that form one of the world's largest breeding grounds of greater snow geese. Unlike the murres, their population has increased dramatically over the last century to about 75,000 adults. Soaring lines of outstretched wings, white with black-edged underwings, are a majestic sight.

Because Bylot lies next to the Northwest Passage, a strategic transportation corridor, the potential for oil spills and the noise associated with drilling and shipping pose threats to its diverse bird population.

Like winged torpedoes, thick-billed murres explode from coastal cliffs overlooking Canada's Baffin Bay. Some 320,000 of the murres summer in Bylot Island Bird Sanctuary, laying their pear-shaped eggs on its steep rock ledges.

GLACIERS, MUSK OXEN, PEARY CARIBOU

QUTTINIRPAAQ
(ELLESMERE ISLAND)
NAT. PARK, Nunavut

QUTTINIRPAAQ NATIONAL PARK

Above latitude 80° N, Quttinirpaaq (Top of the World) National Park, known as Ellesmere Island National Park until its name was changed in 1999, stretches to about 500 miles from the North Pole. The park encompasses Ellesmere Island north of Greely Fiord and a third of its northern coastline, which is delineated by deeply cut valleys and seven major fjords. Because of its proximity to the former Soviet Union, the island housed a Canadian military listening station during the Cold War.

Most of Ellesmere's mountains—including 8,543-foot Barbeau Peak, the continent's highest mountain east of the Rockies—are nunataks, their peaks jutting from beneath a vast ice cap nearly 3,000 feet thick. Glaciers move down the sides of some mountains and into the valleys below, gripping the land with fingers of ice. Here, too, are most of North America's major ice shelves—ancient deposits of frozen fresh water, some more than 250 feet thick. Frozen to the land for thousands of years, they extend out a mile or more over the Arctic Ocean like a crust. Huge pieces sometimes break away to float free for years, pushed by ocean currents, providing scientists with floating research stations, complete with aircraft landing strips.

Much of this 14,581-square-mile expanse is polar desert, with some areas receiving less precipitation in a year than the Sahara. But glacial meltwater is plentiful enough to support grass-sedge meadows, wildflowers, and diverse wildlife habitats.

Dwarf willow twigs and tough grasses are the mainstay of Quttinirpaaq's musk oxen, a species little changed since they walked among prehistoric mastodons and mammoths. Weighing as much as 800 pounds, the musk ox is distinguished by a Roman-emperor profile and downcurved horns that sit like an understated crown on its high, shaggy forehead. The musk ox strategy of standing shoulder to shoulder in defensive circles, facing outward with a buttress of horns, is an excellent defense against wolves but proved the species' undoing when firearms were introduced, which facilitated a market for the meat and hide. Protected in Canada since 1917, musk oxen have repopulated their original ranges.

Arctic foxes contribute to the contours of the landscape. Some of their dens have existed for decades, even for as many as three centuries. Accumulated droppings and food remains have enriched the otherwise nitrogen-poor soil around their entrances, creating luxurious green patches of mountain sorrel, bladder campions, mouse-ear chickweed, and stitchwort. Similarly, elusive arctic wolves den at sites used by previous generations, but in their case, the sites date back two to three hundred years.

One of the most important members of Quttinirpaaq's food chain is also one of its smallest—the lemming. Their mercurial population, which seems to peak and crash in four-year cycles, has a profound impact on

ARCTIC OCEAN

LINCOLN SEA

N

miles 40
kilometers 60

Cape Fanshawe Martin
Cape Richards
Bromley I.
Cape Discovery
Borup Pt.
Ward Hunt I.
Cape Albert Edward
Cape Columbia
Cape Aldrich
Parr Bay
Stubbs Point
Good Point
Point Moss
Cape Colan
Parker Bay
Cape Hecla
Crozier I.
James Ross Bay
Cape Joseph Henry
Feilden Peninsula
Porter Bay
Cape Cresswell
Cape Richardson

Marvin Is.
Markham Fiord

Ayles Fiord

CHALLENGER MOUNTAINS

Marvin Peninsula

McClintock Inlet

Disraeli Fiord

Clements Markham Inlet

James Ross

ALERT
Cape Sheridan

Milne Glacier

QUTTINIRPAAQ

Commonwealth Mountain 7,201 ft

Disraeli Glacier

Clements Markham

Grant 6,276 ft Ice Cap

Cape Union

BRITISH EMPIRE RANGE

UNITED STATES RANGE

Cape Frederick VII

Mt. Oxford 7,251 ft

(ELLESMERE ISLAND)

Barbeau Peak 8,543 ft

Henrietta Nesmith Glacier

Range

Kilbourne Lake

Fort Conger Historic Site

Lake Hazen Camp and Warden Station

Craig Lake

Heintzelman Lake

Discovery Harbour

Distant Cape

Bellot Island

ROBESON CHANNEL

Garfield

Lake Hazen

Ruggles

Ekblaw Lake

Chandler Fiord

Miller Island

Lady Franklin Bay

Cape Baird

HALL BASIN

Osborn Range

Viking Ice Cap

NATIONAL PARK

HAZEN PLATEAU

Very

Conybeare Fiord

Keppel Head

Cape Cracroft

CANADA
GREENLAND (DENMARK)

Tanquary Fiord Camp and Warden Station

MacDonald

Mount Thompson 4,701 ft

Dodge

Archer Fiord

Judge Daly Promontory

Kap Morton

NUNAVUT

Beatrix Bay

Ella Bay

Cape Defosse

Kap Bryan

Bessels Fiord

Tanquary Fiord

Lake Tuborg

John Brown Ice Cap

Greely Fiord

Antionette Bay

Antionette Glacier

AGASSIZ ICE CAP

VICTORIA AND ALBERT MOUNTAINS

5,840 ft

Cape L. Von Buch

Hans Island

KENNEDY CHANNEL

Kap Ulrich

Fossil Bay

Franklin Island

WASHINGTON LAND

Crozier Island

Lafayette Bay

Kap Jefferson

Cape Lawrence

Radmore Harbour

Wilderness of white: Blowing
snow caps the Grant Land
Mountains in Canada's
Quttinirpaaq National Park.
The stony peaks erupt from
100,000-year-old ice fields
that blanket the Nunavut
park. Quttinirpaaq lies
only 500 miles from the
North Pole, northernmost
of hundreds of lands that
preserve cherished pockets
of natural America.

lemming predators—arctic foxes, ermines, snowy owls, glaucous gulls, and pomarine jaegers (a seabird with twisted tail feathers)—that may not mate when prey is scarce.

Experienced park guides and outfitters maximize wildlife viewing opportunities on tours lasting from a day to more than a week. With limited experience around humans, Quttinirpaaq's animals are often curious and approach closely, as they do in the Galápagos Islands. Visitors should not confuse this "ecological naïveté," as it is called, with tameness. Against the law to touch or feed the park's wildlife, it is also dangerous; vaccinations against rabies and tetanus before arrival are recommended as precautions against any accidental contact that might break the skin.

Polar bears loom enormous and white against the vast frozen seascape. They enjoy a life span of 25 years or more, and males can grow to 1,400 pounds. Ferocious predators, they can sprint at nearly 30 miles an hour. Some campers set up tripwire alarm systems to warn of their approach during the night or keep dogs staked on the downwind side of their tents.

Biologists have determined that the polar bear is genetically similar to the north's ubiquitous brown bear. The current theory is that during the Pleistocene era (roughly 200,000 to 250,000 years ago) a large segment of the population of the mostly vegetarian brown bear became isolated by glaciers. Survivors apparently experienced accelerated evolutionary changes, developing smaller, jagged teeth suited to a carnivorous diet, the ability to swim more than 60 miles nonstop (aided by long necks for keeping their heads above water), a buoyant, two-layered white coat, and partially webbed toes. Excellent divers, they can swim powerfully to a depth of 15 feet in their relentless pursuit of seals.

Some 30 species of birds frequent Quttinirpaaq, including gyrfalcons (the world's largest falcon, some of which are spectacularly white) and European migrants like red knots and ringed plovers. But arctic terns hold pride of place among the region's long-haul migrants. Distinguished by black caps and napes and blood-red beaks, these elegant "sea swallows" travel almost from Pole to Pole twice a year—a straight-line journey of nearly 25,000 miles. They may see more hours of daylight than any other creature, as they breed during Quttinirpaaq's summer months, which are virtually without darkness, then cross the Equator to the Antarctic Ocean, where they again encounter almost perpetual light. Their colonies, sometimes thousands strong, are often located on remote beaches that offer protection from predators with a taste for eggs and chicks.

Lake Hazen, at the park's core, is one of the largest freshwater lakes in the circumpolar world—50 miles long and 3 to 12 miles wide. A thermal oasis, its waters are abundant with arctic char and are generally ice free in summer. The Lake Hazen warden station is a good starting point for backpacking into the Garfield Mountains, and the north shore has a tent site. Exquisite Tanquary Fiord offers a campsite, many scenic views

within a day's walk, and the opportunity to observe Inuit stone ruins and roaming herds of endangered, diminutive Peary caribou, named after the American polar explorer. Stout, waterproof footwear and an ample supply of insect repellent are essential for traversing the soggy tundra, where mosquitoes breed in profusion.

As with all Arctic parks, self-reliance is essential. Visitors to the rugged, challenging terrain of Quttinirpaaq are strongly urged to carry single-side-band radios and are expected to provide their own equipment and supplies. Should it become necessary, emergency air evacuation is expensive and problematic, particularly in inclement weather. Park access is most often via Twin Otter, a sturdily built and durable turboprop aircraft with an earned reputation as the Canadian Arctic's workhorse, which can be chartered in the town of Resolute, on Cornwallis Island, about 520 miles away.

SITE DIRECTORY

For official information, go to the following Web sites, or use a search engine and type in a site name.

For U.S. National Parks: **www.nps.gov**
For U.S. Forests and Grasslands: **www.fs.fed.us**

For U.S. National Wildlife Refuges: **www.fws.gov**
For Canadian National Parks: **www.parkscanada.pch.gc.ca**

THE EAST

Gros Morne National Park
P.O. Box 130
Rocky Harbor, NF A0K 4N0
Canada
709-458-2417

Cape Breton Highlands National Park
Ingonish Beach, NS B0C 1L0
Canada
888-773-8888

Acadia National Park
P.O. Box 177
Bar Harbor, ME 04609
207-288-3338

Moosehorn National Wildlife Refuge
RR 1, Box 202, Suite 1
Baring, ME 04694
207-454-7161

White Mountain National Forest
719 Main St.
Laconia, NH 03246
603-528-8721

Green Mountain National Forest
231 N. Main St.
Rutland, VT 05701
802-747-6700

Cape Cod National Seashore
99 Marconi Site Road
Wellfleet, MA 02667
508-349-3785

Adirondack Park
Box 99
Ray Brook, NY 12977
518-891-4050

Cape Hatteras National Seashore
Route 1, Box 675
Manteo, NC 27954
919-473-2111

Assateague Island National Seashore
7206 National Seashore Lane
Berlin, MD 21811
410-641-1441

Chincoteague National Wildlife Refuge
P.O. Box 62
Chincoteague Island, VA 23336
757-336-6122

Bombay Hook National Wildlife Refuge
2591 Whitehall Neck Road
Smyrna, DE 19977
302-653-6872

Great Dismal Swamp National Wildlife Refuge
P.O. Box 349
Suffolk, VA 23439
757-986-3705

Monongahela National Forest
200 Sycamore St.
Elkins, WV 26241
304-636-1800

Shenandoah National Park
3655 U.S. Hwy. 211E
Luray, VA 22835
540-999-3500

Delaware Water Gap National Recreation Area
Bushkill, PA 18324
570-588-2451

Great Smoky Mountains National Park
Gatlinburg, TN 37738
865-436-1200

Chattahoochee-Oconee National Forests
1755 Cleveland Hwy.
Gainesville, GA 30501
770-297-3000

Cape Romain National Wildlife Refuge
5801 Hwy. 17 N
Awendaw, SC 29429
843-928-3264

Francis Marion National Forest
4931 Broad River Road
Columbia, SC 29212
803-561-4000

Carolina Sandhills National Wildlife Refuge
Route 2, Box 100
McBee, SC 29101
843-335-8401

Cumberland Island National Seashore
P.O. Box 806
St. Marys, GA 31558
912-882-4335

Okefenokee National Wildlife Refuge
Route 2, Box 3330
Folkston, GA 31537
912-496-7836

Lower Suwanee National Wildlife Refuge
16450 Northwest 31 Place
Chiefland FL 32626
352-493-0238

Everglades National Park
40001 State Road 9336
Homestead, FL 33034
305-242-7700

Big Cypress National Preserve
HCR 61, Box 110
Ochopee, FL 33943
941-695-4111

Biscayne National Park
P.O. Box 1369
Homestead, FL 33090
305-230-7275

Mammoth Cave National Park
Mammoth Cave, KY 42259
270-758-2328

Reelfoot Lake National Wildlife Refuge
Route 2, Hwy. 157
Union City, TN 38261
901-538-2481

THE MIDLANDS

Pukaskwa National Park
Highway 627
Hattie Cove
Heron Bay, 0N P0T 1R0
Canada
888-773-8888

La Mauricie National Park
794 5th Street, P.O. Box 758
Shawinigan, QC G9N 6V9
Canada
888-773-8888

Isle Royale National Park
800 E. Lakeshore Drive
Houghton, MI 49931
906-482-0984

Sleeping Bear Dunes National Lakeshore
9922 Front Street
Empire, MI 49630
231-326-5134

Pictured Rocks National Lakeshore
P.O. Box 40
Munising, MI 49862
906-387-3700

Apostle Islands National Lakeshore
Route 1, Box 4
Bayfield, WI 54814
715-779-3397

Superior National Forest and Boundary Waters Canoe Area Wilderness
8901 Grand Avenue Place
Duluth, MN 55808
218-626-4300

Quetico Provincial Park
Ministry of Natural Resources
Atikokan, 0N P0T 1C0
Canada
807-597-2735

Voyageurs National Park
3131 Highway 53
International Falls, MN 56649
218-283-9821

St. Croix National Scenic Riverway
P.O. Box 708
St. Croix Falls, WI 54024
715-483-3284

Ozark National Forest
605 West Main Street
Russellville, AR 72801
501-968-2354

Buffalo National River
402 N. Walnut Street
Suite 136
Harrison, AR 72601
870-741-5443

Wichita Mountains National Wildlife Refuge
Route 1, Box 448
Indiahoma, OK 73552
580-429-3222

Flint Hills National Wildlife Refuge
P.O. Box 128
Hartford, KS 66854
316-392-5553

Big Thicket National Preserve
3785 Milam
Beaumont, TX 77701
409-839-2689

Padre Island National Seashore
P.O. Box 181300
Corpus Christi, TX 78480
361-949-8068

Aransas National Wildlife Refuge
P.O. Box 100
Austwell, TX 77950
361-286-3559 or 3533

Sabine National Wildlife Refuge
3000 Holly Beach Highway
Hackberry, LA 70645
337-762-3816

Black Hills National Forest
RR 2, Box 200
Custer, SD 57730
605-673-2251

Badlands National Park
P.O. Box 6
Interior, SD 57750
605-433-5361

Wood Buffalo National Park
Box 750
Fort Smith, NWT X0E 0P0
Canada
888-773-8888

Little Missouri National Grassland
Medora Ranger District
161 21st Street W.
Dickinson, ND 58601
701-225-5151

Grasslands National Park
P.O. Box 150
Val Marie, SK S0N 2T0
Canada
888-773-8888

Charles M. Russell National Wildlife Refuge
P.O. Box 110
Lewistown, MT 59457
406-538-8706

Thelon Wildlife Sanctuary
Nunavut Tourism
P.O. Box 1450
Iqaluit, NT X0A 0H0
Canada
1-800-491-7910

THE GREAT DIVIDE

Rocky Mountain National Park
Estes Park, CO 80517
970-586-1206

White River National Forest
900 Grand Ave.
P.O. Box 948
Glenwood Springs, CO 81602
970-945-2521

Black Canyon of the Gunnison National Park
102 Elk Creek
Gunnison, CO 81230
970-249-1914 ext. 23

Grand Teton National Park
P.O. Drawer 170
Moose, WY 83012
307-739-3300

Yellowstone National Park
P.O. Box 168
Yellowstone National Park
WY 82190
307-344-7381

Banff National Park
P.O. Box 900
Banff, AB T0L 0C0
Canada
888-773-8888

Jasper National Park
P.O. Box 10
Jasper, AB T0E 1E0
Canada
888-773-8888

Yoho National Park
P.O. Box 99
Field, BC V0A 1G0
Canada
888-773-8888

**Kootenay
National Park**
P.O. Box 220
Radium Hot Springs, BC
V0A 1M0
Canada
888-773-8888

**Glacier National Park
National Park Service**
P.O. Box 128
West Glacier, MT 59936
406-888-7800

**Waterton Lakes
National Park**
Waterton Park, AB
T0K 2M0
Canada
888-773-8888

**Sawtooth National
Recreation Area**
HC 64, Box 8291
Ketchum, ID 83340
208-727-5000

**Hells Canyon National
Recreation Area**
88401 Hwy. 82
Enterprise, OR 97828
541-426-4978

**Frank Church-
River of No Return
Wilderness Area**
Payette National Forest
Krassel Ranger District
P.O. Box 1026
McCall, ID 83638
208-634-0600

**Selway-Bitterroot
Wilderness Area**
Nez Perce National Forest
Route 2, Box 475
Grangeville, ID 83530
208-983-1950

**Gospel Hump
Wilderness Area**
Nez Perce National Forest
Route 2, Box 475
Grangeville, ID 83530
208-983-1950

THE SOUTHWEST

**Grand Canyon
National Park**
P.O. Box 129
Grand Canyon, AZ 86023
520-638-7888

**Petrified Forest
National Park**
P.O. Box 2217
Petrified Forest, AZ 86028
520-524-6228

**Paria Canyon-Vermilion
Cliffs Wilderness Area**
Arizona Strip Field Office
Bureau of Land Management
345 E. Riverside Dr.
St. George, UT 84780
435-688-3246

Coconino National Forest
Beaver Creek/Sedona
Ranger District
P. O. Box 300
250 Brewer Road
Sedona, AZ 86339
520-282-4119

Saguaro National Park
3693 S. Old Spanish Trail
Tucson, AZ 85730
520-733-5153

**Cabeza Prieta National
Wildlife Refuge**
1611 N. 2nd Avenue
Ajo, AZ 85321
520-387-6483

**Carlsbad Caverns
National Park**
3225 National Parks Hwy.
Carlsbad, NM 88220
505-785-2232

**Guadalupe Mountains
National Park**
HC 60 Box 400
Salt Flat, TX 79847
915-828-3251

**Big Bend
National Park**
P.O. Box 129
Big Bend National Park, TX
79834
915-477-2251

**Canyonlands
National Park**
2282 S. West Resource Blvd.
Moab, UT 84532
435-719-2313

**Bryce Canyon
National Park**
P.O. Box 170001
Bryce Canyon, UT 84717
435-834-5322

Zion National Park
Springdale, UT 84767
435-772-3256

Arches National Park
P.O. Box 907
Moab, UT 84532
435-719-2299

**Great Basin
National Park**
Baker, NV 89311-9702
775-234-7331

**Death Valley
National Park**
P.O. Box 579
Death Valley, CA 92328
760-786-2331

**Joshua Tree
National Park**
74485 National Park Drive
29 Palms, CA 92277
760-367-5500

Inyo National Forest
White Mountain
Ranger Station
798 N. Main St.
Bishop, CA 93514
760-873-2500

THE FAR WEST

**Channel Islands
National Park**
1901 Spinnaker Dr.
Ventura, CA 93001
805-658-5730

Yosemite National Park
P.O. Box 577
Yosemite National Park, CA
95389
209-372-0200

**Sequoia-Kings Canyon
National Parks**
47050 Generals Hwy.
Three Rivers, CA 93271
559-565-3719

Redwood National Park
1111 Second Street
Crescent City, CA 95531
707-464-6101

**Hart Mountain
National Antelope Refuge**
P.O. Box 11
18 South G St.
Lakeview, OR 97630
541-947-3315

**Klamath Basin
National Wildlife Refuges**
Hill Road, Route 1, Box 74
Tulelake, CA 96134
530-667-2231

**Crater Lake
National Park**
P.O. Box 7
Crater Lake, OR 97604
541-594-2211

**North Cascades National
Park Service Complex**
2105 State Route 20
Sedro-Woolley, WA 98284
360-856-5700

**Mount Baker-Snoqualmie
National Forest**
21905 64th Ave. West
Mountlake Terr., WA 98043
800-627-0062

**Mount Rainier
National Park**
Tahoma Woods
Star Route
Ashford, WA 98304
360-569-2211

**Mount Hood
National Forest**
65000 E. Highway 26
Welches, OR 97067
888-622-4822

Olympic National Park
600 East Park Avenue
Port Angeles, WA 98362
360-452-0330

Olympic National Forest
1835 Black Lake Blvd. SW
Olympia, WA 98512
360-956-2400

**Pacific Rim
National Park Reserve**
Box 280
Ucluelet, BC V0R 3A0
Canada
888-773-8888

**Nahanni National
Park Reserve**
P.O. Bag 348
Fort Simpson, NWT
X0E 0N0
Canada
888-773-8888

**Glacier Bay National Park
and Preserve**
P.O. Box 140
Gustavus, AK 99826
907-697-2230

Tongass National Forest
Southeast Discovery Center
South Main St.
Ketchika, AK 99901
907-228-6220

**Kluane National
Park and Preserve**
P.O. Box 5495
Haines Junction YT
Y0B 1L0
Canada
888-773-8888

**Wrangell-St. Elias
National Park and
Preserve**
P.O. Box 439
Copper City, AK 99573
907-822-5234

**Denali National Park
and Preserve**
P.O. Box 9
Denali Park, AK 99755
907-683-2294

**Yukon Delta National
Wildlife Refuge**
P.O. Box 346
Bethel, AK 99559
907-543-3151

THE ARCTIC NORTH

**Arctic National
Wildlife Refuge**
101 12th Ave., Rm. 236
Fairbanks, AK 99701
907-428-0250

Ivvavik National Park
Western Arctic District,
Parks Canada
Box 1840
Inuvik, NWT X0E 0T0
Canada
888-773-8888

Vuntut National Park
Yukon District Office
Elijah Smith Building
205-300 Main St.
Whitehorse, YT Y1A 2B5
Canada
888-773-8888

**Auyuittuq
National Park**
P.O. Box 353
Pangnirtung, NT X0A 0R0
Canada
888-773-8888

**Bylot Island
Bird Sanctuary
Sirmilik National Park**
P.O. Box 353
Pangnirtung, NT
X0A 0R0
Canada
888-773-8888

**Quttinirpaaq
(Ellesmere Island)
National Park**
P.O. Box 353
Pangnirtung, NT X0A 0R0
Canada
888-773-8888

INDEX

ILLUSTRATIONS CREDITS

Dust jacket, Dennis Flaherty

Front Matter: Pp. 2–3, James Randklev; 5, Phil Schermeister; 6, Michael Melford; 7, W. Perry Conway.

CHAPTER I
THE EAST

Pp. 12–13, Michael Melford; 14 (upper), Nicole Duplaix/NGS Image Collection; 14 (lower), Tony Arruza; 18, Tom Bean; 19, Raymond Gehman/NGS Image Collection; 22–23, Jack Dykinga; 24, David Muench; 25, Peter Essick/AURORA; 26–27 (both), David Muench; 30, David Muench; 30–31, José Azel/AURORA; 34–35, David Muench; 38–39, Jack W. Greene/Transparencies, Inc.; 39, Mike Booher/Transparencies, Inc.; 40, A. Blake Gardner; 41, Medford Taylor/NGS Image Collection; 42, Jake Rajs; 43, David Muench; 46–47, Charles Gurche; 48, Raymond Gehman/NGS Image Collection; 49, H. Mark Weidman; 52, Pat O'Hara; 56, Tony Arruza; 57, Bates Littlehales/NGS Image Collection; 58–59, Raymond Gehman/NGS Image Collection; 62, Fred Hirschmann; 63, Raymond Gehman/NGS Image Collection; 64–65, David Muench; 68, Tony Arruza; 69, Tom & Pat Leeson; 71, Doug Perrine/Innerspace Visions; 74–75, Stephen Alvarez; 76–77, David Muench; 77, Dennis Flaherty.

CHAPTER II
THE MIDLANDS

Pp. 78–79, Fred Hirschmann; 80 (upper), Tom Bean; 80 (lower), Stephen Sharnoff/NGS Image Collection; 84, John & Ann Mahan; 85, Richard Olsenius/NGS Image Collection; 88–89 (both), Phil Schermeister; 90, Phil Schermeister; 91, Melissa Farlow/NGS Image Collection; 92, Phil Schermeister – Photographers/Aspen; 93, Larry Ulrich; 96, Raymond Gehman/NGS Image Collection; 97, Craig Blacklock/Larry Ulrich Stock Photography; 98, David Muench; 99, Richard Olsenius/NGS Image Collection;

104–105, Charles Gurche; 106, Richard Olsenius/NGS Image Collection; 107, David Muench; 110, John Cancalosi; 110–111, David Muench; 114, David Muench; 114–115, George H.H. Huey; 115, John Cancalosi; 116, Joel Sartore/NGS Image Collection; 117, David Muench; 118, Joel Sartore/www.joelsartore.com; 118–119, Joel Sartore/NGS Image Collection; 122, David Hiser—Photographers/Aspen; 123, Craig Blacklock/Larry Ulrich Stock Photography; 124–125, stone/Larry Ulrich; 128–129 (both), Raymond Gehman/NGS Image Collection; 130, Raymond Gehman/NGS Image Collection; 132–133, Joel Sartore/www.joelsartore.com; 136, Tom & Pat Leeson; 137, Art Wolfe.

CHAPTER III
THE GREAT DIVIDE

Pp. 138–139, James Randklev; 140 (left), Raymond Gehman/NGS Image Collection; 140 (right), Art Wolfe; 144, Beth Wald/AURORA; 145, James Randklev; 146, Fred Hirschmann; 147, Willard Clay; 150–151, Scott T. Smith; 151, Willard Clay; 152, Dennis Flaherty; 154, Raymond Gehman/NGS Image Collection; 155, Michael Melford; 158, Marc Muench; 159, Raymond Gehman/NGS Image Collection; 160, Fred Hirschmann; 161, Paul Chesley/NGS Image Collection; 162–163, stone/Art Wolfe; 166, Dennis Flaherty; 168, Phil Schofield; 169, Michael Melford.

CHAPTER IV
THE SOUTHWEST

Pp. 170–171, Charles Gurche; 172 (upper), Chuck Place; 172 (lower), Art Wolfe; 176–177, Jack Dykinga; 178, Kerrick James; 179, David Muench; 182, Larry Ulrich; 183, Jack Dykinga; 184, David Muench; 184–185, Tom Bean; 188, Jack Dykinga; 188–189, Art Wolfe; 191, Willard Clay; 194, Michael Nichols/NGS Image Collection; 194–195, David Muench; 198–199 (both), Willard Clay; 202, George H.H. Huey; 204, Fred Hirschmann; 205, Raymond Gehman/NGS

Image Collection; 206, Scott T. Smith; 206–207, Chuck Place; 210, David Muench; 212, David Muench; 213, Phil Schermeister—Photographers/Aspen; 214–215, Chuck Place.

CHAPTER V
THE FAR WEST

Pp. 216–217, stone/Kim Heacox; 218, Dennis Flaherty; 222, Bob Cranston; 223, George H.H. Huey; 226, Ira Meyer/Danita Delimont, Agent; 227, Pat O'Hara; 228–229 (both), Phil Schermeister; 232, James P. Blair/NGS Image Collection; 233, David Muench; 236–237, Tom & Pat Leeson; 240–241, Raymond Gehman/NGS Image Collection; 243, Charles Gurche; 244, Larry Carver; 246, Charles Gurche; 248, David Hiser–Photographers/Aspen; 250, F. Stuart Westmorland/Danita Delimont, Agent; 251, Jim Corwin/ Ken Graham Agency; 254, David Muench; 255, Pat O'Hara; 256, Pat O'Hara; 257, Raymond Gehman/NGS Image Collection; 262, Marc Muench; 263, stone/Kim Heacox; 264, Art Wolfe; 266, Tom Bean; 268, Ira Meyer/Danita Delimont, Agent; 270–271, stone/ Theo Allofs; 274, John Eastcott & Yva Momatiuk/ NGS Image Collection; 274–275, Darrell Gulin/Danita Delimont, Agent; 278–279, stone/Natalie Fobes; 279, Joel Sartore/NGS Image Collection.

CHAPTER VI
THE ARCTIC NORTH

Pp. 280–281, stone/Jerry Kobalenko; 282, Paul Nicklen/Ursus; 286–287, George Mobley/ NGS Image Collection; 288–289 (both), Raymond Gehman/NGS Image Collection; 292–293 (both), Eugene Fisher; 296–297, Eugene Fisher.

NOTES on AUTHORS

RON FISHER, born and educated in Iowa, devoted some 30 years to writing and editing for the National Geographic Book Division before retiring in 1994. Titles with Fisher's byline include *The Appalachian Trail, Mountain Adventure, Still Waters/White Waters, Our Threatened*

Inheritance, Blue Ridge Range. Various writing assignments took him to many of the sites included in this book: He canoed the Boundary Waters, hiked the Appalachians, rafted western rivers, listened to yipping coyotes in grasslands of the Great Plains, and stalked rare whooping cranes in Texas. Fisher now lives in Virginia and occasionally freelances.

MARK MILLER is a contributing editor of *National Geographic Traveler* magazine. He has written for Society books and publications, including NATIONAL GEOGRAPHIC magazine, since 1977, his assignments ranging across North America from Alaska to Florida's Dry Tortugas, as well as to the Hawaiian Islands, the Caribbean, and Europe. A resident of Los Angeles, Miller has also served as a reporter for Reuters and the CBS Radio Network.

As writer, publisher, and photographer, JEREMY SCHMIDT specializes in natural history, outdoor subjects, and adventure travel. He spends part of every year traveling the world on assignment, but he finds the natural areas of the U.S. among his favorites. One of his recent books is *A Natural History Guide: Grand Canyon National Park*, published by Houghton Mifflin in 1993. Schmidt has spent years exploring the Southwest in boats, trucks, and on foot. At home in the Rockies, he lives with his wife and daughter in Wyoming's Jackson Hole.

THOMAS SCHMIDT has wandered the Rocky Mountains most of his life— backpacking, climbing, paddling, biking, and fishing. He is the author of five books and co-author of more than 15 others covering the plants, animals, geology, and human history of the region. He wrote *National Geographic's Guide to the Lewis and Clark Trail* and *The Rockies* title in Geographic's *Driving Guides to America* series, as well as books about Glacier, Grand Teton, and Rocky Mountain National Parks. Schmidt now lives in Bozeman, Montana, with his wife and two children.

BARBARA SZERLIP is a two-time National Endowment for the Arts Writing Fellow, as well as an editor. A resident of San Francisco, she has tackled topics ranging from literacy, technology, and international business practices to Pulitzer Prize winners and Hollywood costume designers. Most recently, Szerlip contributed to *Michelin's Green Guide to the Pacific Northwest*.

MEL WHITE is a contributing editor for *National Geographic Traveler* and writes frequently for the National Geographic Book Division. Over the years he has covered natural-history destinations from Amazonia to Belize to the national parks of New Zealand, but some of his favorite assignments have taken him to such American wild places as Acadia National Park, Okefenokee Swamp, the Sand Hills of Nebraska, and the Big Bend Country of Texas. Mel White lives in Little Rock, Arkansas.

ACKNOWLEDGMENTS

The Book Division acknowledges the invaluable assistance of contributing editor **Bonnie S. Lawrence** at the project's inception. We also appreciate the skills of consulting editor **Lyn Clement** and also those of **Michele Tussing Callaghan** in reviewing the book in its final stages. In addition, we thank the many park, preserve, forest, and refuge staff members who carefully read parts of the text.

For most generously sharing their expertise and assistance, the Book Division acknowledges **Sue Hirschfeld,** professor emerita, the Geology Department, California State University, Hayward; and **Kenneth R. Young,** the Department of Geography, University of Texas, Austin.

In addition, we acknowledge the help of the **Library,** the **Indexing Division,** the **National Geographic Image Collection,** and the **National Geographic Photographic and Imaging Laboratory.**

NATIONAL GEOGRAPHIC
ATLAS *of* NATURAL AMERICA

The world's largest nonprofit scientific and educational organization, the National Geographic Society was founded in 1888 "for the increase and diffusion of geographic knowledge." Since then it has supported scientific exploration and spread information to its more than nine million members worldwide.

The National Geographic Society educates and inspires millions every day through magazines, books, television programs, videos, maps and atlases, research grants, the National Geography Bee, teacher workshops, and innovative classroom materials.

The Society is supported through membership dues and income from the sale of its educational products. Members receive NATIONAL GEOGRAPHIC magazine—the Society's official journal—discounts on Society products, and other benefits.

For more information about the National Geographic Society and its educational programs and publications, please call 1-800-NGS-LINE (647-5463), or write to the following address:

National Geographic Society
1145 17th Street N.W.
Washington, D.C. 20036-4688 U.S.A.

Visit the Society's Web site at
www.nationalgeographic.com.

Composition for this book by the National Geographic Society Book Division. Printed and bound by R. R. Donnelley & Sons, Willard, Ohio. Color separations by NEC, Nashville, Tennessee. Dust jacket printed by Miken Inc., Cheektowaga, New York.

Contributing Authors
Ron Fisher
Mark Miller
Jeremy Schmidt
Thomas Schmidt
Barbara Szerlip
Mel White

Published by the National Geographic Society
John M. Fahey, Jr., *President and Chief Executive Officer*
Gilbert M. Grosvenor, *Chairman of the Board*
Nina D. Hoffman, *Senior Vice President*

Prepared by the Book Division
William R. Gray, *Vice President and Director*
Charles Kogod, *Assistant Director*
Barbara A. Payne, *Editorial Director and Managing Editor*
Marianne R. Koszorus, *Design Director*

Staff for this Book
Martha Crawford Christian, *Editor*
Melissa G. Ryan, *Illustrations Editor*
Marty Ittner, *Art Director*
Carl Mehler, *Director of Maps*
Sallie M. Greenwood, *Researcher*
Toni Eugene, *Captions Writer*
Gregory Ugiansky, *Map Production Manager*
Matt Chwastyk, Thomas L. Gray, Joseph F. Ochlak, *Mapping Specialists, Map Research, Edit, and Production*
Tibor G. Tóth, *Map Relief*

R. Gary Colbert, *Production Director*
Richard S. Wain, *Production Project Manager*
Meredith C. Wilcox, *Illustrations Assistant*
Peggy Candore, *Assistant to the Director*
Julia Marshall, *Indexer*

Manufacturing and Quality Control
George V. White, *Director*
John T. Dunn, *Associate Director*
Vincent P. Ryan, *Manager*
Phillip L. Schlosser, *Financial Analyst*

Library of Congress Cataloging-in-Publication Data
National Geographic Society (U.S.)
   National geographic atlas of natural America.
     p. cm.
   Includes bibliographical references and index.
   Contents: The East / Mel White -- The Midlands / Ron Fisher -- The Great Divide /
  Thomas Schmidt -- The Southwest / Jeremy Schmidt -- The Far West / Barbara Szerlip
  and Mark Miller -- The Arctic North / Barbara Szerlip and Mark Miller.
   ISBN 0-7922-7955-7 (Regular ed.) -- ISBN 0-7922-7973-5 (Deluxe ed.)
   1. North America--Maps. 2. National parks and reserves--North America--Maps. 3.
Recreation areas--North America--Maps. I. Title.

G1105 .N4 2000
912.7--dc21

00-042385